Abbreviations and acronyms

AATA	Animal Air Transportation Association
ABI/INFORM	Database of abstracts from over 800 business and management journals
ADITUS	North West Health Knowledge Portal
AHIS UK&I	Animal Health Information Specialists UK & Ireland
ALCID	Academic Libraries Co-operating in Dublin
ALL	Access to Libraries for Learning
AMED	Allied and Complementary Medicine
ANGLES	Anglian Libraries Information Exchange Scheme
ASSIA	Applied Social Sciences Index and Abstracts
ASSIGN	ASLIB Social Science Information Group and Network
ASVIN	Assessing and Supporting Veterinary Information Needs
ATLAS	Access to Libraries in Swansea
AULIC	Avon University Libraries in Co-operation
AVSL	Association of Vision Science Libraries
AWHILES	All Wales Health Information Library Extension Services
AWHL	Association of Welsh Health Librarians
BHLG	Berkshire Health Libraries Group
BIDS	Bath Information and Data Services
BL	British Library
BLDSC	British Library Document Supply Centre
BLIP	Berkshire Libraries in Partnership
BMA	British Medical Association
BNF	British National Formulary
BNI	British Nursing Index
CAL	Computer Assisted Learning
CALIM	Consortium of Academic Libraries in Manchester
CHILL	Consortium of Health Independent Libraries in London
CINAHL	Cumulated Index to Nursing and Allied Health Literature
CONARLS	Circle of Officers of National and Regional Library Systems
CSA	Common Services Agency of NHS Scotland
CURL	Consortium of University Research Libraries
DARE	Database of Abstracts of Reviews of Effectiveness
DIG	Derbyshire Information Group
DMLS	Defence Medical Library Services
EAHIL	European Association of Health Information Libraries
EBMR	Evidence Based Medicine Reviews
Embase	Excerpta Medica
eNAMHeL	e-version of NAMHeL
ERIC	Educational Resources Information Centre

EVLG	European Veterinary Libraries Group
FIRST	Forum for Information Resources in Staffordshire
GHI	Glasgow Health Information
GHIN	Grampian Health Information Network
GI	Grampian Information
GIN	Glasgow Information Network
HATRICS	Business-related information providers in Central Southern England
HCLU	Health Care Libraries Unit
HCN	Health Communications Network
Health CD	Department of Health circulars
HEBSWEB	Health Education Board for Scotland Website
HEED	Health Economic Evaluations Database
HeLIN	Health Libraries Information Network
HIFULOP	Health Information Forum Union List of Periodicals
HLN	Health Libraries North
HMIC	Health Management Information Consortium
HMLF	Health Management Librarians Forum
HOWIS	Health of Wales Information Service
HPRG	Health Promotion Reference Group
IBSS	International Bibliography of the Social Sciences
IfM Healthcare	Information for the Management of Healthcare, Health Libraries Group, Library Association
IHLG	Irish Healthcare Libraries Group
IHLJHI	Irish Healthcare Libraries Journal Holdings Index
IMID	Institute of Management International Databases
INFAH	Information Focus for Allied Health
IPATA	Independent Pet and Animal Transportation Association
ISTP	Index to Scientific & Technical Proceedings
JCR	Journal Citation Reports
JHLS	Joint Healthcare Library Services (Yorkshire)
JR	John Rylands University Library
KILN	Kent Information Library Network
LAI – HSLG	Library Association of Ireland Health Sciences Libraries Group
LC	Library of Congress
LfN	Libraries for Nursing, Health Libraries Group, Library Association
LIBNEL	North East London Workforce Development Confederation
LIHNN	Libraries and Information for Health Network Northwest
LILACS	Latin American & Caribbean Health Sciences
LIRC	Library and Information Resources
LISN	Lincolnshire Information Services Network
LLIDU	London Library and Information Development Unit
London LINKS	London Libraries Information and Knowledge Service
LRC	Learning Resource Centre
M25 Consortium	A group of about 125 libraries from 40 universities in the M25 area
MIRON	Bibliographic/full-text database service on NHSNet provided by HCN UK
MRC	Medical Research Council Libraries Network

NAMHEL	National Association of Mental Health Libraries (previously PLCS – Psychiatric Libraries Collaborative Scheme)
NeLH	National Electronic Library for Health
NETHRA	North East Thames Regional Health Authority
NEWLIS	Newport Libraries
NEYAL	North East & Yorkshire Academic Libraries Purchasing Consortium
NLM	National Library of Medicine
NRR	National Research Register
NTLISN	North Thames Library and Information Services Network
NTRLS	North Thames Regional Library Service
NULJ	Nursing Union List of Journals
NYRLAS	Northern and Yorkshire Regional Library Advisory Service
OATA	Ornamental and Aquatic Traders Association
PCG	Primary Care Groups
PCT	Primary Care Trust
PGMC	Postgraduate Medical Centre
PLCS	*See* NAMHEL
RDD	Regional Documents Database
RESCOLINC	Research Councils Library Information Consortium
RIDING	Yorkshire and Humberside Universities Association
RLG	Regional Librarians' Group
RLG	Research Libraries Group
RPS e-PIC	Royal Pharmaceutical Society of Great Britain and HCN, a suite of databases covering journals, new products, discontinued products and pharmaceutics.
SCURL	Scottish Confederation of University & Research Libraries
SEDBASE	Meyler's Side Effects of Drugs
SEeLH	South Essex Electronic Library for Health
SERFILE	Companion database to MEDLINE
SHAIR	Shropshire Access to Information Resources
SHINE	Scottish Health Information Network
SHINE	Shropshire Health Information Network
SIGLE	System for Information on Grey Literature in Europe
SILLR	Scottish ILL rate
SINTO	Sheffield Information Organization
SLIC	Scottish Library & Information Council
SMART	Sports Medicine & Related Research
SOSIG	Social Sciences Information Gateway
STLIS	South Thames Library & Information Services
STN	Scientific and Technical Information Network
SWRLIN	South West Region Library Network
SYBILS	Swansea Bay Health Information and Library Services
TRAHCLIS	Trent Region Association of Health Care Libraries and Information Specialists
UCL	University College London
UKSG	UK Serials Group
UMSLG	University Medical School Librarians Group
VOLSIF	Voluntary Sector Information Forum

WeBNF	Web version of BNF (British National Formulary)
WILCO	Wiltshire Libraries in Co-operation
WISH	West Midlands Information Service for Health
WMRHLN	West Midlands Regional Health Library Network
YJHLS	Yorkshire Joint Healthcare Libraries Service
ZETOC	Provides access to BL's Electronic Table of Contents

Questionnaire

Directory of Health Library and Information Services in the United Kingdom and the Republic of Ireland

Library name   If you do not have a distinct name, please give the name of the institution followed by library, pgmc, etc. If the library name has changed since 1996 please include the former name where shown.

Present library name: Former name if applicable:

Address   Please give the address of the library. There are separate boxes for Town, County, Postcode, and Country (England, Ireland, Northern Ireland, Scotland, Wales, Jersey, Guernsey and Isle of Man).

Address:

Town:	County:

Postcode:	Country:

Communications   In this section, please give the main telephone, fax, & e-mail contact points. If you have a home page on the internet, please give the URL address in the box provided.

Telephone Number:
Fax Number:
E-mail Address:
Web Page URL:

Staff   Please list the name of the Librarian (or person in charge), the names of the professional staff, how many are full time or part time. If there are more than 8 professional staff, list heads of sections only and give the number of other professional staff.

Librarian:
Professional Staff:

Full Time: Part Time:

How Many Library Assistants/Support Staff:
Full Time: Part Time:

Founded   Please indicate in which year the library was founded.

Year Library Was Founded:

Library type   Please indicate type of library, (e.g. multidisciplinary, clinical medicine, health management, dentistry, veterinary, etc).

Type of Library:

Opening hours   Please list when you are open.

Opening Hours:

Users   Please indicate who your users/readers are and whether anyone who does not work in, or is not a member of your organization, can use your library.

Users:

Lending   To whom do you lend stock? Any restrictions? Non-members?

Lending:

Stock policy What happens to old stock? Do you dispose of it or pass it on to other libraries, etc.?

Stock Policy:

Holdings   Please give figures for the amount of stock you have in each of the categories below.

Holdings
Books:
Journals (current subscriptions):
Journals (total holdings):
Films & Videos:
CD-ROMs:
Other Material:

Classification scheme/s   Please enter the name of the classification scheme/s you use for stock arrangement. If you use your own, simply enter 'Own'.

Classification Scheme Used:

Computerized services   Please enter the name of the Library Management System used to control stock, (e.g. Dynix, Libertas, etc.). Also list which online services you have access to and which major CD-ROM databases.

Computerized Services
Library Management System:
Computerized Search Facilities:
Online:
CD-ROM or internet database subscriptions:

Publications   Please list any publications that your library produces.

Publications:

Branches   Please enter below the names of any branches your library has. Please ensure that each branch also fills out one of these questionnaires.

Branches:

Special collections   Please list any special collections which your library keeps.

Special Collections:

Collaborative networks   Please list any local, regional or national schemes of which your library is a member. Please give the name in full plus the acronym used.

Local/Regional/National Collaborative Networks:

If there are any parts of this form which are unclear please contact Julie Ryder on 01428 683448 or e-mail julie.ryder@lineone.net

Directory of Health Library and Information Services in the United Kingdom and the Republic of Ireland

2002–2003

Aberdeen University Medical Library

Polwarth Building
Aberdeen University
Foresterhill
Aberdeen AB25 2ZD
Tel: 01224 552488
Fax: 01224 685157
E-mail: medlib@abdn.ac.uk
URL: www.abdn.ac.uk/diss/library/geninfo/
sites/medical/
Librarian: Keith Nockels
Prof. staff: Mrs Wendy Pirie
Founded: 1495
Type: Clinical Medicine.
Hours open: Mon–Thurs: 9am–10pm; Fri:
9am–8pm; Sat: 9am–10pm; Sun:
1pm–10pm.
Users: University staff and students; staff of
Grampian University Hospitals Trust and
Grampian Primary Care Trust. Open to all for
reference.
Lending: As above. Lending possible to any-
one on payment of an annual fee.
Stock policy: Much old stock kept. Some
surplus disposed of.
Holdings: 36,000 books; 750 current journal
subscriptions; 500 videos; 100 CD-ROMs.
Classification: Dewey.
Library management system: Dynix.
Computerized services: Online access to
AMED via Ovid; CINAHL; Cochrane Library;
MEDLINE; SportDiscus.
Library publications: A range of fact-
sheets.
Special collections: The University has
major historical collections kept in Special
Libraries and Archives and elsewhere in the
city.
Collaborative networks: GHIN;
SCURL/NHS; links with Grampian Primary
Care Trust Library at Royal Cornhill Hospital,
Aberdeen.

Action for Myalgic Encephalomyelitis

PO Box 1302
Wells
Somerset BA5 1YE
Tel: 01749 670799
Fax: 01749 672561
E-mail: info@afme.org.uk
URL: www.afme.org.uk
Librarian: Alison Graham
Type: Charity.
Lending: To members.
Holdings: Small collection of books and
information.

Adelaide & Meath Hospital Library

Tallaght
Dublin 24
Republic of Ireland
Tel: +353 1 414 4852
Fax: +353 1 414 3184
E-mail: library@amnch.ie
Librarian: Anne Murphy
Prof. staff: Anna Craig; Denise Duffy
Founded: Moved to new site 1998.
Type: Multidisciplinary.
Hours open: Mon–Thurs: 8am–10pm; Fri:
8am–5pm; Sat: 9.30am–1.30pm. July–Aug:
Mon–Fri: 8am–5pm.
Users: Hospital staff. Psychiatric Unit staff.
Trinity College medical and nursing under-
graduate students and personnel based in
the hospital.
Lending: Registered borrowers as above.
Stock policy: Superseded editions discard-
ed. Books over 10 years reviewed for reten-
tion in collection. Books by staff
automatically retained.
Holdings: 4,000 books; 300 current journal
subscriptions; 15 videos.
Classification: Dewey 21.
Library management system: Heritage IV.
Computerized services: Internet available to users. Online access to King's Fund
electronic journal and ZETOC service.

Internet access to ASSIA; CINAHL; ClinPsych; EBMR; MEDLINE. Full-text access to Ovid CBC and Nursing I.

Library publications: New books list; current journals list; library guide.

Collaborative networks: Irish Health Libraries Network.

Notes: The Eric Doyle Library, National Children's Hospital Library and the Meath Hospital Library have amalgamated.

Age Concern England Library

Astral House
1268 London Road
London SW16 4ER
Tel: 020 8765 7200
Fax: 020 8764 6594
E-mail: infodep@ace.org.uk
URL: www.ace.org.uk
Librarian: Cherry-Ann Dowling (Library Resources Manager)
Prof. staff: Marian Chinn; Elizabeth Johnston (jobshare)
Founded: 1974
Type: Dealing with issues concerning older people; Social Policy.
Hours open: Mon–Fri: 9.30am–5pm.
Users: Staff and members of the Age Concern Federation. Professionals, students and researchers may use the library for reference purposes.
Lending: Age Concern and Federation staff only.
Stock policy: Some disposal; some archived.
Holdings: 10,000 books; 100 current journal subscriptions, 150 journal titles; 130 videos; 5 CD-ROMs; over 500 subject information files.
Classification: Own.
Library management system: DB/TextWorks.
Computerized services: Online access to internet. Access to AgeInfo, Bookwise.
Library publications: Library guide; fact-sheets; reading lists.

Collaborative networks: BL; BMA Library; NULJ.

Age Concern Scotland Library

Leonard Small House
113 Rose Street
Edinburgh EH2 3DT
Tel: 0131 220 3345
Fax: 0131 220 2779
E-mail: library@acscot-org.uk
URL: www.ageconcernscotland.org.uk
Librarian: John Urquhart
Prof. staff: Jenni Campbell (Information Manager)
Founded: 1943
Type: Gerontological.
Hours open: Mon–Fri: 10am–5pm.
Users: Open to all.
Lending: Postal and personal loans available to all UK users.
Stock policy: Part dispose, part pass on to Age Concern Edinburgh.
Holdings: 7,000 books; 50 current journal subscriptions; 75 videos.
Classification: Own.
Library management system: CAIRS.
Computerized services: Internet access.
Library publications: Library Bulletin. Full publications list available on request.

Ailsa Hospital Medical Library

Ailsa Hospital
Ayrshire & Arran Primary Care Trust
Dalmellington Road
Ayr KA6 6AB
Tel: 01292 513022
Fax: 01292 513027
E-mail: angela.hissett@aapct.scot.nhs.uk
Librarian: Angela Hissett
Founded: 1996
Type: Mental Health and Multidisciplinary.
Hours open: Mon: 9.00am–5.30pm; Tues–Fri: 8.30am–5pm.
Users: Members of staff. Outside users reference only.

Lending: Members of staff; students.
Stock policy: Dispose of.
Holdings: 4,500 books; 58 journals; 75 films and videos; 7 CD-ROMs; 2,000 pamphlets.
Classification: Own and Royal College of Psychiatrists.
Library management system: DS CALM.
Computerized services: Internet and intranet. Online access to BIDS; CINAHL; MEDLINE. Access to AMED; CINAHL; Cochrane Library; Embase: Psychiatry; MEDLINE; National Research Register; PsycINFO.
Library publications: Library bulletin; journals list; library information leaflet.
Special collections: Mental health.
Collaborative networks: SHINE.

Aintree Library & Information Resource Centre

1st Floor, Clinical Sciences Centre
University Hospital Aintree
Aintree Hospitals NHS Trust
Lower Lane
Liverpool L9 7AL
Tel: 0151 529 5851
Fax: 0151 529 5856
E-mail: buryr@edgehill.ac.uk
Librarian: Rachel Bury (LIRC Manager)
Prof. staff: Leo Appleton
Founded: 2000
Type: Multidisciplinary.
Hours open: Mon–Thurs: 8.30am–7pm; Fri: 8.30am–5pm.
Users: Edgehill staff and students; Aintree hospitals NHS Trust staff; Walton Centre for Neurology and Neurosurgery NHS Trust Staff; University of Liverpool Faculty of Medicine undergraduate medical students based at Aintree.
Lending: As above. Staff from other organizations or NHS hospitals can use the library for reference only.
Stock policy: Disposed of.

Holdings: 22,340 books; 300 current journal subscriptions; 707 videos.
Classification: NLM.
Library management system: GEAC.
Computerized services: Online access to AMED; BNI; ChildData; CINAHL; Cochrane Library; Expanded Academic Index; Medical Litiga; MEDLINE; PsycINFO; Web of Science (all available on the Edgehill Network); ADITUS Information Portal available to NHS staff.
Special collections: Neurological material at the Walton Centre for Neurology and Neurosurgery.
Collaborative networks: LIHNN.

Airedale Library Information Service

Airedale NHS Trust
Airedale General Hospital
Steeton, Keighley
West Yorkshire BD20 6TD
Tel: 01535 294412
Fax: 01535 292196
E-mail: hannah.rossall@groupwise.airedale.northy.nhs.uk
Librarian: Vacant
Prof. staff: Anne Troth; Hannah Rossall-Boyle; Hugh Hanchard
Founded: 1974
Type: Health and Medical.
Hours open: Mon–Thurs: 8.30am–7pm; Fri: 8.30am–4pm.
Users: Members of Airedale NHS Trust and placement students. Those not employed by the Trust may use for reference only.
Lending: Members of Airedale NHS Trust and placement students. Restricted borrowing for medical students.
Stock policy: Out-of-date books discarded, donated or sold off.
Holdings: 8,000 books; 200 current journal subscriptions, 230 journal titles; 20 videos; 103 CD-ROMs.
Classification: NLM.

Library management system: Heritage.
Computerized services: Internet, intranet, databases, library catalogue. Access to AMED, Best Evidence, BNI, CINAHL; Cochrane Library; Embase: Psychiatry; King's Fund; MEDLINE; PsycINFO.
Library publications: Journal holdings; study guides; internet guides, user guides on website.
Collaborative networks: Libraries for Nursing SubGroup; NYRLAS.

Alexandra Hospital: Wynne Davies Clinical Library

Worcestershire Acute Hospitals NHS Trust
Woodrow Drive
Redditch
Worcestershire B98 7UB
Tel: 01527 503030 ext. 4646
Fax: 01527 518489
E-mail: PGMClibrary@worcsacute.wmids.nhs.uk
Librarian: Samantha Lloyd
Type: Multidisciplinary.
Hours open: Mon–Fri: 8.30am–5.30pm.
Users: Employees of the Trust. Others at librarian's discretion.
Lending: As above.
Stock policy: Offered to BL BookNet, EducationAid, own users.
Holdings: 3,119 books; 114 current journal subscriptions, 143 journal titles; 60 films and videos; 22 CD-ROMs.
Classification: NLM (Wessex adaptation).
Library management system: Heritage IV.
Computerized services: Online access to Biomed. Access to CINAHL; Cochrane Library; MEDLINE.
Library publications: Guides to library service, EBM, literature searching, search filters.
Collaborative networks: NULJ; WMRHLN.

Altnagelvin Multidisciplinary Education Centre Library

Altnagelvin Hospital
Londonderry
Northern Ireland BT47 1SB
Tel: 02871 611224
Fax: 02871 611261
E-mail: b.a.allen@qub.ac.uk; ccregan@alt.n-i.nhs.uk
URL: www.qub.ac.uk/lib
Librarian: Brenda Allen; Ciaran Cregan
Founded: 1981
Type: Multidisciplinary/University Campus.
Hours open: Mon: 9am–5.30pm; Tues–Thurs: 9am–9.30pm; Fri: 9am–5pm (term time only). Vacations: 9am–5pm only.
Users: University students, mainly nursing and all healthcare staff.
Lending: University students and healthcare staff. Non-members may apply to become associate readers.
Stock policy: Disposed of.
Holdings: 6,000 books; 113 current journal subscriptions, 140 journal titles; 100 videos.
Classification: LC.
Library management system: Talis.
Computerized services: Online access to BNI; CINAHL; Cochrane Library. Access to MEDLINE.

Alzheimer's Disease Society

Ann Brown Memorial Library
Gordon House
10 Greencoat Place
London SW1P 1PH
Tel: 020 7306 0606
Fax: .020 7306 0808
E-mail: Library@alzheimers.org.uk
Librarian: Lesley Mackinnon
Founded: 1993
Type: Health and Social Care of Dementia.
Hours open: Mon–Fri: 9am–5pm.
Users: Staff of Alzheimer's Disease Society. Others can use library for reference only.
Lending: To staff only.

Stock policy: Pass on to branches, other libraries or archive.
Holdings: 6,000 books; 60 current journal subscriptions; 20 films and videos.
Classification: In-house scheme.
Library management system: InMagic.
Computerized services: CD-ROM access to Cochrane Library; Centre for Policy on Ageing; HMIC.
Library publications: Professionals and carers reading lists; current awareness by e-mail.
Special collections: Dementia.

Ambless Cares Library

Shalom House
Lower Celtic Park
Enniskillen
Co. Fermanagh
Northern Ireland BT74 6HP
Tel: 028 66320320
Fax: 028 66320320
Librarian: John Wood
Founded: 1984
Type: Multidisciplinary.
Hours open: Mon–Fri: 10am–5pm.
Users: Open to members only. Mainly research purposes.
Lending: Reference only.
Stock policy: Sold to members at reduced price.
Classification: Own.
Library publications: Our Companion – a quarterly newsletter; Ambless Fund Raising Fact Pack; Somebody Cares cards.
Special collections: Ambless historical material.
Collaborative networks: CLA.

Amersham Hospital Staff Library

Amersham Hospital
Whielden Street
Amersham
Buckinghamshire HP7 0JD
Tel: 01494 734000
Fax: 01494 734293
E-mail: aflo@amlib.demon.co.uk
Librarian: Mrs Ann Flood
Founded: 1978
Type: Multidisciplinary.
Hours open: Mon–Wed, and Fri: 9.15am–5pm; Thurs: 10am–4pm.
Users: Staff of South Bucks NHS Trust; students of the University of Luton; employees of Buckinghamshire Mental Health Trust, subject to SLA in process of being set up. Others reference only by prior arrangement.
Lending: To registered users only.
Stock policy: Discarded.
Holdings: 3,600 books; 61 current journal subscriptions, 75 journal titles.
Classification: NLM.
Library management system: DB/TextWorks.
Computerized services: CD-ROM access to AMED; BNI; Caredata; CINAHL; Cochrane; Embase: Psychiatry; HMIC; MEDLINE; PsycINFO.
Collaborative networks: HeLIN; NAMHEL; NULJ.

Anglia Support Partnership

Health Information and Library Services
Clinical Governance Support Team
Doddington Community Hospital
Benwick Road
Doddington
Cambridgeshire PE15 0UG
Tel: 01354 644276
Fax: 01354 644277
E-mail: library@nwahc-tr.anglox.nhs.uk
Librarian: Lydia Crick
Founded: 1998
Type: Multidisciplinary.
Hours open: Mon–Fri: 8.30am–5pm.
Users: All staff employed by North West Anglia Healthcare NHS Trust; North and South Peterborough PCTs; Fenland PCT; Community staff West Norfolk PCT; Lifespan Healthcare NHS Trust.
Lending: All of the above.

Stock policy: A 'virtual library'.
Holdings: 50 books; 12 current journal subscriptions; 6 videos; 6 CD-ROMs.
Classification: Own.
Library management system: DB/TextWorks.
Computerized services: Access to AMED; ASSIA for Health; CINAHL; Embase; HMIC; MEDLINE; PsycINFO.
Collaborative networks: BLDSC; BMA; Health Care Libraries Unit – Anglia and Oxford; 'Blue Token Scheme'.

Anglo-European College of Chiropractic Library

Anglo-European College of Chiropractic
Parkwood Road
Bournemouth
Dorset BH5 2DF
Tel: 01202 436307
Fax: 01202 436308
E-mail: library@aecc.ac.uk
URL: www.aecc.ac.uk
Librarian: David O'Neill (Head of Learning Resources)
Founded: 1986
Type: Chiropractic; Medicine.
Hours open: Mon–Thurs: 8.45am–9pm; Fri: 8.45am–7pm; Sat: 9.30am–12.30pm.
Users: Reference resource only to students or researchers from other institutions.

Animal Health Trust Harris Library

Animal Health Trust
Lanwades Park
Kentford, Newmarket
Suffolk CB8 7UU
Tel: 01638 751000
Fax: 01638 750410
E-mail: sandra.tatum@aht.org.uk
URL: www.aht.org.uk
Librarian: Sandra Tatum
Founded: 1947
Type: Veterinary.

Hours open: Mon–Fri: 9am–5pm.
Users: Animal Health Trust staff; others by appointment with Librarian.
Lending: Staff only.
Stock policy: Offered to other libraries in the subject area world-wide.
Holdings: 3,000 books; 40 current journal subscriptions, 60 journal titles; 20 videos; 10 CD-ROMs.
Classification: UDC (modified).
Computerized services: Access to PubMed and VETCD.
Collaborative networks: AHIS UK&I.

Animal Transportation Association

AATA European Office
PO Box 251
Redhill
Surrey RHI 5FU
Tel: 01737 822249
Fax: 01737 822954
E-mail: 111257.1720@compuserve.com
URL: www.tim-harris.co.uk
Librarian: Tim Harris
Founded: 1986
Type: Animal Transportation and associated legislative issues.
Hours open: Not open to the public.
Users: AATA and IPATA members. Public telephone enquiries.
Lending: Reference only.
Stock policy: Pass to US office.
Classification: Own.
Library publications: AATA manual for the transportation of animals; AATA conference proceedings.
Collaborative networks: AATA; IPATA; OATA.

Anna Freud Centre

21 Maresfield Gardens
Hampstead
London NW3 5SD
Tel: 020 7794 2313
Fax: 020 7794 6506
E-mail: Charlotte.Turner@annafreud.org
URL: www.annafreudcentre.org
Librarian: Charlotte Turner
Type: Psychoanalysis and Child
Development.
Hours open: Mon: 9.50am–2.20pm; Tues:
9.50am–1.20pm; Wed: 3.30pm–6.30pm; Fri:
10am–4.30pm.
Users: Members and students of AFC.
Lending: As above. Interlending using BL
form.
Holdings: 5,000 books.
Library management system: CALM
2000.
Computerized services: Access to PEP.
Library publications: Library guides; new
title lists.

Archway Healthcare Library

Holborn Union Building
The Archway Campus
Highgate Hill
London N19 5LW
Tel: 020 7288 3580
Fax: 020 7288 3571
E-mail: AHL@mdx.ac.uk
URL: www.archway.ac.uk/AHL
Librarian: Beverley Chapman
Prof. staff: Richard Peacock; Jane Stephen
Founded: New library opened 1999
Type: Multidisciplinary.
Hours open: Mon, Fri: 9am–5pm; Tues,
Wed, Thurs: 9am–8pm; Sat: 10am–2.30pm.
Users: Staff and students in the Middlesex
University, Royal Free and UCL Medical
School; Whittington Hospital; Camden and
Islington Community Health Services Trust
and institutions covered by North London
Education Consortium.
Lending: As above.

Stock policy: Disposed of or passed on to
other libraries.
Holdings: 15,000 books; 300 current journal
subscriptions; 12 films, videos, CD-ROMs;
UCL theses.
Classification: NLM.
Library management system: Horizon.
Computerized services: Online access to
Ovid Biomed; PubMed and other internet
resources. Access to AMED; Best Evidence;
BNI; CINAHL; Cochrane Library; MEDLINE;
OSH-Rom; PsychLit.
Collaborative networks: NTRLS; UK
Libraries Plus.
Notes: Former name: Whittington Hospital
Library.

Argyll & Bute Hospital Professional Library

Lomond and Argyll PCT
Argyll & Bute Hospital
Lochgilphead
Argyll PA31 8LD
Tel: 01546 602323 ext. 2140
Fax: 01546 606452
E-mail: jacki.stewart@aandb.sco.nhs.uk
Librarian: Jacki Stewart
Founded: 1980
Type: Multidisciplinary with Psychiatry spe-
ciality.
Hours open: Mon–Fri: 9am–5pm.
Users: All Health Service staff within the
Trust in general and within Argyll in particu-
lar. Or by arrangement with Librarian.
Lending: Books to users only. Journals not
loaned.
Stock policy: Dispose of after consultation
with Physician Superintendent. Some sent to
Romania.
Holdings: 1,846 books; 52 current journal
subscriptions, 72 journal titles; 1 video; 4
CD-ROMs.
Classification: Own.
Library management system: Own.
Computerized services: Access to Ovid
databases; SHOW; Clib; Paisley University;

NHSNet. Access free through SLIC to HEBS; NRR; Nature; Genome.
Library publications: Literature news sheet – psychiatry.
Collaborative networks: NAMHEL; SHINE; SLIC.

Argyll & Clyde Health Board: Public Health Library

Ross House
Hawkhead Road
Paisley
Renfrewshire PA2 7BN
Tel: 0141 842 7200
Fax: 0141 848 0165
Librarian: Lynn Easton
Type: Public Health; Health Management.
Hours open: 9am–5pm.
Users: Employees of organization only.
Lending: Employees only.
Stock policy: Dispose of.
Holdings: 4,500 books; 8 current journal subscriptions, 36 journal titles; 3 CD-ROMs.
Classification: Own.
Library management system: Cardbox.
Collaborative networks: SHINE.

Arthritis Care

18 Stephenson Way
London NW1 2HD
Tel: 020 7380 6500
Fax: 020 7380 6505
E-mail: lizzie@arthritiscare.org.uk
URL: www.arthritiscare.org.uk
Librarian: Lizzie Eastwood
Type: Charity.
Hours open: Not open to public. Office hours 9am–5pm.
Users: Internal staff; health professionals; public.
Lending: Lend stock to internal staff and occasionally public.
Stock policy: Try to pass on useful stock.
Holdings: 600 books; 20 current journal subscriptions, 35 journal titles; 50 videos.

Classification: DISS.
Library management system: DB/TextWorks; InMagic.
Library publications: Current awareness for staff.
Special collections: Archive of Arthritis Care.
Collaborative networks: BL; BMA.

Arthur Rank House Library

Lifespan Healthcare NHS Trust
351 Mill Road
Brookfields Hospital
Cambridge CB1 3DF
Tel: 01223 723110
Fax: 01223 723111
E-mail: night@pallcareresource.demon.co.uk
URL: www.pallcareresource.demon.co.uk
Librarian: Marit Jones (Information/Liaison Nurse)
Founded: 1983
Type: Multidisciplinary.
Hours open: Mon–Fri: 9am–5pm.
Users: In-house staff/nurses, doctors, therapists, counsellors, social services staff, students, community nursing teams.
Lending: In-house staff, students, community staff,
Stock policy: Old stock is disposed of.
Holdings: 300 books; 7 current journal subscriptions; 30 videos.
Classification: Own.
Computerized services: Access to internet. Three databases via Lifespan. Access to CINAHL; Cochrane Library and MEDLINE via intranet.

ASH Scotland Library & Information Service

8 Frederick Street
Edinburgh EH2 2HB
Tel: 0131 225 4725
Fax: 0131 220 6604
E-mail: ashscotland@ashscotland.org.uk
URL: www.ashscotland.org.uk

Librarian: Sheila Duffy
Founded: 1979
Type: Health; Tobacco.
Hours open: Mon–Fri: 9am–5pm.
Users: Reference only, by appointment.
Lending: Internal only.
Stock policy: Passed to National Library of Scotland as archive.
Classification: Own.
Library management system: Idealist.
Computerized services: Access to PubMed; Tobaccopedia.
Library publications: Weekly bulletin; see also website.
Special collections: All aspects of tobacco and tobacco use.
Collaborative networks: Links with Health Promotion Library Scotland and Edinburgh City Libraries; SHINE.

Ashford & St Peter's Hospital NHS Trust Health Sciences Libraries

Postgraduate Education Centre
St Peter's Hospital
Guildford Road
Chertsey
Surrey KT23 4DB
Tel: 01932 723196
Fax: 01932 723197
E-mail: sylvia.stafford@stph-tr.sthames.nhs.uk
URL: http://stlis.thenhs.com/sthames/stlis/Ascy.htm
Librarian: Sylvia Stafford
Prof. staff: Sandy Komiliades
Founded: 1991
Type: Multidisciplinary.
Hours open: Mon–Fri: 9am–5pm.
Users: Staff of Acute and 2 Community and Mental Health Trusts, 4 PCGs, Health Authority. Affiliated membership available.
Lending: Members only and interlibrary loans.
Stock policy: Disposal.

Holdings: 14,000 books; 215 current journal subscriptions, 229 journal titles; 597 films and videos and CD-ROMs.
Classification: NLM.
Library management system: Heritage IV.
Computerized services: Online access via Ovid to AMED; Best Evidence; CINAHL; Cochrane Library; MEDLINE; PsycINFO. Access to BNI; HMIC.
Collaborative networks: Nursing; PLCS; STLIS.
Notes: The Health Sciences Libraries at Ashford Hospital and St Peter's Hospital are two libraries operating cross-sites.

Ashurst Hospital Staff Library

Southampton University Hospitals NHS Trust
Snowdon House
Ashurst Hospital
Southampton
Hampshire SO40 7AR
Tel: 02380 293636 ext. 212
Fax: 02380 743033
Librarian: Ann Woodford
Prof. staff: Alison Roache
Hours open: Thurs: 9.30am–11.30am.
Collaborative networks: STLIS.

Ashworth Hospital Library

Ashworth Hospital Authority
Parkbourn
Maghull
Liverpool L31 1HW
Tel: 0151 471 2431
Fax: 0151 471 2435
Librarian: Christine Bradshaw
Prof. staff: Claire Hazzard; Catherine McCafferty
Founded: 1975
Type: Multidisciplinary with Forensic Mental Health focus.
Hours open: Mon–Tues: 9am–5.30pm; Wed–Thurs: 8.30am–6.30pm; Fri: 10am–4.30pm

Users: Staff of the Hospital and students undertaking academic programmes run by the Hospital. Reference-only facilities for others.
Lending: To staff and students only.
Stock policy: Dispose.
Holdings: 6,161 books; 51 current journal subscriptions, 94 journal titles; 108 films and videos; networked CD-ROMs.
Classification: Dewey.
Library management system: Heritage.
Computerized services: Online access to ADITUS. Access to CINAHL; Cochrane Library; HMIC; MEDLINE; PsycINFO; National Research Register.
Library publications: Guide to Library and Useful Resources; Current Awareness Bulletin.
Branches: Patients' library service, run by Sefton Public Libraries.
Collaborative networks: LIHNN; PLCS.

Avon & Wiltshire Mental Health Partnership NHS Trust Staff Library

Barrow Hospital
Barrow Gurney
Bristol BS48 3SG
Tel: 0117 928 6528
Fax: 0117 928 6650
E-mail: jill.johnson@awwt.swest.nhs.uk
Librarian: Jill Johnson
Type: Psychiatric.
Hours open: Mon–Thurs: 8.30am–4.30pm; Fri: 8.30am–4pm.
Users: Staff only.
Lending: Staff only.
Holdings: 1,606 books; 30 current journal subscriptions, 106 journal titles.
Classification: NLM (Wessex adaptation).
Special collections: History of Psychiatry, especially in Bristol.
Collaborative networks: PLCS; SWR-LIN.

Ayr Hospital Library

MacDonald Education Centre
Ayr Hospital
Dalmellington Road
Ayr KA6 6DX
Tel: 01292 610555 ext. 4119
Librarian: Mrs Janice Grant
Founded: 1991
Type: Multidisciplinary.
Hours open: Mon–Fri: 8am–4.30pm.
Users: Staff and students within the local Health Board area. Other users by arrangement, on reference basis only.
Lending: To Trust staff and students on placement only.
Stock policy: Disposed of.
Holdings: 3,000 books; 150 current journal subscriptions.
Classification: NLM.
Library management system: Heritage.
Computerized services: Online access to CINAHL; Cochrane Library; MEDLINE.
Collaborative networks: SHINE.

Ayrshire & Arran Health Board Library

Boswell House
10 Arthur Street
Ayr KA7 1QJ
Tel: 01292 885823
Fax: 01292 610636
E-mail: mcmillanm@aapct.scot.nhs.uk
Librarian: Mrs Mhairi McMillan
Founded: 1995
Type: Health Management.
Hours open: Mon–Fri: 9am–5pm.
Users: NHS staff in Ayrshire. Others by appointment only.
Lending: Ayrshire and Arran Health Board staff. Non-members, reference only.
Stock policy: Some disposed of, some passed on.
Holdings: 4,000 books; 40 current journal subscriptions, 45 journal titles; 4 CD-ROMs.
Classification: Dewey 20.

Library management system: CALM for Libraries.

Computerized services: Online access to Ovid. Access to Clinical Evidence; Cochrane Library; HEBS; HMIC; National Research Register; PubMed; Wilson's Social Science Abstracts.

Library publications: Library Guide; Additions to Stock; Official Publications Update; Searching the Literature.

Collaborative networks: Ayrshire Healthcare Libraries Co-operative; BL; BMA; SHINE.

Barnet & Chase Farm Hospitals NHS Trust

Medical Library
Postgraduate Medical Centre
Barnet Hospital
Barnet
Hertfordshire EN5 3DJ
Tel: 020 8216 4834
Fax: 020 8216 4678
E-mail: guy@barnet2.demon.co.uk
URL: www.bhctlib.demon.co.uk
Librarian: Guy Robinson
Founded: 1960s
Type: Multidisciplinary.
Hours open: Mon–Fri: 9am–5pm.
Users: All Trust staff.
Lending: To Trust staff only.
Stock policy: Passed on to other libraries.
Holdings: 3,500 books; 125 current journal titles; 40 videos; 5 CD-ROMs.
Classification: NLM.
Computerized services: Online access to CINAHL; Cochrane; MEDLINE.
Collaborative networks: NTRLS.

Barnsley District General Hospital Education Centre Library

Barnsley District General Hospital NHS Trust Education Centre
Gawber Road
Barnsley
South Yorkshire S75 2EP
Tel: 01226 777973
Fax: 01226 779319
Librarian: Miss R C Merrill
Prof. staff: Mr Stefan Chadwick
Founded: 1992
Type: Multidisciplinary Healthcare.
Hours open: Mon, Wed and Thurs: 8.30am–8pm; Tues and Fri: 8.30am–5pm.
Users: Employees and students of the Acute Trust, Community Trust, Health Authority and GPs. Non-employees reference use only.
Lending: As above – staff 10 books; students 4 books.
Stock policy: Sold or disposed of.
Holdings: 8,000 books; 123 current journal subscriptions; 30 videos.
Classification: NLM.
Library management system: Heritage IV
Computerized services: Online access to Ovid Biomed – includes AMED; CINAHL and PsycINFO. Access to BNI.
Collaborative networks: BL; BMA; JHLS (Yorkshire and Humberside)

Bart's & The London: Queen Mary's Medical School

Turner Street
Whitechapel
London E1 2AD
Tel: 020 7882 7115
Fax: 020 7882 7113
E-mail: p.s.hockney@qmw.ac.uk
a.besson@qmw.ac.uk
URL: www.mds.qmw.ac.uk
Librarian: Paul Hockney
Prof. staff: Alain Besson
Type: University Medical and Dental School.

Users: Staff and students of Queen Mary: University of London; staff of the Bart's and the London NHS Trust; staff of other associated NHS Trusts. Staff and students of other universities may have access to material not available locally.

Lending: Registered members with current ID. Or via interlibrary loans.

Stock policy: Reviewed annually. Out-of-date material discarded.

Classification: NLM.

Library management system: Unicorn.

Computerized services: Online access to AMED; ASSIA; Caredata; Cochrane Library; MEDLINE; PsycINFO.

Branches: Charterhouse Square; West Smithfield; Whitechapel.

Collaborative networks: M25 Consortium; North Thames Regional (NHS) Library Service.

Bart's & The London: Queen Mary's Medical School, Charterhouse Square Library

Charterhouse Square
London EC1M 6BQ
Tel: 020 7882 6019
Fax: 020 7490 2851
E-mail: f.moussavi@qmw.ac.uk
Librarian: Farideh Moussavi
Prof. staff: 1 other member of staff.
Founded: 1962
Type: Medical Research.
Hours open: Mon–Thurs: 9am–6pm; Fri: 9am–5pm. Vacations: Mon–Fri: 9am–5pm.
Holdings: 5,000 books; 55 current print journal subscriptions.
Notes: For details of URL, users, lending arrangements, stock policy, classification scheme, library management system, computerized services and collaborative networks see entry for Bart's and The London: Queen Mary's Medical School.

Bart's & The London: Queen Mary's Medical School, West Smithfield Library

West Smithfield
London EC1A 7BE
Tel: 020 7601 7849
Fax: 020 7606 2137
E-mail: m.b.montague.qmw.ac.uk
Librarian: Marie Montague
Prof. staff: 4 staff
Founded: 1800
Type: Clinical Medicine/Multidisciplinary.
Hours open: Mon–Thurs: 9am–9pm; Fri: 9am–6pm. Vacations: Mon–Fri: 9am–6pm.
Holdings: 10,000 books; 205 current journal subscriptions.
Special collections: Historical collection; Athenae Collection of material about 'Bart's Men'.
Notes: For details of URL, users, lending arrangements, stock policy, classification scheme, library management system, computerized services and collaborative networks see entry for Bart's and The London: Queen Mary's Medical School.

Bart's & The London: Queen Mary's Medical School, Whitechapel Library

Turner Street
Whitechapel
London E1 2AD
Tel: 020 7882 7116
Fax: 020 7882 7113
E-mail: j.h.thomas@qmw.ac.uk
Librarian: Jacquelyn Thomas
Prof. staff: 10 other staff
Founded: 1785
Type: Medical; Clinical Medicine; Dentistry; Occupational Therapy; Multidisciplinary.
Hours open: Mon–Thurs: 9am–10pm; Fri: 9am–8pm; Sat: 10am–5pm. Vacations: Mon–Fri: 9am–6pm.
Holdings: 18,000 books; 424 current print titles; 180 films and videos.

Special collections: Historical collection; 'Old Londoners' Collection; Camps/Cameron Collection in Forensic Medicine; British Society for Orthodontics Collection.

Notes: For details of URL, users, lending arrangements, stock policy, classification scheme, library management system, computerized services and collaborative networks see entry for Bart's and The London: Queen Mary's Medical School.

Basildon Healthcare Library

Robert Brown Postgraduate Medical Centre
Basildon Hospital
Nethermayne
Basildon
Essex SS16 5NL
Tel: 01268 593594
Fax: 01268 593988
Librarian: Sarah Perthon
Prof. staff: Dawn Bradley; Christine Coley
Type: Multidisciplinary.
Hours open: Mon–Fri: 9am–6.30pm.
Users: All staff of Basildon and Thurrock NHS Hospital Trust; NHS staff in South Essex.
Lending: Members; Region.
Stock policy: Dispose to be recycled.
Holdings: 3,500 books; 80 current journal subscriptions, 100 journal titles; 6 CD-ROMs.
Classification: NLM.
Library management system: 2020.
Computerized services: Online access via Ovid to CINAHL; HCN; STAT REF; Harrisons Online; MEDLINE.
Collaborative networks: NETHRA.

Bassetlaw District General Hospital Postgraduate Centre Library

Postgraduate Centre
Bassetlaw District General Hospital
Worksop
Nottinghamshire S81 0BD
Tel: 01909 500990 ext. 2917
Fax: 01909 480879
E-mail: hazel.croucher@bhcs-tr.trent.nhs.uk
Librarian: Hazel Croucher
Hours open: Mon–Fri: 9am–5pm; Sat: 9.30am–12 noon.
Notes: For further details see website www.telh.nhs.uk

Bateman Centre Library

Bateman Centre
Birch Hill Hospital
Rochdale
Lancashire OL12 9QB
Tel: 01706 517058
Fax: 01706 370403
E-mail: library.bateman@exchange.rhc-tr.nwest.nhs.uk
Librarian: Graham Titley
Founded: 1968
Type: Multidisciplinary.
Hours open: Mon–Fri: 9am–5pm; 24-hour access, but unsupervised outside the above times.
Users: All staff of Rochdale Healthcare NHS Trust; local primary care staff; healthcare students on placements. Others by prior arrangement.
Lending: Unrestricted.
Stock policy: Usually offered to readers and other libraries and discarded if not sold.
Holdings: 7,000 books; 102 current journals subscriptions; 40 videos; 10 CD-ROMs.
Classification: Dewey 20.
Computerized services: Online access to ISI Web of Science; PubMed. Internet access to AMED; BNIPlus; CINAHL; Clinical Evidence; Cochrane Library; Embase; HMIC; MEDLINE; PsychLit.
Collaborative networks: BLDSC; BMA; LIHINN; Lis-medical; Lis-medjournal-duplicates.

Beatson Oncology Centre Library

Western Infirmary
Glasgow G11 6NT
Tel: 0141 211 1917
E-mail: gpra08@udcf.gla.ac.uk
URL: www.northglashealthinfo.org.uk
Librarian: Annette Thain
Founded: 1994
Type: Multidisciplinary – Oncology.
Hours open: Mon–Fri: 9.15am–5.30pm.
Librarian available 9.15am–2pm.
Users: Doctors, nurses, radiographers,
researchers. Visitors may use for reference.
Lending: Members only.
Stock policy: Dispose of old books. Journal
exchange scheme.
Holdings: 750 books; 42 current journal sub-
scriptions, 60 journal titles; 10 videos; 10
CD-ROMs.
Classification: NLM.
Library management system: Heritage.
Computerized services: Online access to
MD Consult and Ovid.
Library publications: Cancer resources
on the internet.
Collaborative networks: North Glasgow
Trust; SHINE.

Bedford Hospital NHS Trust, Bevan Library

Ampthill Road
Bedford MK42 9DJ
Tel: 01234 792114
Fax: 01234 795708
E-mail: bevan@bedhos.anglox.nhs.uk
URL: www.beds-med.demon.co.uk
Librarian: Mrs Yvette de Souza
Type: Multidisciplinary.
Hours open: Mon–Fri: 9am–8pm; Sat:
9am–1pm.
Users: NHS staff, GPs and dentists working
in Bedfordshire.
Lending: To registered users only.
Stock policy: Books discarded. Journals
offered to other libraries.

Holdings: 4,000 books; 110 current journal
subscriptions.
Classification: NLM.
Library management system:
DB/TextWorks.
Computerized services: Online access to
internet. Access to CINAHL; Cochrane
Library; MEDLINE; PsycINFO; Rehabilitation
and Physical Medicine.
Library publications: Annual Report; user
guidelines.

Benenden Hospital Library

Staff Development Centre
Benenden Hospital
Benenden
Cranbrook
Kent TN17 4AX
Tel: 01580 240333 ext. 2206
Librarian: Lesley J Downs
Hours open: Mon, Tues, Wed, Fri:
9am–1pm.

Berkshire Health Authority Library

57–59 Bath Road
Reading
Berkshire RG30 2BA
Tel: 0118 982 2785
Fax: 0118 982 2783
E-mail: chrissy.allott@berks-ha.nhs.uk
Librarian: Christine Allott
Type: Multidisciplinary.
Hours open: Mon–Fri: 9am–5pm.
Users: Health Authority, Primary Care
Groups/Trusts, Berkshire Shared Services
Organisation. Also open to other Berkshire
NHS staff and members of the public. Ring
for appointment.
Lending: All NHS staff in Berkshire.
Stock policy: Disposed of.
Holdings: 5,500 books; 36 journal titles.
Classification: NLM.
Library management system:
DB/TextWorks.

Computerized services: Access to Best Evidence; BNI; Cochrane Library; HMIC; MEDLINE.
Library publications: Current awareness service on county intranet.
Special collections: Public Health ONS Statistics.
Collaborative networks: Berkshire Health Libraries; HeLIN.

Berkshire Shared Services Organization Professional Library

Fair Mile Hospital
Cholsey
Oxfordshire OX10 9HH
Tel: 01491 651281 ext. 4125
Fax: 01491 652155
E-mail: library@fairmile-library.demon.co.uk
Librarian: Caroline Papi
Prof. staff: Vacant
Type: Multidisciplinary.
Hours open: Mon–Thurs: 9am–5pm; Fri: 9am–4.30pm.
Users: Berkshire NHS employees.
Lending: All NHS staff in Berkshire.
Stock policy: Dispose of old medical information which can be dangerous.
Holdings: 5,167 books; 117 current journal subscriptions, 200 journal titles; 7 CD-ROMs.
Classification: NLM.
Library management system: Heritage IV.
Computerized services: Search facilities on Heritage OPAC. Internet access to AMED; CINAHL; Cochrane Library; Embase: Psychiatry; HMIC; National Research Register; PsycINFO.
Collaborative networks: Assist Information Technology; BHLG; BLIP; HeLIN; NULJ; PLCS.

Bethlem Royal Hospital Multidisciplinary Library

Bethlem Royal Hospital
Monks Orchard Road
Beckenham
Kent BR3 3BX
Tel: 020 8776 4817
Fax: 020 8776 4818
E-mail: marco.isetta@slam–tr.nhs.uk
URL: www.kcl.ac.uk/depsta/iss/sites/den-markhill/topbethlem.html
Librarian: Marco Isetta
Type: Multidisciplinary.
Hours open: Mon–Fri: 9am–5pm.
Users: South London and Maudsley Trust members; KCL staff and students; others by arrangement.
Lending: Members only.
Holdings: 6,000 books; 40 current journal subscriptions.
Classification: NLM.
Library management system: LIBRARIAN .

Bexley Hospital Library

Bexley Hospital
Oxleas NHS Trust
Old Bexley Lane
Bexley
Kent DA5 2BW
Tel: 01322 625700 ext. 5886
Fax: 01322 557664
E-mail: oxleaslibrary@hotmail.com
Prof. staff: Russell Gray (volunteer)
Hours open: Mon–Fri: 9am–1pm; 2pm–5pm.
Holdings: 27 journal titles.
Computerized services: Access to CINAHL; Cochrane Library; MEDLINE; PsychLit.

Birmingham Children's Hospital NHS Trust

Children's Hospital Library
Steelhouse Lane
Birmingham B4 6NH
Tel: 0121 333 8642
Fax: 0121 333 8641
E-mail:
ursula.ison@bhamchildrens.wmids.nhs.uk
Librarian: Mrs Ursula Ison
Type: Multidisciplinary.
Hours open: Mon–Fri: 9am–5pm. 24-hour access for Trust staff.
Users: All members of the Trust staff. Non-Trust staff can use as reference library during opening hours.
Lending: All Trust staff.
Stock policy: Old stock is disposed of.
Holdings: 1,396 books; 171 current journal subscriptions.
Classification: LC.
Library management system: Heritage.
Computerized services: Ovid website.
Collaborative networks: NULJ; WMRHLN.

Birmingham Women's Hospital Information Service

Birmingham Women's NHS Trust
ERC: Information Service
Metchley Park Lane
Edgbaston
Birmingham B15 2TG
Tel: 0121 472 1377 ext. 4250
Fax: 0121 623 6922
E-mail: mary.publicover@bham-womens.
thenhs.com
derek.yates@bham-womens.thenhs.com
Librarian: Mary Publicover
Prof. staff: Derek Yates
Founded: 2000
Type: Multidisciplinary.
Hours open: Mon–Thurs: 9am–5pm; Fri: 9am–4.30pm. Out-of-hours access for Trust staff.

Users: All Trust staff and trainees; staff of University Hospital Birmingham, staff of Queen Elizabeth and Queen Elizabeth Psychiatric.
Lending: All Trust staff. Staff of Queen Elizabeth and Queen Elizabeth Psychiatric with restrictions.
Stock policy: Dispose of it.
Holdings: 704 books; 44 current journal subscriptions, 50 journal titles; 7 videos; 8 CD-ROMs.
Classification: NLM.
Library management system: Soutron 20/20. DB/TextWorks.
Computerized services: Catmaker and Catbank. Access to Ovid and Cochrane Library.
Collaborative networks: WISH.

Blackburn Royal Infirmary Trust Library

Education Centre
Blackburn Royal Infirmary
Bolton Road
Blackburn
Lancashire BB2 3LR
Tel: 01254 294065
Fax: 01254 294065
E-mail:
Clare.Morton@mail.bhrr.nwest.nhs.uk
Librarian: Mrs Catherine Linda Riley
Prof. staff: Mrs Margaret Webster
Type: Multidisciplinary.
Hours open: Mon–Thurs: 8.45am–4.30pm; Fri: 8.30am–4pm.
Users: Any employee of the Trust, GPs, Community Healthcare Trust, student nurses of the University of Central Lancashire.
Lending: To all staff. Reference only for non-members, if appropriate.
Stock policy: Old stock is disposed of.
Holdings: 7,332 books; 143 current journal subscriptions, 184 journal titles; 112 videos; 20 CD-ROMs.
Classification: Dewey 20.
Library management system: Heritage.

Computerized services: Online access to AMED; BNIPlus; CINAHL; Embase; HMIC; MEDLINE; PsycINFO. Access to ClinPsych; EMIMS; HealthStar; MEDLINE; Rehab and Physical Medicine.
Library publications: In-house library bulletin.
Collaborative networks: BL; BMA; JRULM; LIHNN; RCSE.

Bon Secours Hospital: Potel Library

College Road
Cork
Republic of Ireland
Tel: +353 21 4801736
Fax: +353 21 4801661
E-mail: Tkenny@cork.bonsecours.ie
Librarian: Tara Kenny
Founded: 1997
Type: Nursing and Medical.
Hours open: Mon–Fri: 9am–1.30pm; 2.30pm–5pm.
Users: Hospital staff only: nurses, doctors, consultants, administrative staff, dieticians, care assistants, etc.; nursing students, senior house officers and interns.
Lending: As above.
Stock policy: Very old/obsolete material is disposed of. Other material is circulated among interested parties.
Holdings: 2,500 books; 35 current journal subscriptions, 45 journal titles; 10 films and videos; 3 CD-ROMs.
Classification: Dewey.
Library management system: Manage Your Books.
Computerized services: Internet connection on 4 PCs. Online access to MEDLINE. Access to CINAHL.
Library publications: Newsletter.
Collaborative networks: Irish Healthcare Libraries Interlibrary Loan Co-operative.

Bradford Community Health NHS Trust Library & Health Promotion Resources

Lynfield Mount Hospital
Heights Lane
Bradford
West Yorkshire BD16 1LZ
Tel: 01271 363194
Fax: 01272 363194
E-mail: hugh.hanchard@bcht.northy.nhs.uk
Librarian: Hugh Hanchard
Founded: 1998
Type: Psychiatry; Mental Health; Community Nursing; Health Promotion.
Hours open: Mon–Thurs: 8.30am–5pm; Fri: 8.30am–4.30pm.
Users: Open to all NHS staff in the Bradford area and all 'health promoters' working in the area. Open for reference to anyone.
Lending: Registered borrowers only as above.
Stock policy: Offered to staff; remaining items binned.
Holdings: 5,000 books; 60 current journal subscriptions, 80 journal titles; 240 films and videos; 10 CD-ROMs; 1,000 training packs.
Classification: NLM (Wessex adaptation). Own for health promotion stock.
Library management system: Heritage IV.
Computerized services: Access via internet Ovid to AMED; Best Evidence; CINAHL; Cochrane Library; MEDLINE; PsychINFO; NRR.
Collaborative networks: JHLS; NULJ; NYRLAS.

Bradford Health Authority Library

New Mill, Victoria Road
Saltaire, Shipley
West Yorkshire BD18 3LD
Tel: 01274 366051
Fax: 01274 539232
E-mail: kwhite@bradford-ha.nhs.uk
URL: www.bradford-ha.nhs.uk

Librarian: Mrs Kim White
Founded: 1996
Type: Health Management.
Hours open: Open access during office hours. Staffed 9am–3pm.
Users: All NHS staff in the district. Non-members by arrangement.
Lending: As above.
Stock policy: Shared/archived locally. If not, disposed of.
Holdings: 5,000 books; 30 current journal subscriptions.
Classification: NLM.
Library management system: Heritage IV.
Computerized services: Access to Ovid interface via regional deal.
Collaborative networks: Bradford NHS Libraries; NYRLAS; Yorkshire Health Libraries; YJHLS.

Bradford Royal Infirmary Medical Library

Bradford Royal Infirmary
Bradford
West Yorkshire BD9 6RJ
Tel: 01274 364130
Fax: 01274 364704
E-mail: medical.library@bradfordhospitals.nhs.uk
Librarian: Ian P G King
Prof. staff: Michael A Reid
Founded: 1800s
Type: Multidisciplinary.
Hours open: Mon and Wed: 8.30am–6pm; Tues: 8.30am–8pm; Thurs: 8.30am–7pm; Fri: 8.30am–4pm.
Users: Anyone working with the NHS in the Bradford area can join the library. Others may use it for reference and may join, if they can demonstrate need. Backup service on medical information offered to public library.
Lending: To registered members. Libraries via interlibrary loans.
Stock policy: Superseded, or out-of-date, stock is sold, where possible.

Holdings: 14,000 books; 210 current journal subscriptions; 120 videos; 30 CD-ROMs.
Classification: NLM (Wessex adaptation).
Library management system: InMagic. Heritage (coming soon).
Computerized services: Online access to Dialog and Data-Star. CD-ROM access to CINAHL; MEDLINE. Ovid web gateway – AMED; Best Evidence; CINAHL; Cochrane Library; DARE: Embase: Psychiatry; MEDLINE; PreMEDLINE.
Library publications: Ethnic Minorities Health: Current Awareness Bulletin (quarterly).
Special collections: Ethnic minorities health.
Collaborative networks: YJHLS.

Bristol Cancer Help Centre Library

Grove House
Cornwallis Grove
Clifton
Bristol BS8 4PG
Tel: 0117 980 9500
Fax: 0117 923 9184
E-mail: info@bristolcancerhelp.org
URL: www.bristolcancerhelp.org
Librarian: Chrissy Jones
Founded: 1982
Type: Complementary medicine, focusing on cancer.
Hours open: Mon–Fri: 9am–5.30pm.
Users: Open to staff, patients and students of the Centre.
Lending: As above.
Stock policy: Old stock withdrawn unless classic.
Holdings: 800 books; 10 current journal subscriptions, 20 journal titles; 55 films and videos; 210 cassettes.
Classification: NLM.
Computerized services: Online access to Biomed.
Special collections: Complementary medicine; Psycho-Oncology.

Collaborative networks: Bristol Healthcare Librarians Group; SWRLIN.

British Association of Psychotherapists Library

37 Mapesbury Road
London NW2 4HJ
Tel: 020 8452 9823
Fax: 020 8452 5182
E-mail: library@bap-psychotherapy.org
URL: www.bap-psychotherapy.org
Librarian: Lucia Asnaghi
Founded: 1991
Type: Psychotherapy.
Hours open: Mon–Fri: 9.30am–5pm.
Users: Members of BAP and external students. Non-members by prior arrangement with the librarian.
Lending: Members of BAP and external students.
Stock policy: Ad hoc decisions – Wellcome, sell, charity.
Holdings: 4,000 books; 19 current journal subscriptions, 29 journal titles; 30 videos; 1 CD-ROM; tapes.
Classification: BLISS.
Library management system: Cardbox on PC.
Computerized services: Internet access; PsycINFO via Tavistock; CD-ROM access to PEP.
Library publications: Library guide; list of member publications.

British Dental Association Information Centre

64 Wimpole Street
London W1G 8YS
Tel: 020 7563 4545
Fax: 020 7935 6492
E-mail: infocentre@bda-dentistry.org.uk
URL: www.bda-dentistry.org.uk
Librarian: Roger Farbey
Prof. staff: Andy Duggan; Helen Nield; Damyanti Raghvani; Nikki West

Founded: 1920
Type: Dentistry/Oral Health.
Hours open: Mon–Fri: 9am–6pm.
Users: Members. Non-dentists by appointment only.
Lending: Members only.
Stock policy: Retain most stock.
Holdings: 13,000 books; 200 current journal titles, 1,075 journal titles; 323 videos; 16 CD-ROMs; 30 CAL packages on disk.
Classification: Black and NLM.
Library management system: AMLIB.
Computerized services: Online access to Knight Ridder (Data-Star). Access to Ovid – MEDLINE.
Library publications: BDA Centre: A Potted Guide.
Special collections: Rare book collection.
Collaborative networks: BL; BMA; CHILL.

British Homeopathic Association

15 Clerkenwell Close
London EC1R 0AA
Tel: 020 7566 7800
Fax: 020 7566 7815
E-mail: info@trusthomeopathy.org
URL: www.trusthomeopathy.org
Librarian: Sue Pearce (Marketing Assistant)
Type: Charity promoting medical homeopathy.
Users: Welcomes public and media enquiries on any aspect of homeopathy.
Lending: Supports the work and services of the Faculty of Homeopathy.
Library publications: Information pack on homeopathy, which includes advice on how to get homeopathic treatment on the NHS and a list of homeopathic doctors, dentists and vets. Quarterly magazine called Health and Homeopathy.

British Homoeopathic Library (HOM-INFORM)

Homoeopathic Information Resource Centre
Glasgow Homoeopathic Hospital
1053 Great Western Road
Glasgow G12 0XQ
Tel: 0141 211 1617
Fax: 0141 211 1610
E-mail: hom-inform@dial.pipex.com
URL: www.hom-inform.org
Librarian: Mrs Mary Gooch
Prof. staff: Ms Sandra Davies
Founded: c1930
Type: Homoeopathy and some complementary medicine.
Hours open: Mon–Fri: 9.30am–5.30pm.
Users: Members and Associates of the Faculty of Homoeopathy and staff of the Glasgow Homoeopathic Hospital. Anyone can become an associate member, for an annual charge.
Lending: Members and Associates of the Faculty of Homoeopathy and staff of the Glasgow Homoeopathic Hospital.
Stock policy: Pass to other homoeopathic libraries.
Holdings: 2,600 books; 47 current journal subscriptions; 10 CD-ROMs.
Classification: Own.
Library management system: InMagic; DB/TextWorks
Computerized services: Hom-Inform information service, computerized repertories. Fee-based literature searches. Online access to Ovid; EBSCO; electronic journal access via NHS Glasgow E-Library. Access to IBIS.
Library publications: Database of indexed journal references published online via website.
Special collections: 19th-century homoeopathic books and journals.
Collaborative networks: SHINE.
Notes: This organization requests the use of the third 'o' in homoeopathy.

British Institute of Radiology (BIR)

Information Centre
36 Portland Place
London W1B 1AT
Tel: 020 7307 1405
Fax: 020 7307 1414
E-mail: infocentre@bir.org.uk
URL: www.bir.org.uk
Librarian: Mrs Kate Sanders
Type: Learned Society.
Hours open: Mon, Wed, Fri: 9am–7pm; Tue and Thurs: 10am–6pm.
Users: Institute members, radiographers, radiologists, members of British Medical Ultrasound Society.
Lending: Reference only.
Stock policy: Some given to a School of Radiography, some disposed of.
Holdings: 10,000 books; 80 current journal subscriptions, 100 journal titles.
Classification: Own.
Library management system: Horizon epixtech.
Computerized services: Access to Health; Radiology and Nuclear Medicine; RADLINE.
Library publications: Library information leaflet.
Special collections: K C Clark slide collection (5,000 glass slides).
Collaborative networks: CHILL Serials Consortium.

British Library: Health Care Information Service

96 Euston Road
London NW1 2DB
Tel: 020 7412 7489
Fax: 020 7412 7923
E-mail: hcis@bl.uk
URL: www.bl.uk/services/stb/hcis.html
Librarian: Bruce Madge
Prof. staff: Tony McCulloch; Fiona McLean; Philippa Seaton; Les Wilkinson; Helen Wills
Founded: 1995

Type: Multidisciplinary.
Users: Open to anyone. BL Reading Rooms require a pass.
Lending: Through BLDSC.
Classification: Own.
Library management system: AMICUS.
Computerized services: Online services via Dialog, Data-Star, STN. Access to AMED; BNI; BIOSIS; CINAHL; Embase; MEDLINE.
Library publications: Leaflets on Health Care Information Service, AMED; healthcare updates.

British Library: Science Reading Rooms

96 Euston Road
London NW1 2DB
Tel: 020 7412 7288
Fax: 020 7412 7217
E-mail: scitech@bl.uk
URL: www.bl.uk
Librarian: Lynne Brindley (Chief Executive)
Founded: 1973
Type: Multidisciplinary.
Hours open: Mon: 10am–8pm; Tues–Thurs: 9.30am–8pm; Fri and Sat: 9.30am–5pm.
Users: To use the Reading Rooms you need a British Library reader's pass. These are issued to people undertaking research who need to see items in the Library's collections which are not readily available elsewhere.
Lending: Stock is for reference only.
Holdings: 263,000 books; 20,000 current journal subscriptions; 46 million patents (figures are for all the Science Reading Rooms).
Classification: Own.
Computerized services: Online access to all major hosts. Access to AMED; BNI; BIO-SIS; CINAHL; Embase; International Pharmaceutical Abstracts; Life Sciences; MEDLINE; OSH-ROM; PsycINFO; Web of Science and many more.
Branches: British Library: Document Supply Centre; British Library: Health Care Information Service.

British Medical Association Library

BMA House
Tavistock Square
London WC1H 9JP
Tel: 020 7383 6625
Fax: 020 7388 2544
E-mail: bma-library@bma.org.uk
URL: www.library.bma.org.uk
Librarian: Tony McSeán
Prof. staff: Jane Smith (Deputy Librarian); Richard Jones; Jane Rowlands (Head of Development); Fiona Robertson; Lina Coelho – total 14 professional staff.
Founded: 1887
Type: Clinical Medicine.
Hours open: Mon–Fri: 9am–6pm.
Users: BMA members and staff. Institutional members. Others at the Librarian's discretion.
Lending: Members and institutional members.
Stock policy: Discarded when no longer used.
Holdings: 38,000 books; 1,200 current journal subscriptions, 3,000 journal titles; 3,500 films and videos.
Classification: NLM.
Library management system: Dynix.
Computerized services: See website for details.
Library publications: BMA Library Bulletin; catalogues.

British Optical Association Library

College of Optometrists
42 Craven Street
London WC2N 5NG
Tel: 020 7839 6000
Fax: 020 7839 6800
E-mail: librarian@college-optometrists.org
URL: www.college-optometrists.org
Librarian: Mrs Jan Ayres
Founded: 1901
Type: Medical/Professional.

Hours open: Mon–Fri: 9am–1pm;
2pm–5pm.
Users: Mostly members. Non-members by
arrangement.
Lending: Members only.
Holdings: 6,000 books; 70 current journal
subscriptions, 112 journal titles; 20 films and
videos; 4 CD-ROMs; DOCET tapes and
videos.
Classification: Dewey 21.
Library management system: Libero.
Computerized services: Catalogue to be
online soon.
Special collections: BCLA Library – reference only. OIAAC Library – reference only.

British Psychological Society Collection

c/o University of London Library
Senate House, Malet Street
London WC1E 7HU
Tel: 020 7862 8451/8461
Fax: 020 7862 8480
E-mail: enquiries@ull.ac.uk
URL: www.ull.ac.uk
Librarian: Susan Tarrant
Type: Psychology; Psychiatry.
Hours open: Mon–Fri: 9am–9pm; Sat:
9.30am–5.30pm. Vacations: Mon–Fri:
9am–6pm; Sat: 9.30am–5.30pm.
Users: British Psychological Society mem-
bers and staff and students of University of
London. Others can use library on payment
of fee.
Lending: Reference only.
Stock policy: Dispose of.
Holdings: Combined Society and University
Psychology Collection of 30,000 books; 250
current journal subscriptions, 350 journal
titles.
Classification: BLISS .
Library management system:
INNOPAC.
Computerized services: Access to
PsycINFO.

British School of Osteopathy Library

275 Borough High Street
London SE1 1JE
Tel: 020 7407 0222
Fax: 020 7839 1098
E-mail: library@bso.ac.uk
URL: www.bso.ac.uk
Librarian: Will Podmore
Prof. staff: Les Fagan
Founded: 1917
Type: Medicine.
Hours open: Mon–Tues: 9am–7.30pm;
Wed–Thurs: 9am–9.30pm; Fri: 9am–5pm.
Vacations: Mon–Fri: 9am–5pm.
Users: BSO staff and students.
Lending: To BSO staff and students. Open
to public.
Stock policy: Pass on to other libraries.
Holdings: 10,000 books; 40 current journal
subscriptions, 90 journal titles; 300 videos;
30 CD-ROMs.
Classification: Dewey.
Library management system: AutoLib.
Computerized services: Internet access;
Online access to MEDLINE. Access to
AMED.
Library publications: Index to British
Osteopathic Journal; bibliographies on
osteopathy and cranial osteopathy; spinal
manipulation: outcome studies.
Special collections: Osteopathy and its
history.
Collaborative networks: South Thames
Library and Information Services.

Bromley Hospital Medical Education Centre Library

Bromley Hospital
Cromwell Avenue
Bromley
Kent BR2 9AL
Tel: 020 8289 7208
Fax: 020 8289 7004
E-mail: carol.serginson@bromleyh-
tr.sthames.nhs.uk

Librarian: Vacant
Prof. staff: Carol Serginson
Hours open: Mon–Fri: 9am–3pm.
Computerized services: Access to MEDLINE.
Collaborative networks: STLIS.

Bronglais General Hospital Library Services

Bronglais General Hospital
Caradoc Road
Aberystwyth
Ceredigion SY23 1ER
Tel: 01970 635803
Fax: 01970 635923
E-mail: bronglais-library@ceredigion-tr.wales.nhs.uk
URL: www.ceredigion-tr.wales.nhs.uk/all/services/library
Librarian: Tricia Chapman
Founded: 1973
Type: Multidisciplinary.
Hours open: Mon–Fri: 9am–5pm.
Users: Employees of Ceredigion and Mid Wales NHS Trust. Students on clinical placement. Access to others by appointment.
Lending: Members only. Non-members reference only.
Stock policy: Pass it on to overseas libraries where possible or recycle.
Holdings: 4,000 books; 100 current journal subscriptions.
Classification: NLM.
Library management system: Libero.
Computerized services: Search facilities – internet; HOWIS; Ovid; SilverPlatter. Online access to AMED; ASSIA for Health; Best Evidence; BNIPlus; CancerLit; CINAHL; HealthStar; HMIC; MEDLINE; PsycINFO; RCN; World Information Nursing. Access to Cochrane Library.
Library publications: New acquisitions.
Collaborative networks: AWHL; AWHILES; HOWIS.

Bronllys Hospital Medical Library

Education, Training and Research Department
Bronllys
Powys LD3 0LU
Tel: 01874 711255 ext. 4527
Fax: 01874 712053
Librarian: To be appointed
Prof. staff: To be appointed
Founded: 1979
Type: Medicine; Psychiatry.
Hours open: Mon–Fri: 9am–5pm.
Users: NHS staff of Powys Healthcare NHS Trust.
Lending: As above.
Stock policy: Retained on site.
Holdings: 4,000 books; 40 current journal subscriptions; 200 videos; 30 CD-ROMs.
Classification: Dewey.
Computerized services: Online access to Ovid; MEDLINE; standard medical databases.
Collaborative networks: NULJ; AWHL; PLCS.

Broomfield Hospital: Warner Library

Court Road
Chelmsford
Essex CM1 7ET
Tel: 01245 443651/2
Fax: 01245 442140
E-mail: carol.roberts@meht.nhs.uk
Librarian: Carol Roberts
Prof. staff: Michelle Cotton; Deborah Lepley
Type: Multidisciplinary.
Hours open: Mon–Thurs: 8.30am–6pm; Fri: 8.30am–5.30pm.
Users: Employees of the Trusts. Students and other users can have reference use only.
Lending: To members only.
Stock policy: Distribute to branch libraries and book sales to staff.

Holdings: 3,950 books; 107 current journal subscriptions, 198 journal titles; 54 videos; 15 CD-ROMs; 60 reports.
Classification: NLM.
Library management system: DB/TextWorks.
Computerized services: Online access via Ovid to Best Evidence; CINAHL; Cochrane Library; MEDLINE; 12 full-text journals. Access to 150 full-text electronic journals.
Collaborative networks: North Thames Books and Journals Catalogue (RDD and ULS); NULJ.

Brunel University: Osterley Campus Library

Borough Road
Isleworth
Middlesex TW7 5DU
Tel: 020 8891 0121 ext. 2815
Fax: 020 8891 8251
E-mail: library@brunel.ac.uk
URL: www.brunel.ac.uk/depts/lib
Librarian: Robert Elves
Founded: 1966
Type: Academic.
Hours open: Mon–Thurs: 9am–9pm; Fri: 9am–5pm; Sat: 9.30am–1pm. Vacations: Mon–Fri: 9am–5pm.
Users: Staff and students of the University. Visitors can use library for reference purposes, by arrangement.
Lending: To members only.
Stock policy: Old stock is disposed of.
Holdings: 48,000 books; 500 journal titles (250 health related); 200 videos.
Classification: LC.
Library management system: Unicorn.
Computerized services: Online access to BIDS: CINAHL; First Search; HealthStar; MEDLINE; OSH-ROM; PsychLit plus others.
Library publications: Various library guides.
Collaborative networks: M25 Consortium.

Buckinghamshire Chilterns University College: Chalfont Campus Library

Newland Park
Gorelands Lane
Chalfont St Giles
Buckinghamshire HP8 4AD
Tel: 01494 605135
Fax: 01494 603082
E-mail: challib@bcuc.ac.uk
URL: www.bcuc.ac.uk/library/index.htm
Librarian: Lizanne Thackary
Prof. staff: Michael King; Mrs Susan Morris; Mr Roland Scales
Founded: 1973
Type: Academic; Multidisciplinary – Health and Nursing.
Hours open: Term time: Mon–Thurs: 8.30am–12 midnight; Fri: 8.30am–9pm; Sat: 10am–5pm; Sun: 12 noon – 7pm.
Users: Registered students of BCUC, staff and researchers. Non-members can use library stock and catalogue but not net-worked databases.
Lending: 10 books to students; staff/researchers entitled to total of 16 items. External borrowers entitled to 4 items only.
Stock policy: Academic staff have first refusal. Some sent to Africa. Other titles are discarded.
Holdings: 58,058 books; 440 current journal subscriptions; 3,818 videos; 5 CD-ROMs.
Classification: Dewey.
Library management system: SIRSI Unicorn.
Computerized services: Search facilities – networked PCs; online access via Ovid for CINAHL; EBMR; MEDLINE; PsycINFO. Access to Butterworths; CITELINE; Proquest. CD-ROM being phased out and replaced with internet database subscriptions where possible.
Library publications: Factsheets for online subscription databases; guides for particular subject specialisms and to subject journal titles – both printed and electronic; subject-specific bookmarks.

Collaborative networks: BMA; NULJ.

Buckinghamshire Health Authority Library

Verney House
Gatehouse Road
Aylesbury
Buckinghamshire HP19 8ET
Tel: 01296 318604
Fax: 01296 310121
E-mail: library@bha.powernet.co.uk
Librarian: Deirdre MacGuigan (Knowledge Officer)
Founded: 1992
Type: Health Management; Public Health.
Hours open: Mon–Fri: 9am–5pm.
Users: Health Authority staff. Others for reference use only.
Lending: Health Authority staff. Other libraries.
Stock policy: Offer to other libraries where appropriate. Dispose of the rest.
Holdings: 8,000 items; 30 current journal subscriptions; 4 CD-ROMs.
Classification: NLM (Modified).
Library management system: IDEAL-IST; converting to DB/TextWorks.
Computerized services: Internet access. Online access via Ovid to AMED; CINAHL; Embase; MEDLINE; PsycINFO. CD-ROM access to ASSIA; Cochrane Library; HMIC; National Research Register.
Collaborative networks: Buckinghamshire Collaboration for Knowledge Solutions; HCLU; HeLIN.

Burton Graduate Medical Centre Library

Queen's Hospital
Burton Hospitals NHS Trust
Belvedere Road
Burton-on-Trent
Staffordshire DE13 0RB
Tel: 01283 511511 ext. 2104
Fax: 01283 510347

E-mail: 0198@dial.pipex.com
Librarian: Liza Alderman
Founded: 1973
Type: Medical.
Hours open: Mon and Fri: 9am–5pm; Tues–Thurs: 9am–8pm.
Users: All Trust members. Others on request.
Lending: To members of the Burton Hospitals NHS Trust only.
Stock policy: Old stock sold or shipped to Uganda.
Holdings: 3,142 books; 120 current journal subscriptions, 130 journal titles; 10 videos; 4 CD-ROMS.
Classification: LC.
Library management system: Heritage.
Computerized services: Intranet access. Access to Best Evidence; Cochrane Library; MEDLINE; National Research Register.
Collaborative networks: WMRHLN.

Bury Postgraduate Medical Library

Postgraduate Medical Institute
Bury General Hospital
Bury
Lancashire BL9 6PG
Tel: 0161 705 3375
Fax: 0161 761 4702
E-mail: burylibrary@yahoo.co.uk
Librarian: Sue Locke
Type: Multidisciplinary.
Hours open: Mon–Thurs: 8.45am–5pm; Fri: 8.45am–4.30pm.
Users: Staff working for the Bury Health Care NHS Trust. Others by arrangement and reference only.
Lending: Staff working for the Bury Health Care NHS Trust. Interlibrary loans.
Stock policy: Old stock is donated overseas or discarded.
Holdings: 5,500 books; 77 current journal subscriptions, 120 journal titles; 30 videos; 20 CD-ROMs.
Classification: NLM.

Library management system: InMagic; DB/TextWorks 2.2.

Computerized services: Access to AMED; BNI; CINAHL; Cochrane Library; Embase; HMIC; MEDLINE; PsycINFO; SEDBASE.

Collaborative networks: LIHNN; NULJ; PLCS.

Bushey Fields Hospital: Tariq Saraf Library

Russell's Hall
Dudley
West Midlands DY1 2LZ
Tel: 01384 457373 ext. 1307
E-mail: tariqsaraf.library@dudleyph-tr.wmids.nhs.uk
Librarian: Mrs Susan Hume
Type: Mental Health and Psychiatry.
Hours open: Tues: 2pm–5pm; Thurs: 9am–12 noon.
Users: All grades working at Bushey Fields Hospital and local Community Mental Health Services. All other local healthcare and social service staff. Those not in hospital, by appointment only.
Lending: Registered readers as above. Interlibrary lending within West Midlands Regional Health Libraries.
Stock policy: Disposal.
Holdings: 1,325 books; 14 current journal subscriptions, 26 journal titles; 43 films and videos.
Classification: NLM.
Library management system: AMLIB.
Computerized services: 1 NHSNET PC connected. Online access to AMED; Biomed Nursing; CINAHL; Embase: Psychiatry; MEDLINE via Regional WISH subscription; NeLH; Electronic DTB.
Library publications: Guides for users.
Special collections: Local community mental health.
Collaborative networks: Dudley Online Health Libraries; WMRHLN.

Caerphilly District Miners Hospital Library

Caerphilly District Miners Hospital
St Martins Road
Caerphilly
Mid Glamorgan CF83 2WW
Tel: 02920 807104
Fax: 02920 807101
E-mail: claire.powell@gwent.wales.nhs.uk
Librarian: Mrs Claire Powell
Founded: 1991
Type: Nursing and Clinical Medicine.
Hours open: Mon–Thurs: 8.30am–5pm; Fri: 8.30am–4.30pm.
Users: Trust staff and placements only.
Lending: Gwent Healthcare NHS Trust.
Stock policy: Dispose of it or offer to other libraries.
Holdings: 1,000 books; 21 current journal subscriptions; 100 videos; 6 CD-ROMs.
Computerized services: Internet access to CINAHL; Cochrane; MEDLINE, etc.
Special collections: Full set MRCP 11 videos.

Cairns Library: John Radcliffe Hospital

University of Oxford
John Radcliffe Hospital
Headington
Oxford OX3 9DU
Tel: 01865 221936
Fax: 01865 221941
E-mail: library@cairns.ox.ac.uk
URL: www.medicine.ox.ac.uk/cairns
Founded: 1950
Type: Health Sciences.
Hours open: Staffed Mon–Fri: 9am–9pm. Vacations: Mon–Fri: 9am–5pm. 24-hour access.
Users: Staff and students attached to the Faculty of Medicine, University of Oxford. Staff and students from other services who have contracted the Library Services.
Lending: Members only.

Stock policy: Sold or otherwise disposed of.
Holdings: 12,409 books; 457 current journal subscriptions. CD-ROMs and electronic journals networked through the University of Oxford.
Classification: NLM.
Library management system: GEAC.
Computerized services: Internet and database access. Search facilities via Silverplatter. Online access to Dialog. Access to CINAHL; Embase; MEDLINE, etc.
Branches: Cairns Library, Radcliffe Infirmary, Oxford; Cairns Library, Churchill Hospital, Oxford.
Collaborative networks: HeLIN; University of Oxford.

Cairns Library: Radcliffe Infirmary

University of Oxford
Radcliffe Infirmary
Woodstock Road
Oxford OX2 6HE
Tel: 01865 224478
Fax: 01865 224789
E-mail: library@cairns-library.ox.ac.uk
URL: www.medicine.ox.ac.uk/cairns
Founded: 1950
Type: Health Sciences.
Hours open: Open 24 hours. Staffed: Mon–Fri: 9am–5pm.
Users: Staff and students attached to the Faculty of Medicine, University of Oxford. Staff and students from other services who have contracted the Library Services.
Lending: Members only.
Stock policy: Sold or otherwise disposed of.
Holdings: 3,734 books; 83 current journal subscriptions; CD-ROMs and electronic journals networked through the University of Oxford.
Classification: NLM.
Library management system: GEAC.

Computerized services: Internet and database access. Search facilities via SilverPlatter. Online access to Dialog. Access to CINAHL; Embase; MEDLINE etc.
Branches: Cairns Library, Churchill Hospital, Oxford; Cairns Library, John Radcliffe Hospital, Oxford.
Collaborative networks: HeLIN; University of Oxford.

Cairns Library: Research Institute

University of Oxford
The Churchill Hospital
Oxford OX3 7LJ
Tel: 01865 225815
Fax: 01865 225834
E-mail: library@cairns-library.ox.ac.uk
URL: www.medicine.ox.ac.uk/cairns
Founded: 1950
Type: Multidisciplinary.
Hours open: Mon–Fri: 9am–5pm.
Users: Staff and students attached to the Faculty of Medicine, University of Oxford. Staff and students from other bodies who have contracted the Library Services.
Lending: Members only.
Stock policy: Withdrawn as appropriate. Sold or otherwise disposed of.
Holdings: 994 books; 36 current journal subscriptions.
Classification: NLM.
Library management system: GEAC.
Computerized services: Online access to Dialog and SilverPlatter. Access to CINAHL; Embase; MEDLINE. Electronic journals and CD-ROMs networked through University of Oxford.
Branches: Cairns Library, John Radcliffe Hospital, Oxford; Cairns Library, Radcliffe Infirmary, Oxford.
Collaborative networks: HeLIN; University of Oxford.
Notes: Previously George Wiernik Library.

Calderdale Royal Hospital Library Learning and Development Centre

Calderdale Royal Hospital
Salterhebble
Halifax
West Yorkshire HX3 0PW
Tel: 01422 224191
Fax: 01422 366889
Librarian: Helen Curtis; Chris Jackson (job-share)
Founded: 1982
Type: Multidisciplinary.
Hours open: Mon, Fri: 8.30am–5pm; Tues–Thurs: 8.30am–8pm; Sat: 8.30am–1pm.
Users: Employees of Calderdale and Huddersfield NHS Trust; local GPs and primary care staff. Others may use for reference purposes.
Lending: To library members and other medical libraries (by arrangement).
Stock policy: 10-year discard policy.
Holdings: 5,500 books; 130 current journal subscriptions.
Classification: NLM (Wessex adaptation).
Library management system: Heritage.
Computerized services: Access to AMED; Best Evidence; BNI; CINAHL; Cochrane Library; Embase: Psychiatry; MEDLINE.
Library publications: Current Awareness Bulletin; library guides.
Collaborative networks: BL; BMA; NULJ; Yorkshire Health Libraries.
Notes: Previously Halifax General Hospital Postgraduate Medical Library.

Cambridge Health Authority Knowledge Centre

Kingfisher House
Hinchingbrooke Business Park
Huntingdon
Cambridgeshire PE29 6FH
Tel: 01480 398622
Fax: 01480 398501
E-mail: Hilary.Jackson@camsha.nhs.uk
Librarian: Hilary Jackson
Prof. staff: Gill Curtis (Library Assistant)
Founded: 2000
Type: Health Management.
Hours open: 8.30am–5.30pm.
Users: Health Authority staff; PCG/Ts management.
Lending: As above.
Classification: Own.

Camden & Islington Health Authority Library

Insull Wing
110 Hampstead Road
London NW1 2LJ
Tel: 020 7853 5395
Fax: 020 7853 5369
E-mail: mandy.guest@cai-ha.nthames.nhs.uk
URL: www.cai-ha.nthames.nhs.uk
Librarian: Mandy Guest
Type: Health Management.
Hours open: Mon–Fri: 9am–4pm.
Users: Members of the Health Authority, Primary Care Groups, primary care staff in Camden and Islington.
Lending: Members only. Interlibrary loans.
Stock policy: Disposed of.
Holdings: 6,000 books; 60 current journal subscriptions, 75 journal titles; 25 films and videos; 20 CD-ROMs.
Classification: BLISS.
Library management system: DB/TextWorks.
Computerized services: Access to ASSIA for Health; Cochrane Library; HMIC; MEDLINE.
Collaborative networks: London Region; RDD.

Cancer BACUP: Resources

3 Bath Place
Rivington Street
London EC2A 3JR
Tel: 020 7696 9003
Fax: 020 7696 9002

E-mail: info@cancerbacup.org
URL: www.cancerbacup.org.uk
Librarian: Valerie Norrish
Prof. staff: Sandra Harwood
Founded: 1986
Type: Cancer.
Hours open: Not open. Office hours 9am–5.30pm.
Users: Staff of Cancer BACUP.
Lending: Reference only.
Stock policy: Often donated overseas.
Holdings: 1,160 books; 33 current journal subscriptions; 75 videos; 4 CD-ROMs.
Classification: Own.
Library management system: STATUS.
Computerized services: Online access to NCI; MEDLINE. Access to Cochrane Library.
Collaborative networks: CHILL; VOLSIF.

Canterbury Christ Church University College Library

Christ Church College
North Holmes Road
Canterbury
Kent CT1 1QU
Tel: 01227 782354
Fax: 01227 767530
E-mail: lib1@cant.ac.uk
URL:
www.cant.ac.uk/depts/services/library/library. htm
Librarian: Dr A Conyers
Prof. staff: Mr D Dorman; Mrs R Lewis; Mrs K Pounder; Mrs K Smith
Founded: 1962
Type: Multidisciplinary.
Hours open: Mon: 9.30am–9.30pm; Tues–Thurs: 8.30am–9.30pm; Fri: 8.30am–7pm; Sat: 10am–5pm; Sun: 2pm–7pm. Vacations: Mon: 9.30am–7pm; Tues–Thurs: 9am–7pm; Fri: 9am–5pm; Sat: 10am–1pm.
Users: Students and staff of the College. Members of the public may use the library for reference purposes, on application to the Director of Library Services. Those who wish

to borrow must apply to register as external readers.
Lending: As above.
Stock policy: Disposed of.
Holdings: 247,950 books; 1,152 journal titles.
Classification: Dewey.
Library management system: ALEPH.
Computerized services: Online access to Ovid Biomed services. Access to ASSIANet; BNI; CancerLit; Caredata; CINAHL; Cochrane Database of Systematic Reviews; MEDLINE; PsycINFO; SportDiscus.
Special collections: The Gaskell Collection.
Branches: Salomons Library, Tunbridge Wells; Thanet Campus, Broadstairs.
Collaborative networks: Canterbury Circle of Libraries; M25 Consortium; SCONUL Vacation Access Scheme; UK Libraries Plus.

Cefn Coed Hospital Staff Library

Cefn Coed Hospital
Swansea NHS Trust
Waunarlwydd Road
Cockett
Swansea SA2 0GH
Tel: 01792 516546
Fax: 01792 516410
E-mail: cefncoedlibrary@hotmail.com
Librarian: Miss Emma L James
Founded: 1950
Type: Multidisciplinary.
Hours open: Staffed Mon–Thurs: 8.45am–4.45pm; Fri: 8.45am–4.15pm. 24-hour access.
Users: Doctors, nurses, PAMs, scientific and community management. Others at discretion of Librarian and service level agreement.
Lending: Members of Swansea NHS Trust. Others, reference only.
Stock policy: Old stock archived.

Holdings: 2,500 books; 30 current journal subscriptions, 45 journal titles; 60 videos; 10 CD-ROMs.
Classification: NLM (Wessex adaptation).
Computerized services: Online access to AMED; ASSIA; BNI; CancerLit; CINAHL; Embase; HealthStar; MEDLINE; PsycINFO. Access to ClinPsych; Cochrane Library; Embase: Psychiatry.
Library publications: Library services guide; guides to internet, intranet, audio-visual services. Guide to using ClinPsych/Embase: Psychiatry; Evidence Based Medicine.
Collaborative networks: ATLAS; AWHL; PLCS; SYBILS.

Central Manchester & Manchester Children's University Hospitals NHS Trust Library Service

Postgraduate Health Sciences Centre
Manchester Royal Infirmary
Oxford Road
Manchester M13 9WL
Tel: 0161 276 4344
Fax: 0161 276 6918
E-mail: jefferson@central.cmht.nwest.nhs.uk
Librarian: Christine Thornton (Service Manager)
Prof. staff: Rini Banerjee; Ruth Silman; Debra Thornton
Founded: 1971
Type: Multidisciplinary.
Hours open: Mon–Wed: 9.30am–7pm; Thurs–Fri: 9.30am–5pm. St Mary's and Royal Eye Hospital vary.
Users: Staff of the Trust and students on placement. Reference access for members of other health libraries in Manchester – passport scheme.
Lending: Non-members cannot borrow. Reference books not available for loan.
Stock policy: Old stock is passed on or disposed of.

Holdings: 6,000 books; 204 current journal subscriptions.
Classification: NLM.
Library management system: Heritage IV.
Computerized services: Access to Cochrane Library via NeLH. Access via ADITUS to AMED; BNI; CINAHL; Embase; HMIC; MEDLINE; PsycINFO.
Library publications: In-house bulletin.
Special collections: Obstetrics, gynaecology, paediatrics. Ophthalmology.
Branches: Booth Hall Children's Hospital Library; Royal Manchester Children's Hospital Library.
Collaborative networks: LIHNN.
Notes: The Jefferson, St Mary's and Royal Eye Hospital Libraries are now a single service – three service points on the same site.

Central Manchester & Manchester Children's University Hospitals NHS Trust: Booth Hall Children's Hospital Medical Library

Manchester Children's Hospitals NHS Trust
Charlestown Road
Blackley
Manchester M9 7AA
Tel: 0161 220 5018
Fax: 0161 220 5579
Librarian: Jennifer Kelly
Type: Multidisciplinary.
Hours open: Open 24 hours via digital lock.
Users: Trust staff.
Lending: As above.
Stock policy: Dispose of.
Holdings: 1,400 books; 30 journal subscriptions.
Classification: NLM.
Library management system: DB/TextWorks
Computerized services: Catalogue. Internet access. Access to MEDLINE and Cochrane Library.

Collaborative networks: LIHNN.

Central Manchester & Manchester Children's University Hospitals NHS Trust: Royal Manchester Children's Hospital Medical Library

Giving for Living Research and Postgraduate Centre
Royal Manchester Children's Hospital
Hospital Road, Pendlebury
Manchester M27 4HA
Tel: 0161 727 2387
Fax: 0161 727 2387
E-mail: jenny1@rmch.fsnet.co.uk
Librarian: Jennifer Kelly
Founded: 1977
Type: Multidisciplinary.
Hours open: Mon–Thurs: 9am–7.30pm; Fri: 9am–4.30pm.
Users: Trust staff.
Lending: As above.
Stock policy: Dispose of.
Holdings: 2,500 books; 98 current journal subscriptions; small collection of videos.
Classification: NLM.
Library management system: DB/TextWorks.
Computerized services: Catalogue. Internet access. Access to CINAHL; Cochrane Library; MEDLINE.
Library publications: Journals list; Library Bulletin; acquisitions list.
Collaborative networks: LIHNN; NULJ.

Central Middlesex Hospital: Avery Jones Postgraduate Centre Library

Central Middlesex Hospital
North West London Hospitals NHS Trust
Acton Lane
London NW10 7NS
Tel: 020 8453 2504
Fax: 020 8453 2503
E-mail: library@cmhlib.demon.co.uk
URL: www.cmhlib.demon.co.uk
Librarian: Barbara Cumbers (Library Manager)
Prof. staff: Alan Fricker
Type: Multidisciplinary.
Hours open: Mon: 9am–5pm; Tues–Wed: 9am–7pm; Thurs and Fri: 9am–5pm.
Users: Staff of NWLH NHS Trust, Parkside Health, BKCW Mental Health Trust, Brent PCGs, Brent and Harrow HA and medical and nursing staff on placement.
Lending: To members.
Stock policy: Old stock discarded after ten years.
Holdings: 3,000 books; 180 current journal subscriptions, 223 journal titles; 300 films and videos; 30 CD-ROMs.
Classification: NLM.
Library management system: InMagic; DB/TextWorks.
Computerized services: Online access to Ovid Biomed; Embase; Cochrane Library; NeLH; PsycINFO. Access to British Nursing Index; CINAHL; MEDLINE.
Library publications: Library guide; CINAHL guide; MEDLINE guide; Embase guide; Current Awareness Bulletin.
Collaborative networks: London Region; PLCS; West London Workforce Development Confederation.

Charles Hastings PGMC Clinical Library

Worcestershire Acute Hospitals NHS Trust
Worcester Royal Infirmary
Ronkswood Branch
Newtown Road
Worcester WR5 1HN
Tel: 01905 760602
Fax: 01905 767834
E-mail: chpgc@freenetname.co.uk
Librarian: Mrs C Spencer-Bamford
Prof. staff: Miss Emma Brant (Information and Library Assistant)
Founded: 1972
Type: Multidisciplinary.
Hours open: 8am–5pm.
Users: Bona fide medical staff only.
Lending: Staff only.
Stock policy: On offer to staff before disposal.
Holdings: 1,946 books; 140 current journal subscriptions; 5 CD-ROMs.
Classification: NLM (Wessex adaptation).
Library management system: Heritage.
Computerized services: Online access to Biomed. Access to Ovid MEDLINE.
Collaborative networks: BL; BMA; WMRHN.

Chartered Society of Physiotherapy Information Resource Centre

14 Bedford Row
London WC1R 4ED
Tel: 020 7306 6619/6605/6604
Fax: 020 7306 6611
E-mail: millerc@csphysio.org.uk or sewernia-ka@csphysio.org.uk
URL: www.csp.org.uk
Prof. staff: Caroline Miller; Anna Sewerniak
Founded: 1991
Type: Physiotherapy.
Hours open: Mon–Fri: 9am–5pm.
Users: Members of the Chartered Society of Physiotherapy, including students.
Lending: Reference only.

Stock policy: Sent to Wellcome Institute.
Holdings: 500 books; 140 current journal subscriptions; 10 CD-ROMs; 2,000 grey literature; 200 dissertations and theses.
Classification: Own
Library management system: GLAS; OSI.
Computerized services: CD-ROM access to AMED; Book Data; CINAHL; Cochrane Library; Embase; HMIC; MEDLINE; SMART.
Library publications: Current awareness bulletins on the Information Resource Centre; dissertations and theses; software packages; internet websites; sources of consumer health information and many more.
Special collections: Physiotherapy Research Database (ongoing and completed).
Collaborative networks: INFAH.

Chase Health Information Centre

Block C4, Chase Farm Hospital
The Ridgeway
Enfield
Middlesex EN2 8JL
Tel: 020 8967 5982
Fax: 020 8366 2245
E-mail: LIBCF@mdx.ac.uk
Librarian: Vacant
Prof. staff: Mrs Helen Frankel
Founded: 1999
Type: Multidisciplinary.
Hours open: Mon and Fri: 9.30am–5pm; Tues–Thurs: 9.30am–6pm. August: 9.30am–5pm.
Users: Staff and students of Middlesex Hospital; NHS staff working in the Hospital and local community.
Lending: To Library members.
Stock policy: Some sent overseas; some discarded.
Holdings: 6,000 books; 100 current journal subscriptions, 130 journal titles.
Classification: NLM.

Library management system: Horizon.
Computerized services: Online access to CINAHL; Cochrane Library; MEDLINE; PsycINFO.
Library publications: Library guide; new books list.
Collaborative networks: London Region; UK Libraries Plus.

Cheltenham General Hospital Trust Library

Alexandra House
Cheltenham General Hospital
Sandford Road
Cheltenham
Gloucestershire GL53 7AN
Tel: 01242 273036
Fax: 01242 273060
E-mail: dorothy.curtis@cghst.org.uk
Librarian: Dorothy Curtis
Founded: 1990
Type: Multidisciplinary.
Hours open: Mon–Thurs: 8.30am–5pm; Fri: 8.30am–4.30pm.
Users: Staff of Gloucestershire NHS Trusts.
Lending: To staff only or local interlending scheme.
Stock policy: Offered to other libraries.
Holdings: 3,500 books; 72 current journal subscriptions, 150 journal titles; 10 CD-ROMs.
Classification: NLM (Wessex adaptation).
Library management system: Headfast plus Webcat on Regional Website.
Computerized services: Access to AMED; ASSIA; BNI; CINAHL; Embase; HMIC; MEDLINE; PsycINFO.
Collaborative networks: SWRLIN.

Chester College School of Nursing & Midwifery: Arrowe Park Hospital Nursing Library

School of Nursing & Midwifery
Chester College
Arrowe Park Hospital

Upton
Wirral
Merseyside CH49 5PE
Tel: 0151 604 7291
Fax: 0156 678 5322
E-mail: lr.arrowe@chester.ac.uk
URL: www.chester.ac.uk
Librarian: Christine Holly
Founded: 1990
Type: Nursing.
Hours open: Mon–Thurs: 8.30am–4.30pm; Fri: 8.30am–4pm.
Users: Student and trained nurses on Chester College courses; Wirral Hospital Trust staff, except medics; Community Trust; practice nurses; BUPA Hospital.
Lending: As above.
Stock policy: Disposed of, if considered useless by teaching staff.
Holdings: 21,000 books; 35 current journal subscriptions; 100 films and videos.
Classification: Dewey.
Library management system: INNOPAC
Computerized services: ADITUS for access to CINAHL. Online access to AMED; Cochrane Library; Embase; Web of Science. Online journals: Infotrac; Internurse; Synergy.
Library publications: Library publicity leaflets.
Special collections: General nursing; psychology; health promotion; nurse education and research.
Collaborative networks: LIHNN.

Chesterfield & North Derbyshire Royal Hospital NHS Trust

Education Centre Library
Calow, Chesterfield
Derbyshire S44 5BL
Tel: 01246 277271
Librarian: Julia Nicholson
Prof. staff: Jonathan Phillips
Founded: 1984

Type: Medical/Health.
Hours open: Mon–Thurs: 8.30am–6.30pm;
Fri: 8.30am–5pm.
Users: Trust staff and other health workers in North Derbyshire on application. Anyone can have access to library for reference.
Lending: To members only.
Stock policy: Book sale where appropriate. Disposed of if doesn't sell.
Holdings: 8,000 books; 102 current journal subscriptions, 200 journal titles; 200 videos; 5 CD-ROMs.
Classification: NLM.
Library management system: Heritage.
Computerized services: Internet access to Biomed. CD-ROM access to BNI; CINAHL; Cochrane Library; MEDLINE; NRR.

Chiltern Medical Library

Chiltern Medical Education Centre
Wycombe General Hospital
Queen Alexandra Road
High Wycombe
Buckinghamshire HP11 2TT
Tel: 01494 426364
Fax: 01494 424376
E-mail: lesleymartyn@wyclib.demon.co.uk
Librarian: Mrs Lesley Martyn
Founded: 1965
Type: Multidisciplinary.
Hours open: Mon–Fri: 8.30am–5.30pm.
Users: Staff of the Buckinghamshire NHS Trust, of the Buckinghamshire Mental Health Trust, primary care staff in the area, students on placement with the South Buckinghamshire Trust. Public on application.
Lending: Registered readers.
Stock policy: Exchange list for journals, then disposal. Books offered for sale, donated to developing countries or disposed of.
Holdings: 5,087 books; 80 current journal subscriptions, 135 journal titles; 109 videos; 33 audio tapes.
Classification: NLM.

Library management system: DB/TextWorks.
Computerized services: Online access to Data-Star and Ovid. Access to AMED; BNI; CINAHL; Cochrane Library; Embase; HMIC; MEDLINE; PsycINFO.
Library publications: Library guide; Union List of Periodicals; guide to searching MEDLINE and Cochrane.
Branches: Staff Library, Amersham Hospital.
Collaborative networks: HeLIN.

Chorley & South Ribble NHS Trust Postgraduate Education Centre Library

Chorley & South Ribble NHS Trust
Preston Road
Chorley
Lancashire PR7 1PP
Tel: 01257 245607
Fax: 01257 245623
E-mail: kathyturtle@csrtr.nhs.uk
Librarian: Mrs Kathleen M Turtle
Founded: 1994
Type: Multidisciplinary.
Hours open: Mon, Wed, Fri: 9am–5pm; Tues and Thurs: 9am–6pm.
Users: Trust staff; general practice staff; students and staff of the University of Central Lancashire; medical students at University of Manchester. All others, reference facilities only by arrangement.
Lending: To members only.
Stock policy: Old stock discarded.
Holdings: 3,800 books; 91 current journal subscriptions, 141 journal titles; 26 videos; 13 CD-ROMs.
Classification: Dewey 20.
Library management system: Talis.
Computerized services: Online access via ADITUS; Ovid Biomed; REGISS. Access to Best Evidence, Cochrane Library; NRR.
Library publications: Quarterly Library Bulletin.
Collaborative networks: BL; BMA; LIHNN; Royal College of Surgeons.

Christie Hospital NHS Trust: Kostoris Medical Library

Wilmslow Road
Withington
Manchester M20 4BX
Tel: 0161 446 3452
Fax: 0161 446 3454
E-mail: sglover@picr.man.ac.uk
URL: www.christie.man.ac.uk/library.htm
Librarian: Melanie Hinde
Prof. staff: Steve Glover; Jenny Russell
Type: Multidisciplinary.
Hours open: Mon–Wed: 9am–7pm; Thurs: 8am–5.30pm; Fri: 8am–5pm; Sat: 9am–1pm.
Users: Doctors, nurses, PAMs, scientists, medical students, junior doctors.
Lending: To full members only.
Stock policy: Disposed of.
Holdings: 5,300 books; 145 current journal subscriptions, 223 journal titles; 15 CD-ROMs.
Classification: Barnard.
Library management system: Winchill.
Computerized services: Access to AMED; BNI; CINAHL; Embase; MEDLINE; PsycINFO.
Library publications: In-house newsletter: Library Link.
Collaborative networks: LIHNN.

City Hospital NHS Trust: Bevan Library

Dudley Road
Birmingham B18 7QU
Tel: 0121 507 4491
Fax: 0121 507 4602
E-mail: bevan.library@cityhospbham.wmids.nhs.uk
Librarian: Karen Bowen
Prof. staff: Sally Barley
Founded: 1960s.
Type: Multidisciplinary.
Hours open: Mon–Fri: 8.30am–5pm. 24-hour access for staff.

Users: All CHT staff; visitors to the Trust; PCGs. Others by appointment or prior arrangement.
Lending: Staff and students of CHT only.
Stock policy: Book sales.
Holdings: 168 books; 180 current journal subscriptions, 180 journal titles; 6 CD-ROMs.
Classification: LC/NLM.
Library management system: Heritage.
Computerized services: Access via Ovid online to AMED; CINAHL; Cochrane Library; Embase: Psychiatry; MEDLINE.
Library publications: Newsletter.
Collaborative networks: WMRHLN.

City Hospitals Sunderland Medical Library

Sunderland Royal Hospital
Kayll Road
Sunderland
Tyne and Wear SR4 7TP
Tel: 0191 565 6256 ext. 42430/42218/42577
Fax: 0191 569 9786
E-mail: library@chs.northy.nhs.uk
Librarian: Catherine Fisher
Prof. staff: Mrs Gwyneth Fleming (Library Manager)
Type: Multidisciplinary.
Hours open: Mon–Fri: 8am–8pm; Sat: 10am–5pm.
Users: City Hospital staff with some external members. No public service.
Lending: Members only.
Stock policy: Usually disposal.
Holdings: 5,000 books; 250 journal titles; 50 films and videos; 20 CD-ROMs; 500 reports.
Classification: Dewey.
Library management system: Dynix.
Computerized services: Online access to AMED; CINAHL; Cochrane Library; Embase: Psychiatry; MEDLINE. Access to BNI.
Library publications: Annual Report; user guides.
Collaborative networks: HLN.

College of Occupational Therapists Library (DISC)

106–114 Borough High Street
Southwark
London SE1 1LB
Tel: 020 7450 2316
Fax: 020 7450 2364
E-mail: library@cot.co.uk
URL: www.cot.co.uk
Librarian: Ann Mason
Founded: 1991
Type: Specialist Healthcare.
Hours open: Mon–Fri: 9am–5pm.
Users: Members of the College of Occupational Therapists. Anyone with a legitimate interest in occupational therapy.
Lending: Library is reference only. Theses/dissertation loan collection – members only.
Stock policy: Keep occupational therapy material for archive. Offer duplicates to other libraries.
Holdings: 5,880 books; 75 current journal subscriptions, 85 journal titles; 60 videos.
Classification: Dewey.
Library management system: Limes.
Computerized services: Access to AMED; CINAHL; ClinPsych; Cochrane Library; HMIC; OTDBASE.
Library publications: Carr, P. Thesis Collection: The National Collection of Unpublished Occupational Therapy Research. London: COT,1999.
Special collections: Historical collection of occupational therapy literature. BAOT/COT archive held at Wellcome Institute for History of Medicine.
Collaborative networks: INFAH.

Corbett Clinical Library

Medical Services Centre
Corbett Hospital
Stourbridge
West Midlands DY8 4JB
Tel: 01384 456111 ext. 4819
Fax: 01384 443631
E-mail: cor.library@dudleyph-tr.wmids.nhs.uk
Librarian: Sue Hume (Assistant Librarian to Dudley Group of Hospitals NHS Trust)
Type: Multidisciplinary.
Hours open: Mon–Fri: 9am–5pm. (Librarian available: Mon: 10am–5pm; Tues: 9am–12.30pm; Wed: 9am–5pm; Thurs: 2pm–5pm; Fri: 10am–2pm.)
Users: All multidisciplinary staff of Dudley Group Hospitals; healthcare staff working in the locality; local social services staff. Visitors by appointment only.
Lending: Registered readers as above only. Interlibrary loan to other Regional Health Libraries.
Stock policy: Try to sell, then pass to GAZA Library project.
Holdings: 1,360 books; 59 current journal subscriptions, 104 journal titles; 76 videos; 1 CD-ROM.
Classification: NLM.
Library management system: AMLIB.
Computerized services: Connected to internet via NHSNet. Biomed services via Regional WISH subscription. Access to AMED; Biomed Nursing; CINAHL; Embase: Psychiatry; MEDLINE.
Collaborative networks: Dudley Online Health Libraries; WMRHLN.
Notes: The library is a branch of Dudley Group of Hospitals NHS Trust Clinical Library Service.

Cork University Hospital Medical Library

Wilton
Cork
Republic of Ireland
Tel: +353 21 490 2976
Fax: +353 21 434 5826
E-mail: r.buttimer@ucc.ie
URL: http://booleweb.ucc.ie
Librarian: Rosarii Buttimer
Founded: 1979
Type: Primarily Medicine, Dentistry and Nursing.

Hours open: Oct–mid-June: 9am–8.30pm; mid-June–end June: 9am–5pm; July–Aug: 9am–4.30pm; Sept: 9am–7pm.

Users: Staff and students registered with UCC (primarily medicine, dentistry and nursing); staff of Southern Health Board; external readers, primarily those who have graduated from UCC.

Lending: Registered users can borrow stock. Other libraries can borrow books through interlibrary loan. Reference material, non-book material or journals may not be borrowed.

Stock policy: Old stock is placed in storage with UCC and can be accessed within 48 hours of placing a faxed request.

Holdings: 10,000 books; 350 current journal subscriptions, 400 journal titles; 80 films and videos; 50 CD-ROMs.

Classification: Dewey.

Library management system: INNOPAC.

Computerized services: Online access to Biomed via Ovid; OCLC First Search; Science Direct and Web of Science Citation Databases (ISI).

Collaborative networks: IHLG.

Cornwall Health Library Service

Cornwall Postgraduate Medical Centre
Royal Cornwall Hospital
Truro
Cornwall TR1 3LJ
Tel: 01872 252610
Fax: 01872 222838
E-mail: medical.library@rcht.swest.nhs.uk
Librarian: Pam Kitch
Prof. staff: Sue Richards
Founded: 1966
Type: Multiprofessional.
Hours open: Mon–Thurs: 8.30am–6.30pm; Fri: 8.30am–5.30pm; Sat: 9.30am–5pm.
Users: Healthcare professionals and other students. Personal/institutional members by subscription.

Lending: Members only.

Stock policy: Stock revision policy for all stock over 15 years.

Holdings: 11,300 books; 241 current journal subscriptions; 50+ videos.

Classification: NLM (Wessex adaptation).

Library management system: Headfast.

Computerized services: Search facilities via Data-Star and HCN. Online access to Cochrane Library; PubMed. Internet access to AMED; ASSIA; BNI; CINAHL; Cochrane Library; Embase; HMIC; MEDLINE; PsycINFO.

Branches: Staff library, St Lawrence's Hospital, Bodmin.

Collaborative networks: SWRLIN.

County Durham & Darlington Health Authority Library

Appleton House
Lanchester Road
Durham DH1 5XZ
Tel: 0191 333 3395
Fax: 0191 333 3398
E-mail: linda.snowdon@public-health. durham–ha.northy.nhs.uk
Librarian: Ms Linda Snowdon
Founded: 2000
Type: Multidisciplinary.
Hours open: Mon–Fri: 9am–5pm.
Users: Any NHS employee working in County Durham and Darlington.
Lending: As above.
Stock policy: Dispose of it.
Holdings: 7,000 books; 50 current journal subscriptions; 100 journal titles; 10 videos.
Classification: Own.
Computerized services: All Ovid databases.
Collaborative networks: Alliance of Health Library and Information Services; Durham and Teeside Workforce Confederation; HLN.

Crawley Hospital Health Sciences Library

Crawley Hospital
Surrey and Sussex NHS Trust
West Green Drive
Crawley
West Sussex RH11 7DH
Tel: 01293 600300 ext. 3368/01293 600368
Fax: 01293 600317
E-mail: library@crawley@sysx-tr.eshcare-tr.sthames.nhs.uk
Librarian: Sheila Marsh (based at East Surrey)
Prof. staff: Anne Gardener; Carole Iles
Hours open: Mon–Fri: 9am–5pm.
Holdings: 122 journal titles.
Collaborative networks: STLIS.

Crosshouse Hospital Medical Library

Crosshouse Hospital
Kilmarnock
Ayrshire KA2 0BE
Tel: 01563 577092
Fax: 01563 577096
E-mail: Susan.Cuthbertson@aaaht.scot.nhs.uk
Librarian: Ms Susan Cuthbertson
Type: Multidisciplinary.
Hours open: Mon–Thurs: 8.45am–5pm; Fri: 8.45am–4.30pm. Open 24 hours to members only.
Users: Staff in the Ayrshire and Arran NHS Trust, Ayrshire Primary Care Trust, GPs.
Lending: Members only.
Stock policy: Withdrawn stock is normally sent to developing countries.
Holdings: 4,000 books; 100 current journal subscriptions; 100 videos; 20 CD-ROMs.
Classification: NLM.
Library management system: ALICE for Windows.
Computerized services: Library home page on Hospital and Trust intranet. Online access to CINAHL; Cochrane Library; HEBS; NRR. Access to AMED.

Library publications: Library guide; internet guide.
Special collections: Historical collection.
Collaborative networks: Ayrshire Health Libraries Co-operative; SHINE.

Croydon Health Promotion Library

Croydon and Surrey Downs Community NHS Trust
12–18 Lennard Road
Croydon
Surrey CR9 2RS
Tel: 020 8680 2008 ext. 256
Fax: 020 8666 0495 (attn Library)
E-mail: jmclean@jmclean.demon.co.uk
Librarian: Janet McLean
Founded: 1986
Type: Multidisciplinary.
Hours open: Mon–Thurs: 10am–4pm.
Users: NHS staff in Croydon. Other professionals involved in health promotion.
Lending: Members only.
Stock policy: Offered to other libraries and readers, then disposed of.
Holdings: 4,500 books; 40 current journal suscriptions, 57 journal titles.
Classification: NLM.
Library management system: DB/TextWorks.
Computerized services: Online access to Ovid. Access to AMED; ASSIA; CINAHL; Cochrane Library; MEDLINE.
Collaborative networks: BL; NULJ; STLIS Union Lists.

Croydon Health Sciences Library

Mayday University Hospital
London Road
Thornton Heath
Surrey CR7 7YE
Tel: 020 8401 3197
Fax: 020 8401 3883
E-mail: ray.phillips@mhc-tr.sthames.nhs.uk

Librarian: Ray Phillips
Prof. staff: Arpita Banerjee; David Hayes
Type: Multidisciplinary.
Hours open: Mon–Fri: 9am–5pm. After-hours access available by application.
Users: All Croydon NHS workers. Largest user group is nurses followed by doctors. Non-NHS persons may apply for affiliated membership.
Lending: To all registered users. No restriction by discipline.
Stock policy: Journals offered nationally. Books usually no longer safe to use so disposed of.
Holdings: 5,000 books; 140 current journal subscriptions, 170 journal titles; 40 films and videos; 20 CD-ROMs.
Classification: NLM.
Library management system: DB/TextWorks.
Computerized services: Access to Ovid and Dialog.

Darlington Memorial Hospital Education Centre Library

Darlington Memorial Hospital
Hollyhurst Road
Darlington
Co Durham DL3 6HX
Tel: 01325 743222
Fax: 01325 743222
E-mail: librarydmh@hotmail.com
Librarian: Carol Houghton; Claire Masterman
Founded: 1972
Type: Multidisciplinary.
Hours open: Mon–Fri: 8.45am–5.30pm. 24 hour access via key at switchboard.
Users: All Trust employees; all members of the Community Mental Health Trust; GPs and practice staff; University of Teesside students on placement at the Trust. Others reference only.
Lending: As above.
Stock policy: Discard all stock over 10 years old unless of some archival value.

Holdings: 6,000 books; 100 current journal subscriptions; 12 videos; 6 CD-ROMs.
Classification: Dewey 21.
Library management system: Manual at present.
Computerized services: Online access to AMED; CINAHL; Embase: Psychiatry; MEDLINE. Access to Cochrane Library.
Collaborative networks: DAR; Northern and Yorkshire Union List; PLCS.

Dartford & Gravesham NHS Trust Library

Philip Farrant Education Centre
Darent Valley Hospital
Darenth Wood Road
Dartford
Kent DA2 8DA
Tel: 01322 428549
Fax: 01322 428547
E-mail: Carole.Smith@dag-tr.sthames.nhs.uk
Librarian: Carole Smith
Founded: 2000
Type: Multidisciplinary.
Hours open: Mon and Wed: 8.30am–5pm; Tues and Thurs: 8.30am–8pm; Fri: 8.30am–4.30pm.
Users: The library provides services to staff of Dartford and Gravesham NHS Trust; Thames Gateway NHS Trust and Dartford and Gravesham and Swanley PCT staff. Others at the discretion of the Librarian, for reference use only.
Lending: As above plus interlibrary loans to regional library network.
Stock policy: Dispose of it.
Holdings: 8,000 books; 78 current journal subscriptions; 200 films and videos; 20 CD-ROMS.
Classification: NLM.
Library management system: LIBRARIAN and DB/TextWorks.
Computerized services: Regional database for catalogue and union list of journals. Online access to Data-Star and Ovid. CD-ROM access to BNI; CINAHL; MEDLINE.

Library publications: Library guide.
Collaborative networks: BL; BMA; Institute of Psychiatry; STLIS.
Notes: This library replaces libraries at Gravesend and North Kent Hospital, Joyce Green Hospital, Stone House Hospital and West Hill Hospital.

De Montfort University: Charles Frears Campus Library

266 London Road
Leicester LE2 1RQ
Tel: 0116 201 3905
Fax: 0116 201 3822
E-mail: bfreeman@dmu.ac.uk
URL: www.library.dmu.ac.uk
Librarian: Barbara Freeman
Prof. staff: Jill Bentley; Andrew Gerrard; Deirdre Hayward; Beryl Welding
Founded: 1978
Type: Academic – Nursing and Midwifery.
Hours open: Mon–Thurs: 8.30am–8pm; Fri: 8.30am–5pm.
Users: Staff and students of De Montfort University. Leicestershire NHS staff have reference access only.
Lending: To De Montfort University members only.
Stock policy: Disposed of.
Holdings: 22,000 books; 230 current journal subscriptions; 700 videos; 12 CD-ROMs.
Classification: NLM.
Library management system: Talis.
Computerized services: Online access to ASSIA; BNI; Caredata; CINAHL; Cochrane Library; HMIC; MEDLINE; PsycINFO. CD-ROM no longer used.
Library publications: Library guide; databases worksheets.
Collaborative networks: LeHLA; NULJ; TRAHCLIS.

De Montfort University: Scraptoft Library

Scraptoft Campus
Leicester LE7 9SU
Tel: 0116 257 7865
Fax: 0116 257 7866
Librarian: Ms Olwyn Reynard
Hours open: Mon–Thurs: 8.45am–9pm; Fri: 8.45am–5pm; Sat: 9am–12 noon (summer term). Vacations: Mon–Fri: 9am–5pm.
Notes: For further details see website www.telh.nhs.uk

Defence Medical Services Training Centre

MacLaughlin Library
Keogh Barracks
Ash Vale
Aldershot
Hampshire GU12 5RQ
Tel: 01252 340259
Fax: 01252 340262
E-mail: library@dmstc.demon.co.uk
Librarian: Carol Hobbs
Hours open: Mon–Thurs: 8.30am–5pm; Fri: 8.30am–12.30pm.
Holdings: 70 journal titles.

Dementia Service Development Centre

Library and Information Service
University of Stirling
Stirling FK9 4LA
Tel: 01786 467740
Fax: 01786 466846
E-mail: a.e.harrison@stir.ac.uk
URL: www.stir.ac.uk/dsdc
Librarian: Averil Harrison (Information Officer)
Founded: 1990
Type: Specialist – Dementia Care.
Hours open: Mon–Fri: 10am–4pm.
Users: Those working or in training in the field of dementia care service provision.

Lending: Users within Scotland. Loan service not available to those in the education sector or users outside Scotland. Anyone can use the resource as a reference library.
Stock policy: Everything archived at the moment.
Holdings: 7,000 books; 53 current journal subscriptions, 75 journal titles.
Classification: Own.
Computerized services: Windows and web version of Dataware BRS SEARCH.
Library publications: A range of publications produced. List available.
Collaborative networks: DSDC Network; SHINE.

Department of Health Library: Quarry House

Room 5C05
Quarry House
Quarry Hill
80 London Road
Leeds LS2 7UE
Tel: 0113 2545080
Fax: 0113 2545084
E-mail: kerry.hanson@doh.gsi.gov.uk
Librarian: Kerry Hanson (Acting Senior Librarian)
Type: Health Management, Policy and associated subjects.
Hours open: 9am–5pm.
Users: As Skipton House below.
Lending: As Skipton House.
Stock policy: As Skipton House.
Computerized services: Variety of CD-ROM and online services.

Department of Health Library: Skipton House

Skipton House
80 London Road
London SE1 6LW
Tel: 020 797 26541
Fax: 020 797 25976
URL: www.doh.gsi.gov.uk

Librarian: Pek Lan Bower (Head of Library and Information Services)
Prof. staff: Gill Baker; John Scott Cree; Philip Defriez; Karen George; Martin Gilbert; Jennifer Goodfellow
Founded: 1834
Type: Public Health; Health Services; Medicine; Hospitals; Social Care.
Hours open: 9am–5pm.
Users: Department of Health staff; other government libraries for borrowing. Not open to the public.
Lending: Internal staff only.
Stock policy: Weeded material is offered to various organizations such as BL, BookAid, Education Aids and interested libraries.
Holdings: 200,000 monographs; 2,000 journals; a variety of CD-ROMs and online and internet services.
Classification: BLISS 2nd edition.
Computerized services: Variety of CD-ROM and online services.
Library publications: Health Service Abstracts; Electronic – Health CD; HMIC CD; DH-Data.
Branches: Quarry House, Quarry Hill, Leeds; Wellington House, London. See other entries.
Collaborative networks: Health Management Information Consortium.

Department of Health Library: Wellington House

Room G42
Wellington House
133–155 Waterloo Road
London SE1 8UG
Tel: 020 797 24204
Fax: 020 797 24209
Librarian: Melanie Peffer
Hours open: 9am–5pm.
Users: As Skipton House above.
Lending: As Skipton House.
Stock policy: As Skipton House.

Holdings: Small collection on health and social services.
Computerized services: Variety of CD-ROM and online services.

Derby City General Hospital Library & Knowledge Service

Derby City General Hospital NHS Trust
Derby DE22 3NE
Tel: 01332 340131
Fax: 01332 200318
Librarian: David Watson
Type: Multidisciplinary.
Hours open: Mon–Thurs: 8am–6pm; Fri: 8am–5pm.
Users: Trust employees only.
Lending: Trust employees only.
Stock policy: Old stock disposed of.
Holdings: 7,500 books; 104 current journal subscriptions, 200 journal titles; 20 CD-ROMs.
Classification: NLM.
Library management system: Heritage.
Computerized services: Search facilities via Ovid Biomedical Service – access to AMED; Best Evidence; CINAHL; Cochrane Library; DARE; Embase; MEDLINE; PsycINFO.
Collaborative networks: DIG; TRAH-CLIS.

Derbyshire Royal Infirmary Library & Knowledge Service

Devonshire House
Derbyshire Royal Infirmary
Derby DE1 2QY
Tel: 01332 254788
Fax: 01332 254608
Librarian: Maxine Lathbury
Prof. staff: David Watson; Caroline White
Type: Multidisciplinary.
Hours open: Mon–Fri: 8am–6pm; Sat: 9am–12.30pm.
Users: Trust employees and other contracted users.

Lending: To Trust employees.
Stock policy: Disposed of.
Holdings: 8,500 books; 160 current journal subscriptons, 250 journal titles; 12 films and videos; 80 CD-ROMs.
Classification: NLM.
Library management system: Heritage.
Computerized services: Online access to Ovid Biomedical Service.
Library publications: Library and Knowledge Service Newsletter.
Collaborative networks: DIG; TRAH-CLIS; Trent Regional Libraries.

Dewsbury Health Care NHS Trust Library & Information Service

Oakwell Centre
Dewsbury Health Care NHS Trust
Halifax Road
Dewsbury
West Yorkshire WF13 4HS
Tel: 01924 816073
Fax: 01924 816173
E-mail: library@dhc-tr.northy.nhs.uk
Librarian: Ms Francesca Pendino
Founded: 1973
Type: Multidisciplinary.
Hours open: Mon: 9.30am–5pm; Tues and Thurs: 9am–6.30pm; Wed: 9am–5pm; Fri: 9am–4.30pm.
Users: Trust staff. Other users, reference only.
Lending: All eligible users.
Stock policy: Superseded and out-of-date stock is sold. Ongoing stock revision.
Holdings: 14,000 books; 180 current journal subscriptions, 200 journal titles; 200 videos; 3,000 35mm slides.
Classification: NLM (Wessex adaptation).
Library management system: T- Series.
Computerized services: Online access to Data-Star. Access to AMED; BNI; Bookwise; CINAHL; EBMR; Embase; HMIC; MEDLINE.
Collaborative networks: Health Libraries North; JHLS.

Diabetes UK Library

Research and Information Dept
10 Queen Anne Street
London W19 9LH
Tel: 020 7462 2601
Fax: 020 7637 5444
E-mail: infoscience@diabetes.org,uk
URL: www.diabetes.org.uk
Librarian: Miss M Benson
Prof. staff: Mrs K Campion; Miss J Elsom
Type: Medical; Healthcare.
Hours open: Mon–Fri: 9am–5pm. No public access.
Users: No public access. All enquiries taken by phone, fax, e-mail and letter.
Lending: Reference only.
Stock policy: Where possible passed to other libraries.
Holdings: 300 books; 20 current journal subscriptions; Diabetes UK reports and publications.
Classification: Own.
Computerized services: Access via Ovid to CINAHL; Cochrane Library; MEDLINE; PsycINFO; Sociological Abstracts.
Special collections: Focus on Diabetes Mellitus.

Doncaster Royal Infirmary Medical & Professional Library

Doncaster Royal Infirmary
Armthorpe Road
Doncaster
South Yorkshire DN2 5LT
Tel: 01302 553118
Fax: 01302 553250
E-mail: library.admin@dbh.nhs.uk
Librarian: Margaret Evans
Prof. staff: Janet Sampson
Founded: 1968
Type: Multidisciplinary.
Hours open: Mon–Fri: 9am–5pm.
Users: NHS staff employed or working within Doncaster Health Authority. Student nurses and midwives. Others may use for reference only by appointment.

Lending: To members of the user groups, other libraries within existing networks. Non-members have reference use only.
Stock policy: Books and journals discarded after varying intervals.
Holdings: 12,500 books; 170 current journal subscriptions.
Classification: NLM (Wessex adaptation).
Library management system: Heritage IV.
Computerized services: Online access to BNI; Best Evidence; CINAHL; ClinPsych; Cochrane Library; DARE; Embase; MEDLINE; PreMEDLINE; PsychLit. Access to HMIC.
Special collections: Health Information Unit specializing in child health; Health Information Unit at Doncaster Health Authority specializing in public health.
Collaborative networks: BLDSC; BMA; Trent Knowledge and Library Information Unit; YJHLS.
Notes: From 2003, plans to integrate this library and Nursing Library below to one site.

Doncaster Royal Infirmary Nursing Library

School of Nursing and Midwifery
C Block, Doncaster Royal Infirmary
Armthorpe Road
Doncaster
South Yorkshire DN2 5LT
Tel: 01302 553118
Fax: 01302 553250 (in Medical and Professional Library)
E-mail: libdon@sheffield.ac.uk
Librarian: Margaret Evans
Prof. staff: Janet Sampson
Founded: 1986
Type: Nursing and Midwifery.
Hours open: Tues–Thurs: 9am–5pm.
Users: Student nurses and midwives attached to the University of Sheffield School of Nursing and Midwifery; NHS staff in the District Health Authority. Others use for reference only by appointment.

Lending: To members of the user groups. Other libraries within existing networks. Non-members have reference use only.
Stock policy: Books and journals discarded after varying intervals.
Holdings: 5,800 books; 57 current journal subscriptions.
Classification: NLM (Wessex adaptation).
Library management system: Heritage IV.
Computerized services: NHS staff as Medical and Professional Library above. Students separate access to University of Sheffield Network. Access to BNI; CINAHL.
Collaborative networks: JHLS; TRACH-LIS.

Dorset County Hospital: Thomas Sydenham Education Centre Library

Williams Avenue
Dorchester
Dorset DT1 1TS
Tel: 01305 255248
Fax: 01305 254690
E-mail: library.managers@dorch.wdgh-tr.swest.nhs.uk
Librarian: Patricia Graham; Judi Tighe (Acting Librarians)
Type: Multidisciplinary.
Hours open: Mon–Thurs: 8.45am–5pm; Fri: 8.45am–4.30pm.
Users: Employees of WDGH NHS Trust; Dorset primary care, mental health and Health Authority staff; nursing and midwifery students attending Bournemouth University. NHS personnel may join for an annual fee.
Lending: As above.
Stock policy: Usually dispose of.
Holdings: 6,100 books; 120 current journal subscriptions, 136 journal titles; 8 videos; 2 CD-ROMs.
Classification: NLM (Wessex adaptation).
Library management system: Heritage.
Computerized services: All computers linked to internet through NHSNet. Search

facilities include AMED; ASSIA; BNI; CINAHL; Embase; HMIC; MEDLINE; PsycINFO. Cochrane Library via NeLH.
Branches: The Library, Forston Clinic, Herrison, Dorchester, DT2 9TB.
Collaborative networks: NULJ; SWRLIN.

Dublin Dental School & Hospital: Library & Information Service

Lincoln Place
Dublin 2
Republic of Ireland
Tel: +353 1 6127205
Fax: +353 1 6127205
E-mail: aobyrne@dental.tcd.ie
Librarian: Anne M O Byrne
Prof. staff: Vera Kershaw; Timothy Lawless; Claire McLaughlin; Lorna Shields
Founded: 1968
Type: Dental/Academic.
Hours open: Mon–Fri: 10am–10pm; Sat: 10am–12.30pm. Vacations: Mon–Fri: 10am–5pm.
Users: Clinical staff and students of the Dublin Dental School and Hospital. Limited external reader registration by application. Staff of university libraries by referral.
Lending: To staff and students only. Not available on interlibrary loans.
Stock policy: Retention and archive policy. Occasionally issued for Third World development. Internal book sales on occasion.
Holdings: 94 current journal subscriptions; 50 videos; 25 CD-ROMs; 20 CAL programmes.
Classification: Black's Medical and Dental Classification (adapted from Dewey).
Library management system: Horizon (interleaf).
Computerized services: Internet access to free MEDLINEs e.g. PubMed, etc. MEDLINE on CD-ROM: Ovid.
Library publications: Library guide; journal subscriptions list; guide to the internet; recent additions list.

Special collections: Archive collection; Problem Based Learning Collection.

Dudley Health Authority Library

12 Bull Street
Dudley
West Midlands DY1 2DD
Tel: 01384 239376
Fax: 01384 455068
E-mail: david.law@dudley-ha.wmids.nhs.uk
URL: www.dudley.nhs.uk
Librarian: David Law
Founded: 1996
Type: Health Management.
Hours open: Mon–Fri: 8.30am–4pm.
Users: Health Authority employees and primary care group management. Health staff employed within Dudley. Other access by prior appointment.
Lending: Healthcare staff within Dudley. Various restrictions apply. Non-members reference only.
Stock policy: Generally discarded due to nature of holdings. Some journals may be passed to other libraries.
Holdings: 2,700 books; 39 current journal subscriptions, 72 journal titles; 5 CD-ROMs.
Classification: NLM (Wessex adaptation).
Library management system: AMLIB.
Computerized services: WebOPAC. Online access to WISH. Access to Best Evidence; Cochrane Library; Oxford Textbook of Medicine; NRR.
Library publications: Daily Health Information Digest; Newsletter.
Special collections: Maureen Airey Memorial Trust Collection for Practice Nurses.
Collaborative networks: Black Country Accreditation group; Dudley Online Libraries Network; WMRHLN.

Dunhill Library, St Richard's Hospital

St Richard's Hospital

Royal West Sussex Trust
Spitalfield Lane
Chichester
West Sussex PO19 4SE
Tel: 01243 831506
Fax: 01243 831553
E-mail: dunhill.library@rws-tr.sthames.nhs.uk
Librarian: Mike Roddham
Prof. staff: Sue Hayler; Darrell Mason
Hours open: Mon: 10am–6pm; Tues–Wed: 9am–6pm; Thurs–Fri: 9am–5pm. 24-hour key access.
Holdings: 197 journal titles.
Library publications: District list of journals.
Collaborative networks: STLIS.

Earlsfort Terrace Library

University College Dublin
Earlsfort Terrace
Dublin 2
Republic of Ireland
Tel: +353 1 706 7372
Fax: +353 1 475 4568

East & North Herts NHS Trust Library & Information Service: Lister Site

Level 2, Lister Hospital
Coreys Mill Lane
Stevenage
Hertfordshire SG1 4AB
Tel: 01438 781092
Fax: 01438 781247
E-mail: sallyk@sklister.demon.co.uk
Librarian: Sally Knight
Prof. staff: Maureen Alexander; Carol Milton
Founded: 1972
Type: Multidisciplinary.
Hours open: Mon–Fri: 9am–5pm.
Users: All members of staff across the Trust.
Lending: To members of staff. Non-members reference only.
Stock policy: All superseded editions and stock older than 10 years are discarded.

Holdings: 3,000 books; 180 current journal subscriptions.
Classification: NLM.
Library management system: BookFind.
Computerized services: Online access to NHSNet and Ovid. CD-ROM access to Cochrane Library; MCQs; MEDLINE Hospital Collection; several full texts.
Library publications: Journal holdings; new publications in stock; user guide.
Collaborative networks: LLIDU.

East & North Herts NHS Trust: Queen Elizabeth II Hospital

Postgraduate Medical Centre Library and Learning Resource Centre
Queen Elizabeth II Hospital
Howlands, Welwyn Garden City
Hertfordshire AL7 4HQ
Tel: 01707 365046
Fax: 01707 390425
E-mail: joan@qeliza.demon.co.uk
Librarian: Joan Lomas
Prof. staff: Gill Jones
Type: Multidisciplinary.
Hours open: PGMC Mon–Thurs: 9.30am–5.15pm; Fri: 9.30am–4pm. LRC Mon–Thurs:10am–4.30pm; Fri: 10am–4pm.
Users: Staff working for East and North Herts NHS Trust; community medical staff, medical and nursing students.
Lending: As above. Limited lending to full-time students.
Stock policy: Old editions are passed on to departments or individuals if useful.
Holdings: 7,000 books; 150 current journal subscriptions; 100 videos; 7 networked data-bases. Various other electronic textbooks and packages.
Classification: NLM (Wessex adaptation).
Library management system: DB/TextWorks.
Computerized services: Online access to NHSNet and Ovid. Access to Bioethicsline; CancerLit; CINAHL; Cochrane Library; HealthStar; MEDLINE; STAT REF.

Library publications: Holdings list; welcome leaflet.
Collaborative networks: Eastern Region (West) Workforce Development Confederation; Hertfordshire Library Working Group; LLIDU.

East Kent Hospitals NHS Trust: Canterbury Centre for Health & Clinical Sciences Library

Kent and Canterbury Hospitals NHS Trust
Canterbury
Kent CT1 3NG
Tel: 01227 864156
Fax: 01227 864154
E-mail: sue.cover@ekh-tr.sthames.nhs.uk
Librarian: Rhiannon Cox (Knowledge Services Manager)
Prof. staff: Sue Cover
Founded: 2001 as Multidisciplinary; originally 1967.
Type: Multidisciplinary.
Hours open: Mon–Thurs: 8.30am–5pm; Fri: 8.30am–4.30pm.
Users: All East Kent Hospitals NHS Trust staff, local GPs, dentists and vets.
Lending: To members and other South Thames libraries.
Stock policy: Regional withdrawal policy used. Old books sold to readers.
Holdings: 10,000 books; 250 current journal subscriptions; 250 videos; 50 CD-ROMs; plus slides and anatomical models.
Classification: NLM.
Library management system: LIBRARIAN.
Computerized services: Online access via Ovid to AMED; Best Evidence; CINAHL; ClinPsych; Cochrane Systematic Reviews; DARE; MEDLINE, PreMEDLINE. CD-ROM access to BNI.
Library publications: Introductory library guide; journal holdings list.
Special collections: History of medicine.
Collaborative networks: STLIS.

Notes: Linacre Library and Kent and Canterbury Nurse Education Centre Library have combined.

East Kent Hospitals NHS Trust: Queen Elizabeth the Queen Mother Hospital Clinical Studies Library

Queen's Centre for Clinical Studies
Ramsgate Road
Margate
Kent CT9 4AN
Tel: 01843 225544 ext. 62536
Fax: 01843 296082
E-mail: jonathan.baker@ekh-tr.sthames.nhs.uk
Librarian: Mr Jonathan Baker
Type: Multidisciplinary.
Hours open: Mon–Thurs: 9am–6pm; Fri: 9am–4.30pm.
Users: Primarily NHS staff and employees of East Kent Hospitals NHS Trust. Patients and their representatives reference only.
Lending: As above.
Stock policy: Books sold to staff if possible. Journals offered to other libraries.
Holdings: 2,000 books; 47 current journal subscriptions; 200 films and videos; 10 CD-ROMs.
Classification: NLM (modified).
Library management system: LIBRARIAN.
Computerized services: Internet subscriptions to AMED; Best Evidence (including Cochrane); CINAHL; ClinPsych; MEDLINE.
Collaborative networks: STLIS.

East Kent Hospitals NHS Trust: William Harvey Hospital Library

Education Centre Library
Kennington Road
Ashford
Kent TN24 0LZ
Tel: 01233 616695
Fax: 01233 613597
Librarian: Vacant
Founded: 1975
Type: Multidisciplinary.
Hours open: Mon–Fri: 9am–5pm. 24-hour access by key.
Users: East Kent Hospitals NHS Trust; East Kent Community NHS Trust; East Kent Health Authority; PCGs in the area.
Lending: To all full library members. Interlibrary loans via South Thames region.
Stock policy: Discarded or sold.
Holdings: 5,000 books; 105 current journal subscriptions, 120 journal titles.
Classification: NLM.
Library management system: LIBRARIAN.
Computerized services: Internet and intranet available. Online access to Data-Star databases. Access to AMED; BNI; CINAHL, Cochrane Library; ClinPsych; MEDLINE.
Library publications: Guide to Library Services; Current Journal Holdings.
Branches: Buckland Hospital Library, Dover.
Collaborative networks: STLIS.

East Lancashire Health Authority Library

31–33 Kenyon Road
Lomeshaye Estate
Nelson
Lancashire BB9 5SZ
Tel: 01282 610248
Fax: 01282 610213
E-mail: elaine.walton@elancs-ha.nwest.nhs.uk
Librarian: Mrs Elaine Walton
Prof. staff: Liz Walton
Founded: 1994
Type: Multidisciplinary.
Hours open: Open to ELHA staff 24 hours a day. Staffed Mon–Fri: 8am–5pm.
Users: All health professionals within East Lancashire Health Authority, plus all PCG/T staff.

Lending: To those above. Occasionally non-members by special arrangement.
Stock policy: Usually dispose of it.
Holdings: 5,500 books; 25 current journal subscriptions, 52 journal titles; 2 CD-ROMs.
Classification: Own.
Library management system: Dataflex (an in-house system).
Computerized services: Online access to Ovid Biomed and Data-Star web.
Collaborative networks: BL; BMA; LIHNN.

East Riding Medical Education Centre Library

Hull Royal Infirmary
Anlaby Road
Hull
East Yorkshire HU3 2JZ
Tel: 01482 674337
Fax: 01482 674342
E-mail: ermedlibr.sbx.co.uk/rhh-tr.northy.nhs.uk
Librarian: Mr D I Thompson
Prof. staff: Mrs P Clarke
Founded: 1970
Type: Multidisciplinary.
Hours open: Mon, Thurs: 9am–7pm; Tues, Wed, Fri: 9am–5pm.
Users: Employees of Trusts locally; university staff and healthcare students; associate members on payment of fee.
Lending: Members only.
Stock policy: Discards passed to Third World countries.
Holdings: 20,000 books; 280 current journal subscriptions; 300 videos; 50 CD-ROMs.
Classification: Dewey.
Library management system: Heritage.
Computerized services: Online access to AMED; CINAHL; Cochrane Library; Embase: Psychiatry; MEDLINE; Ovid journals.
Special collections: Medical history.
Collaborative networks: NYRLAS.

East Somerset NHS Trust Library Service

Marsh Jackson Education Centre
Yeovil District Hospital
Yeovil
Somerset BA21 4DE
Tel: 01935 384495
Fax: 01935 384995
E-mail: hillj@est.nhs.uk
Librarian: Jean Hill
Prof. staff: Linda Foote
Founded: 1974
Type: Multidisciplinary.
Hours open: Mon–Fri: 9am–5pm. 24-hour access for staff.
Users: All NHS healthcare professionals and students on placement within the Somerset, Devon and Cornwall Workforce Development Confederation.
Lending: To the above. Corporate and private members may be subscribing members.
Stock policy: Stock over 10 years old is disposed of.
Holdings: 6,500 books; 160 current journal subscriptions; 50 videos; 50 CD-ROMs.
Classification: NLM (Wessex adaptation).
Library management system: DB/TextWorks and Web publisher.
Computerized services: Online access to AMED; ASSIA; BNI; CINAHL; Cochrane Library; Embase; HMIC; MEDLINE; PsycINFO using HCN.
Collaborative networks: SWRLIN.

East Surrey Health Authority Library

Ramsay
West Park Hospital
Horton Lane
Epsom
Surrey KT19 8PB
Tel: 01372 731111
Fax: 01372 748914
Librarian: Gordon Smith (based at Epsom District Hospital)

East Surrey Library and Information Services

Surrey and Sussex Healthcare NHS Trust
Maple House
East Surrey Hospital
Canada Road
Redhill
Surrey RH1 5RH
Tel: 01737 768511 ext. 6057
Fax: 01737 231790
E-mail: library.esh@sysx-tr.eshcare-tr.
sthames.nhs.uk
Librarian: Sheila Marsh
Prof. staff: Freda Knight
Hours open: Mon, Thurs, Fri: 9am–5pm;
Tues, Wed: 9am–7pm. Open 24 hours by
arrangement.
Holdings: 200 journal titles.
Special collections: Learning disabilities
material; local historical collection.
Collaborative networks: STLIS.

East Sussex, Brighton & Hove Health Authority Library

36–38 Friars Walk
Lewes
East Sussex BN7 2PB
Tel: 01273 403508
Fax: 01273 403508
E-mail: alackey@esbhhealth.cix.co.uk
Librarian: Amanda Lackey
Founded: 1998
Type: Health Management.
Hours open: Mon, Tues, Thurs:
8.30am–3.30pm; Fri: 9.30am–3.30pm. Wed:
Closed.
Users: Main users are staff of the Health
Authority. Staff from the local NHS and local
authority organizations can register and
receive a restricted service.
Lending: No restrictions to Health Authority
staff. Three items only to non-Health
Authority members.
Stock policy: All old stock is passed on to
the Sussex Postgraduate Medical Centre
Library.

Holdings: 5,000 books; 10 current journal
subscriptions, 120 journal titles; 5 CD-
ROMs.
Classification: NLM.
Library management system:
LIBRARIAN
Computerized services: Access to
ASSIA for Health; Cochrane Library; HMIC;
MEDLINE.
Library publications: New Titles in the
Library – monthly.
Collaborative networks: STLIS.

Eastbourne District General Hospital Health Sciences Library

Eastbourne District General Hospital
Kings Drive
Eastbourne
East Sussex BN21 2UD
Tel: 01323 417400 ext. 4048
Fax: 01323 435740
E-mail: s.e.hardwick@bton.ac.uk
m.f.d.sibson@bton.ac.uk
Librarian: Sue Hardwick
Prof. staff: Anne Harvey; Neil Iden;
Christine Selmes; Mike Sibson; Lorraine
Worland
Hours open: Mon, Wed: 8.30am–8pm;
Tues, Thurs, Fri: 8.30am–5pm.
Collaborative networks: STLIS.

Eastern Region

Queen Elizabeth Hospital
Gayton Road
King's Lynn
Norfolk PE30 4ET
Tel: 01553 613792
Fax: 01553 613883
E-mail: a.osborne@klshosp.anglox.nhs.uk
Librarian: Ann Osborne (Chair of Health
Care Librarians of East Anglia)

Eastern Regional Health Authority

Regional Library and Information Service
Eastern Health Shared Services
Dr Stevens Hospital
Dublin 8
Republic of Ireland
Tel: +353 1 6352555/556/558
Fax: +353 1 6352557
E-mail: library@erha.ie
Librarian: Bennary Rickard
Prof. staff: Fiona McCarthy; Ciaran Quinn
Founded: 1998
Type: Multidisciplinary.
Hours open: Mon, Tues, Thurs, Fri: 10am–1pm, 2pm–4.45pm; Wed: 2pm–4.45pm.
Users: Health Authority employees, including medical and nursing staff, public health, social workers, psychiatric services, health management.
Lending: Members of Health Authority.
Holdings: 2,381 books; 76 current journal subscriptions; 2 videos; 5 CD-ROMs.
Classification: Dewey.
Library management system: Unicorn.
Computerized services: Access to ASSIA; BNI; Caredata; CINAHL; Cochrane Library; ERIC; Evidence Based Medicine; HMIC; MEDLINE; PsycINFO.
Special collections: Official health-related publications.
Collaborative networks: Irish Health Libraries.

Eastman Dental Institute Information Centre

Gray's Inn Road
London WC1X 8LD
Tel: 020 7915 1045/1262
Fax: 020 7915 1147
E-mail: ic@eastman.ucl.ac.uk
URL: www.eastman.ucl.ac.uk
Librarian: Heather Lodge
Type: Postgraduate Dental.

Hours open: Mon–Thurs: 8am–8pm; Fri: 8am–5.30pm; Sat: 11am–3pm.
Users: Staff and students of Eastman Dental Institute and Eastman Dental Hospital. Visitors by appointment – charge of £10 per day.
Lending: To registered members only.
Stock policy: Withdrawn stock offered to readers first then to other libraries.
Holdings: 3,000 books; 100 current journal subscriptions; 44 videos; 30 CD-ROMs; 100 PhD theses.
Classification: Own.
Library management system: Heritage.
Computerized services: Online access to Cochrane Library; Embase; PsycINFO; Web of Science. Access to CAL; MEDLINE.
Library publications: Staff publications on web.
Collaborative networks: Part of University College London.

Edgehill College Learning Resources Centre

St Helens Road
Ormskirk
Lancashire L39 4QP
Tel: 01695 584298
Fax: 01695 584550
E-mail: penstc@edgehill.ac.uk
URL: www.edgehill.ac.uk/ims/
Librarian: Sue Roberts (Head of Information and Media Services)
Prof. staff: Coral Black (Support Services Manager); Anna Forsyth; Lyndsey Martin; Helen Miles; Maureen Richardson; Ruth Wilson
Founded: 1993
Type: HE college with a School of Health collection.
Hours open: Mon–Fri: 8.45am–9pm; Sat, Sun: 1pm–5pm. See website for vacation opening hours.
Users: Staff and students only. Members of UK Libraries Plus Scheme. Other organizations, reference only.

Lending: Staff and students. Do not lend to non-members unless they have a UK Libraries Plus card.

Stock policy: Discarded stock sent for recycling.

Holdings: 249,173 books; 1,000 print journal titles, 3,000 electronic journal titles. 231 films and videos; 240 CD-ROMs.

Classification: Dewey.

Library management system: GEAC.

Computerized services: 30 online databases. See website for details.

Branches: Aintree Library and Information Resource Centre.

Collaborative networks: ALLIS; LIHNN; UK Libraries Plus Scheme.

Edinburgh & South East Scotland Blood Transfusion Service Library

41 Lauriston Place
Edinburgh EH3 9HB
Tel: 0131 536 5337 (Contact, not library)
Fax: 0131 536 5352 (Contact, not library)
E-mail: june.macleod@subts.csa.scot.nhs.uk
Librarian: Library unstaffed since 1999.
Founded: 1986
Type: Blood Transfusion Service.
Hours open: 24-hour access by security card.
Users: Service staff – consultants, clinicians, donor nurses, laboratory staff. Outside users would need to contact June MacLeod.
Lending: As above.
Stock policy: Old stock stored.
Holdings: 828 books; 26 current journal subscriptions, 53 journal titles; 2 CD-ROMs.
Classification: Eileen R Cunningham Classification for Medical Literature
Library management system: InMagic.
Computerized services: No internet access. CD-ROM access to Cochrane Library and MEDLINE on the BTS Network.
Collaborative networks: SHINE.

Edinburgh University Library: Centre for Tropical Veterinary Medicine Library

Royal (Dick) School of Veterinary Studies
Easter Bush
Roslin
Midlothian EH25 9RG
Tel: 0131 650 6410
URL: www.lib.ed.ac.uk
Librarian: Fiona Brown (Senior Library Assistant)
Hours open: Mon–Thurs: 9am–10pm; Fri, Sat: 9am–5pm; Sun: 12noon–5pm.
Computerized services: See website.
Notes: For further details see website and Erskine Medical Library entry.

Edinburgh University Library: Easter Bush Veterinary Centre Library

Royal (Dick) School of Veterinary Studies
Easter Bush Veterinary Centre
Easter Bush
Roslin
Midlothian EH25 9RG
Tel: 0131 650 6405
URL: www.lib.ed.ac.uk
Librarian: Dorie Wilkie (Library Assistant)
Hours open: Mon–Thurs: 9am–10pm; Fri, Sat: 9am–5pm; Sun: 12noon–5pm. Vacations: Mon–Fri: 9am–5pm.
Computerized services: See website.
Notes: For further details see website and Erskine Medical Library entry.

Edinburgh University Library: Erskine Medical Library

Hugh Robson Building
George Square
Edinburgh EH8 9XE
Tel: 0131 650 3684
Fax: 0131 650 6841
E-mail: eml@ed.ac.uk
URL: www.lib.ed.ac.uk

Librarian: Irene McGowan (Medical Librarian)

Prof. staff: Marshall Dozier (Reader Services Librarian)

Founded: 1931

Hours open: Mon–Thurs: 9am–10pm; Fri and Sat: 9am–5pm; Sun: 12pm–7pm. Vacations: Mon–Thurs: 9am–7pm; Fri: 9am–5pm; Sat: 10am–1pm.

Users: Staff and students of Medical Faculty; NHS in Lothian staff and all other staff and students of Edinburgh University are eligible. For details of facilities offered to external users see website.

Lending: As above.

Stock policy: Selective weeding of older monograph material, which goes into book sales.

Holdings: 45,000 books; 900 current journal subscriptions.

Library management system: Voyager.

Computerized services: Access to AMED; CINAHL; Cochrane Library; Embase; MEDLINE; PsycINFO; Web of Science, etc.

Library publications: Erskine Medical Library Guide.

Branches: Edinburgh University Library – Psychiatry Library, Department of Psychiatry; Royal Hospital for Sick Children Library; Royal Infirmary Edinburgh Postgraduate Education Centre; Western General Hospital Medical Library.

Special collections: Lothian Health Services Archives kept in Main Library, Dept Special Collections and Archives, George Square, Edinburgh.

Edinburgh University Library: Psychiatry Library

Department of Psychiatry
Royal Edinburgh Hospital
Morningside Park
Edinburgh EH10 5HF
Tel: 0131 537 6285
Fax: 0131 447 6860
E-mail: psychlib@srv4.lib.ed.ac.uk

URL: www.lib.ed.ac.uk

Librarian: Wendy Mill (Senior Library Assistant)

Founded: 1836 (present building since 1965)

Hours open: Mon–Fri: 9am–5pm.

Users: Staff and students of Edinburgh University, employees of Lothian Primary Care Trust. Students from other universities may consult stock during vacations. Other users have to pay for access to the Library.

Lending: To registered borrowers and to other libraries through interlibrary loans using BLDSC.

Stock policy: Old stock sent to the main library at Edinburgh University and either sold or disposed of.

Holdings: 7,500 books; 105 current journal subscriptions; 9 films and videos; 4 CD-ROMs.

Classification: NLM

Library management system: Voyager.

Computerized services: Access to Athens databases including BIDS; Biomed Web of Science; First Search; MIMAS; EDINA. Access to Edinburgh University networked CD-ROMs. Access to ClinPsych; Cochrane Library.

Library publications: Psychiatry Library: A Brief Guide.

Collaborative networks: PLCS.

Edinburgh University Library: Royal (Dick) School of Veterinary Studies, Veterinary Library

Summerhall
Edinburgh EH9 1QH
Tel: 0131 650 6175
URL: www.lib.ed.ac.uk
Librarian: M Anne R Kennett
Founded: 1874
Hours open: Mon–Thurs: 9am–10pm; Fri, Sat: 9am–5pm; Sun: 12noon–5pm. Vacations: Mon–Fri: 9am–5pm.
Computerized services: See website.

Notes: See website and Erskine Medical Library entry for further details.

Edinburgh University Library: Royal Hospital for Sick Children Library

9 Sciennes Road
Edinburgh EH9 1LF
Tel: 0131 536 0839
Fax: 0131 536 0839
URL: www.lib.ed.ac.uk
Librarian: Anne Donnelly; Sheila Fiskin (job-share)
Founded: 1995
Type: Paediatric nursing, medical, surgical and paramedical.
Hours open: Mon–Fri: 8.30am–4.30pm.
Users: NHS Trust employees; nursing and medical students taking training at hospital; Edinburgh University staff and students.
Lending: As above.
Stock policy: Dispose of it.
Holdings: 1,500 books; 60 current journal subscriptions; 10 CD-ROMs.
Classification: NLM.
Computerized services: See Erskine Medical Library
Collaborative networks: Edinburgh University Library; SHINE.

Edinburgh University Library: Royal Infirmary of Edinburgh Postgraduate Education Centre

Lauriston Place
Edinburgh EH3 9YW
Tel: 0131 536 4513
Fax: 0131 536 4512
E-mail: anne.donnelly@ed.ac.uk
URL: www.lib.ed.ac.uk/lib/sites/riepgl.shtml
Librarian: Anne Donnelly
Founded: 1996
Type: Clinical Medicine.
Hours open: Mon–Fri: 9am–5pm.

Users: Royal Infirmary staff and students; Edinburgh University staff and students. Others at the discretion of the Librarian.
Lending: As above.
Stock policy: Pass it on and sell at a nominal sum to Hospital departments and students.
Holdings: 500 books; 11 current journal subscriptions, 23 journal titles; 20 films and videos; 6 CD-ROMs.
Classification: NLM.
Library management system: Voyager.
Computerized services: Intranet of hospital information. Online access via Edinburgh University to Biomed; BIDS; Web of Science. CD-ROM access to Ovid – CINAHL.
Collaborative networks: University of Edinburgh; SHINE.
Notes: Site library of Edinburgh University.

Edinburgh University Library: Western General Hospital Medical Library

Crewe Road
Edinburgh EH4 2XU
Tel: 0131 537 2299
Fax: 0131 537 1144
E-mail: Western.General.Library@ed.ac.uk
URL: www.lib.ed.ac.uk/lib/sites/wghl.shtml
Librarian: Susan Lyle (Senior Library Assistant)
Founded: 1980
Type: Medical and Paramedical.
Hours open: Mon–Thurs: 9am–9pm; Fri: 9am–5pm; Sat: 9am–1pm.
Users: Members of Edinburgh University; staff of NHS Trusts in Lothian according to Service Level Agreements. Free access to staff and students of other UK universities. Charges are in place for other external users.
Lending: As above.
Stock policy: Selective weeding of older material, which goes into book sales.

Holdings: 3,700 books; 173 current journal subscriptions; 8 films and videos; 20 CD-ROMs; slides and audiocassettes.
Classification: NLM.
Library management system: Voyager.
Computerized services: Access to AMED; CINAHL; Cochrane Library; Embase; MEDLINE; PsycINFO; Web of Science, etc.
Library publications: Library guides and guides to databases.
Collaborative networks: SHINE.

Eli Lilly & Co. Ltd

Information Centre
Erl Wood Manor
Sunninghill Road
Windlesham
Surrey GU20 6PH
Tel: 01276 483345
Fax: 01276 483769
E-mail: wickenden@lilly.com
Librarian: Mr John A Wickenden (Information Scientist)
Founded: 1967
Type: Pharmaceutical Research.
Hours open: Mon–Fri: 8am–4.30pm.
Users: Employees only.
Lending: To other libraries only.
Stock policy: Passed to other libraries or disposed of.
Holdings: 225 current journal subscriptions.
Library management system: SIRSI Workflow.
Computerized services: Online access to BLAISE; Data-Star; Dialog; STN; Questel. CD-ROM access to Adonis.
Collaborative networks: HATRICS; SASLIC.

Enuresis Resource & Information Centre (ERIC)

34 Old School House
Britannia Road
Kingswood
Bristol BS15 8DB

Tel: 0117 960 3060
Fax: 0117 960 0401
E-mail: info@eric.org.uk
URL: www.eric.org.uk
Librarian: Molly Haig (Information and Helpline Manager)
Founded: 1988
Type: Charity; Health.
Hours open: Telephone only Mon–Fri:10am–4pm.
Users: Parents, children and health professionals.
Library publications: Newsletters; guides for parents.
Special collections: Research articles on enuresis and encopresis.

Epsom General Hospital: Sally Howell Library

Dorking Road
Epsom
Surrey KT18 7EG
Tel: 01372 735735 ext. 6250
Fax: 01372 735687
E-mail: gsmith.sthelier.sghms.ac.uk
Librarian: Gordon Smith
Prof. staff: Marion Morrison
Founded: 1940s (purpose-built library 1980)
Type: Multidisciplinary.
Hours open: Mon–Fri: 8.45am–4.45pm. Access at other times by arrangement.
Users: Staff of Epsom and St Helier NHS Trust, Surrey Heartlands NHS Trust and East Surrey Health Authority; NHS staff in the area. Others at the Librarian's discretion, for reference.
Lending: As above and members of Psychiatric Libraries Cooperative Scheme. No lending of reference books nor copies of whole journals.
Stock policy: With new amalgamated library, disposal of most duplicates over 10 years old, retaining at least one copy.
Holdings: 12,000 books; 135 current journal subscriptions, 200 journal titles; 30 videos;

CD-ROMs: 6 databases; 3 teaching packages.
Classification: NLM.
Library management system: Heritage.
Computerized services: 6 PCs with internet access; 2 standalone workstations.
Library publications: Introduction to the Library; various handouts.
Collaborative networks: BLDSC; BMA; NULJ; PLCS; RCS; STLIS at present but changing to London region.
Notes: The expanded library is an amalgamation of the old Sally Howell Library and West Park Postgraduate Medical Library; Farmside Resources Centre, West Park and East Surrey Health Authority Library. The librarian for the whole Epsom and St Helier Trust is at St Helier.

European School of Osteopathy Library (ESO)

Boxley House
Boxley
Kent ME14 3DZ
Tel: 01622 671558
Fax: 01622 662165
E-mail: raysmith@eso.ac.uk
URL: www.eso.ac.uk
Librarian: Ray Smith
Founded: 1982
Type: Alternative Medicine; Osteopathy.
Hours open: Mon–Fri: 9am–8pm. Vacations: Mon–Fri: 9am–1pm.
Users: Staff and students of the School. Other users for reference only, by prior appointment.
Lending: Books and videos loaned internally. Photocopies provided.
Stock policy: Old stock is normally sold off to ESO students.
Holdings: 2,300 books; 60 current journal subscriptions, 70 journal titles; 250 videos; 30 CD-ROMs.
Classification: Own.
Library management system: ALICE.

Computerized services: Access to AMED; CINAHL; MEDLINE.
Special collections: Osteopathy; other manipulative therapies.
Collaborative networks: NULJ; STLIS.

Evesham Community Hospital Education Centre Library Service

Waterside
Evesham
Worcestershire WR11 6JT
Tel: 01386 502353
E-mail: martin.blewett@worcsh-tr.wmids.nhs.uk
Librarian: Hilary Johnson
Prof. staff: David Chamberlain
Founded: 2001
Type: Multidisciplinary.
Hours open: Mon–Fri: 9am–5pm.
Users: All Community Trust staff professions.
Lending: Anyone within the West Midlands Health Region.
Stock policy: New service.
Holdings: 474 books.
Classification: NLM (Wessex adaptation).
Library management system: SIRSI.
Computerized services: Ovid Biomed database service; NHSNet.
Branches: Newtown Library, Newtown Hospital, Worcester.
Collaborative networks: WMRHLN.

Exeter Medical Library

Exeter Postgraduate Medical Centre
Barrack Road
Exeter
Devon EX2 5DW
Tel: 01392 403002
Fax: 01392 403007
E-mail: medlib@ex.ac.uk
URL: www.ex.ac.uk/library/eml
Librarian: Virginia Newton
Prof. staff: Marjorie Brewer; Jill Maxted
Type: Multidisciplinary.

Hours open: Mon–Fri: 9am–5.30pm.
Users: NHS staff working in Somerset, Devon and Cornwall. Students on placement in Royal Devon Exeter Healthcare NHS Trust. Staff and students of Exeter School of Postgraduate Medicine and Health Science.
Lending: Registered users.
Stock policy: Put in store or disposed of.
Holdings: 6,300 books; 181 current journal subscriptions; 30 CD-ROMs.
Classification: NLM (Wessex adaptation).
Library management system: INNOPAC.
Computerized services: Internet search facilities to AMED; ASSIA; British Education Index; BNI; Caredata; CINAHL; Embase; ERIC; HMIC; IBSS; JCR; MEDLINE; PsycINFO; Web of Science; ZETOC. Large number of electronic journals.
Collaborative networks: SWRLIN.

Falkirk & District Royal Infirmary Postgraduate Medical Library

1 Major's Loan
Falkirk FK1 5QE
Tel: 01324 616169
Fax: 01324 616168
E-mail: efotheringham@sri.scot.nhs.uk
Librarian: Mrs Emily Fotheringham
Prof. staff: Mr Mark Ullrich
Type: Multidisciplinary.
Hours open: Mon–Fri: 9am–1pm.
Users: Consultant staff; students, nurses, etc. Non-members can use on request.
Lending: No restrictions.
Stock policy: Dispose of and pass on to various departments.
Holdings: 300-400 books; 31 current journal subscriptions, 70 journal titles; 50 videos; 20 CD-ROMs.
Classification: Own.
Library management system: Card Index.

Computerized services: Online access to MEDLINE. UpToDate medicine.
Collaborative networks: BMA; SHINE.

Fife Health Board Library

Fife Health Board
Springfield House
Cupar
Fife KY15 5UP
Tel: 01334 421106
Librarian: Catherine Smith
Type: Public Health; Health Management.
Hours open: Mon–Thurs: 9am–5pm; Fri: 9am–4.30pm.
Users: Staff at Fife Health Board; NHS staff in Fife.
Lending: NHS staff in Fife.
Stock policy: Pass on if possible. Out-of-date material discarded.
Holdings: 5,000 books; 20 current journal subscriptions, 50 journal titles.
Classification: DH/DSS Data.
Library management system: Heritage.
Computerized services: Access to Cochrane Library; HMIC; MEDLINE.
Collaborative networks: SHINE.

Food Safety Authority of Ireland Information Centre

Abbey Court
Lower Abbey Street
Dublin 1
Republic of Ireland
Tel: +353 1 817 1300
Fax: +353 1 817 1301
E-mail: info@fsai.ie
URL: www.fsai.ie
Prof. staff: Anne McMahon; Noeleen Murtagh
Founded: 1998
Type: Food Safety.
Hours open: Mon–Fri: 9am–5pm.
Users: Staff; food safety professionals; food industry; students; public.
Lending: Staff.

Holdings: 1,000 books; 110 current journal subscriptions, 115 journal titles; 20 films and videos; 4 CD-ROMs.
Classification: Own.
Library management system: Unicorn.
Computerized services: Barbour Food Safety Professional. Access to ASFA; CAB; FSTA; Irish Statute Book; Justis Celex.
Collaborative networks: Irish Health Care Libraries Interlibrary Loans Scheme.

fpa Library & Information Service (formerly Family Planning Association)

2–12 Pentonville Road
London N1 9FP
Tel: 020 7923 5228
Fax: 020 7837 3034
E-mail: library&information@fpa.gov.uk
URL: www.fpa.org.uk
Librarian: Margaret McGovern
Founded: 1973
Type: Multidisciplinary.
Hours open: Mon–Fri: 9am–5pm.
Users: Staff. Other users by prior appointment.
Lending: Reference only.
Stock policy: Stock discarded at Librarian's discretion.
Holdings: 3,500 books; 100 current journal subscriptions,130 journal titles.
Classification: Own.
Library management system: Headfast plus own database.
Library publications: Library and Information Service leaflet; series of fact-sheets.

Freeman Hospital Teaching Centre Library

Freeman Hospital
Newcastle-upon-Tyne Hospitals NHS Trust
High Heaton
Newcastle-upon-Tyne NE7 7DN
Tel: 0191 223 1325
Fax: 0191 284 3783
E-mail: library@tfh.nuth.northy.nhs.uk
Librarian: Margaret Valentine
Prof. staff: Mark Chambers; Joanne Mullen; Helen Reed
Founded: 1978
Type: Multidisciplinary.
Hours open: Mon–Wed: 9am–7pm; Thurs, Fri: 9am–5pm; Sat: 10am–1pm.
Users: All NHS staff working within Newcastle-upon-Tyne, medical students, nursing and PAM students. Others may use for reference only.
Lending: All NHS staff working within Newcastle-upon-Tyne. Medical students based at Freeman Hospital may borrow. Others – reference only.
Stock policy: Keep latest edition plus previous one.
Holdings: 11,000 books; 194 current journal subscriptions; 245 CD-ROMs.
Classification: Dewey.
Library management system: SydneyPLUS.
Computerized services: Online access to AMED; BNI; CINAHL; EBMR; Embase; Embase: Psychiatry; HMIC; MEDLINE. Access to Cochrane Library.
Library publications: Library Bulletin; library guides; guides to searching techniques and databases.
Collaborative networks: HLN.
Notes: Linked with Royal Victoria Infirmary Library, Newcastle-upon-Tyne.

Frenchay Hospital Health Facts Centre

Frenchay Hospital
Bristol BS16 1LE
Tel: 0117 918 6567
Fax: 0117 975 3867
E-mail: healthfacts@north-bristol.swest. nhs.uk
Librarian: Arthur Pillay
Founded: 1987
Type: Multidisciplinary.

Hours open: Mon–Fri: 8.30am–5pm.
Users: General public.
Lending: Reference only.
Stock policy: Pass on to other libraries.
Holdings: 5,000 books; 30 current journal subscriptions; 250 videos; 20 CD-ROMs.
Classification: Own.
Library publications: Health News.

Friarage Hospital Library

Study Centre
Friarage Hospital
Northallerton
North Yorkshire DL6 1JG
Tel: 01609 762526
Fax: 01609 771126
E-mail: hlst5@york.ac.uk
Librarian: Mrs Meri Snowdon
Prof. staff: Mrs Janet Gee
Founded: 1968
Type: Multidisciplinary.
Hours open: Mon–Fri: 9am–5pm (Mon, Wed: to 8.30pm). Access by Swipe card outside staffed hours.
Users: Trust staff, staff and students of York University, Department of Health Studies. Others on payment.
Lending: To any registered reader. Journals, reference only.
Stock policy: Most journals discarded after 10 years. Books discarded when outdated. Book sales held. Rest to British Library/Eastern Europe.
Holdings: 7,000 books; 120 current journal subscriptions; 10 videos.
Classification: Dewey.
Library management system: InMagic.
Computerized services: Computerized catalogue. NHSNet link for users. Access to BNI; CINAHL; ClinPsych; Cochrane Library; MEDLINE. Others via regional deal.
Library publications: Subject Index; The Library; Using the Library Catalogue; Borrowing Books; Using the Internet and E-mail; various guides to useful websites.
Collaborative networks: HLN; LfN.

Frimley Park Hospital NHS Trust

Health Sciences Library
Portsmouth Road
Frimley
Surrey GU16 7UJ
Tel: 01276 604168
Fax: 01276 604278
E-mail: suzy.hollaway@fph-tr.nhs.uk
URL: www.lib.surrey.ac.uk/sthames/stlis/Fr2.htm
Librarian: Suzy Hollaway (Library Services Manager)
Founded: 1974
Type: Multidisciplinary.
Hours open: Mon–Thurs: 9am–6pm; Fri: 9am–5pm.
Users: NHS staff employed in West Surrey health community.
Lending: All registered members as above.
Stock policy: Withdrawn in line with regional policy. Offered to other libraries or users.
Holdings: 10,000 books; 140 current journal subscriptions, 157 journal titles; 10 films and videos; 27 CD-ROMs.
Classification: NLM (South Thames version).
Library management system: InMagic.
Computerized services: Online access to AMED; BNI; CINAHL; Cochrane Library; DARE; MEDLINE; PsycINFO and 28 full-text journals via Ovid. CD-ROM access to BNI; Cochrane Library. Subscription for CINAHL, ClinPsych and MEDLINE not renewed as accessible on the internet.
Library publications: Training guides for in-house databases and the internet.
Collaborative networks: BMA; HATRICS; NULJ; STLIS.

Furness General Hospital Education Centre Library

Morecambe Bay Hospitals NHS Trust
Furness General Hospital
Dalton Lane
Barrow-in-Furness LA14 4LF

Tel: 01229 491297
Fax: 01229 491070
E-mail: fgh.library@b.bay-tr.nwest.nhs.uk
Librarian: Pam Rigden; Jenny Tancock (job-share)
Type: Multidisciplinary.
Hours open: 24-hour access for journals, reference and internet.
Users: Morecambe Bay Hospitals NHS Trust staff; staff of former Bay Community Trust; medical students on placement in the Acute and Community Trusts; staff and students of St Martin's College taught and on placement at Furness General Hospital.
Lending: As above. Other libraries within the Trust.
Stock policy: Usually withdrawn. Sometimes pass on to libraries in the Third World.
Holdings: 10,644 books; 152 current journal subscriptions; 30 films and videos.
Classification: Dewey.
Library management system: Heritage.
Computerized services: Internet and e-mail access. Search facilities for MEDLINE online and ADITUS databases. Access to CINAHL; Cochrane Library; MEDLINE.
Collaborative networks: LIHNN; Morecambe Bay Hospitals NHS Trust – Bay Librarians Group.

Gartnavel Royal Hospital: Maria Henderson Library

Primary Care Trust
Gartnavel Royal Hospital
Great Western Road
Glasgow G12 0XH
Tel: 0141 211 3913
Fax: 0141 211 3814
E-mail: d.burns@clinmed.gla.ac.uk
URL: www.show.scot.nhs.uk/ggpct/library
Librarian: Catriona Denoon (Library Services Manager)
Prof. staff: David Burns (Divisional Librarian)
Type: Multidisciplinary.

Hours open: Mon, Tues, Thurs, Fri: 9am–5pm; Wed: 9am–7pm.
Users: Members of Trust staff; postgraduate students at Glasgow University, some University staff; other Glasgow NHS staff.
Lending: Library members.
Stock policy: Selected volumes added to historical collection; some disposed of.
Classification: NLM.
Library management system: Heritage.
Computerized services: Online access to EBSCONet; Ovid; MD Consult; Science Direct Online. CD-ROM and internet access to Cochrane, NRR.
Special collections: Herrington Collection – historical.
Branches: Douglas Inch Centre; Leverndale Hospital; MacKinnon Hospital; Parkhead Hospital – all unstaffed but library staff visit regularly.
Collaborative networks: GHI; GIN; NULJ; PLCS; SHINE.

Gateshead & South Tyneside Health Authority

Health Information and Library Services
Ingham House
Horsley Hill Road
South Shields
Tyne and Wear NE33 3DP
Tel: 0191 401 4539
Fax: 0191 401 4520
E-mail: susan.austin@gwise.gast-ha.northy.nhs.uk
Librarian: Susan Austin
Founded: 1993
Type: Health Authority.
Hours open: Health Authority office hours. External visitors by arrangement.
Users: Health Authority staff; primary care staff in Gateshead and South Tyneside; external users with enquiries relating to Health Authority data, information and reports.
Lending: Eligible users; other libraries.
Stock policy: Disposal.

Holdings: 50 books; 15 current journal subscriptions; 1,300 reports and documents.
Classification: Own.
Library management system: Manual and Endnote 2.
Computerized services: Access to HMIC. Access to AMED; CINAHL; EBMR; Embase: Psychiatry; MEDLINE via Ovid. Access to Clinical Evidence and Cochrane Library via NeLH.
Library publications: Introductory leaflet; journals holdings list.
Collaborative networks: HLN.

Gateshead Health NHS Trust Library

Queen Elizabeth Hospital
Sheriff Hill
Gateshead
Tyne and Wear NE9 6SX
Tel: 0191 403 2935
Librarian: Joanne Stemp
Founded: 2000
Type: Clinical Medicine.
Hours open: Mon, Wed, Fri: 9am–5pm; Tues, Thurs: 9am–7.30pm.
Users: Trust staff only. Visitors by appointment only.
Lending: To Trust staff and students on placement.
Stock policy: Disposed of.
Holdings: 3,700 books; 77 current journal subscriptions, 136 journal titles; 13 CD-ROMs.
Classification: Dewey.
Library management system: SydneyPLUS.
Computerized services: Access to AMED; CINAHL; Cochrane Library; Embase: Psychiatry; HMIC; MEDLINE.
Collaborative networks: HLN.

George Eliot Hospital NHS Trust Postgraduate Education Centre Library

George Eliot Hospital NHS Trust
College Street
Nuneaton
Warwickshire CV10 7DJ
Tel: 024 76865024
Fax: 024 76865464
E-mail: debbie.towle@geh-tr.wmids.nhs.uk
Librarian: Deborah Towle (Library Services Manager)
Type: Multidisciplinary.
Hours open: Staffed Mon–Fri: 9am–5pm. 24-hour access with swipe card
Users: Hospital employees; North Warwickshire NHS Trust employees; local GPs; students on placement in the hospital.
Lending: To registered users only.
Stock policy: Offer it to departments and other libraries.
Holdings: 5,000 books; 95 current journal subscriptions; 17 films and videos; 15 CD-ROMs; 23 audiotapes.
Classification: Dewey.
Library management system: Heritage.
Computerized services: Access to regional internet database – WISH; CD-ROM access to Best Evidence; MEDLINE.
Collaborative networks: West Midlands Self-Help Photocopy Scheme.

Glan Clwyd Hospital Library

Conwy and Denbighshire NHS Trust
Bodelwyddan
Denbighshire LL18 5UJ
Tel: 01745 534882
Fax: 01745 534731
E-mail: mainpc.library@cd-tr.wales.nhs.uk
Librarian: Mrs Eryl M Smith
Prof. staff: Miss Catrin G Jones; Miss Nia Morris
Founded: 1980
Type: Multidisciplinary.

Hours open: Mon, Wed: 9am–7pm; Tues, Thurs, Fri: 9am–5pm. 24-hour access via swipe card.

Users: NHS staff in North Wales, plus students on Project 2000/BN courses at University of Wales Bangor and North East Wales Institute. GPs and dentists in North Wales. Others may join on payment of a fee.

Lending: Registered users. Restrictions on some students on short placements.

Stock policy: Sell old stock over 15 years old to users or dispose of it.

Holdings: 14,600 books; 287 current journal subscriptions, 641 journal titles; 150 videos; 40 CD-ROMs.

Classification: NLM.

Library management system: Libertas.

Computerized services: CD-ROM access to CINAHL; Med6. Networked access via NHS Cymruweb to AMED; ASSIA; BNI; BookFind; CancerLit; CINAHL; Cochrane Library; Embase; HMIC; HealthStar; MEDLINE; PsycINFO.

Library publications: Quarterly newsletter; library guide; introduction to internet; database guide.

Branches: Abergele Hospital; H M Stanley Hospital, St Asaph. Both are unmanned and occupy a small library/seminar room. Staffed and supervised from Glan Clwyd.

Collaborative networks: AWHILES; AWHL; NULJ; PLCS.

Glasgow Caledonian University Library & Information Centre

Cowcaddens Road
Glasgow G4 0BA
Tel: 0141 331 3867
Fax: 0141 331 3968
E-mail: library@gcal.ac.uk
URL: www.lib.gcal.ac.uk
Librarian: Flora Smith
Prof. staff: Liz Banks; Paul Blount; Carol Carver; John Crawford; Jan Howden; Eileen McKee; Marian Miller; John Powles
Founded: 1993

Type: Multidisciplinary.

Hours open: Mon–Thurs: 8.30am–9pm; Fri: 8.30am–5pm; Sat–Sun: 11am–7pm. Vacations: Mon: 9am–8pm; Tues–Fri: 9am–5pm. Sun: 11am–4pm.

Users: University staff and students. Reciprocal access to staff and students of other named institutions. Open for a fee to others.

Lending: To staff and students. External paying members.

Stock policy: Mixture of disposal, book sale, transfer to libraries in developing countries.

Holdings: 315,000 books; 6,243 current journal subscriptions; 4,452 films and videos; 321 electronic media.

Classification: Dewey.

Library management system: Dynix.

Computerized services: All library operations are computerized. Mediated searches are carried out for staff and students. Access to ABI/Inform; ANBAR; ASSIA; BHI net; Biomed; BIOSIS; BNI; CSA; Caredata; CINAHL; Cochrane Library; ISI and more. See website for complete list.

Library publications: Wide range of user guides.

Special collections: Gallagher Memorial Library; George H Johannes Collection; Norman and Janey Buchan Collection; Queen's College Collection; Scottish and Northern Book Distribution Centre Collection plus 10 others.

Collaborative networks: SCURL; SHINE.

Glenfield Hospital Medical Library

Groby Road
Leicester LE3 9QP
Tel: 0116 256 3672
Fax: 0116 256 3334
E-mail: library@earthling.net
URL: www.glenlib.demon.co.uk
Librarian: Dr Humphrey Dunn

Librarian: Jacqueline Verschuere (Clinical Librarian)
Founded: 1984
Type: Medical; Nursing.
Hours open: Mon–Thurs: 8.30am–7pm; Fri: 8.30am–6pm; Sat: 9am–1pm.
Users: Staff of University Hospitals of Leicester, Leicestershire and Rutland Trust. Others by applying to Librarian.
Lending: To members only.
Stock policy: Sold to members.
Holdings: 8,000 books; 180 current journal subscriptions; 200 videos.
Classification: NLM.
Library management system: Heritage.
Computerized services: Internet access to AMED; Best Evidence; CINAHL; Cochrane Library; EBMR; Embase; HMIC; MEDLINE; PsycINFO.
Library publications: Nursing Union List of Journals.
Special collections: Cardiology; respiratory medicine; orthopaedics; cardiothoracic surgery.
Collaborative networks: BMA; NULJ; PLCS; TRAHCLIS.

Gloucestershire Royal NHS Trust Library

Redwood House
Gloucestershire Royal NHS Trust
Great Western Road
Gloucester GL1 3NN
Tel: 01452 394495
Fax: 01452 394170
E-mail: library@gloucr-tr.swest.nhs,uk
URL: www.grhlib.demon.co.uk
Librarian: Claire Harman
Founded: 1975
Type: Health Care.
Hours open: Mon–Thurs: 8.30am–5pm; Fri: 8.30am–4pm.
Users: Trust members; members of other Trusts; students.
Lending: As above.

Stock policy: Discarded stock offered to other libraries or disposed of.
Holdings: 80 current journal subscriptions; other figures unknown.
Classification: NLM.
Computerized services: Access to BNI; CINAHL; Embase; HMIC; MEDLINE; PsycINFO.
Collaborative networks: NULJ; SWRLIN.

Good Hope Hospital Education Centre Library

Good Hope Hospital NHS Trust
Rectory Road
Sutton Coldfield
West Midlands B75 7RR
Tel: 0121 378 2211 ext. 3540/41/44/45
Fax: 0121 378 6039
E-mail: gwen.giles@goodhot.wmids.nhs.uk
sue.peacock@goodhot.wmids.nhs.uk
Librarian: Gwen Giles
Prof. staff: Sue Peacock
Founded: PMC and Nurses' Library merged 2001.
Type: Multidisciplinary.
Hours open: Mon–Fri: 8.30am–5pm.
Users: All Trust staff; community and primary care staff. Non-NHS staff pay annual fee. Others for reference only.
Lending: To library members. Restrictions apply to students.
Stock policy: Books discarded after 15 years after consultation. Disposals lists circulated to regional network. Remainder sold to users.
Holdings: 6,000 books; 130 current journal subscriptions, 201 journal titles; 110 videos; 10 CD-ROMs.
Classification: NLM (Wessex adaptation).
Library management system: Heritage.
Computerized services: Online access to WISH. Access to BNI; CINAHL; Cochrane Library; MEDLINE.
Library publications: Booklist; library guide; newsletter; courses and conferences list.

Collaborative networks: WMRHLN.

Grantham & District Hospital Staff Library

101 Manthorpe Road
Grantham
Lincolnshire NG31 8DG
Tel: 01476 565232 ext. 4321
E-mail: library.grantham@ulh.nhs.uk
Librarian: Vacant
Librarian: Sheila Stevens (Assistant Librarian)
Founded: 1981
Type: Multidisciplinary.
Hours open: Mon–Fri: 9am–5pm.
Users: NHS staff, staff and students of University of Nottingham; School of Nursing; Academic Division of Midwifery. Others for reference only, at the discretion of the Librarian.
Lending: Registered members.
Stock policy: Dispose.
Holdings: 11,797 books; 104 current journal subscription titles.
Computerized services: Web access via Trent Consortium Ovid Biomed Service and University of Nottingham Networked Resources.
Library publications: Mental Health Current Awareness Service.
Collaborative networks: United Lincolnshire Hospitals NHS Trust.

Graylingwell Library

Sussex Weald and Downs NHS Trust
Eastergate Building
Graylingwell Hospital
College Lane
Chichester
West Sussex PO19 4PQ
Tel: 01243 815338
Fax: 01243 815228
E-mail: gwell_library@yahoo.com
Librarian: Patricia Ingham
Prof. staff: Iris Rooth; Paula Sands

Hours open: Mon: 10am–5pm; Tues-Fri: 9am–5pm.
Holdings: 38 journal titles.
Collaborative networks: STLIS.

Guild Community Healthcare NHS Trust Medical Library

Guild Academic Centre
Royal Preston Hospital
Sharoe Green Lane, Fulwood
Preston
Lancashire PR2 4HT
Tel: 01772 710270
Fax: 01772 710772
E-mail: carmel.smith@gchc-tr.nwest.nhs.uk
Librarian: Carmel Smith
Founded: 1984
Type: Mental Health; Multidisciplinary.
Hours open: Mon–Fri: 9am–5pm.
Users: Staff within the Trust; students on placement.
Lending: As above.
Stock policy: Old stock is disposed of.
Holdings: 4,210 books; 41 current journal subscriptions; 20 videos; 11 CD-ROMs.
Classification: NLM.
Library management system: Heritage.
Computerized services: Online access to ADITUS and NeLH. Access to Ovid: Cochrane Library.
Library publications: Library Bulletin.
Collaborative networks: LIHNN; Northwest Regional Learning Network.

Gwent Healthcare NHS Trust Library Services

Royal Gwent Hospital
The Friars, Friars Road
Newport
Gwent NP9 4EZ
Tel: 01633 238134
Fax: 01633 238123
E-mail: Joanna.Grey_Lloyd@gwent.wales.nhs.uk
URL: www.uwcm.ac.uk

Librarian: Miss Joanna Grey-Lloyd (Library Services Manager)
Prof. Staff: Maureen Williams (Assistant Librarian)
Founded: 1967
Type: Multidisciplinary.
Hours open: Mon–Thurs: 9am–6pm; Fri: 9am–5pm.
Users: Trust staff; GPs; dentists; primary care; private/hospice; Health Authority in South Gwent; students on placement in Trust; Newport librarians and the public with letter of introduction from librarian in own area.
Lending: Full lending rights to above. 2 books for 2 weeks for students on placements in Trust. Reference only for public.
Stock policy: Fairly new stock on shelves but if over 15 years disposed of or kept for historic reasons. Keep latest and previous edition of core textbooks but rest are removed from shelves. Departments sometimes ask for older editions to be kept in their offices.
Holdings: 7,000 books; 210 current journal subcriptions, 300 journal titles; 250+ videos; 20 CD-ROMs.
Classification: Dewey.
Library management system: In-house access database.
Computerized services: Online access to AMED; ASSIA; BNI; CancerLit; CINAHL; Cochrane Library; EBMR; Embase; HealthStar; HMIC; MCE; MICROMEDEX; NeLH; NHSCRD; NRR; Ovid MEDLINE; PsycINFO; WeBNF.
Library publications: Library Guide; Handy Hints on Searching and on Harvard Referencing (also on intranet); Trust-wide journal holdings and weblinks to table of contents (also on intranet); Careers Information (Powerpoint file on intranet).
Special collections: Archive of Royal Gwent Hospital.
Collaborative networks: AWHL; AWHILES; BMA; INFAH; NEWLIS; RCSE.

Halton Education Centre Library

Halton General Hospital
North Cheshire Hospitals NHS Trust
Runcorn
Cheshire WA7 2DA
Tel: 01928 753318
Fax: 01928 753268
E-mail: linda.chapelhow@halton-tr.nwest.nhs.uk
Librarian: Linda Chapelhow
Founded: 1985/6
Type: Multidisciplinary.
Hours open: Mon: 9am–5pm; Tues–Thurs: 9am–6.30pm; Fri: 9am–4.30pm.
Users: Medical staff; nursing staff; community staff; PAMs; social services; nursing home staff; students – medical and nursing.
Lending: Library members only.
Stock policy: Dispose of it.
Holdings: 3,897 books; 89 current journal subscriptions, 94 journal titles; 6 CD-ROMs.
Classification: Own and Dewey.
Library management system: Heritage.
Computerized services: Online access to AMED; ASSIA; BNI; CINAHL; Cochrane Library; HMIC; MEDLINE; NeLH; PsycINFO; RCN.
Collaborative networks: ADITUS.

Harefield Hospital Library

Harefield Hospital
Royal Brompton and Harefield NHS Trust
Hill End Road
Harefield
Middlesex UB9 6JH
Tel: 01895 828947
Fax: 01895 828993
E-mail: deptlibraryharefield@rbh.nthames.nhs.uk
URL: www.rbh.nthames.nhs.uk/library
Librarian: Richard Osborn
Founded: 1993
Type: Multidisciplinary.
Hours open: Mon–Fri: 9am–5pm. Key access at other times.

Users: All Trust staff; Imperial College research staff on site. Other users on application.

Lending: Books and journals loaned to library members and other libraries. Photocopies provided.

Stock policy: Books and journals discarded at varying intervals – offered to other libraries.

Holdings: 1,000 books; 114 current journal subscriptions.

Classification: NLM (Wessex adaptation).

Library management system: DB/TextWorks.

Computerized services: Internet access available (NHSNet). Consortium-funded access to Ovid databases via internet. AMED, MEDLINE and PsycINFO via Ovid online. Access to CINAHL. Cochrane Library via NeLH and Ovid. Range of full-text journals.

Library publications: Annual Report; periodicals holdings list.

Special collections: Cardiothoracic medicine and surgery.

Collaborative networks: London Library and Information Network co-ordinated by LLIDU.

Harold Bridges Library

University College of St Martin
Bowerham Road
Lancaster LA1 3JD
Tel: 01524 384243
Fax: 01524 384588
E-mail: library@ucsm.ac.uk
URL: www.ucsm.ac.uk
Librarian: David Brown
Prof. staff: Judy Dyer; Margaret Gill; Janet Henderson
Type: Higher Education.
Hours open: Mon–Thurs: 8.45am–9pm; Fri: 8.45am–5.30pm; 9.30am–4pm.
Users: Staff and students of the College. Open as a reference library to anybody else, or option to join as an external borrower.

Lending: Staff and students. Do not lend to non-members.

Stock policy: Dispose of stock.

Holdings: 140,497 books; 557 current journal subscriptions, 945 journal titles.

Classification: BLISS.

Library management system: Talis.

Computerized services: Online access to internet and MEDLINE. Access to CINAHL, Community Wise; EBMR; Infotrac; Journals @ Ovid; PreMEDLINE.

Collaborative networks: LIHNN; NULJ.

Harold Wood Hospital Multidisciplinary Library & Information Services

Academic Centre
Harold Wood Hospital
Gubbins Lane
Harold Wood
Essex RM3 0BE
Tel: 01708 708113
Fax: 01708 708113
E-mail: jackie@hwhlibrary.demon.co.uk
URL: www.libnel.nhs.uk
Librarian: Miss Jackie Blanks
Prof. staff: Mrs Karen Johnston (Old Church Site Branch Library)
Type: Multidisciplinary.
Hours open: Mon–Fri: 9am–5pm. 24-hour coded access for registered users.
Users: Employees of Barking, Havering and Redbridge NHS Trust. Reference only for some other healthcare workers in the local area who are not employed by the Trust.
Lending: To registered members.
Stock policy: Withdrawn and offered to other libraries or to library users – minimum charge 50p.
Holdings: 1,998 books; 76 current journal subscriptions, 110 journal titles; 59 videos; 23 CD-ROMs; 10 cassette tapes.
Classification: NLM.
Library management system: DB/TextWorks.

Computerized services: Card-operated internet access. Online access via Ovid to AMED; CINAHL; MEDLINE; PsycINFO. Access to Cochrane Library.
Branches: Multidisciplinary Library and Information Service, Oldchurch Hospital.
Collaborative networks: LIBNEL.

Harrogate District Hospital Library & Information Service

Strayside Education Centre
Harrogate District Hospital
Knaresborough Road
Harrogate
North Yorkshire HG2 7SX
Tel: 01423 553104
Fax: 01423 883094
E-mail: hslibhg@york.ac.uk
Librarian: Gillian Jarrett
Type: Multidisciplinary.
Hours open: Mon–Thurs: 8.30am–5.30pm; Fri: 8.30am–4.30pm; Sat: 9.30am–12.30pm. 24-hour access.
Users: Staff of Harrogate Health Care NHS Trust; staff and students of the University of York Department of Health Studies. External membership available to other healthcare professionals who are not part of above organizations.
Lending: All users and external users – no restrictions. Non-members not allowed to borrow.
Stock policy: Older material disposed of. Book sale for recently published material.
Holdings: 6,000 books; 124 current journal subscriptions, 148 journal titles; 40 films and videos.
Classification: Dewey.
Library management system: Dynix.
Computerized services: Access to AMED; BNI; CINAHL; Cochrane Library; Embase: Psychiatry; HMIC; MEDLINE; NRR.
Collaborative networks: LfN – Yorkshire; Northern and Yorkshire Regional Libraries.

Hastings & Rother NHS Trust: Rosewell Library

Education Centre
Conquest Hospital
The Ridge
St Leonards-on-Sea
East Sussex TN37 7RD
Tel: 01424 755255 ext. 8672
Fax: 01424 758010
E-mail: rosewell.library@mail.har-tr.sthames.nhs.uk
Librarian: Jenny Turner
Prof. staff: Margaret Ellis; Rachel Haddock; Tony Moses; Marion Vernon-Gill; Maureen Wycherley.
Hours open: Mon–Thurs: 8.30am–8pm; Fri: 8.30am–5pm; Sat: 10am–4pm.
Holdings: 200 journal titles.
Collaborative networks: STLIS.

Health Education Board for Scotland: Health Promotion Library Scotland

Health Education Board for Scotland
The Priory, Canaan Lane
Edinburgh EH10 4SG
Tel: 0845 912 5442
Fax: 0131 536 5502
E-mail: library.enquiries@hebs.scot.nhs.uk
URL: www.hebs.com/library
Librarian: Margaret Forrest
Prof. staff: Katie McGlew
Founded: 1971
Type: Multidisciplinary.
Hours open: Mon–Thurs: 9am–4.30pm; Fri: 9am–4pm.
Users: The library is open to everyone who lives and/or works in Scotland.
Lending: As above – no restrictions.
Stock policy: Old books are passed to local University Donations Department to use in other libraries or to sell.
Holdings: 12,000 books; 370 current journal subscriptions; 30 CD-ROMs.
Classification: UDC.
Library management system: Olib.

Computerized services: Online access to Caredata; Cochrane Library and Data-Star. Access to ASSIA Plus; Best Evidence; CINAHL; Current Research in Britain; Helpbox; MEDLINE; OECD Health Data; plus many more.
Library publications: Bi-monthly Library Bulletin. Full list of publications on website.
Collaborative networks: SHINE.

Health Information East London Library & Information Centre

81–91 Commercial Road
London E1 1RD
Tel: 020 7655 6686
Fax: 020 7655 6687
E-mail: library@elcha.nhs.uk
URL: www.thpct.org/hiel
Librarian: Sarah Lawson (Library Manager)
Founded: 2000
Type: Health Management; Health Promotion; Public Health.
Hours open: Mon, Tues, Thurs, Fri: 10am–4pm.
Users: Health Authority staff, professional and student health professionals in East London working on health promotion issues. Cross-sector – voluntary, local authority, NHS, GPs, etc. Anyone else for reference only.
Lending: As above.
Stock policy: Dispose of it.
Holdings: 5,000 books; 50 current journal subscriptions, 500 journal titles; 1,000 videos.
Classification: Own.
Library management system: Integer.
Computerized services: Online access to Ovid Biomed to CINAHL; Cochrane Library; MEDLINE; full-text journals.
Library publications: Website list; internet training pack; Current Awareness Bulletin; Acquisitions Bulletin.
Special collections: East London Public Health Collection.
Collaborative networks: London-wide network; Health Management Forum; Health Promotion Libraries Forum; IfM Healthcare.

Health Information in the Weald

Sevenoaks Hospital
Hospital Road
Sevenoaks
Kent TN13 3PG
Tel: 01732 743333
Fax: 01732 452181
E-mail: Pam@hospiceweald.co.uk
Librarian: Pamela Vale-Taylor
Founded: 1991
Type: Patient Information.
Hours open: Mon, Thurs, Fri: 9.30am–12.45pm; Tues, Wed: 9.30am–4pm.
Users: Any member of the public. (70% enquiries are from health or social services professionals.)
Lending: All enquirers, but most are given information.
Stock policy: Dispose of out-of-date stock and information.
Holdings: Some books, journals and videos; leaflets and information sheets.
Classification: Own.
Library management system: Manual.
Computerized services: DISS; PatientWise; Access to various medical search engines.
Library publications: Annual Report.
Branches: Information areas at Edenbridge, Hawkhurst, Kent and Sussex, Pembury and Tonbridge Hospitals.
Collaborative networks: KILN.

Health Promotion Department Information & Resources Centre

Haki House
Cameron Hospital
Leven
Fife KY2 5RA
Tel: 01592 712812 ext. 291/294
Fax: 01592 716858
E-mail: healthpromotion@fife-pct.scot.nhs.uk
URL: www.fife-hpd.demon.co.uk
Librarian: Roberta Simpson (Office and Financial Co-ordinator)

Founded: 1978
Type: Health Promotion.
Hours open: Mon–Thurs: 9am–5pm; Fri: 9am–4.30pm.
Users: Any individual or organization involved in any health promotion activity within the Fife Region.
Lending: As above.
Stock policy: Dispose of or pass to any interested party.
Holdings: 4,000 books; 53 current journal subscriptions, 58 journal titles; 400 films and videos; 1,100 other items.
Classification: DHSS and own.
Library management system: HPLIB2000.
Collaborative networks: SHINE.

Health Promotion Service Avon Resource & Information Centre, Bath

Bath NHS House
Newbridge Hill
Bath BA1 3QE
Tel: 01225 825670
Fax: 01225 825683
E-mail: hpsabath@netcomuk.co.uk
Type: Health Promotion.
Hours open: Mon, Tues, Thurs: 8.30am–12.30, 1pm–5pm.
Users: Health promotion staff in HPSA, plus anyone who has an interest in health promotion in their work. Main users are health visitors, midwives, teachers, youth workers, school nurses, etc.

Health Promotion Service Avon Resource & Information Centre, Central Bristol

Central Health Clinic
Tower Hill
Bristol BS2 0JD
Tel: 0117 9291010 ext. 6872/81
Fax: 0117 9750607
E-mail: hpsachc@netcomuk.co.uk

Librarian: Angelica Anderson (Information Manager)
Prof. staff: Jackie Mitchell
Type: Health Promotion.
Hours open: Mon, Tues, Thurs: 8.30am–12.30pm, 1pm–5pm; Wed: 8.30am–12.30pm; Fri: 8.30am–12.30pm,1pm–4pm.
Users: Health promotion staff in HPSA, plus anyone who has an interest in health promotion in their work. Main users are health visitors, midwives, teachers, youth workers, school nurses, etc.
Lending: As above. Reference only for undergraduate students and the public.
Stock policy: Recycle leaflets, etc; dispose of books when old or superseded.
Holdings: 2,406 books; 53 current journal subscriptions; 406 films and videos; 428 teaching packs; 200 leaflets.
Classification: NLM (Wessex adaptation).
Library management system: Integer: RGM.
Library publications: Annual Report; HPSource – newsletter.
Collaborative networks: SWRLIN.

Health Promotion Service Avon Resource & Information Centre, North Bristol

Somerset House
Southmead Hospital
Bristol BS10 5NB
Tel: 0117 959 5463
Fax: 0117 959 5469
E-mail: hpsasou@netcomuk.co.uk
Type: Health Promotion.
Hours open: Mon, Tues, Thurs: 8.30am–12.30, 1pm–5pm.
Users: Health promotion staff in HPSA, plus anyone who has an interest in health promotion in their work. Main users are health visitors, midwives, teachers, youth workers, school nurses, etc.

Health Promotion Service Avon Resource and Information Centre, Weston-super-Mare

Drove House
Drove Road
Weston-super-Mare
Somerset
BS23 3NT
Tel: 01934 636363
Fax: 01934 416181
E-mail: hpsawest@netcomuk.co.uk
Type: Health Promotion.
Hours open: Mon and Thurs: 8.30am–12.30, 1pm–5pm.
Users: Health promotion staff in HPSA, plus anyone who has an interest in health promotion in their work. Main users are health visitors, midwives, teachers, youth workers, school nurses, etc.

Health Promotion Service, Guildford

The Jarvis Centre
Health Education Centre
60 Stoughton Road
Guildford
Surrey GU1 1NG
Tel: 01483 532828
E-mail:
enquiries@wsurreyhps3.demon.co.uk
URL: www.surreyweb.org.uk/wshp/wshp.htm

Health Promotions

181 Union Street
Aberdeen AB11 6BB
Tel: 01224 551306
Fax: 01224 582947
E-mail: gillian.heron@health-promotions.com
URL: www.health-promotions.com
Librarian: Anne Whitcombe (Health Information Manager)
Prof. staff: Gillian Heron
Founded: 1995
Type: Multidisciplinary.

Hours open: Mon–Thurs: 9am–5pm; Fri: 9am–4pm.
Users: Staff of Health Promotions; health professionals in the Grampian area.
Lending: As above.
Stock policy: Dispose of or pass on.
Holdings: 3,750 books; 50 current journal subscriptions, 100 journal titles; leaflets, posters, models, equipment on a loan/supply basis.
Classification: Own.
Library management system: MS Access.
Computerized services: Access to HNC for ASSIA; HMIC. Access via Ovid for CINAHL; Embase; MEDLINE. Access to Cochrane Library.
Collaborative networks: GHIN; SHINE.

Health Services Management Centre Library & Information Services

University of Birmingham
Park House
40 Edgbaston Park Road
Birmingham B15 2RT
Tel: 0121 414 7060
Fax: 0121 414 7051
E-mail: library-hsmc@bham.ac.uk or s.e.rose@bham.ac.uk
URL: www.bham.ac.uk/hsmc
Librarian: Steve Rose (Library and Information Services Manager)
Prof. staff: Pat Metcalfe; Rachel Posaner
Founded: 1974
Type: Health Management.
Hours open: Mon–Thurs: 9am–7pm; Fri: 9am–5pm. Vacations: Mon–Fri: 9am–5pm.
Users: Staff and postgraduate students at HSMC, staff from the NHS Executive West Midlands Regional Office, staff from Birmingham Health Authority and public health. Others can use the library for reference only, by appointment.
Lending: As above. All journals reference only.

Stock policy: Old or outdated stock would be offered to users and then disposed of.
Holdings: 11,500 books; 100 current journal subscriptions; 50 videos.
Classification: LC.
Library management system: Soutron's 2020.
Computerized services: 2020 catalogue searched using web publisher software also supplied by Soutron. Internet access to Cochrane Library; HealthStar; HMIC; MEDLINE. CD-ROM access to Best Evidence.
Branches: Small collection at West Midlands Regional Office.
Collaborative networks: WMRHLN.

Healthpoint, Poole Central Library

Poole Central Library
The Dolphin Centre
Poole
Dorset BH15 1QE
Tel: 01202 675377
Fax: 01202 667112
E-mail: healthpoint@poole.gov.uk
URL: www.poole.gov.uk/healthpoint
Librarian: Vivienne Grier
Prof. staff: Kay Roderick
Founded: 1989
Type: Health Information Centre.
Hours open: Mon: 10am–5.30pm; Tues–Fri: 9.30am–5.30pm; Sat: 9am–1pm.
Users: The public; health and social care professional students.
Lending: Rarely lend, as collection is a study/reference collection. Occasionally to individuals in need, at Librarian's discretion. Has a small loan collection of videos.
Stock policy: Mainly disposed of or pulped as information must be current.
Holdings: 1,000 books; 52 current journal subscriptions, 120 journal titles; 35 videos. Leaflets and some cassettes.
Classification: Own.

Computerized services: Internet access. Access to DISSbase; Helpbox; UK Advice Finder.
Library publications: Annual Report; Healthpoint leaflet.
Collaborative networks: CHIC; NHS Direct; SWRLIN.

Heatherwood & Wexham Park Hospitals NHS Trust: John Jamison Library

Slough
Berkshire SL2 4HL
Fax: 01753 634189
E-mail: wxlibrary@hwph-tr.nhs.uk
Librarian: Sarah Pallot
Prof. staff: Claire Coverson
Type: Multidisciplinary; Health and Medicine including Management.
Hours open: Mon, Wed, Fri: 9am–5.30pm; Tues and Thurs: 9am–8pm.
Users: Mainly healthcare professionals employed in the NHS. Others may subscribe and become library members.
Lending: Any registered member of the library; other libraries.
Stock policy: Offer old books for sale and discard unwanted stock; offer journals to other libraries through duplicates exchange scheme.
Holdings: 6,000 books; 179 current journal subscriptions, 185 journal titles; 240 films and videos; 10 CD-ROMs.
Classification: NLM.
Library management system: Heritage.
Computerized services: Internet access and NHSNet. Online access to Data-Star. Access to AMED; Best Evidence; CINAHL; Cochrane Library; HMIC on SilverPlatter; MEDLINE.
Library publications: Annual Report; library leaflet; list of journals.
Branches: Heatherwood Library, Heatherwood Hospital, Ascot.
Collaborative networks: BLIP; HeLIN.

Hemel Hempstead General Hospital Library

Hillfield Road
Hemel Hempstead
Hertfordshire HP2 4AD
Tel: 01442 287185
Fax: 01442 287992
Librarian: Diane Levey
Type: Multidisciplinary.
Hours open: Mon–Fri: 9am–5pm.
Users: Healthcare staff working in hospitals, community, mental health and primary care; students. Reference use for others.
Lending: Members only.
Stock policy: Old stock discarded locally or passed to overseas libraries if suitable.
Holdings: 6,000 books.
Classification: NLM.
Library management system: DB/TextWorks.
Computerized services: Access to AMED; BNI; CINAHL; ClinPsych; Cochrane Library; HMIC; MEDLINE; NRR.
Collaborative networks: London North Thames.

Herefordshire Clinical Library

Postgraduate Medical Centre
Hereford County Hospital
Hereford HR1 2ER
Tel: 01432 355444 ext. 5840
Fax: 01432 355265
E-mail: library@hh-tr.wmids.nhs.uk
Librarian: Janet Ball (Lead Health Librarian)
Prof. staff: Lindsey Baker (Training and Resource Development Librarian); Elise Collins (Assistant Information Librarian); Sue Powell (Library Assistant).
Founded: 1968
Type: Multidisciplinary.
Hours open: Mon–Fri: 9am–5pm. Out-of-hours access via a swipe card.
Users: All Herefordshire NHS staff. On request non-Herefordshire NHS staff may be granted access for reference purposes.

Lending: Clinical staff. Non-clinical staff on occasions. Only Herefordshire NHS staff have borrowing rights.
Stock policy: Disposed of to clinical department, to stock Muheza hospital library or clinical staff.
Holdings: 2,500 books; 80 current journal subscriptions; 50 films and videos; 210 CD-ROMs; 250 reports, etc.
Classification: Dewey, but changing to NLM.
Computerized services: Access to Cochrane Library; MEDLINE; WISH which includes AMED, CINAHL, Embase.
Special collections: A local historical section.
Collaborative networks: WMRHLN.

Hesketh Centre Library

The Hesketh Centre
51–55 Albert Road
Southport
Merseyside PR9 0LT
Tel: 01704 547471 ext. 3177
Fax: 01704 502014
Librarian: Matthew Leigh (Library Manager)
Type: Psychiatry; Nursing.
Hours open: Mon–Fri: 12pm–3pm.
Users: Doctors, SHOs, Project 2000 nurses, medical students.
Lending: Local libraries.
Stock policy: Old stock is placed in an area where people can take as many as they wish.
Holdings: 2,500 books; 38 current journal subscriptions, 50 journal titles; 20 videos; 60 CD-ROMs.
Classification: NLM.
Library management system: Heritage.
Computerized services: Internet and NHSNet. Access to BNI; CINAHL; Embase; MEDLINE; PsycINFO.

Hexham Hospital Library

Corbridge Road
Hexham
Northumberland NE46 1QJ
Tel: 01434 655046
Fax: 01434 655048
Librarian: Mrs S Ellingham
Founded: 1975
Type: Multidisciplinary.
Hours open: Mon–Fri: 8.45am–4.45pm.
Users: Northumbria Healthcare NHS Trust staff and students on placement.
Lending: To hospital staff and students in situ.
Stock policy: Offered to other local regional libraries and then to hospital staff. Anything remaining is disposed of.
Holdings: 642 books; 57 current journal titles, 64 journal titles; 40 videos; 8 CD-ROMs.
Classification: Dewey.
Library management system: SydneyPLUS.
Computerized services: Access via Ovid to AMED; CINAHL; MEDLINE, etc. Access to Clinical Evidence and Cochrane Library via NeLH.
Collaborative networks: BL; BMA; HLN; Northumbria Healthcare NHS Trust.

High Royds Hospital Medical & Professional Library

High Royds Hospital
Menston
Ilkley
West Yorkshire BD23 4DA
Tel: 0113 3056227
Fax: 01943 870471
E-mail: medlib.leedscmht-leedscmht@btinternet.com
Librarian: Mrs Shirley Robinson
Type: Multidisciplinary.
Hours open: Mon: 9am–8.30pm; Tues–Thurs: 9am–4.30pm; Fri: 9am–4.00pm.
Users: Mainly Leeds CMHT and College of Health students.

Lending: Employees of Leeds CMHT only at present.
Stock policy: Dispose of it.
Classification: Own.
Computerized services: Access to CINAHL; Cochrane Library; MEDLINE; NRR.
Collaborative networks: PLCS; YHL.

Highlands Health Sciences Library

University of Stirling
Highland Campus
Old Perth Road
Inverness IV2 3FG
Tel: 01463 705269
Fax: 01463 713471
E-mail: hhsl1@stir.ac.uk
URL: www.nm.stir.ac.uk/HHSL/HHSLibrary.htm
Librarian: Anne Gillespie (Campus Librarian)
Prof. staff: Kathleen Irvine; Rob Polson
Founded: 1971
Type: Multidisciplinary.
Hours open: Mon–Fri: 9am–9pm; Sat: 10am–5pm.
Users: Staff and students of Stirling University; employees of Highland Health Board and its associated NHS Trusts; employees of Highland Council Social Work Department. Other persons who are working in related fields, who are unemployed, or are retired from the Health Service in the Highland Region may apply to join and pay appropriate charges. Public access is for reference only.
Lending: As above.
Stock policy: Passed to libraries in developing countries if appropriate; otherwise discarded.
Holdings: 25,000 books; 250 current journal subscriptions, 350 journal titles; 500 videos.
Classification: NLM and LC.
Library management system: Dynix.
Computerized services: Access to BNI; CINAHL; Cochrane Library; HEBS; MEDLINE and NRR. Also available for University staff and students only: BIDS PsycINFO;

Biomed Nursing Collection; Biomed Sport; CSA Internet Database Service; ISI Web of Science.

Library publications: Library guides; various database guides; Library Regulations.

Collaborative networks: BMA; GI; SHINE; PLCS.

Hillingdon Hospital Trust Library

Postgraduate Medical Centre
Hillingdon Hospital
Pield Heath Road
Uxbridge
Middlesex UB8 3NN
Tel: 01895 279250
Fax: 01895 234150
E-mail: peter@hil21.demon.co.uk
Librarian: Peter Lovegrove
Founded: 1989
Type: Multidisciplinary.
Hours open: Mon–Fri: 9am–5pm.
Users: All Trust staff and NHS staff in the locality. Other users on application.
Lending: To registered members only.
Stock policy: Offered to departments/consultants. Offered to sister libraries within the region. Offered to Third World countries.
Holdings: 3,000 books; 125 current journal subscriptions.
Classification: NLM (Wessex adaptation).
Library management system: DB/TextWorks.
Computerized services: Ovid databases and some full-text journals; NHSNet access. Access to AMED; CINAHL; ClinPsych; Cochrane Library; MEDLINE.
Collaborative networks: LLIDU.

Hinchingbrooke Hospital NHS Trust

Education Centre Library
Hinchingbrooke Hospital
Huntingdon
Cambridgeshire PE29 6NT
Tel: 01480 416412
Fax: 01480 363552
Librarian: Kerry Herbert
Type: Multidisciplinary.
Hours open: Mon–Fri: 9am–5pm.
Users: Staff of Hinchingbrooke Hospital NHS Trust, GPs and Homerton School of Health staff and students.
Lending: As above.
Stock policy: Try to sell it initially.
Holdings: 4,000 books; 168 current journal subscriptions; 5 CD-ROMs; leaflets for Patient Information Service.
Classification: NLM.
Library management system: Soutron 2020 (just converting).
Computerized services: Access to BNI; CINAHL; Cochrane Library; Embase: Psychiatry; MEDLINE.
Special collections: Healthlink, a patient information service and a Health Promotion Resources Service which is funded separately.
Collaborative networks: Anglia Library Group; Cambridgeshire Librarians Group.

Homerton Health Library: Cambridge

Victoria House
Capital Park
Fulbourn
Cambridge CB1 5XA
Tel: 01223 885995
Fax: 01223 885990
E-mail: camblibrary@health-homerton.ac.uk
URL: www.health-homerton.ac.uk
Librarian: Graham C Haldane (Health Studies Librarian)
Prof. staff: Kathy Cook (Librarian); Caroline Dethridge (Assistant Librarian)
Founded: 2001 (merger of three previous libraries)
Type: Nurse, Midwifery and Health Visiting Education.

Hours open: Mon: 8.30am–5pm; Tues–Thurs: 8.30am–6.30pm; Fri: 8.30am–5pm; Sat: 9.30am–1pm.

Users: Staff and students of the School. Also open to all local healthcare staff.

Lending: All registered users. Higher borrowing limit for School staff and students. Borrowing facilities under review for other users.

Stock policy: Stock over 10 years old reviewed, but retained if of archival or research interest. Discarded stock sold or disposed of.

Holdings: 11,723 books and other items; 150 current journals subscriptions.

Classification: NLM.

Library management system: Heritage IV.

Computerized services: Internet access to ASSIA; BNI; BookFind; ChildData; CINAHL; Cochrane Library; Embase; HMIC; MEDLINE. Ingenta Journals; ZETOC via Athens system.

Library publications: Citation and Referencing Guidelines; Study Skills Guide; various printed guides to databases; Searching the Literature Unit of Homerton Health Online: Exploring Research.

Branches: Homerton Health Library: Papworth; Homerton Health Library: Peterborough.

Collaborative networks: Anglia and Oxford; BL; Cambridgeshire Health Librarians Group; Health Librarians of Anglia.

Homerton Health Library: Papworth

Education Centre
St Peter's Nursing Home
Church Lane
Papworth Everard
Cambridge CB3 8QT
Tel: 01480 830541 ext. 4294
Fax: 01480 831154
E-mail: coates@health-homerton.ac.uk

URL: www.health-homerton.ac.uk

Librarian: Graham C Haldane (Health Studies Librarian – Cambridge based)

Prof. staff: Joy Coates (Administrative Assistant)

Type: Cardiovascular and Transplant Nursing.

Hours open: Mon–Thurs: 10am–3pm.

Users: Staff and students of the School. Also open to all nursing staff of Papworth NHS Trust.

Lending: All registered users. Higher borrowing limit for School staff and students. Borrowing facilities under review for other users.

Stock policy: Stock review policy still to be implemented on this site.

Holdings: 431 books and other items; 10 current journal subscriptions.

Classification: NLM.

Library management system: Heritage IV.

Computerized services: Internet access to ASSIA; BNI; BookFind; ChildData; CINAHL; Cochrane Library; Embase; HMIC; MEDLINE. Ingenta Journals; ZETOC via Athens system.

Library publications: See Homerton Health Library: Cambridge.

Collaborative networks: Anglia and Oxford; BL; Cambridgeshire Health Librarians Group; Health Librarians of Anglia.

Homerton Health Library: Peterborough

Education Centre
Peterborough District Hospital
Gables Drive
Thorpe Road
Peterborough
Cambridgeshire PE3 6DA
Tel: 01733 874766
Fax: 01733 897731
E-mail: pblibrary@health-homerton.ac.uk
URL: www.health-homerton.ac.uk

Librarian: Graham C Haldane (Health Studies Librarian – Cambridge based)
Prof. staff: Peter Stokes (Assistant Librarian)
Type: Nurse, Midwifery and Health Visiting Education.
Hours open: Mon and Fri: 8.30am–5pm; Tues–Thurs: 8.30am–6.30pm; Sat: 9.30am–1pm.
Users: Staff and students of the School. Also open to all local healthcare staff.
Lending: All registered users. Higher borrowing limit for School staff and students. Borrowing facilities under review for other users.
Stock policy: Stock policy: Stock over 10 years old reviewed, but retained if of archival or research interest. Discarded stock sold or disposed of.
Holdings: 9,705 books and other items; 109 current journal subscriptions.
Classification: NLM.
Library management system: Heritage IV.
Computerized services: Internet access to ASSIA; BNI; BookFind; ChildData; CINAHL; Cochrane Library; Embase; HMIC; MEDLINE. Ingenta Journals; ZETOC via Athens system.
Library publications: Citation and Referencing Guidelines; Study Skills Guide; various printed guides to databases; Searching the Literature Unit of Homerton Health Online: Exploring Research.
Collaborative networks: Anglia and Oxford; BL; Cambridgeshire Health Librarians Group; Health Librarians of Anglia.

Huddersfield Learning Centre Library

Calderdale and Huddersfield NHS Trust
Huddersfield Royal Infirmary
Acre Street, Lindley
Huddersfield
West Yorkshire HD3 3EA

Tel: 01484 342869
Fax: 01484 347085
E-mail: richard.heywood@hudderfd-tr.northy.nhs.uk
Librarian: Richard Heywood
Founded: 1972
Type: Multidisciplinary.
Hours open: Mon–Fri: 9am–5pm.
Users: Trust staff. Open to others for reference purposes.
Lending: Trust staff.
Stock policy: Obsolete stock discarded.
Holdings: 8,000 books; 160 current journal subscriptions.
Classification: NLM (Wessex adaptation).
Library management system: SydneyPLUS.
Computerized services: Internet available. Access to AMED; BNI; CINAHL; ClinPsych; Cochrane Library; Embase: Psychiatry; HMIC; MEDLINE; Speech and Language Database.
Library publications: Various resource lists and self-training manuals.
Collaborative networks: YJHLS.

Hull & East Riding Community Health NHS Trust

Healthcare Library
RED Unit
Bridlington and District Hospital
Bessingby Road
Bridlington
East Yorkshire YO16 4QP
Tel: 01262 423144
Fax: 01262 423417
E-mail: Julie.Williams@herch-tr.nhs.uk
Librarian: Julie Williams (Communication Support Manager)
Prof. staff: Margery Sidell
Founded: 1997
Type: Multidisciplinary.
Hours open: Mon–Fri: 8.30am–5pm. 24-hour access for members.

Users: Local patch NHS family; pre-registration and postgraduate medical, clinical and nursing students.

Lending: Patch-wide access to acute and Health Authority staff. Restricted access to Scarborough and North East Yorkshire NHS Trust.

Stock policy: Old stock disposed of depending on type. Some medical textbooks e.g. anatomy passed on to charities.

Holdings: 3,000 books; 20 current journal subscriptions; 10 films and videos; 500 reports and papers.

Classification: Dewey.

Library management system: Heritage.

Computerized services: Ovid regional deal databases.

Library publications: Clinical Matters – Best Practice.

Branches: 5 electronic libraries.

Collaborative networks: East Riding Medical Education Centre; NYRLAS.

Imperial Cancer Research Fund

Library and Information Services
PO Box No 123
Lincoln's Inn Fields
London WC2A 3PX
Tel: 020 7269 3206
Fax: 020 7269 3084
E-mail: lib_info@icrf.icnet.uk
URL: www.icnet.uk
Librarian: Julia Chester
Prof. staff: Angela Aldam; Jane Falconer; Fiona Hutchison; Jane Milligan; Samantha Murray; Susan Osborne
Founded: 1910
Type: Medical; Research.
Hours open: Mon–Fri: 9am–5.30pm. 24-hour access for users.
Users: ICRF staff only.
Lending: Books and photocopies to other libraries on repayment.
Stock policy: No formal disposal policy. Suitable items are used for charitable purposes where possible.

Holdings: 5,000 books; 185 current journal subscriptions, 300 journal titles.

Classification: NLM.

Library management system: TechLib Plus (BASIS).

Computerized services: All library services available via the organizational intranet. Online access to Cochrane Library; MEDLINE; SciSearch; Web of Science.

Library publications: ICRF Annual Scientific Report; ICRF Research Prospectus.

Special collections: ICRF Staff Publications Database; ICRF Staff Theses.

Branches: ICRF Laboratories, Clare Hall, South Mimms, Potters Bar, Hertfordshire, EN6 3LD.

Collaborative networks: CHILL.

Imperial College of Science Technology & Medicine: Charing Cross Campus Library

The Reynolds Building
St Dunstan's Road
London W6 8RP
Tel: 020 7594 0755
Fax: 020 7594 0851
E-mail: librarycx@ic.ac.uk
URL: www.lib.ic.ac.uk
Librarian: Susan V Howard
Prof. staff: Christopher Awre; Sarah Deakin; Helen Gilmour; Howard Hague; Rebecca Mackle; Paul Morrell; Jennifer Randall
Founded: 1818 (1997 as part of IC)
Type: Multidisciplinary.
Hours open: Mon–Thurs: 9am–9pm; Fri: 9am–8pm; Sat: 9am–12 noon (term time only).
Users: Staff and students of the Imperial College, staff of associated NHS Trusts, local GPs. Others may use the library for reference – fee may be levied.
Lending: To full members only.
Stock policy: Dispose of or sell.

Holdings: 20,000 books; 480 current print journal subscriptions, 4,000 electronic journal subscriptions; 500 videos.
Classification: NLM.
Library management system: Unicorn.
Computerized services: See www.lib.ic.ac.uk/eiindex.htm
Library publications: Newsletter.
Collaborative networks: CURL; M25 Consortium; London NHS Region; University of London.

Imperial College School of Medicine: Chelsea & Westminster Campus Library

369 Fulham Road
London SW10 9NH
Tel: 020 8746 8107
Fax: 020 8746 8215
E-mail: librarycw@ic.ac.uk
URL: www.lib.ic.ac.uk
Librarian: Reinhard Wentz
Prof. staff: Ruilian Chen; Kate Ogden
Founded: 1834 (1997 as part of IC)
Type: Multidisciplinary.
Hours open: Mon–Fri: 9am–9pm; Sat: 9pm–5pm (term time only).
Users: Staff and students of the Imperial College, staff of associated NHS Trusts, local GPs. Others may use the library for reference (fee may be levied).
Lending: To full members only.
Stock policy: Dispose of or sell.
Holdings: 4,500 books; 177 current print journal subscriptions, 4,000 electronic journal subscriptions; 500 films and videos.
Classification: NLM.
Library management system: Unicorn.
Computerized services: See www.lib.ic.ac.uk/eiindex.htm
Library publications: Newsletter.
Collaborative networks: CURL; M25 Consortium; London NHS Region; University of London.

Imperial College School of Medicine: Hammersmith Campus

Wellcome Library
Hammersmith Hospital
Du Cane Road
London W12 0NN
Tel: 020 8383 3246
Fax: 020 8383 2195
E-mail: lib.hamm@ic.ac.uk
URL: www.lib.ic.ac.uk/hammersmith/
Librarian: Liz Davis
Prof. staff: Fereshteh Afshari; Georgina Going; Tricia Gwynn-Jones; Angela Jefkins; John Matthews; Paul Stokes; Judith Stone
Founded: 1935
Type: Clinical Medicine.
Hours open: Mon–Fri: 9am–9pm; Sat: 9.30am–12.30pm. August: Mon–Fri: 9am–6pm; Sat: 9.30am–12.30pm.
Users: Staff and students of Imperial College. Staff of Hammersmith Hospitals NHS Trust. Other users by arrangement.
Lending: To staff and postgraduate students of Imperial College and staff of Hammersmith Hospitals NHS Trust.
Stock policy: Out-of-date stock is discarded.
Holdings: 8,000 books; 900 current journal subscriptions; 50 videos.
Classification: NLM.
Library management system: Unicorn.
Computerized services: See www.lib.ic.ac.uk/eiindex.htm
Collaborative networks: M25 Consortium; University of London.

Imperial College School of Medicine: Royal Brompton Campus, National Heart & Lung Institute Library

National Heart and Lung Institute
Dovehouse Street
London SW3 6LY
Tel: 020 7351 8150

Fax: 020 7351 8117
E-mail: nhli.library@ic.ac.uk
URL: www.lib.ic.ac.uk/depts/nhindex.htm
Librarian: Rachel C Shipton
Prof. staff: Marina Stylianides
Founded: 1948 (1997 as part of IC)
Type: Multidisciplinary.
Hours open: Mon–Fri: 9am–9pm.
Users: Staff and students of the Imperial college; staff of associated NHS Trusts. Others may use the library for reference (fee may be levied).
Lending: Staff and students of Imperial College; staff of the Royal Brompton and Harefield NHS Trust.
Stock policy: Superseded editions discarded.
Holdings: 10,800 books; 209 current journal subscriptions; 24 CD-ROMs.
Classification: NLM.
Library management system: Unicorn.
Computerized services: See www.lib.ic.ac.uk/eiindex.htm
Collaborative networks: CURL; London NHS Region; M25 Consortium; University of London.

Imperial College School of Medicine: St Mary's Campus Library

Norfolk Place
London W2 1PG
Tel: 020 7594 3692
Fax: 020 7402 3971
E-mail: sm.lib@ic.ac.uk
URL: www.lib.ic.ac.uk/depts/stindex.htm
Librarian: Nigel Palmer
Prof. staff: John Nyman; Dale Russell; Sally Smith
Founded: 1854 (1988 as part of IC)
Type: Multidisciplinary.
Hours open: Mon–Fri: 9am–9pm; Sat: 9am–1pm. Vacations: Mon–Fri: 9am–7pm.
Users: Staff and students of the Imperial College, staff of associated NHS Trusts,

local GPs. Others may use the library for reference (fee may be levied).
Lending: To full members only.
Stock policy: Disposed of within Imperial College Libraries.
Holdings: 8,000 books; 350 current journal subscriptions; 300 videos.
Classification: Own.
Library management system: Unicorn.
Computerized services: See www.lib.ic.ac.uk/eiindex.htm
Collaborative networks: CURL; London NHS Region; M25 Consortium; University of London.

Institute of Cancer Research Library

Chester Beatty Laboratories
Royal Cancer Hospital
237 Fulham Road
London SW3 6JB
Tel: 020 7352 8133
Fax: 020 7352 6283
E-mail: fullib@icr.ac.uk
URL: www.icr.ac.uk
Librarian: Neroli Wolland (Acting)
Prof. staff: Christina Lockley; Richard Murphy
Type: Multidisciplinary.
Hours open: Mon–Fri: 9am–5.30pm. 24-hour access to staff.
Users: Staff. Other readers, reference only by appointment.
Lending: To staff, books only.
Holdings: 5,000 books; 200 journal titles; 4 CD-ROMs.
Classification: NLM.
Library management system: Unicorn.
Computerized services: Access to BIDS, Cancer CD; CINAHL; Embase; JCR; Web of Science.
Branches: Franz Bergel Library, 15 Cotswold Road, Sutton, Surrey, SM2 5NG.

Institute of Cancer Research Library: Franz Bergel Library

15 Cotswold Road
Sutton
Surrey SM2 5NG
Tel: 020 8722 4230
Fax: 020 8661 1823
E-mail: sutlib@icr.ac.uk
URL: www.icr.ac.uk
Librarian: Sue Sugden
Prof. staff: Barry Jenkins; Sue Rogers
Founded: 1960s
Type: Medical; Scientific; Nursing.
Hours open: Mon–Fri: 9am–5.30pm (open access for staff only).
Users: Members of the Institute and Royal Marsden Hospital; bona fide researchers by appointment.
Lending: To staff only.
Stock policy: Dispose of it.
Holdings: 8,000 books; 500 current journal subscriptions; 800 journal titles; 20 CD-ROMs.
Classification: NLM.
Library management system: SIRSI/Unicorn.
Computerized services: Online access to BIDS; Chemical Abstracts; Embase; MEDLINE; Web of Science. Access to BNI; CINAHL. Access to Cancer CD.
Special collections: Historical collection of cancer books and pamphlets.

Institute of Child Health: Friends of the Children of Great Ormond Street Library

Institute of Child Health
30 Guilford Street
London WC1N 1EH
Tel: 020 7242 9789 ext. 2424
Fax: 020 7831 0488
E-mail: library@ich.ucl.ac.uk
URL: www.gosh.nhs.uk/library/
Librarian: John Clarke
Prof. staff: Anna Mitman; Sue Woodburn
Founded: 1946

Type: Medical; Nursing.
Hours open: Mon–Fri: 9am–6pm.
Users: Staff and students of ICH, University College London (UCL) and Great Ormond Street Hospital (GOSH). Other users at discretion of Librarian.
Lending: Books loaned to members only. Journals for reference only (all users).
Stock policy: Older stock may be discarded.
Holdings: 25,500 books and pamphlets; 250 current journal subscriptions, 300 journal titles; 150 videos.
Classification: Healthlink and NLM.
Library management system: Unicorn.
Computerized services: 10 PCs with Internet and database access. Access to Ovid MEDLINE; SilverPlatter MEDLINE; BNI; ChildData; CINAHL; Cochrane Library; ERIC; Popline; PsychLit.
Special collections: Historical material relating to ICH and GOSH; Teaching Aids at Low Cost (TALC) materials; Source – an international information support centre supporting health and disability activities worldwide.
Collaborative networks: UCL.

Institute of Laryngology & Otology Library

Royal National Throat, Nose and Ear Hospital
330–332 Gray's Inn Road
London WC1X 8EE
Tel: 020 7915 1445
E-mail: ilolib@ucl.ac.uk
URL: www.ucl.ac.uk/library/ilo
Librarian: Alex Stagg
Founded: 1946
Type: Clinical medicine – Otorhinolaryngology speciality.
Hours open: Mon–Tue: 9.30am–7pm; Wed–Fri: 9.30am–5.30pm. Vacations: 9.30-5pm.
Users: University College London staff and students; University College London hos-

pitals NHS Trust staff and students. Others by appointment.

Lending: To registered members only. No journal loans.

Stock policy: All stock retained – sent for storage within UCL facility as necessary.

Holdings: 2,500 books; 56 current journal subscriptions; 1,110 films and videos; 10 CD-ROMs.

Classification: Barnard.

Library management system: ALEPH – catalogue held as part of UCL Library Services.

Computerized services: Access to Cochrane Library; Embase; MEDLINE; PsychLit.

Special collections: Historical collection of ENT material.

Collaborative networks: NULJ.

Institute of Neurology: Rockefeller Medical Library

The National Hospital for Neurology and
Neurosurgery
Queen Square
London WC1N 3BG
Tel: 020 7829 8709
Fax: 020 7278 1371
E-mail: library@ion.ucl.ac.uk
URL: www.ion.ucl.ac.uk/library/
Librarian: Louise Shepherd
Prof. staff: Ingrid Aubry
Founded: 1948
Type: Multidisciplinary.
Hours open: Mon–Fri: 9am–6pm. Extended hours for users on site.
Users: Staff and students of the Institute of Neurology, the National Hospital for Neurology and Neurosurgery, University College London Hospitals Trust, other Trusts associated with UCL. Anyone else, for reference use only, who has a need to use highly specialized collections.
Lending: To registered users.

Stock policy: Specialist neurology/neurosciences stock retained. Other subjects disposed of, to other libraries where possible.

Holdings: 17,000 books; 180 current journal subscriptions, 440 titles; 40 videos; 35 CD-ROMs.

Classification: NLM. UDC for older material.

Library management system: Unicorn.

Computerized services: Online access to CINAHL; Cochrane Library; Embase; MEDLINE; PsycINFO plus others via UCL library.

Library publications: Newsletter; Catalogue of Historical Collection. Patient Support Database and Staff Publications Database on web.

Special collections: Historical neurology, neurosurgery and neuroscience. Staff publications.

Collaborative networks: UCL Medical Libraries. Many other informal links.

Institute of Occupational Health Library

Institute of Occupational Health
University of Birmingham
Edgbaston
Birmingham B15 2TT
Tel: 0121 414 6029
Fax: 0121 414 6217
E-mail: c.a.mcroy@bham.ac.uk
URL: www.bham.ac.uk/ioh
Librarian: Christine McRoy
Founded: 1990
Type: Occupational Health.
Hours open: Mon–Thurs: 9am–4.30pm; Fri: 9am–4pm.
Users: Staff and students of the Institute; others by appointment only at the discretion of the Librarian.
Lending: Staff and students of the Institute.
Stock policy: Offered to users before being disposed of.
Holdings: 3,000 books; 40 current journal subscriptions; 2 CD-ROMs.
Classification: LC.
Library management system: In-house.

Computerized services: OSH-ROM and TOXLINE CD-ROM.
Library publications: Guide to Library; Journal holdings.

Institute of Occupational Medicine Library

8 Roxburgh Place
Edinburgh EH8 9SU
Tel: 0131 667 5131
Fax: 0131 667 0136
E-mail: iom@iomhq.org.uk
Librarian: K Dixon
Founded: 1969
Type: Occupational Health.
Hours open: Mon–Fri: 9am–5pm.
Users: Staff of the Institute. External users by appointment.
Lending: Members as above.
Stock policy: Retain for archival needs.
Holdings: 6,000 books; 36 current journal subscriptions; 8 CD-ROMs.
Classification: UDC.
Library management system: Heritage.
Computerized services: Online access to Data-Star and Dialog. Access to ACGIH; Barbour Health and Safety Professional; CCINFO; WINIPINS OHROM.
Library publications: Research reports.

Institute of Orthopaedics: Francis Costello Library

Robert Jones and Agnes Hunt Orthopaedic and District Hospital NHS Trust
Oswestry
Shropshire SY10 7AG
Tel: 01691 404388
Fax: 01691 404071
E-mail: mcarter@ortholib.demon.co.uk
Librarian: Marie Carter
Founded: 1971
Type: Multidisciplinary.
Hours open: Staffed: Mon–Thurs: 8.45am–5pm; Fri: 8.45am–4pm. 24-hour access.

Users: Staff and students based at the Hospital. Nursing students from Staffordshire University. Others by arrangement with the librarian.
Lending: Open to all except students on short-term clinical placements and non-members.
Stock policy: Orthopaedic books sent to World Orthopaedic Concern or other charities in developing countries. Some sent to other libraries or sold for library funds.
Holdings: 3,740 books; 69 current journal subscriptions, 111 journal titles; 161 videos; 10 CD-ROMs; 200 items in historical collection.
Classification: NLM.
Library management system: Heritage.
Computerized services: Online access to AMED; CINAHL; Embase: Psychiatry via Biomed. Access to Cochrane Library; MEDLINE.
Library publications: Library Bulletin; published abstracts and papers by Hospital staff.
Special collections: History of Orthopaedics; History of the Hospital and its Founders.
Collaborative networks: SHAIR; SHINE; WMRHLN.

Institute of Orthopaedics Library

Royal National Orthopaedic Hospital
Brockley Hill
Stanmore
Middlesex HA7 4LP
Tel: 020 8909 5351
Fax: 020 8954 1213
E-mail: orthlib@ucl.ac.uk
URL: www.ucl.ac.uk/
Librarian: Bethan Adams
Founded: 1946
Type: Orthopaedics.
Hours open: Mon–Fri: 9am–5pm.
Users: University College London registered staff and students; Royal National

Orthopaedic Hospital employees. Members of public/private researchers may use the library for reference purposes. Please telephone in advance.

Lending: As above. Non-members have reference rights only.

Stock policy: Keep majority of stock. Some duplicates are passed on to World Orthopaedic Concern.

Holdings: 3,000 books; 160 current journal subscriptions; 30 videos.

Classification: NLM.

Library management system: ALEPH.

Computerized services: Online access for registered NHS users only to AMED; CINAHL; Cochrane Library; Embase; MEDLINE.

Special collections: Collection of over 500 volumes significant to the development of the field of orthopaedics. Kept in store so please phone in advance.

Collaborative networks: North Thames (IOR).

Institute of Psycho-Analysis Library

114 Shirland Road
London W9 2EQ
Tel: 020 7563 5008
Fax: 020 7563 5001
E-mail: ipa_library@compuserve.com
URL: www.pyschoanalysis.org.uk
Librarian: Andrea Chandler
Founded: 1900
Type: Psycho-analysis.
Hours open: Mon–Thurs: 12 noon–9pm.
Users: Open to members of the Institute. Open to all researchers for reference by appointment.
Lending: To members.
Holdings: 15,759 books; 80 current journal subscriptions, 172 journal titles.
Classification: Own.
Library management system: Calm.
Computerized services: Access to Jourlit; PEP.

Inverclyde Royal Hospital: Robert Lamb Library

Larkfield Road
Greenock
Inverclyde PA16 0XN
Tel: 01475 656011
Fax: 01475 635810
E-mail: morag.wright@irh.scot.nhs.uk
Librarian: Mrs Morag H Wright
Founded: 1962 (as Medical Reference Library)
Type: Multidisciplinary.
Hours open: Mon–Thurs: 8.30am–7pm; Fri: 8.30am–4.30pm. Extended access to 11pm to keyholders and at weekends 9am–11pm.
Users: All staff in the Hospital and university students on placement at Inverclyde. External membership, costing £30 per annum is available at the discretion of the Librarian.
Lending: All registered members.
Stock policy: Old stock is offered to hospital departments and/or to charitable organizations for libraries abroad.
Holdings: 3,500 books; 81 current journal subscriptions; 85 videos; 20 CD-ROMs; 12 cassette tapes; 14 slide collections.
Classification: Dewey.
Library management system: Heritage IV.
Computerized services: Online access to AMED; CINAHL; Cochrane Library; EBMR; Embase; MEDLINE; PreMEDLINE; PsycINFO; SportDiscus. Access to NRR.
Library publications: Annual Report; information leaflets.
Collaborative networks: BL; BMA; North Glasgow Hospital Libraries Consortium; SHINE.

Ipswich Hospital Library & Information Service

Ipswich Hospital NHS Trust
Heath Road
Ipswich
Suffolk IP4 5PD

Tel: 01473 702545
Fax: 01473 702548
E-mail: medical.library@ipsh-tr.anglox.nhs.uk
Librarian: Paula Althorpe
Prof. staff: Tracey Hunter
Type: Multidisciplinary Healthcare.
Hours open: Mon–Thurs: 9am–5pm; Fri: 9am–4.30pm. 24-hour access for members.
Users: All healthcare NHS professionals in East Suffolk including students on placement. Others for reference only by appointment.
Lending: To members only.
Stock policy: Dispose of or sell.
Holdings: 8,000 books; 322 current journal subscriptions; 40 videos; 15 CD-ROMs.
Classification: NLM.
Library management system: Cardbox.
Computerized services: Access to AMED; Best Evidence; CINAHL; ClinPsych; MEDLINE; NNR.
Library publications: Library Bulletin; Union List of Journals of Healthcare Libraries in Ipswich.
Branches: Ivy House; St Clements Hospital.
Collaborative networks: HeLIN.

Irish Nurses Organization Library

11 Fitzwilliam Place
Dublin 2
Republic of Ireland
Tel: +353 1 6760137
Fax: +353 1 6615012
E-mail: library@ino.ie
URL: www.ino.ie
Librarian: Muriel Haire
Prof. staff: Niamh Adams
Founded: 1998
Type: Nursing.
Hours open: Mon, Wed: 9am–8pm; Tues, Thurs, Fri: 9am–5pm.
Users: INO members and some non-members.
Lending: Reference only.
Stock policy: Pass on to other libraries.

Holdings: 4,263 books, reports, legislation; 38 current print journal subscriptions, 28 online subscriptions, 70 journal titles; 4 CD-ROMs.
Classification: Royal College of Nursing.
Library management system: DB/TextWorks.
Computerized services: Access to BNI; CINAHL; Cochrane Library; MEDLINE.
Collaborative networks: Irish Healthcare Libraries Journal Holdings.

James Connolly Memorial Hospital Medical Library

Blandchardstown
Dublin 15
Republic of Ireland
Tel: +353 1 821 3844 ext. 5620
Fax: +353 1 822 6318
Librarian: Honora Faul
Founded: 1999
Type: Clinical medicine.
Hours open: Mon–Fri: 9am–5pm.
Users: Hospital staff; students of the Royal College of Surgeons in Ireland
Lending: To members as above.
Holdings: 1,000 books; 83 current journal subscriptions, 92 journal titles; 51 videos; 2 CD-ROMs.
Classification: Dewey.
Library management system: Calm 2000 Plus
Computerized services: Access to Cochrane Library; EBMR; MEDLINE.
Collaborative networks: IHLG.

James Ireland Memorial Library

Glasgow Dental Hospital and School NHS Trust
378 Sauchiehall Street
Glasgow G2 3JZ
Tel: 0141 211 9705
Fax: 0141 331 2798
E-mail: library@dental.gla.ac.uk

URL: http:// intranet.dental.gla.ac.uk/library/
index.html
Librarian: Ms Beverly Rankin
Prof. staff: Dr Helen S Marlborough
Founded: 1949
Type: Dentistry and Allied Sciences.
Hours open: Mon–Thurs: 9am–9pm; Fri and
Vacations: 9am–5pm.
Users: Staff and students of the University of
Glasgow; Glasgow Dental Hospital and
School NHS Trust staff and students.
Lending: To members only.
Stock policy: Old stock is retained unless it
falls outside the scope of the Dental
Historical Collection.
Holdings: 5,000 books; 261 current journal
subscriptions, 294 journal titles; 85 videos;
10 CD-ROMs; 182 theses;12 tape/slide.
Classification: Modified LC.
Library management system:
INNOPAC.
Computerized services: Access to
Embase; MEDLINE; SCI.
Special collections: Dental Historical
Collection.
Collaborative networks: North Glasgow
University Hospitals Trust; SHINE; UK
Dental Librarians Group.

Janssen Glag Ltd

Library
Saunderton
High Wycombe
Buckinghamshire HP14 4HJ
Tel: 01494 567472
Fax: 01494 567445
E-mail: library@jacgb.jnj.com
Founded: 1989
Type: Pharmaceutical.
Hours open: Mon–Fri: 9am–5pm.
Users: All employees.
Lending: All employees.
Stock policy: Disposed of to Community
Heart who send to South Africa.
Holdings: 3,000 books; 150 current journal
subscriptions; 30 CD-ROMs.

Classification: NLM.
Library management system: In-house.
Computerized services: Online access to
Ovid and MEDLINE.

Jersey General Hospital Library: Harvey Besterman Education Centre Library

Jersey General Hospital
St Helier
Jersey JE1 3QS
Tel: 01534 622664
Fax: 01534 622510
E-mail: hss13@itl.net
Librarian: Mrs Sylvia Tillman
Type: Multidisciplinary.
Hours open: Mon–Fri: 9am–5pm. Key avail-
able to staff after hours.
Users: All island health personnel.
Lending: To registered borrowers, no restric-
tions.
Stock policy: Disposed of.
Holdings: 5,000 books; 150 current journal
subscriptions.
Classification: NLM.
Library management system: In-house
Computerized services: Internet access
available. Online access to EBSCO services.
Access to BNI; CINAHL; Cochrane Library;
MEDLINE.
Collaborative networks: NULJ; SWRLIN.

John Rylands University Library of Manchester

Oxford Road
Manchester M13 9PP
Tel: 0161 275 3738
Fax: 0161 273 7488
E-mail: libtalk@fs1.li.man.ac.uk
URL: http://rylibweb.man.ac.uk
Librarian: Christopher Hunt
Prof. staff: Alastair Flett (Assistant Librarian,
Health Sciences); Eleri Strittmatter (Nursing
Information Development Manager); Katy

Woolfenden (Faculty Librarian for Medicine, Dentistry, Nursing and Pharmacy)
Founded: 1851
Type: Multidisciplinary.
Hours open: See website for details.
Users: Members of University of Manchester. Non-members must apply to Membership Office – charges may be levied.
Lending: Members only.
Stock policy: Various arrangements for disposal.
Holdings: 3,700,000 books; 8,900 current print journal subscriptions; 300 films and videos; 800 CD-ROMs; 352,000 microforms; 1,300,000 manuscripts.
Classification: Dewey.
Library management system: Talis.
Computerized services: See website for details.
Library publications: Library Bulletin; various monographs.
Special collections: Various.
Branches: Gateway House Library.
Collaborative networks: CALIM; CURL; Research Libraries Group.

Keele University Site Library

Department of Nursing and Midwifery Library
Keele University
City General Hospital
Newcastle Road
Stoke-on-Trent
Staffordshire ST4 6QG
Tel: 01782 552949
Fax: 01782 712941
E-mail: nsa17@keele.ac.uk
Librarian: David Bird
Type: Higher Education – Nursing and Midwifery.
Hours open: Mon–Thurs: 8.45am–7.30pm; Fri: 8.45am–4.45pm; Sat: 10am–2pm.
Users: University staff and students, practising nurses and midwives working for local NHS Trusts. Other NHS Trust staff and members of the public have access.

Lending: University staff and students and eligible local NHS staff, as covered in service level agreements.
Stock policy: Withdrawn stock is destroyed if obsolete or misleading. Otherwise offered to users.
Holdings: 25,000 books; 220 current journal subscriptions, 305 journal titles. 150 films and videos; 20 CD-ROMs.
Classification: LC.
Library management system: INNOPAC.
Computerized services: Access to Ageline; Aids and Cancer Research Abstracts; AMED; Biological Sciences; Cambridge Scientific Abstracts; Child Abuse and Neglect; CINAHL; Cochrane Library; MEDLINE; PsycINFO.
Collaborative networks: PLCS.

Kennedy Institute of Rheumatology Division Library

1 Aspenlea Road
Hammersmith
London W6 8LH
Tel: 020 8383 4494
Fax: 020 8383 4499
E-mail: k.bull@ic.ac.uk
Librarian: Ms K Bull (Information Scientist)
Founded: 1966
Type: Multidisciplinary.
Hours open: Mon–Fri: 9.15am–4.45pm.
Users: Staff. Other users by application for reference only.
Lending: Staff only.
Stock policy: Journals discarded at variable intervals.
Holdings: 1,000 books; 80 current journal subscriptions, 100 journal titles.
Classification: Own.
Computerized services: CD-ROM access to Ovid MEDLINE.

Kensington, Chelsea, & Westminster Health Authority: Health Improvement Information & Resource Centre

50 Eastbourne Terrace
London W2 6LX
Tel: 020 7725 3456
Fax: 020 7725 3385
E-mail: info-centre@ha.kcw-ha.nthames.nhs.uk
URL: www.kcwhealth.org.uk
Librarian: David Whiting
Prof. staff: Ruth Rodigan
Founded: 1986
Type: Health Management and Health Promotion.
Hours open: Mon, Wed, Thurs: 9am–5pm; Tues: 12 noon–5pm; Fri: 9am–4.45pm.
Users: Open to all with an interest in health matters in Kensington and Chelsea and Westminster, except the general public. Reference-only service to students.
Lending: Members only.
Stock policy: Dispose of it.
Holdings: 4,200 books; 100 current journal subscriptions; 500 films and videos; 50 CD-ROMs.
Classification: Own.
Library management system: DB/TextWorks.
Computerized services: Online access to Dialog. Access to Ovid Biomed for AMED; CINAHL; MEDLINE; PsychLit plus access to ASSIA for Health; BNI; Cochrane Library; HMIC.
Collaborative networks: LLIDU; North Thames Regional Library Unit Network.

Kettering General Hospital NHS Trust Library Service

Prince William Postgraduate Medical Education Centre
Kettering General Hospital NHS Trust
Kettering
Northamptonshire NN16 8UZ
Tel: 01536 492861
Fax: 01536 492611
E-mail: wayne.sime@kgh-trust.anglox.nhs.uk
URL: http://alpha5/intranet/kett.htm
Librarian: Wayne Sime
Type: Multidisciplinary.
Hours open: Mon–Fri: 9am–9pm; Sat and Sun:10am–4pm.
Users: All NHS staff. External membership available – charge applicable.
Lending: As above.
Stock policy: Sent to Bansang Hospital in Gambia.
Holdings: 17,833 books; 225 current journal subscriptions; 245 videos; 67 CD-ROMs.
Classification: NLM.
Library management system: SIRSI-Unicorn.
Computerized services: Online access to BNIPlus. Access via Ovid to CINAHL; Embase; EBMR plus Best Evidence; MEDLINE. Access also to Book Data and SPSS.
Collaborative networks: HeLIN.

Kidderminster Hospital Clinical Library

Postgraduate Medical Centre
Kidderminster Hospital
Bewdley Road
Kidderminster
Worcestershire DY11 6BY
Tel: 01562 747965 ext. 3295
Fax: 01562 825733
E-mail: jan.brown@worcsacute.wmids.nhs.uk
Librarian: Mrs Jan Brown
Type: Multidisciplinary.
Hours open: Mon–Fri: 9am–5pm.
Users: Acute hospital staff, community and mental health staff, local GPs and practice staff.
Classification: NLM (Wessex adaptation).
Computerized services: Access to AMED; CINAHL; Clinical Evidence;

Cochrane Library; Embase: Psychiatry; MEDLINE; Ovid Nursing Collection.

Library publications: Journals list; Library guide.

Collaborative networks: WMRHLN.

King Edward VII Hospital Library: Cassel Library & Information Service

King Edward VII Hospital
Midhurst
West Sussex GU29 0BL.
Tel: 01730 812341 ext. 2128
Fax: 01730 816333
E-mail: kevii@line.net
Librarian: Amanda Brookman
Founded: 1906
Type: Medical.
Hours open: Mon–Fri: 9am–5pm.
Accessible at other times, key with porters.
Users: Staff; students on clinical placement; students from other organizations on courses run by the Hospital's training department; local GPs.
Lending: To staff; non-staff for the duration of the course; students on clinical placement while at the Hospital; GPs by arrangement.
Stock policy: Stock is reviewed by the stock selection group. Old stock is disposed of.
Holdings: 1,667 books; 47 current journal subscriptions, 117 journal titles.
Classification: NLM.
Library management system: DB/TextWorks.
Computerized services: Access to BNI; Cochrane Library. Access via Ovid to CINAHL and MEDLINE.
Special collections: Several runs of old journals relating to tuberculosis.
Collaborative networks: BMA; BLDSC; NULJ; STLIS.

King George Hospital: Goldberg Library

King George Hospital
Barley Lane
Goodmayes
Essex IG3 8YB
Tel: 020 8970 8239
Fax: 020 8970 8237
E-mail: kghlibrary@dial.pipex.co.uk
URL: www.libnel.nhs.uk
Librarian: Jim Moore
Founded: 1993
Type: Multidisciplinary.
Hours open: Mon, Fri: 9am–5pm; Tues, Thurs: 9am–6pm; Wed: 9am–7pm.
Users: NHS staff of all local Trusts and specified students. Reference available to all with a genuine need.
Lending: To all members and other NHS libraries.
Stock policy: Old stock is discarded.
Holdings: 6,000 books; 170 current journal subscriptions, 274 journal titles.
Classification: NLM.
Library management system: DB/TextWorks.
Computerized services: CD-ROM access to CINAHL; Cochrane Library; MEDLINE.
Library publications: Annual Report; journals listing; library guide.
Collaborative networks: NTRLS; PLCS.

King's College Institute of Psychiatry Library

De Crespigny Park
London SE5 8AF
Tel: 020 7848 0202
Fax: 020 7848 0209
E-mail: spyllib@iop.kcl.ac.uk
Librarian: Martin Guha
Prof. staff: Elda Caldarone; Clare Martin.
Founded: 1890
Type: Psychiatry.
Hours open: Mon–Fri: 9am–8pm; Sat: 9am–1pm.

Users: Owing to enormous pressures, access is very restrictive.
Lending: King's College London members only.
Stock policy: Stock is retained.
Holdings: 40,000 books; 450 current journal subscriptions.
Classification: BLISS .
Library management system: ALEPH.

King's College London: Calnan Dermatology Library

Block 7, St Thomas' Hospital
London SE1 7EH
Tel: 020 7928 9292 ext. 1313
URL: www.kcl.ac.uk/deptsta/iss/sites/
stthomas/topthomascalnan.html
Librarian: Angela Gunn
Prof. staff: Pat Tharratt
Type: Dermatology.
Hours open: Mon–Fri: 9am–5.30pm.
Users: KCL staff and students; staff of specified Trusts. Others on application.
Lending: Books only, to members.
Holdings: 7,000 books; 100 current journal subscriptions.
Library management system: ALEPH.
Computerized services: A full list is available at www.kcl.ac.uk/deptsta/iss/library/databases/atoz/dba.html

King's College London: Franklin-Wilkins Information Services Centre

150 Stamford Street
London SE1 9NN
Tel: 020 7848 4378
Fax: 020 7848 4290
E-mail: peter.walsh@kcl.ac.uk
URL: www.kcl.ac.uk/deptsta/iss/sites/
waterloo/topwaterloo.html
Librarian: Peter Walsh
Prof. staff: Angus Brown; Kate Brunskill; Joan Lovenack; Sheelagh Merritt; Anne Monkcom; Gill Ritchie; Sue Rugg

Founded: 1829
Type: Multidisciplinary – Gerontology, Nursing, Nutrition, Pharmacy.
Hours open: Mon–Fri: 9am–9pm; Sat: 9.30am–5.30pm; Vacations: Mon–Fri: 9am–7pm; Sat: 9.30am–5.30pm.
Users: Staff and Students of King's College London, staff of specified Trusts. Others on application.
Lending: As above – books only.
Holdings: 44,000 books; 1,000 current journal subscriptions; 426 videos; 284 CD-ROMs.
Classification: NLM.
Library management system: ALEPH.
Computerized services: A full list is available at www.kcl.ac.uk/depsta/iss/library/databases/atoz/dba.html

King's College London: New Hunt's House Information Services Centre

New Hunt's House
Guy's Hospital
St Thomas Street
London SE1 9RT
Tel: 020 7848 6600
Fax: 020 7848 6743
E-mail: andrew.baster@kcl.ac.uk
Librarian: Andrew Baster
Prof. staff: Jeremy Claridge; Lara Dennison; Guy Etherington; David Hodgson; Gary Horrocks; Derek MacKenzie; Andrea McGrath; Margaret Samman
Founded: 1903
Type: Medical; Biomedical Science, Physiotherapy.
Hours open: Mon–Fri: 9am–8.45pm; Sat: 9am–4.45pm; Sun: 1pm–4.45pm.
Users: KCL staff and students; staff of specified Trusts. Others on application.
Lending: Books only, to members.
Holdings: 32,000 books; 830 current journal subscriptions; 41 videos; 186 CD-ROMs.
Classification: NLM.
Library management system: ALEPH.

Computerized services: A full list is available at www.kcl.ac.uk/depsta/iss/library/databases/atoz/dba.html

Special collections: Books by Guy's and St Thomas' people; history of medicine.

Branches: Warner Dental Library.

King's College London: St Thomas' Medical Library

St Thomas' Hospital
Lambeth Palace Road
London SE1 7EH
Tel: 020 7928 9292 ext. 2367
Fax: 020 7401 3932
E-mail: angela.gunn@kcl.ac.uk
URL: www.kcl.ac.uk/deptsta/iss/sites/stthomas/topthomas.html
Librarian: Angela Gunn
Prof. staff: Tammy Ashcroft; Robert Foster; Christine Lawes; Stephen Prowse; Catrin Sly; Robert Watt
Founded: 1903
Type: Medical.
Hours open: Mon–Fri: 9am–8.45pm; Sat: 9am–4.45pm.
Users: KCL staff and students, staff of specified Trusts. Others on application.
Lending: Books only, to members.
Stock policy: Old stock disposed of.
Holdings: 12,500 books; 300 current journal subscriptions; 6 videos; 19 CD-ROMs.
Classification: NLM.
Library management system: ALEPH.
Computerized services: A full list is available at www.kcl.ac.uk/depsta/iss/library/databases/atoz/dba.html
Special collections: Books by Guy's and St Thomas' people; History of medicine.
Branches: Calnan Dermatology Library.

King's College London: Warner Dental Library

27th Floor, Guy's Tower
Guy's Hospital
London SE1 9RT
Tel: 020 7955 4238
Fax: 020 7848 6743
E-mail: andrew.baster@kcl.ac.uk
Librarian: Andrew Baster
Prof. staff: Jeremy Claridge; Lara Dennison; Guy Etherington; David Hodgson; Gary Horrocks; Derek MacKenzie; Andrea McGrath; Margaret Samman
Type: Dental.
Hours open: Mon and Fri: 9am–7pm; Tues–Thurs: 9am–8pm.
Users: KCL staff and students; staff of specified Trusts. Others on application.
Lending: Books only, to members.
Holdings: 11,000 books; 109 current journal subscriptions; 65 videos; 6 CD-ROMs.
Classification: NLM.
Library management system: ALEPH.
Computerized services: A full list is available at www.kcl.ac.uk/depsta/iss/library/databases/atoz/dba.html

King's College London: Weston Education Centre Information Services Centre

Bessemer Road
London SE5 9PJ
Tel: 020 7848 5541
Fax: 020 7848 5550
E-mail: jean.yeoh@kcl.ac.uk
URL: www.kcl.ac.uk/deptsta/iss/denmarkhill/topdenmarkhill.html
Librarian: Jean Yeoh
Prof. staff: Shaeli Ball; Christine Bell; Martin Hewitt; Sue Isaac; Naomi Paterson; Anne Tobin
Founded: 1915
Type: Multidisciplinary.
Hours open: Mon–Fri: 9am–9pm; Sat: 10am–1.30pm.
Users: KCL staff and students. Staff of specified Trusts. Others on application.
Lending: As above, books only.
Holdings: 12,500 books; 350 current journal subscriptions; 197 videos; 41 CD-ROMs.
Classification: NLM.

Library management system: ALEPH.

Computerized services: A full list is available at www.kcl.ac.uk/depsta/iss/library/databases/atoz/dba.html

Special collections: Small Historical Collection (16th to 19th centuries); collection of material written by, or about, King's 'men'.

Branches: Bethlem Hospital Library.

King's Fund Centre Library

11–13 Cavendish Square
London W1G 0AN
Tel: 020 7307 2568/2569
Fax: 020 7307 2805
E-mail: library@kingsfund.org.uk
URL: www.kingsfund.org.uk
Librarian: Lynette Cawthra
Prof. staff: Sue Duffy; Liz James; Kathy Johnson; Lucy Johnson; Valerie Wildridge
Founded: 1970s
Type: Health Management.
Hours open: Mon,Tues, Thurs and Fri: 9.30am–5.30pm; Wed: 11am–5.30pm; Sat: 9.30am–5pm.
Users: NHS; social services; voluntary sector; academics including students, commercial. The library is open to all.
Lending: Staff only.
Stock policy: Stock disposed of, via BookNet where possible.
Holdings: 30,000 books; 350 current journal subscriptions, 600 journal titles; 50 videos; 50 CD-ROMs.
Classification: BLISS (modified).
Library management system: Unicorn.
Computerized services: Online access to Data-Star. Access to ASSIA; CINAHL; Cochrane Library; HMIC; MEDLINE; Urbadisc.
Library publications: Current Awareness Bulletin; reading lists.
Collaborative networks: CHILL; HMIC; NULJ.

Kingston & Richmond Health Authority Library

22 Hollyfield Road
Surbiton
Surrey KT5 9AL
Tel: 020 8339 8000
Fax: 020 8339 8100 (FAO Patricia East, Library)
Librarian: Patricia East (based at Tolworth Hospital Library)
Hours open: Friday afternoons only.

Kingston Hospital: Stenhouse Library

Esher Wing
Kingston Hospital NHS Trust
Galsworthy Road
Kingston-upon-Thames
Surrey KT2 7QB
Tel: 020 8546 7711 ext. 2856
Fax: 020 8974 5763
E-mail: irene.chalmers@kh-tr.sthames.nhs.uk
Librarian: Irene Chalmers
Prof. staff: Frances Cocks; Terry Hillier; Flora Nawaz; Bobby Preston; Olga Rak; Nooria Ravalia; Richard Rickford; Les West
Hours open: Mon–Thurs: 9.15am–7.30pm; Fri: 9.15am–5pm; Sat: 9.30am–11.30pm.
Holdings: 120 journal titles.
Collaborative networks: STLIS.

Knee Foundation Library

2nd Floor, Orchard House,
Victoria Square
Droitwich
Worcestershire WR9 8BS
Tel: 01905 776676
Fax: 01905 793807
E-mail: thekneefoundation@kneeclinics.co.uk
Prof. staff: Dr Sheila Strover; Mr Mohi El Shazly; Mrs Lesley Hall; Miss Ellen Beales
Founded: 1990
Type: Medical – knee specialist.

Hours open: By private arrangement.
Users: Research fellows and staff associated with Droitwich Knee Clinic. Any other person by arrangement.
Lending: As above.
Stock policy: Dispose of it.
Holdings: 150 books; 2,000 videos; 1 CD-ROM; 4,000 35mm slides.
Library publications: In House Research.

Lambeth Southwark & Lewisham Health Authority

1 Lower Marsh
London SE1 7NT
Tel: 020 7716 7000 ext. 7660
URL: www.lslha.nhs.uk
Librarian: Gina McHale
Prof. staff: Linda Kalinda
Founded: 1992
Type: Health Management.
Hours open: Mon–Fri: 9am–5pm.
Users: Health Authority and local NHS staff only.
Lending: Health Authority staff only.
Stock policy: Disposed of.
Holdings: 8,000 books; 76 current journal subscriptions, 131 journal titles.
Classification: NLM.
Library management system: DB/TextWorks.
Computerized services: Library catalogue. Access to AMED; CINAHL; HMIC; MEDLINE.
Collaborative networks: LLIDU.

Lanarkshire NHS Trust Health Promotion Resource Library

Strathclyde Hospital
Arbles Road
Motherwell
Lanarkshire MLI 3BW
Tel: 01698 263219
Fax: 01698 266758
E-mail:
resource.library@lanarkshirelib.scot.nhs.uk

Librarian: Carol Hallesy; Clare Scanlan (job-share)
Founded: 1995
Type: Health Promotion.
Hours open: Mon–Thurs: 9.30am–4.30pm; Fri: 9.30am–4pm.
Users: Health professionals; health promotion staff; students; the public.
Lending: To members.
Stock policy: Regularly reviewed. Passed to other libraries if appropriate.
Holdings: 6,000 books; 800 films and videos; 4 CD-ROMs.
Classification: Own.
Library management system: ADLIB.
Computerized services: Access to Dialog; CINAHL; HEBSWEB; MEDLINE.
Special collections: Displays, demonstration models and equipment for hire.
Collaborative networks: SHINE.

Lancaster Royal Infirmary Education Centre Library

Postgraduate Medical Centre
Royal Lancaster Infirmary
Ashton Road
Lancaster LA1 4RR
Tel: 01524 583954
Fax: 01524 848289
E-mail: rli.library@l.bay-tr.nwest.nhs.uk
Librarian: Paul Longbottom
Type: Multidisciplinary.
Hours open: Mon–Fri: 9am–5pm.
Users: NHS staff in the Morecambe Bay Health Community.
Lending: NHS staff and placement students working in a clinical setting.
Stock policy: Disposed of.
Holdings: 2,189 books; 48 current journal subscriptions, 87 journal titles; 47 videos.
Classification: Dewey 19th.
Library management system: Heritage.
Computerized services: Through ADITUS North West Portal access to AMED; BNI; CINAHL; Embase; HMIC; MEDLINE; PsycINFO.

Library publications: Library guide; Journal holdings list.

Collaborative networks: BL; BMA; LIHNN; Morecambe Bay Hospitals NHS Trust.

Lea Castle Centre Medical Library

North Warwickshire NHS Trust
Wolverley
Kidderminster
Worcestershire DY10 3PP
Tel: 01562 850461
Fax: 01562 859010
E-mail: Janette.Hill@nw-tr.wmids.nhs.uk
Librarian: Janette Hill
Type: Multidisciplinary – all aspects of Learning Disabilities and related topics.
Hours open: Mon, Tues, Fri: 10am–2pm; Wed, Thurs: 9am–5pm.
Users: Doctors, nurses, therapists, care staff, psychiatrists, psychologists, community workers, etc. Available by appointment only to non-staff at the Librarian's discretion.
Lending: To members only.
Stock policy: Offered to staff, then disposed of.
Holdings: 3,000 books; 50 current journal subscriptions; 55 films and videos.
Classification: NLM (Wessex adaptation).
Computerized services: CD-ROM access to ClinPsych and Cochrane Library. Access to CINAHL, MEDLINE, etc., via WISH.
Collaborative networks: PLCS; WMRHLN.

Leeds Health Authority

Blenheim House
West One
Duncombe Street
Leeds LS1 4PL
Tel: 0113 295 2127
Fax: No. 0113 295 2222

E-mail: Helen.Thompson@lh.leeds-ha.northy.nhs.uk
URL: www.leedshealth.org.uk
Librarian: Helen Thompson
Founded: 1997
Type: Health Management.
Hours open: Mon–Fri: 8.30am–5pm.
Users: Health Authority and Leeds PCG staff. Ad hoc external queries considered if for local information.
Lending: Health Authority and PCG staff. Other libraries.
Stock policy: Check with Regional Office in case relevant to them, then disposed of.
Holdings: 4,600 books; 100 journal titles.
Classification: Dewey.
Library management system: ALICE.
Computerized services: Access to Dialog. Access to Ovid – MEDLINE; AMED; CINAHL; Cochrane Library; Embase; HMIC.
Collaborative networks: Collaboration of NHS Librarians in Northern and Yorkshire Region; Collaboration of Health Authority Librarians in Northern and Yorkshire Region.

Leeds Health Promotion Service

St Mary's Hospital
Greenhill Road
Armley
Leeds LS12 3QE
Tel: 0113 305 5366
Fax: 0113 305 5360
E-mail: janecarlton@cwcom.net
Librarian: Lynne Hellewell (Manager)
Prof. staff: Jane Carlton
Type: Health Promotion.
Hours open: Mon, Wed, Fri: 9am–4pm; Tues, Thurs: 10am–5pm.
Users: Anyone in the Leeds area who is involved in health promotion has borrowing rights. Others, including students, can use for reference and study.
Lending: As above.
Stock policy: Disposed of. If still current might be passed to other libraries.

Classification: Own.
Library management system: Integer.
Collaborative networks: Leeds Library
Development Group.

Leeds Teaching Hospitals NHS Trust: Chapel Allerton Hospital Library

Chapel Allerton Hospital
Chapeltown Road
Leeds LS7 4RB
Tel: 0113 392 4662
E-mail: dominic.gilroy@leedsth.nhs.uk
URL: www.nyrlas.nhs.uk
Librarian: Dominic Gilroy
Type: Multidisciplinary.
Hours open: 24-hour access. Staffed Tues:
9am–1pm; Thurs: 9am–5pm; Fri:
1.30pm–5pm.
Users: Any members of Leeds Teaching
Hospitals Trust staff.
Lending: All users.
Stock policy: Old stock is sold or disposed
of.
Holdings: 1,082 books; 25 current journal
subscriptions, 36 journal titles plus access to
Trustwide electronic journals.
Classification: NLM.
Computerized services: Access to LTHT
intranet and internet. Online access to
AMED; CINAHL; Cochrane Library; DARE;
EBMR; Embase; MEDLINE; PsycINFO.
Collaborative networks: NYRLAS.

Leeds Teaching Hospitals NHS Trust: Cookridge Hospital Medical Library

Cookridge Hospital
Hospital Lane
Leeds LS16 6QB
Tel: 0113 3924293
Fax: 0113 3924293
E-mail: dominic.gilroy@leedsth.nhs.uk
URL: www.nyrlas.nhs.uk
Librarian: Dominic Gilroy

Type: Multidisciplinary; Cancer speciality.
Hours open: 24-hour access. Staffed: Mon:
9am–5pm; Wed: 1.30pm–5pm; Fri:
9am–1pm.
Users: Members of staff of Leeds Teaching
Hospitals NHS Trust, local GPs and practice
nurses.
Lending: Members of staff of LTHT.
Stock policy: Some items offered to library
users, others disposed of.
Holdings: 1,500 books; 43 current journal
subscriptions plus access to online journals;
NHS/DOH reports.
Classification: NLM.
Computerized services: Online access to
AMED; CINAHL; Cochrane Library; Embase:
Psychiatry; MEDLINE.
Collaborative networks: NYRLAS.

Leeds Teaching Hospitals NHS Trust: Leeds General Infirmary Postgraduate Medical Library

Old Nurses' Home
Leeds General Infirmary
Leeds LS1 3EX
Tel: 0113 392 6445
Fax: 0113 392 2930
E-mail: sheila.leadbeater@leedsth.nhs.uk
URL: www.nyrlas.nhs.uk
Librarian: Sheila Leadbeater
Founded: 1992
Type: Clinical Medicine.
Hours open: Mon–Thurs: 8.30am–5pm; Fri:
8.30am–4.30pm.
Users: Postgraduate medical staff only at
present.
Lending: Reference collection only.
Stock policy: Either passed to satellite
library or sold.
Holdings: 4,000 books; 91 current journal
subscriptions, 160 journal titles including
electronic journals; 10 CD-ROMs.
Classification: NLM.
Computerized services: Access to LTHT
intranet; MRCP Masterclass.

Collaborative networks: Northern and Yorkshire Regional Library Service ILL Scheme.

Leeds Teaching Hospitals NHS Trust: Seacroft Hospital Medical Library

Education Centre
Seacroft Hospital
York Road
Leeds LS14 6UH
Tel: 0113 206 3675
Fax: 0113 206 3675
E-mail: seacroft.library@gw.sjsuh.northy.nhs.uk
URL: www.nyrlas.nhs.uk
Librarian: Christine Reid
Type: Multidisciplinary.
Hours open: Mon–Thurs: 9am–5pm; Fri: 9am–4.30pm.
Users: Acute Trust staff; Community and Mental Health Trust; Public Health Laboratory Service; National Blood Service; Breast Screening Unit; medical and nursing students.
Lending: To all users.
Stock policy: Old stock is disposed of.
Holdings: 1,800 books; 50 current journal subscriptions; 30 videos; 10 CD-ROMs.
Classification: NLM (abbreviated).
Library management system: InMagic.
Computerized services: Online access to AMED; CINAHL; Cochrane Library; Embase: Psychiatry; MEDLINE.
Collaborative networks: NYRLAS.

Leeds Teaching Hospitals NHS Trust: Wharfedale Medical Library

Wharfedale General Hospital
Newall Carr Road
Otley
Leeds LS21 2LY
Tel: 0113 392 6072
Fax: 01943 468314

E-mail: val.williams@leedsth.nhs.uk
URL: www.nyrlas.nhs.uk
Librarian: Valerie Williams
Type: Multidisciplinary.
Hours open: Mon–Fri: 9am–5pm.
Users: Hospital staff, PCG staff, local NHS staff.
Lending: See above.
Stock policy: Sale, dispose of, pass on – where appropriate.
Holdings: 1,700 books; 60 current journal subscriptions, 97 journal titles; 25 videos; 10 CD-ROMs.
Classification: NLM.
Library management system: Own (using Access database).
Computerized services: Online access to ACP Journal Club; AMED; CINAHL; Cochrane Library; DARE; EBMR; MEDLINE and Pre-MEDLINE; PsycINFO; Journals @ Ovid Full Text.
Library publications: Library guide; Library News.
Collaborative networks: NYRLAS Union List of Periodicals.

Leicester General Hospital

Education Centre Library
University Hospitals of Leicester NHS Trust
Gwendolen Road
Leicester LE5 4PW
Tel: 0116 258 4245
Fax: 0116 258 8078
E-mail: lghlib@hotmail.com
URL: www.le.ac.uk/li/lgh/library.htm
Librarian: Claire Honeybourne
Prof. staff: Sarah Stockton; Linda Ward
Founded: 1994
Type: Multidisciplinary.
Hours open: Mon–Fri: 8.30am–5pm; Sat: 9am–1pm. 24-hour access available.
Users: All staff of the University Hospitals of Leicester and Leicestershire Mental Health.
Lending: As above.
Stock policy: Dispose of it.

Holdings: 7,000 books; 134 current journal subscriptions.
Classification: NLM.
Library management system: SydneyPLUS.
Computerized services: Access to AMED: CINAHL; ClinPsych; Cochrane Library; Embase; MEDLINE; PsycINFO via Biomed. Access via HCNNet to BNI; HMIC.
Collaborative networks: NULJ.

Leicestershire & Rutland Healthcare NHS Trust: Leicester Frith Medical Library

Leicester Frith Hospital
Groby Road
Leicester LE3 9QF
Tel: 0116 225 5244
Fax: 0116 225 5202
E-mail: wendypell@hotmail.com
Librarian: Dr Humphrey Dunn
Prof. staff: Mrs Wendy Pell (Library Assistant)
Hours open: Mon–Thurs: 10am–2.30pm.
Notes: For further details see website www.telh.nhs.uk

Leicestershire Health Promotion Centre

2nd Floor, 92 Regent Road
Leicester LE1 7PE
Tel: 0116 258 8875
Fax: 0116 258 8852
Librarian: Mr Chris Bigger
Hours open: Mon–Fri: 9am–4pm.
Notes: For further details see website www.telh.nhs.uk

Lewisham Hospital Library

Lewisham Hospital
Lewisham High Street
London SE13 6LH
Tel: 020 8333 3030 ext. 6454
Fax: 020 8333 3247

E-mail: library@uhl.nhs.uk
Librarian: Joy Ellery
Prof. staff: Jane Coyte
Type: Multidisciplinary.
Hours open: Mon–Thurs: 9am–7pm; Fri and Vacations: 9am–5pm.
Users: Employees of Lewisham Hospital NHS Trust; Community Health South London Trust; South London and Maudsley Trust; North Lewisham and South Lewisham Primary Care Trusts; students on placement; other libraries. Non-members by appointment for reference only.
Lending: No restrictions on books if in one of the groups above. Journal issues at the discretion of the Librarian.
Stock policy: Withdrawn stock sold or discarded. Journals mostly discarded after 20 years.
Holdings: 5,000 books; 152 current journal subscriptions, 264 journal titles; 50 films and videos.
Classification: NLM.
Library management system: LIBRARIAN.
Computerized services: Online access to Dialog. Regional Union Catalogues. Access to CINAHL; Cochrane Library; Embase: Psychiatry; MEDLINE.
Library publications: Library guide.
Collaborative networks: London LINKS; STLIS.

Lincoln County Hospital Professional Library

Education Centre
Lincoln County Hospital
Greetwell Road
Lincoln LN2 5QY
Tel: 01522 573954
Fax: 01522 573940
E-mail: library.lincoln@ulh,nhs.uk
Librarian: Marishona Ortega
Founded: 1993
Type: Multidisciplinary.

Hours open: Mon–Thurs: 8.45am–9.15pm; Fri: 8.45am–5.15pm; Sat: 10am–5pm; Sun: 12 noon–5pm.

Users: United Lincolnshire Hospitals NHS Trust staff; students and staff of the University of Nottingham School of Nursing and Division of Midwifery; medical and other students on placement within the Trust; employees of Lincolnshire NHS Trusts.

Lending: To users as indicated above, and to other local hospital libraries.

Stock policy: Old stock is either sold or discarded.

Holdings: 17,000 books; 136 current journal subscriptions.

Classification: Dewey.

Library management system: DS GALAXY.

Computerized services: Members can register for access to the Regional Ovid Biomed service which provides access to AMED; CINAHL; EBMR; Embase; MEDLINE; PreMEDLINE; PsycINFO and a range of full text journals provided by Journals @ Ovid.

Library publications: Library guide.

Branches: Louth County Hospital.

Collaborative networks: NULJ; PLCS.

Lincolnshire Health Authority Library

Cross O'Cliff
Bracebridge Heath
Lincoln LN4 2HN
Tel: 01522 513355 ext. 5476
Fax: 01522 515364
E-mail: sue.williams@lincs-ha.nhs.uk
Librarian: Sue Williams (Alison Price on maternity leave)
Type: Public Health; Primary Care.
Hours open: Mon–Fri: 9am–5pm.
Users: Employees of Health Authority.
Lending: Employees.
Stock policy: Old stock disposed of.

Holdings: 4,000 books; 99 current journal subscriptions, 136 journal titles; 30 films and videos; 15 CD-ROMs.

Classification: Dewey.

Library management system: PENLIB.

Computerized services: Access to Ovid; Cochrane Library and SilverPlatter; HMIC.

Collaborative networks: Health Authorities Librarians Group; LISN.

Lincolnshire Healthcare NHS Trust

Peter Hodgkinson Centre Library
County Hospital
Lincoln LN2 5UA
Tel: 01522 573517
Fax: 01522 525327
E-mail: maria.blakesley@lht.nhs.uk
Librarian: Maria T Blakesley
Founded: 1988
Type: Psychiatry and allied subjects.
Hours open: Mon, Thurs, Fri: 8am–3pm; Tues–Wed: 8am–2.30pm.
Users: Used by Trust staff and staff of Acute Trust at Lincoln County Hospital. Professional visitors welcome but service limited to stock only.
Lending: As above.
Stock policy: Reference books sent to Sudan. Others available for trainees to take or are disposed of.
Holdings: 2,000 books; 15 current journal subscriptions; 14 films and videos; 8 CD-ROMs; government reports.
Classification: Own.
Computerized services: Access via Ovid Biomed databases to AMED; Best Evidence; CINAHL; Cochrane Library; DARE; Embase; MEDLINE; PreMEDLINE; PsycINFO; Journals @ Ovid.
Collaborative networks: BL; BMA; PLCS; TRAHCLIS; Knowledge and Library Services Unit (Trent).

Liverpool Cardiothoracic Centre Library

Thomas Drive
Liverpool L14 3PE
Tel: 0151 228 1616 ext. 2338
Fax: 0151 220 8573
E-mail: mkielty@ccl-tr.nwest.nhs.uk
Librarian: Margaret Kielty
Founded: 1992
Type: Heart and Lung Specialist.
Hours open: Mon, Tues, Wed:
8.30am–4pm. 24-hour access.
Users: All staff.
Lending: Reference only.
Stock policy: Dispose of.
Computerized services: Access to
CINAHL; Cochrane Library; MEDLINE; NRR.
Collaborative networks: BL; BMA;
LIHNN; Liverpool Medical Institute; NULJ.

Liverpool Medical Institution

114 Mount Pleasant
Liverpool L3 5SR
Tel: 0151 709 9125
Fax: 0151 707 2810
E-mail: library@lmi.org.uk
URL: www.lmi.org.uk
Librarian: Mair Pierce Moulton
Prof. staff: Linda Crane
Founded: 1779
Type: Learned Society – Postgraduate
Clinical Medicine; Allied Disciplines; History
of Medicine.
Hours open: Mon–Fri: 9.30am–6pm; Sat:
9.30am–12.30pm.
Users: Members and affiliates of Liverpool
Medical Institution. Researchers (non-mem-
bers) on written application to the Librarian.
Lending: To members and affiliates only.
Stock policy: Retained indefinitely as
medico-legal resource. Stock dates from
16th century to present.
Holdings: 30,000 books; 165 hard-copy journal titles, 65 online; 50 CD-ROMs; plus
archives of the Institution and 5,000 glass
plate xrays.

Classification: Barnard.
Library management system: Heritage.
Computerized services: Access to Ovid
Biomed for CINAHL; EBMR; MEDLINE; full-
text journals. Access to ADITUS (HCN) for
AMED; ASSIA; BNI; CINAHL; Embase;
HMIC; MEDLINE; PsycINFO; RPS e-PIC;
SERFILE; SIGLE.
Library publications: Liverpool Medical
Institution Catalogue (to end of 19th
century); Transactions of the Liverpool
Medical Institution; Shepherd, J A, History of
the Liverpool Medical Institution. 1979.
Special collections: History of medicine;
orthopaedics.
Collaborative networks: LIHNN.

Llyfrgell Uned MDT Unit Library

Ysbyty Gwynedd
Bangor
Gwynedd LL57 2PW
Tel: 01248 384191
Fax: 01248 384191
E-mail: anne.jones2@nww-tr.wales.nhs.uk
Librarian: Anne Jones
Prof. staff: Pamela Jones
Type: Multidisciplinary.
Hours open: Mon–Thurs: 9am–5pm; Fri:
9am–4.30pm. 24-hour access.
Users: All members of Trust staff; GPs and
staff in the Trust area. Students on place-
ment in the Trust.
Lending: Stock is lent to all of the above with
the exception of undergraduate nursing stu-
dents at the University of Bangor.
Stock policy: Some disposed of, some
given to members of staff, some given to
charities – all depending on age and condi-
tion.
Holdings: 5,760 books; 162 current journal
subscriptions, 220 journal titles; 73 videos;
18 CD-ROMs.
Classification: NLM.
Library management system: ALICE.
Computerized services: Access to
AMED; ASSIA; BNI; CINAHL; Cochrane

Library; Embase; HealthStar; HMIC; MED-LINE; PsycINFO.
Special collections: Llandudno General Hospital.
Collaborative networks: AWHL; LIHNN.

London Ambulance Service NHS Trust Library

Clinical Audit and Research Unit
150 Seagrave Road
London SW6 1RX
Tel: 020 7381 4070 ext. 226
Fax: 020 7385 0254
E-mail: hasna.sinancevic@lond.amb.sthames.nhs.uk
Librarian: Hasna Sinancevic
Founded: 1995
Type: Clinical; Medical.
Hours open: Mon–Fri: 9am–5pm.
Users: LAS staff and North Thames Library and Information Services Network.
Lending: As above.
Stock policy: Stock retained.
Holdings: 19 current journal subscriptions.
Classification: Own.
Library management system: Reference Manager.
Computerized services: Access to MED-LINE; Cochrane Library; Health Information on the Internet; medical journals.
Library publications: Clinical audit and research bulletins.
Collaborative networks: NTLISN.

London Foot Hospital & School of Podiatric Medicine Library

33 Fitzroy Square
London W1T 6AY
Tel: 020 7530 4509
Fax: 020 7530 4540
E-mail: r.murphy@ucl.ac.uk
URL: www.ucl.ac.uk/podiatry
Librarian: Ms Ruth Murphy
Founded: 1913
Type: Podiatry; Medical.

Hours open: Mon–Fri: 8.30am–5pm. Not staffed all the time.
Users: Students and staff of the Hospital and School; Camden and Islington Community Health Services NHS Trust. Other users by appointment only.
Lending: Staff and students. Others for reference only.
Stock policy: Non-podiatry journals discarded after 5 years; non-podiatry books discarded after varying intervals.
Holdings: 3,000 books; 33 current journal subscriptions, 68 journal titles; 30 videos; 20 CD-ROMs; 3,000 35mm slides.
Classification: NLM.
Computerized services: Internet access. Access to AMED; Cochrane Library; Embase; MEDLINE; PsycINFO.
Collaborative networks: London LINKS; UCL.

London Library & Information Development Unit

20 Guilford Street
London WC1N 1DZ
Tel: 020 7692 3389
Fax: 020 7692 3393
E-mail: ldnlidu@lidu.ac.uk
URL: www.londonlinks.ac.uk
Librarian: Shane Godbolt (Regional Librarian and Head of Unit)
Prof. staff: Susan Fairlamb; Ruth Fosker; Jane Williamson; Aileen Wood.
Founded: 1995
Type: Regional Strategic Policy Development Unit.
Hours open: Mon–Fri: 8.30am–5.30pm.
Library publications: Regional Documents Database and Union List of Serials are produced quarterly on CD-ROM.
Collaborative networks: London and linked to South East and Eastern Regions.

London School of Hygiene & Tropical Medicine Library

Keppel Street
London WC1E 7HT
Tel: 020 7927 ~~2283~~ 2276
Fax: 020 7927 2273
E-mail: library@lshtm.ac.uk
URL: www.lshtm.ac.uk/as/library/libintro.htm
Librarian: Brian Furner
Prof. staff: David Archer; John Eyers
Founded: 1899
Type: Multidisciplinary.
Hours open: Mon–Fri: 8.30am–11pm; Sat: 9am–12.30pm.
Users: Staff and students of the School of the University of London and of other educational institutions. Open for reference to general public.
Lending: To members of the School. Limited lending to University of London academic staff and research degree students. To external members on payment of fee.
Stock policy: Wherever possible, donate.
Holdings: 60,000 books; 807 current journal subscriptions.
Classification: Barnard.
Library management system: Unicorn.
Computerized services: Online access to BIDS; Cochrane Library; LILACS; Web of Science and Journals Citations Reports. In-house networked databases for HEED; HMIC; MEDLINE; Popline; SIGLE; Topics in International Health.
Library publications: Library guides; Catalogue of the Ross Archives.
Special collections: Reece Collection on Vaccinations; Ross Archives.
Collaborative networks: M25 Consortium; University of London.

Lorn & Islands District General Hospital Health Services Information Library

Education Centre
Lorn and Islands District General Hospital
Glengallan Road
Oban
Argyll PA34 4HH
Tel: 01631 567588
Fax: 01631 567126
E-mail: vmurchison@ablilib.demon.co.uk
Librarian: Ms Vivien Murchison
Founded: 1978
Type: Multidisciplinary; Health.
Hours open: Mon–Fri: 9am–5pm.
Users: All contracted staff in Argyll and Bute district, GPs, and GP registrars, medical students.
Lending: To registered users as above.
Stock policy: Disposed of if out of date. Transferred if still useful to one of the other sites.
Holdings: 3,600 books; 41 current journal subscriptions.
Classification: NLM (Wessex adaptation).
Library management system: Heritage IV.
Computerized services: Access to internet; NHSNet; AMED; Best Evidence; BNI/RCN; CINAHL; Embase; HMIC; Health CD; MEDLINE; Speech and Language Research Database.
Library publications: Information sheets.
Collaborative networks: BLDSC; BMA; CONARLS; LfN; NULJ; RCN; SHINE; SILLR.

Louth County Hospital Medical Library

Postgraduate Education Centre
Louth County Hospital
Louth
Lincolnshire LN11 0EU
Tel: 01507 600100 ext. 324
Fax: 01507 609290 (main hospital fax)
Librarian: Mrs Gill Kettle
Notes: For further details see website www.telh.nhs.uk

Luton & Dunstable Hospital Medical Centre Library

Lewsey Road
Luton
Bedfordshire LU4 0DZ
Tel: 01582 497201
Fax: 01582 497164
E-mail: david.johnson@ldh-tr.anglox.nhs.uk
URL: www.ldmedics.nhs.uk/
library.homepage.htm
Librarian: David Johnson
Founded: 1967
Type: Clinical Medicine.
Hours open: Mon–Fri: 8.30am–6pm.
Users: All NHS employees in South Bedfordshire, including GP practices; University of Luton students. All others by prior arrangement for reference only.
Lending: To NHS staff as above and University of Luton students.
Stock policy: Out-of-date items disposed of.
Holdings: 2,400 books; 93 current journal subscriptions, 122 journal titles; 74 films and videos; 38 CD-ROMs.
Classification: NLM.
Computerized services: Online access to Data-Star. 3 NHSNet-connected PCs with internet access. Access to BNI.
Library publications: List of journals; guide for new users (also on website).
Collaborative networks: Health Librarians of Anglia.

Macclesfield District General Hospital Multi-Professional Health Sciences Library

Education and Training Centre
East Cheshire NHS Trust
Macclesfield District General Hospital
Victoria Road
Macclesfield
Cheshire SK10 3BL
Tel: 01625 661362
Fax: 01625 663923
E-mail: Healthsciences_library@echeshire-tr.nwest.nhs.uk
Librarian: Mrs M Perry
Founded: 1998
Type: Multidisciplinary.
Hours open: Mon–Fri: 9am–5pm. Access available out of staffed hours.
Users: All Trust and primary care staff and students on placement within the Trust.
Lending: Stock lent to all bona fide users.
Classification: Dewey.
Library management system: Heritage.
Computerized services: Internet and NHS access via ADITUS to AMED; BNIPlus; CINAHL; Embase; HMIC; MEDLINE; PsycINFO.
Collaborative networks: LIHNN; NULJ.

MacKenzie Medical Centre Library

Burnley General Hospital
Casterton Avenue
Burnley
Lancashire BB10 2PQ
Tel: 01282 474720
Fax: 01282 474254
E-mail: mackenzielib@yahoo.co.uk
Librarian: Mrs Rose Turner
Founded: 1966
Type: Clinical Medical.
Hours open: Mon–Fri: 9am–5pm.
Users: Any employee of Burnley Health Care Trust and life members of the Mackenzie Medical Association.
Lending: Only to members and life members of the Mackenzie Medical Association.
Stock policy: Pass on to Rossendale and then libraries in Romania.
Holdings: 2,471 books; 22 journal titles; 39 videos; 12 CD-ROMs.
Classification: NLM. Changing to Dewey.
Library management system: Heritage.
Computerized services: Access to ADITUS and Cochrane Library.
Branches: Rossendale.

Collaborative networks: East Lancashire Health Librarians Patch Group; LIHNN.

Macmillan Cancer Relief Library

89 Albert Embankment
London SE1 7UQ
Tel: 020 7840 7840
Fax: 020 7840 7841
E-mail: ubarrett@macmillan.org.uk
Librarian: Ursula Barrett
Founded: 1999
URL: www.macmillan.org.uk
Type: Charity library
Hours open: Mon–Fri: 8.30am–6pm
Users: Macmillan staff only. Visitors by request only
Lending: as above
Holdings: 5,000 books; 70 current journal subscriptions; 80 journal titles; 60 films and videos; 20 CD-ROMs.
Classification: Own
Library management system: Lotus Notes
Computerized services: LEXUS
Library publications: Library services user guide
Special collections: Macmillan Cancer Relief publications
Collaborative networks: CHILL; VOLSIF

Maidstone and Tunbridge Wells NHS Trust: Maidstone Library

Robert Hardwick Postgraduate Centre
Maidstone Hospital
Kent ME16 9QQ
Tel: 01622 224647
Fax: 01622 224120
E-mail: maidlib@netcomuk.co.uk
Librarian: David Copsey (Library Services Manager)
Prof. staff: Jennifer Blackburn (Knowledge Manager – Clinical Support)
Hours open: Mon, Wed, Thurs: 9am–9pm; Tues, Fri: 9am–5pm.
Collaborative networks: STLIS.

Maidstone & Tunbridge Wells NHS Trust: Tunbridge Wells Library

Kent and Sussex Hospital
Tunbridge Wells
Kent TN4 8AT
Tel: 01892 526111 ext. 2384
Fax: 01892 531975
E-mail: jennifer.blackburn@mtw-tr.nhs.uk
Librarian: David Copsey (Library Services Manager)
Prof. staff: Jennifer Blackburn (Knowledge Manager – Clinical Support)
Founded: 1974
Type: Multidisciplinary.
Hours open: Mon–Fri: 9am–5.30pm.
Users: All staff of the Trust; staff of the Invicta Community Care NHS Trust; South West Kent PCT. External, non-NHS readers by prior arrangement only.
Lending: To registered users including external users – 4 books for 6 weeks. To other libraries in South Thames. No loans to non-members.
Stock policy: Regional withdrawals policy. If material is too old, it is disposed of. Some given to BookAid if within their timeframe.
Holdings: 3,000 books; 120 current journal subscriptions.
Classification: NLM.
Library management system: LIBRARIAN.
Computerized services: Online access to BNI and CINAHL through SilverPlatter via MIRON, Cochrane Library via NeLH; MEDLINE.
Collaborative networks: NULJ; STLIS.

Manchester Health Authority Library

Gateway House
Piccadilly South
Manchester M60 7LP
Tel: 0161 237 2544
Fax: 0161 237 2813
E-mail: atkinsok@manchester.nwest.nhs.uk

URL: www.manchesterhealth.co.uk
Librarian: Kathy A Atkinson
Founded: 1991
Type: Health Authority.
Hours open: Mon–Fri: 8.30am–5pm. Staffed: Mon–Thurs: 8.30am–1pm.
Users: Health Authority Staff. Other users (M/CR NHS staff) for reference only.
Lending: To Health Authority staff only.
Stock policy: Disposed of.
Holdings: 3,627 books; 26 current journal subscriptions, 38 journal titles.
Classification: NLM (SW Thames adaptation).
Library management system: Heritage IV.
Computerized services: Access to Manchester ADITUS scheme and Cochrane Library; MEDLINE.
Special collections: City of Manchester Health Reports from 1845.
Collaborative networks: LIHNN.

Manchester School of Physiotherapy Library

Manchester Royal Infirmary
Oxford Road
Manchester M13 9WL
Tel: 0161 276 8716
Fax: 0161 276 8711
E-mail: inform@msop.cmht.nwest.nhs.uk
URL: http://cmhtweb/sop/physiolibrary2.htm
Librarian: Colette King
Type: Physiotherapy.
Hours open: Mon, Wed, Thurs: 8.45am–5pm; Tues: 8.45am–7pm; Fri: 8.45am–4.30pm. Ring to check opening hours during vacations.
Users: Staff and students of the School; certain categories of CMHT staff. Others by appointment.
Lending: As above.
Stock policy: Passed to other libraries, or disposed of, depending on the usefulness of the stock.

Holdings: 5,000 books; 50 current journal subscriptions; 100 films and videos.
Classification: NLM.
Library management system: ALICE.
Computerized services: Access to ADITUS; Cochrane Library; Oxford Textbook of Medicine.
Library publications: Newsletter.
Special collections: 1,000 undergraduate and postgraduate dissertations; hospital profiles for students on placement.
Collaborative networks: LIHNN.

Marie Curie Cancer Care

Library and Information Service
Edenhall
11 Lyndhurst Gardens
London NW3 5NS
Tel: 020 7853 3434
Fax: 020 7431857
E-mail: PEngland@mariecurie.org.uk
Librarian: Pat England (Library and Information Services Manager)
Founded: 1996
Type: Palliative Care.
Hours open: Variable. Please contact the manager for details.
Users: Staff and students. Others by application.
Lending: Staff and students only.
Stock policy: Disposal.
Holdings: 1,000 books; 25 current journal subscriptions, 40 journal titles; 50 videos.
Classification: NLM.
Library management system: LIMES.
Computerized services: Ovid Biomed via Thames Valley University.
Branches: Marie Curie Centre, Caterham, Surrey.
Collaborative networks: CHILL.

Marie Curie Centre, Liverpool Library

Speke Road
Woolton

Liverpool L25 8QA
Tel: 0151 801 1444
Fax: 0151 801 1458
E-mail: lclarke@mariecurie.org.uk
Librarian: Lorna Clarke
Founded: 1992
Type: Cancer and Palliative Care.
Hours open: Mon–Thurs: 9am–5pm; Fri: 9am–4.30pm.
Users: Staff and students registered on an in-house course. Non-members, reference use only.
Lending: As above, libraries from LIHNN and other Marie Curie Centres.
Stock policy: Offer to other Marie Curie Centres and then other libraries in the Region before disposal.
Holdings: 1,700 books; 21 current journal subscriptions, 61 journal titles; 84 films and videos; 36 CD-ROMs.
Classification: NLM.
Library management system: LIMES.
Computerized services: Access to ADITUS; MEDLINE.
Collaborative networks: LIHNN.

Marie Curie Centre, Warren Pearl

Education Department
911–913 Warwick Road
Solihull
West Midlands B91 3ER
Tel: 0121 254 7832
Fax: 0121 254 7840
E-mail: clake@mariecurie.org.uk
Librarian: Christine Lake
Type: Palliative and Cancer Care.
Hours open: 9am–3pm.
Users: Marie Curie nurses, Community Hospital; hospice nurses; student nurses; other healthcare professionals.
Lending: Restricted to members of staff and students on placement or attending MCCC degree courses.
Stock policy: Would pass it on.

Holdings: 500 books; 14 current journal subscriptions; bibliographies and indices of articles on palliative and cancer care.
Classification: NLM.
Library management system: LIMES.
Computerized services: Access to CINAHL; Cochrane Library; Core Biomedical Collection; MEDLINE; Nursing Collection.

McArdle Library

Postgraduate Centre
Arrowe Park Hospital
Arrowe Park Road
Upton
Wirral
Merseyside CH49 5PE
Tel: 0151 604 7223
Fax: 0151 604 7223
E-mail: mcardlelibrary@hotmail.com
Librarian: Ms Amanda Elkerton
Prof. staff: Miss Mona Larkin; Mrs Beryl Stanley.
Founded: 1992
Type: Multidisciplinary.
Hours open: Mon–Thurs: 9am–5pm; Fri: 9am–4.30pm.
Users: All Trust staff.
Lending: To all Trust staff.
Stock policy: Old stock goes into archive.
Holdings: 4,300 books; 130 journal titles.
Classification: Dewey.
Library management system: Heritage.
Computerized services: Access to ADITUS.
Collaborative networks: LIHNN; NULJ.

McTimoney College of Chiropractic Library

McTimoney College of Chiropractic
The Clock House
22–26 Ock Street
Abingdon
Oxfordshire OX14 5SH

Tel: 01235 523336
Fax: 01235 523576
E-mail: library@mctimoney-college.ac.uk
URL: www.mctimoney-college.ac.uk
Librarian: Mrs Heather Woodley
Type: Multidisciplinary; Medical; Chiropractic; Undergraduate.
Hours open: 9am–5.30pm 7 days a week.
Users: College staff, teaching and clinical; practitioners (MCA members); undergraduate students. Others by appointment and application to Librarian.
Lending: To MCC staff and students. Reference use only to others.
Stock policy: Dispose of outdated stock.
Holdings: 2,000 books; 30 current journal subscriptions; 200 films and videos; audiotapes.
Classification: Dewey.
Library management system: ALICE.
Computerized services: Internet access available. Access to AMED; CINAHL; Cochrane Library; Embase; MEDLINE.
Special collections: Chiropractic books; research imprints.
Collaborative networks: HeLIN.

Medical Devices Agency Library

Department of Health
Room 1001
Hannibal House
Elephant and Castle
London SE1 6TQ
Tel: 020 7972 8341
Fax: 020 7972 8079
E-mail: library@medical-devices.gov.uk
URL: www.medical-devices.gov.uk
Librarian: Karen Morgan
Prof. staff: Kay Phillips
Type: Government.
Hours open: Mon–Fri: 9am–5pm.
Users: Medical Devices Agency staff and other government departments. Others by appointment only.

Lending:. Medical Devices Agency staff and other Government Departments.
Stock policy: Disposed of.
Holdings: 5,200 books; 165 current journal subscriptions; 15 CD-ROMs.
Classification: BLISS.
Library management system: Unicorn.
Computerized services: Online access to Data-Star. Access to BSI; Dorlands; Eurolaw; Health Devices Alerts; Healthcare Product Comparison System; Standards Infobase; Stedmans; UK Info Disk.

Medical Research Council: Harwell Library

Medical Research Council
Harwell
Didcot
Oxfordshire OX11 0RD
Tel: 01235 834393 ext. 342
Fax: 01235 834776
E-mail: m.bulman@har.mrc.ac.uk
Librarian: Mrs Maureen Bulman
Founded: 1950
Type: Medical Research.
Hours open: Mon–Thurs: 8.30am–5pm; Fri: 9am–4.15pm.
Users: Research staff; PhD students.
Lending: Mainly to staff. Occasionally non-members on application.
Stock policy: Outdated stock is advertised to other libraries, before being recycled.
Holdings: 5,000 books; 80 current journal subscriptions, 230 journal titles; 2,000 reports.
Classification: UDC.
Library management system: Heritage.
Computerized services: Online access to MEDLINE and Web of Science.
Collaborative networks: MRC.

Medical Research Council: Human Genetics Unit Library

Western General Hospital
Crewe Road
Edinburgh EH4 2XU
Tel: 0131 332 2471 ext. 2214
Fax: 0131 343 2620
E-mail: library@hgu.mrc.ac.uk
Librarian: Siobhan Marron
Founded: 1974
Type: Genetics Research.
Hours open: Mon–Fri: 8.30am–4.45pm.
Users: Unit staff and students. Visitors by appointment.
Lending: No restrictions on lending book stock. Journals reference only. Photocopies provided.
Stock policy: Preferably pass on to other libraries.
Holdings: 2,493 books; 90 journal titles; 12 videos; 38 CD-ROMs; 442 other items
Classification: UDC.
Library management system: Heritage IV.
Computerized services: Online access to Ovid MEDLINE; PubMed; Web of Science.
Library publications: Annual Report; serials holdings list.
Special collections: MRC Human Genetics Unit reprints.
Collaborative networks: BMA; SHINE; UKSG.

Medical Research Council: Social & Public Health Science Unit Library

Medical Research Council
4 Lilybank Gardens
Glasgow G12 8RZ
Tel: 0141 357 3949
Fax: 0141 337 2389
E-mail: library@msoc.mrc.gla.ac.uk
URL: www.msoc-mrc.gla.ac.uk
Librarian: Mary Robins
Founded: 1973
Type: Multidisciplinary; Medical Sociology; Research Methodology; Sociology; Statistics, Government Publications.
Hours open: Mon–Fri: 9am–5pm.
Users: Employees of the Medical Research Council and their collaborators. Others by appointment.
Lending: To staff only. Otherwise reference only.
Stock policy: Prefer to pass on our stock to other libraries providing the item is not out-dated.
Holdings: 4,000 books; 60 current journal subscriptions, 80 journal titles.
Classification: Own.
Library management system: CALM 2000.
Computerized services: Search facilities through Glasgow University. Online access to Embase; GEOBASE; MEDLINE; PsycINFO: Web of Science. Access to HMIC; SIGLE.
Collaborative networks: MRC; SHINE.

Medical Toxicology Unit Library

Guy's and St Thomas NHS Library
Avonley Road
New Cross
London SE14 5ER
Tel: 020 7771 5364
Fax: 020 7771 5363
E-mail: helaina.checketts@gstt.sthames.nhs.uk
Librarian: Helaina Checketts
Type: Toxicological.
Hours open: Mon–Fri: 9am–5pm, strictly by appointment only.
Users: Members of Medical Toxicology Unit staff. Others by appointment only.
Lending: Staff only.
Stock policy: Passed to other poisons centres, other libraries or thrown out, depending on the items.
Holdings: 1,500 books; 48 current journal subscriptions, 80 journal titles.
Classification: NLM.

Medway Maritime Hospital Library

Windmill Road
Gillingham
Kent ME7 5NY
Tel: 01634 833849
Fax: 01634 845640
E-mail: carla.wearing@medway-tr.sthames.nhs.uk
Librarian: Carla Wearing
Prof. staff: Fiona Sinclair
Founded: 1970
Type: Multidisciplinary.
Hours open: Mon–Fri: 8.30am–9pm.
Users: All staff employed by Medway NHS Trust, Thames Gateway NHS Trust, West Kent Health Authority, local PCGs and PCTs. King's medical students and other students at the discretion of the Librarian
Lending: To registered members only and libraries within the South Thames region.
Stock policy: South Thames withdrawals policy adhered to. Latest editions only kept on shelves. Withdrawn books sold to readers.
Holdings: 12,000 books; 195 current journal subscriptions, 250 journal titles; 100 videos; 30 CD-ROMs.
Classification: NLM.
Library management system: LIBRARIAN.
Computerized services: Online access to Data-Star. Internet access available. Access to AMED; Best Evidence; BNI; CINAHL; ClinPsych; Cochrane Library; DARE; Embase: Psychiatry; MEDLINE.
Library publications: Current Awareness Bulletin.
Collaborative networks: STLIS.

Mercy Hospital Medical Library

Mercy Hospital
Grenville Place
Cork City
Republic of Ireland
Tel: +353 21 4271971
Fax: +353 21 4278815
E-mail: rbradfield@mercy-hospital-cork.ie
Librarian: Mr Richard Bradfield
Founded: 1995
Type: Multidisciplinary.
Hours open: Mon–Fri: 9am–5pm.
Users: Hospital staff; University College Cork students.
Lending: To members only.
Stock policy: Dispose and donate.
Holdings: 1,500 books; 54 current journal subscriptions.
Classification: Dewey.
Library management system: ClarisWorks Filemaker Pro.
Computerized services: Internet access available. Access to CINAHL; MEDLINE.
Collaborative networks: Irish Health Sciences Libraries Group.

Mid Cheshire Hospital NHS Trust: Joint Education & Training Library (JET)

Leighton Hospital
Crewe
Cheshire CW1 4QJ
Tel: 01270 255141 ext. 2705/2538
Fax: 01270 252611
E-mail: lr.leighton@chester.ac.uk
Librarian: Elisa Dowey
Founded: 1995
Type: Multidisciplinary.
Hours open: Mon–Fri: 8.30am–5pm.
Users: Medical, nursing, professionals allied to medicine, student nurses, midwives, support staff within the Trust. Anyone outside the Trust, reference only.
Lending: To Trust staff only.
Stock policy: Old stock is usually disposed of.
Holdings: 10,500 books; 105 current journal subscriptions.
Classification: Dewey.
Library management system: INNOPAC.
Computerized services: Regional co-operative ADITUS gives access to AMED;

CINAHL; Embase; HMIC; MEDLINE; PsycINFO.
Collaborative networks: LIHNN.

Mid Kent College of Higher & Further Education Library

Horsted
Maidstone Road
Chatham
Kent ME5 9UQ
Tel: 01634 828625
Fax: 01634 830224
E-mail: jane.beeley@midkent.ac.uk
linda.russell@midkent.ac.uk
Librarian: Jan Loose
Prof. staff: Jane Beeley; Linda Russell; Janette Wastell
Hours open: Mon–Thurs: 9am–8pm; Fri: 9am–4pm.
Collaborative networks: STLIS.

MIDIRS: (Midwives Information & Resource Service)

9 Elmdale Road
Clifton
Bristol BS8 1SL
Tel: 0117 925 1791
Fax: 0117 925 1792
E-mail: info@midirs.org
URL: www.midirs.org
Librarian: Kathy Levine (Information Officer)
Prof. staff: Sarah Boughton; Rob Wilson
Founded: 1985
Type: Midwifery.
Hours open: Mon–Fri: 9am–5pm (telephone access). 24-hour e-mail and web access.
Users: Mostly midwives in the UK and world-wide. Anyone can use the services, although some are charged for on a sliding scale of charges depending on membership status.
Lending: No lending. Photocopy service available.
Stock policy: Retain almost all old stock.

Holdings: 500 books; 250 current journal subscriptions, 300 journal titles; 150 films and videos.
Classification: Own.
Computerized services: Own website which gives access to midwifery databases and web links. Access to BNI; CINAHL; Cochrane Library; MEDLINE; MEDSCAPE.
Library publications: MIDIRS Midwifery Digest; Informed Choice leaflets; website.
Collaborative networks: Bristol Healthcare Librarians Group.

Mildmay Hospital UK Library

Hackney Road
London E2 7NA
Tel: 020 7613 6300
Fax: 020 7729 5361
E-mail: library@mildmay.org.uk
URL: www.mildmay.org.uk
Librarian: Jenny Grove (Education Administrator)
Prof. staff: Claire Troughton (Sessional Librarian)
Type: Multidisciplinary – HIV/AIDS, Palliative Care.
Hours open: Mon–Fri: 11am–1.30pm.
Users: Mainly staff, students on courses, interested parties.
Lending: To staff only.
Stock policy: Books archived or sold cheaply within the Hospital. Journals archived or passed to other libraries.
Holdings: 1,200 books; 23 current journal subscriptions, 41 journal titles; 62 videos; 15 slide collections.
Classification: NLM (adapted).
Library management system: Button File.
Computerized services: Access to Aidsline; CINAHL; MEDLINE.
Library publications: Current Awareness Bulletin 10 times a year.
Special collections: Hospital Archive.
Collaborative networks: NTRLS.

Milton Keynes General NHS Trust Staff Library

Postgraduate Education Centre
Milton Keynes General NHS Trust
Standing Way, Eaglestone
Milton Keynes
Buckinghamshire MK13 7QQ
Tel: 01908 243076
Fax: 01908 671977
E-mail: lis@powernet.co.uk
Librarian: Lorna R Maguire
Prof. staff: Sue Whiteley
Founded: 1984
Type: Multidisciplinary.
Hours open: Mon–Fri: 9.30am–5pm.
Users: All staff groups who are employed by the NHS in the local area, plus GP practices and registered students on NMET contracts. Reference-only access for the public.
Lending: To registered members only.
Stock policy: Old stock is sent to charities to distribute worldwide or destroyed.
Holdings: 12,000 books; 250 current journal subscriptions; 100 videos; 10 CD-ROMs.
Classification: NLM.
Library management system: Heritage.
Computerized services: Ovid Gateway and Dialog. Access to AMED; BNI; CINAHL; Embase; HMIC; MEDLINE; NRR; PsycINFO.
Collaborative networks: HeLIN.

Monklands Hospital Library

Monklands Hospital
Airdrie
Lanarkshire ML6 0JS
Tel: 01236 748748
Fax: 01236 713105
Librarian: J MacLeod
Founded: 1976
Type: Multidisciplinary.
Hours open: Mon–Thurs: 9am–5pm; Fri: 9am–4.30pm.
Users: Employees of the Trust and local NHS personnel.
Lending: To Trust employees and local NHS personnel.

Stock policy: Disposed of.
Holdings: 3,500 books; 100 current journal subscriptions, 110 journal titles.
Classification: NLM (Wessex adaptation).
Library management system: LIBRARIAN.
Computerized services: Access via Ovid to CINAHL and MEDLINE. Access to Cochrane Library.
Collaborative networks: SHINE.

Moorfields Eye Hospital & Institute of Ophthalmology Joint Library

11–43 Bath Street
London EC1V 9EL
Tel: 020 7608 6814
Fax: 020 7608 6814
E-mail: ophthlib@ucl.ac.uk
URL: www.ucl.ac.uk/ioo/library
Librarian: Deborah Heatlie
Prof. staff: Katy Gwyther
Founded: 1999 (Joint Library)
Type: Multidisciplinary; Ophthalmology and Visual Science.
Hours open: Mon: 9am–5pm; Tues–Fri: 9am–6pm.
Users: Employees of the Institute and Moorfields Eye Hospital NHS Trust; Research and undergraduate students of University College London. Visitors may use the library for reference purposes – £5 charge for a day pass.
Lending: To members only.
Stock policy: All Ophthalmology and Visual Science stock is kept. General clinical medicine and nursing texts are offered to other libraries once a new edition is published.
Holdings: 20,500 books; 161 current journal subscriptions, 529 journal titles; 8 films and videos; 2 CD-ROMs.
Classification: Own.
Library management system: ALEPH.
Computerized services: Access to Best Evidence; CINAHL; Cochrane Library;

Embase; MEDLINE. Searches may be carried out for non-members for a charge.

Special collections: Historical collection of works dating from 1585 on vision science and ophthalmology; papers of Nettleship; several thousand reprints from 1800.

Collaborative networks: AVSL (International); North Central Regional Libraries; University College London Group of Libraries; University of London Libraries.

Moorgreen Hospital Staff Library, Countess Mountbatten House

Southampton University Hospitals NHS Trust
Botley Road
West End
Southampton
Hampshire SO30 3JB
Tel: 02380 475129
Fax: 02380 473501
Prof. staff: Fran Smitherman
Hours open: Mon: 11am–3pm; Wed, Thurs: 1pm–3pm.
Collaborative networks: STLIS

Moorgreen Hospital Staff Library, Hawthorn Lodge

Southampton University Hospitals NHS Trust
Botley Road
West End
Southampton
Hampshire SO30 3JB
Tel: 02380 475154
Fax: 02380 475155
Librarian: Frances Little
Prof. staff: Clair Oldrieve; Fran Smitherman
Hours open: Mon–Thurs: 9.30am–4.15pm.
Collaborative networks: STLIS.

Morriston Staff Library

Postgraduate Centre
Morriston Hospital

Swansea NHS Trust
Swansea SA6 6NL
Tel: 01792 703131
Fax: 01792 703211
E-mail: edcent@hotmail.com
Librarian: Anne Powell
Founded: 1969
Type: Multidisciplinary.
Hours open: Mon–Fri: 8.30am–5pm.
Users: All employees of Swansea NHS Trust.
Lending: As above plus regional libraries.
Stock policy: Disposed of.
Holdings: 5,000 books; 150 current journal subscriptions, 200 journal titles; 165 videos; 50 CD-ROMs.
Classification: NLM (Wessex adaptation).
Library management system: Voyager.
Computerized services: Access to HOWIS and networked clinical information within the Hospital. Access via Ovid to AMED; Best Evidence; CancerLit; CINAHL; Cochrane Library; Embase; HealthStar; MEDLINE; PsycINFO. SilverPlatter for ASSIA; BNI; HMIC. CD-ROM access to MEDLINE.
Library publications: User guides; clinical effectiveness guides.
Collaborative networks: AWHILES; AWHL; NULJ.

Mount Vernon Hospital: Les Cannon Memorial Library

Mount Vernon Postgraduate Medical Centre
Mount Vernon Hospital
West Hertfordshire Hospitals NHS Trust
Rickmansworth Road
Northwood
Middlesex HA6 2RN
Tel: 01923 844143
Fax: 01923 827216
E-mail: mvnlib@cs.com
Librarian: Richard Osborn
Prof. staff: Jane McFarlane
Founded: 1973
Type: Multidisciplinary.

Hours open: Mon–Fri: 9am–5pm (Wed: 7pm in term-time). Swipe card access for Trust staff at other times.
Users: All staff from local NHS Trusts. Other users on application.
Lending: Books and journals loaned to library members and other libraries. Photocopies provided.
Stock policy: Books discarded at varying intervals. Offered to other libraries.
Holdings: 3,500 books; 165 current journal subscriptions.
Classification: NLM (Wessex adaptation).
Library management system: DB/TextWorks.
Computerized services: Consortium-funded access to Ovid databases. Access to AMED; CINAHL; ClinPsych; Cochrane Library; MEDLINE.
Library publications: Annual Report; Periodicals Holdings List.
Special collections: Cancer research and treatment; maxillofacial surgery; oral surgery; plastic surgery.
Collaborative networks: LLIDU.

Napier University: Canaan Lane Learning Centre

74 Canaan Lane
Edinburgh EH10 4TB
Tel: 0131 536 4616
Fax: 0131 536 5608
E-mail: s.moffat@napier.ac.uk
URL: www.napier.ac.uk/depts/library/learningcentres/canaanlane/canaanlane.htm
Librarian: Sheena Moffat (Information Services Advisor)
Prof. staff: Margaret Gill (Learning Centre Manager)
Founded: 1969
Type: Nursing; Midwifery.
Hours open: Mon–Thurs: 8.45am–9pm; Fri: 9am–5pm; Sat: 9am–12 noon.
Users: Staff and students of Napier University. NHS staff by arrangement.

Lending: Staff and students of Napier University; others by arrangement.
Stock policy: Disposal
Holdings: 15,000 books; 150 current journal subscriptions; 500 films and videos.
Classification: Dewey.
Library management system: epixtech/Dynix.
Computerized services: Access to BioMedNet; Health on the Net; Medical Matrix; NHS Direct; OMNI; Scottish Health on the Net; SOSIG.
Library publications: Subject guides and resource guides (printed and on web)
Collaborative networks: SHINE.

Napier University: Comely Bank Learning Centre

13 Crewe Road South
Edinburgh EH4 2LD
Tel: 0131 343 7918
Fax: 0131 343 7958
E-mail: s.moffat@napier.ac.uk
URL: www.napier.ac.uk/depts/library/learningcentres/comelybank/comelybank.htm
Librarian: Sheena Moffat (Information Services Advisor)
Founded: 1969
Type: Nursing and Midwifery; Learning Disabilities; Mental Health.
Hours open: Mon–Thurs: 8.45am–9pm; Fri: 9am–5pm; Sat: 9am–12 noon.
Users: University staff and students. NHS Trust staff by arrangement.
Lending: University staff and students. Others by arrangement.
Stock policy: Disposal.
Holdings: 20,000 books; 200 current journal subscriptions; 550 videos.
Classification: NLM.
Library management system: epixtech/Dynix.
Computerized services: Access to BioMedNet; Health on the Net; Medical Matrix; NHS Direct; OMNI; Scottish Health on the Net; SOSIG.

Library publications: Subject guides and resource guides.
Collaborative networks: SHINE.

Napier University: Livingston Learning Centre

St John's Hospital at Howden
Livingston
West Lothian EH54 6PP
Tel: 01506 422831
Fax: 01506 422833
E-mail: s.moffat@napier.ac.uk;
ml.mitchell@napier.ac.uk
URL: www.napier.ac.uk/depts/library/
learningcentres/livingston/livingston.htm
Librarian: Moira Mitchell; Sheena Moffat
(Information Services Advisors)
Prof. staff: Mari Porter (Learning Centre Manager)
Founded: 1969
Type: Nursing; Midwifery; Medical; Multidisciplinary.
Hours open: Mon–Thurs: 8.45am–9pm; Fri: 9am–9pm; Sat: 9am–12 noon.
Users: University staff and students. NHS Trust staff by arrangement.
Lending: University staff and students. NHS Trust staff by arrangement.
Stock policy: Disposal.
Holdings: 15,000 books; 200 current journal subscriptions; 350 films and videos.
Classification: NLM.
Library management system: epixtech/Dynix .
Computerized services: Access to BioMedNet; Health on the Net; Medical Matrix; NHS Direct; OMNI; Scottish Health on the Net; SOSIG.
Library publications: Subject guides and resource guides (printed and on web)
Collaborative networks: SHINE.

Napier University: Melrose Learning Centre

Borders General Hospital
Melrose
Roxburghshire TD6 9BD
Tel: 01896 661632
Fax: 01896 823386
E-mail: ml.mitchell@napier.ac.uk
URL: www.napier.ac.uk/depts/library/
learningcentres/melrose/melrose.htm
Librarian: Moira Mitchell (Information Services Advisor)
Prof. staff: Jennifer MacLaine (Learning Centre Manager)
Founded: 1979
Type: Nursing; Midwifery; Medical; Multidisciplinary.
Hours open: Mon–Thurs: 8.45am–9pm; Fri: 9am–9pm; Sat: 9am–12 noon.
Users: University staff and students. NHS Trust staff by arrangement.
Lending: University staff and students. NHS Trust staff by arrangement.
Stock policy: Disposal.
Holdings: 15,000 books; 200 current journal subscriptions; 250 videos.
Classification: NLM.
Library management system: epixtech/Dynix.
Computerized services: Access to BioMedNet; Health on the Net; Medical Matrix; NHS Direct; OMNI; Scottish Health on the Net; SOSIG.
Library publications: Current Awareness Bulletin; subject guides and resource guides (printed and on the web).
Collaborative networks: SHINE.

National Autistic Society Library

393 City Road
London EC1V 1NG
Tel: 020 7833 2299
Fax: 020 7833 9666
E-mail: nas@nas.org.uk
URL: www.nas.org.uk
Librarian: David Potter (Head of Information and Publications)
Type: Autism Spectrum Disorders.

Hours open: Mon–Fri: 10am–4pm.
Users: Staff; visitors by appointment.
Lending: Reference only.
Holdings: 3,400 books; 48 current journal subscriptions; 80 films and videos.
Classification: Own.
Library management system: InMagic.

National Centre for Training & Education in Prosthetics & Orthotics

Library
University of Strathclyde
Curran Building
131 St James' Road
Glasgow G4 0LS
Tel: 0141 548 3814
Fax: 0141 552 1283
E-mail: h.smart@strath.ac.uk
URL: www.recal.org.uk
Librarian: Heather Smart
Founded: 1983
Type: Medicine.
Hours open: Mon–Fri: 9am–5pm.
Users: Staff and students of the University. Others, reference only.
Lending: To all staff and students of the University. Interlibrary loans.
Stock policy: All stock archived.
Holdings: 8,000 books; 130 current journal subscriptions.
Library management system: ALICE.
Computerized services: RECAL Bibliographic Database. Subscription via website.
Library publications: RECAL Current Awareness (26 issues p.a.).
Special collections: Prosthetics; orthotics; rehabilitation.
Collaborative networks: SHINE.

National Children's Bureau

8 Wakley Street
London EC1V 7QE
Tel: 020 7843 6000

Fax: 020 7843 6008
E-mail: library@ncb.org.uk
URL: www.ncb.org.uk
Librarian: Nicola Hilliard
Prof. staff: Wendy Beecher; Anna Kassman-McKerrell; Tricia Murphy; Claire O'Kane; Jayne Parkin
Founded: 1963
Type: Children; Multidisciplinary.
Hours open: Mon–Fri: 10am–5pm.
Users: Members and staff of the Bureau. Non-members pay a daily charge.
Lending: To staff only.
Stock policy: Disposed of or relegated to basement.
Holdings: 20,000 books; 250 current journal subscriptions, 300 journal titles.
Library management system: InMagic.
Library publications: ChildData CD-ROM; ChildData Abstracts; Childstats; Children in the News; Conferences and Events; Highlights – key research findings.
Special collections: Early years; play.
Collaborative networks: CHILL.

National Information Centre for Speech & Laryngology Therapy

Department of Human Communication Science Library
University College London
Chandler House
2 Wakefield Street
London WC1N 1PG
Tel: 020 76579 4207
Fax: 020 7713 0861
E-mail: hcs.library@ucl.ac.uk
URL: http://library.hcs.ucl.ac.uk
Librarian: Stevie Russell
Type: Academic; Allied Health.
Hours open: Mon–Thurs: 9.30am–5pm; Fri: 10am–5pm.
Users: Staff and students of University College and other academic institutions. Non-members can use the library on payment of a fee.

Lending: To members only. Journals and videos not loaned.

Stock policy: Offered to other libraries within UCL, then within UK, then donated abroad.

Holdings: 6,000 books; 78 current journal subscriptions; 150 videos; 12 CD-ROMs.

Classification: Dewey.

Library management system: ALEPH.

Computerized services: Online access to Web of Science. Access to the Cochrane Library; Embase; Medical Directory; MEDLINE; PsycINFO; Scientific American Medicine.

Special collections: 500 assessment tests in speech and language; archive of historical texts in speech therapy.

Branches: The library is a branch of UCL.

Collaborative networks: North Thames Document Delivery Network; PLCS.

National Institute for Biological Standards & Control (NIBSC)

Blanche Lane
South Mimms
Potters Bar
Hertfordshire EN6 3QG
Tel: 01707 654753 ext. 323/326
Fax: 01707 646845
E-mail: library@nibsc.ac.uk
URL: www.nibsc.ac.uk
Librarian: Anita Brewer
Hours open: Staffed Mon–Fri: 9am–5pm.
Users: Staff of the NIBSC. Other users for reference only by prior arrangement in exceptional circumstances.
Lending: To staff only.
Holdings: 5,000 books; 170 current journal subscriptions, 400 journal titles.
Classification: NLM.
Library management system: Unicorn.
Computerized services: Internet access available. Online access to Dialog. Access to MEDLINE; Web of Science; STN; a few electronic journals.
Library publications: Periodicals catalogue.

Special collections: Subject areas include vaccines, blood products, AIDS, biochemistry, haematology, virology, microbiology, immunology and endocrinology.

National Institute for Medical Research

The Ridgeway
Mill Hill
London NW7 1AA
Tel: 020 8913 8630
Fax: 020 8913 8534
E-mail: library@nimr.mrc.ac.uk
URL: www.nimr.mrc.ac.uk/Library
Librarian: Frank Norman
Prof. staff: Patti Biggs; Ros Wenham
Founded: 1920
Type: Research Institute.
Hours open: Mon–Fri: 9am–5pm.
Users: NIMR staff; MRC staff. Bona fide researchers, on application in writing.
Lending: To recognized libraries only.
Stock policy: Offer to key libraries first, then to lis-medical duplicates or lis-scitech. Then dispose.
Holdings: Approx. 10,000 books; 250 current journal subscriptions, 850 journal titles; 5 CD-ROMs; scientific archives.
Classification: Barnard.
Library management system: Unicorn.
Computerized services: Online access to Crossfire; STN; Ovid MEDLINE/Embase; Web of Science. Access to Current Protocols; Practical Approach.
Library publications: Influenza bibliography.
Special collections: MRC Publications.
Collaborative networks: CHILL; MRC Libraries; RESCOLINC.

National Statistics Information & Library Service

Office for National Statistics
1 Drummond Gate
London SW1V 2QQ

Tel: 0845 6013034
Fax: 01633 652747
E-mail: info@statistics.gov.uk
URL: www.statistics.gov.uk
Founded: 1996
Type: Government; Statistics.
Hours open: Mon–Fri: 9am–5pm.
Users: Free open access to the public.
Lending: To other libraries only.
Stock policy: Will donate to other libraries when appropriate.
Classification: Own.
Special collections: Registrar General reports from 1837; international publications from bodies such as WHO.

National University of Ireland: James Hardiman Library Nursing Library

Galway
Republic of Ireland
Tel: +353 91 544361
Fax: +353 91 527214
E-mail: maire@sulacco.library.nuigalway.ie
Librarian: Maire o hAodha
Founded: 1995
Type: Nursing and Allied Health.
Hours open: Mon–Fri: 9am–8pm; Sat: 9am–1pm.
Users: Nursing students, teaching staff, nurses.
Lending: Students and staff. Clinical co-ordinators on wards.
Stock policy: No old stock as yet.
Holdings: 5,000 books; 76 current journal subscriptions, 80 journal titles; 30 films and videos.
Classification: Dewey.
Library management system: ALEPH.
Computerized services: CINAHL and all at Master Resource Index of James Hardiman Library.
Special collections: Grey literature collection of publications produced in Ireland by voluntary organizations.
Collaborative networks: IHSLG.

National University of Ireland: Medical Library

Clinical Science Institute
National University of Ireland
Galway
Republic of Ireland
Tel: +353 91 524411 ext. 2791
Fax: +353 91 750517
E-mail: timothy.collins@nuigalway.ie
URL: www.library.nuigalsway.ie/mlib.html
Librarian: Tim Collins
Founded: 1970
Type: Medicine; Health Sciences.
Hours open: Mon–Fri: 9.15am–10pm; Sat: 9.15am–1pm. Vacations: Mon–Fri: 9.15am–5.30pm.
Users: Registered students and staff of NUI, Galway. External users by prior appointment.
Lending: To registered students and staff of NUI, Galway only.
Stock policy: Disposal.
Holdings: 6,000 books; 150 current journal subscriptions, 660 journal titles; 120 films and videos; 200 CD-ROMs; 35mm slides; laser discs.
Classification: Dewey.
Library management system: ALEPH.
Computerized services: See website.
Library publications: Factsheets; newsletter.
Special collections: Doherty Collection (obstetrics and gynaecology); grey literature collection.
Collaborative networks: EAHIL; LAI – HSLG; UMSLG.

Neath General Hospital Staff Library

Postgraduate Centre
Bro Morgannwg NHS Trust
Neath General Hospital
Neath SA11 2LQ
Tel: 01639 762369
Fax: 01639 639046
E-mail: sarah.george@bromor-tr.wales.nhs.uk

Librarian: Sarah George
Founded: 1963
Type: Multidisciplinary.
Hours open: Mon–Thurs: 8.30am–4.30pm; Fri: 8.30am–4pm. 24-hour access available with key.
Users: Staff of NHS Trust.
Lending: All staff.
Stock policy: Dispose of it.
Holdings: 5,000 books; 60 current journal subscriptions; 500 films and videos; 20 CD-ROMs.
Classification: NLM (Wessex adaptation).
Computerized services: Access via HOWIS to CINAHL; MEDLINE, etc.
Library publications: Guide to Library Services; Annual Report.
Collaborative networks: AWHILES; AWHL.

Nevill Hall Postgraduate Medical Centre Library

Postgraduate Medical Centre
Nevill Hall Hospital
Brecon Road
Abergavenny
Monmouthshire NP7 7EG
Tel: 01873 732663
Fax: 01873 732662
E-mail: r.benham@virgin.net
Librarian: Mrs Elizabeth Lewis
Founded: 1970s
Type: Clinical Medicine; soon to be fully Multidisciplinary.
Hours open: Mon–Fri: 9am–5pm. 24-hour access for reference.
Users: Trust staff only; local GPs; medical and nursing students on placement.
Lending: As above; other medical libraries within Wales. No lending to anyone else.
Stock policy: Old stock disposed of.
Holdings: 2,400 books; 40 current journal subscriptions; 100 videos; 25 CD-ROMs; pamphlets.
Classification: Dewey.

Library management system: Microsoft Access.
Computerized services: Networked access to intranet and HOWIS. Access to Cochrane Library.
Collaborative networks: AWHILES; AWHL; HOWIS.

Newcastle General Hospital: Neurosciences Library

Regional Neurosciences Centre
Newcastle General Hospital
Westgate Road
Newcastle-upon-Tyne NE4 6BE
Tel: 0191 273 8811
Fax: 0191 256 3150
E-mail: bill.frew@nuth.northy.nhs.uk
Librarian: Bill Frew
Founded: 1964
Type: Clinical Neurosciences.
Hours open: Mon–Thurs: 8am–4pm; Fri: 8am–3.30pm.
Users: Staff.
Lending: Staff.
Stock policy: Pass on.
Holdings: 14 current journal subscriptions, 23 journal titles; 12 films and videos; 20 CD-ROMs.
Classification: Dewey.
Library management system: Microsoft Access.
Computerized services: Trust intranet and local university nets. Access via Ovid to MEDLINE. Online access to journals.
Special collections: Limited edition facsimiles of classic historical medical textbooks.
Collaborative networks: HLN.

Newcastle General Hospital: Tomlinson Teaching Centre Library

Westgate Road
Newcastle upon Tyne NE4 6BE
Tel: 0191 273 8811 ext. 22545

Fax: 0191 219 5044
E-mail: nghlib@nghlib.demon.co.uk
Librarian: Kati Russell
Founded: 1966
Type: Multidisciplinary.
Hours open: Mon, Tues and Wed: 9am–6pm; Thurs–Fri: 9am–5pm. 24-hour key access for medical staff.
Users: All healthcare practitioners working within Newcastle and North Tyneside area. Others at the discretion of the library staff.
Lending: All staff working for the NNN Mental Health Trust and healthcare practitioners working within Newcastle and North Tyneside area.
Stock policy: Old stock discarded.
Holdings: 6,500 books; 124 current journal titles, 150 journal titles; 4 videos; 2 CD-ROMs.
Classification: Dewey.
Library management system: SydneyPLUS.
Computerized services: Online access to Data-Star. Access to BNI; CINAHL; Cochrane Library; Embase: Psychiatry; MEDLINE; PsycINFO.
Library publications: Journal holdings list; library bulletin; library guide.
Special collections: Medical History (120 volumes).
Branches: Mental Health Library, St Nicholas Hospital.
Collaborative networks: HLN; PLCS.

Newcomb Library

Homerton Hospital NHS Trust
Homerton Row
London E9 6SR
Tel: 020 8510 7751
Fax: 020 8510 7281
E-mail: newcomb.library@homerton.nhs.uk
URL: www.newcolib.demon.co.uk
Librarian: Isabel Cantwell
Prof. staff: Heather Mills; Sophie Robinson
Founded: 1986
Type: Multidisciplinary

Hours open: Mon: 11am–8pm; Tues–Fri: 9am–8pm.
Users: All staff from Homerton Hospitals NHS Trust, City and Hackney Primary Care NHS Trust, East London and the City Mental Health NHS Trust. Medical students from the St Bartholomew's and Royal London School of Medicine and Dentistry, Queen Mary and Westfield College. Nursing students from City University. All healthcare personnel in the area served by the Trusts. Members of other organizations which make appropriate contributions to the budget. HA and CHC members of staff.
Lending: Registered members with full library privileges. Reference only to those with reader status who are not staff of Trusts within the health economy or students from affiliated organizations. Regional interlibrary loan scheme.
Stock policy: All books older than 10 years are discarded. They are offered to other libraries; if not required they are sold to library members/visitors having been stamped with a caution notice stating that the information contained within may be out of date.
Holdings: 5,000 books; 148 current journal subscriptions; 405 journal titles, including electronic journals; 6 CD-ROMs.
Classification: NLM.
Library management system: DB/TextWorks.
Computerized services: Access to RCOG Dialog; Medical Directory; NRR. Online access to Binleys. CD-ROM access to Best Evidence; CHAIN; CINAHL; Cochrane Library; MEDLINE; PsycINFO.
Library publications: New books; Annual Report.
Collaborative networks: eNAMHeL; London Region Document Delivery Service; NULJ; North East London Workforce Development Confederation.

Newham Healthcare NHS Trust Library

Newham Hospital
Glen Road
Plaistow
London E13 8SL
Tel: 020 7363 8016
Fax: 020 7363 8087
E-mail: library@newlib.demon.co.uk
URL: www.newlib.demon.co.uk/library.htm
Librarian: Mrs Angela Head
Prof. staff: Mrs Terry Visram
Founded: 1974
Type: Multidisciplinary.
Hours open: Mon, Tues: 8.30am–7pm; Wed–Fri: 8.30am–5pm.
Users: All staff of Newham Healthcare NHS Trust; Newham Primary Care Trust; East London and the City Mental Health Trust. Medical students from St Bartholomews and Royal London School of Medicine. Nursing students from City University. Others for reference use only, by arrangement.
Lending: All full members can borrow books. Reference only for non-members.
Stock policy: Old books are discarded. Journals offered via various co-operative schemes.
Holdings: 7,000 books; 120 current journal subscriptions; 18 videos; 30 CD-ROMs.
Classification: NLM.
Library management system: DB/TextWorks.
Computerized services: Online access to Ovid Biomed. Access to ASSIA for Health; BNI; CINAHL; Cochrane Library; HMIC; London Dysmorphology.
Library publications: Careers Information (Careers Related to Medicine); Careers Information (Nurses); Careers Information (Doctors).
Special collections: Material on postgraduate opportunities in medicine and related topics within the UK. Prospectuses, guidelines from training bodies, etc.
Branches: East Ham Memorial Hospital, Shrewsbury Road, London E7 (psychiatric collection); St Andrew's Hospital Library, Devons Road, London E3.
Collaborative networks: LIBNEL; London Region (NHS).

NHS Direct Online

Highcroft
Romsey Road
Winchester
Hampshire SO22 5DH
Tel: 01962 872208
Fax: 01962 849079
E-mail: nhsdo@hfht.org
URL: www.nhsdirect.nhs.uk
Librarian: Bob Gann (Director)
Prof. staff: Mat Jordan (Content Manager); Gerard Murray (Business Manager)
Founded: 1999
Type: Consumer health information.

NHS Direct West Midlands

West Midlands Ambulance Service NHS Trust
4th Floor, Falcon House
6 The Minories
Dudley
West Midlands DY2 8PN
Tel: 01384 215555
Fax: 01384 215559
E-mail: healthpoint@dial.pipex.com
URL: www.wmas.org
Prof. staff: Edwina Riley; Tim Roberts; John Robinson
Founded: 1992
Type: Public Health Information; Nursing.
Hours open: 24 hours 7 days via NHS Direct. Staffed Mon–Fri: 8am–6pm.
Users: NHS Direct; helpline advisors including nurses.
Lending: Mostly nurses.
Holdings: Small collection of books; 15 current journal subscriptions; Asian language films and videos.
Classification: Adapted Plaintree.

Library management system: Communicator.

Computerized services: Internet access. CD-ROM access to CINAHL; MEDLINE; WM Health Research.

Special collections: Non-English health resources (in development)

Collaborative networks: FIRST; NHS Direct Information Group; WMRHLN.

NHS Executive: London & South East Regional Offices

Library and Information Centre
40 Eastbourne Terrace
London W2 3QR
Tel: 020 7725 5400
Fax: 020 7725 2715
E-mail: ebtlibra@doh.gov.uk
Librarian: Steve Whitlam
Prof. staff: Anh Tran
Founded: 1996
Type: Health Management.
Hours open: Mon–Fri: 9am–5pm.
Users: Staff working at the Regional Offices. Limited self-help enquiry service provided to NHS staff and students in the two regions.
Lending: Members only; other medical libraries in London and South East.
Stock policy: Passed to staff in Regional Offices, remainder offered to other libraries.
Holdings: 6,000 books; 100 current journal subscriptions, 130 journal titles; 20 videos; 20 CD-ROMs.
Classification: BLISS.
Library management system: Unicorn.
Computerized services: Online access to Dialog; Lexis-Nexis. Access to ASSIA; BNI; CancerLit; Caredata; ChildData; CINAHL; Cochrane Library; HealthStar; HMIC; MEDLINE; NRR; PsychLit.
Special collections: NHS Ethnic Health Unit collections.
Collaborative networks: Department of Health Libraries Network; NTRLS; STLIS.

NHS Executive: North West Regional Office

930–932 Birchwood Boulevard
Millennium Park
Birchwood
Warrington WA3 7QN
E-mail: Shan.Annis.doh.gsi.gov.uk
Librarian: Shan Annis

NHS Executive: South East Region (Oxford Unit)

Health Care Libraries Unit
Level 3
Academic Centre
John Radcliffe Hospital
Oxford OX3 9DU
Tel: 01865 221951
Fax: 01865 220040
E-mail: jane.brittain@hclu.ox.ac.uk
URL: http://wwwlibjr2.ox.ac.uk
Librarian: Jane Brittain
Prof. staff: Anne Brice
Founded: 1970
Type: Regional Library Unit.
Hours open: Mon–Fri: 9am–5pm.
Users: Services available to members of the network (HeLIN) in the NHS Region.
Lending: Small professional collection for lending to members of the network.
Stock policy: Outdated stock is disposed of.
Classification: NLM (Wessex adaptation).
Library publications: Anglia and Oxford Union List of Periodicals; Anglia and Oxford Directory of Libraries and Librarians.
Collaborative networks: HeLIN.

NHS Executive: South West Region

Information and Library Services Development
Academic Centre
Frenchay Hospital
Bristol BS16 1LE
Tel: 0117 918 6741

Fax: 0117 975 7060
E-mail: sally.hernando@north-bristol.swest.
nhs.uk
val.trinder@north-bristol.swest.nhs.uk
URL: www.soton.ac.uk/~swhclu/
Librarian: Sally Hernando (Head of Division)
Prof. staff: Valerie Trinder (Assistant Head
of Division)
Founded: 1999
Type: Regional Co-ordinating and
Development Unit.
Hours open: Mon–Fri: office hours.
Answerphone when office unattended.
Users: All NHS library staff in the Region;
NHS Trusts; Health Authorities;
Postgraduate Deaneries and Workforce
Development Confederation; NHS Executive
Regional Office staff.
Computerized services: Online access
via SWICE to AMED; ASSIA for Health; BNI;
CINAHL; Embase; HMIC; Martindale;
MEDLINE; PsychLit and BMJ portfolio of
electronic journals.
Library publications: e-SWRLIN News;
ILSD Annual Report.
Collaborative networks: SWRLIN.

NHS Executive: Trent Library

Fullwood House
Old Fullwood Road
Sheffield S10 3TH
Tel: 0114 282 0481
Fax: 0114 230 6956
Librarian: Glenis Roddis
Hours open: Mon–Fri: 8.30am–5pm.
Notes: For further details see website
www.telh.nhs.uk

NHS Northern & Yorkshire Regional Office

John Snow House
Durham University Science Park
Durham DH1 3YG
Tel: 0191 301 1326
Fax: 0191 301 1460

E-mail: catherine.smith@doh.gsi.gov.uk
Librarian: Mrs Catherine Smith
Prof. staff: Mrs Catherine Graham
Founded: 1979
Type: Health Management and Policy.
Hours open: Mon–Fri: 9am–5pm.
Users: NHS staff are free to visit the library.
Other users by prior appointment. Anyone
can contact the service by telephone.
Lending: Loans to Regional Office staff,
Department of Health staff and NHS staff in
the Region only.
Stock policy: Offered to other libraries and
sent to British Library.
Holdings: 8,500 books; 45 current journal
subscriptions, 80 journal titles; 10 CD-
ROMs.
Classification: UDC.
Library management system: Unicorn
(main catalogue); Lotus Notes for in-house
library services.
Computerized services: Internet and
intranet access. Online access to Dialog.
Regional subscriptions to databases.
Library publications: Monthly Bulletin;
Government Publications Monthly.
Collaborative networks: HLN; HMLF.

Ninewells Medical Library

University of Dundee
Ninewells Hospital and Medical School
Dundee DD1 9SY
Tel: 01382 632515/632519
Fax: 01382 566179
E-mail: medlib@library.dundee.ac.uk
URL: www.dundee.ac.uk/library
Librarian: D A Orrock
Prof. staff: M J Franklin
Founded: 1974
Type: All Medicine, principally Clinical
Medicine.
Hours open: Mon–Fri: 9am–10pm; Sat: 12
noon–5pm. Vacations: Mon–Fri: 9am–5pm;
plus limited evening and weekend hours.
Users: Dundee University staff and students.
Tayside NHS Trusts employees.

Lending: To all registered users.
Stock policy: Disposal.
Holdings: 14,000 books; 500 current journal subscriptions.
Classification: NLM (modified).
Library management system: Dynix.
Computerized services: Online access to Cochrane Library and MEDLINE.
Special collections: Historical collection.
Collaborative networks: SHINE.

Nobles Hospital Postgraduate Medical Library

Postgraduate Medical Centre
Westmoreland Road
Douglas
Isle of Man IM1 4QA
Tel: 01624 642377
Fax: 01624 611922
E-mail: postgrad@dhss.gov.im
Librarian: Mrs Christine Sugden
Founded: 1975
Type: Medical.
Hours open: Mon–Thurs: 8.30am–5pm; Fri: 8.30am–4.30pm. 24-hour access for medical staff.
Users: Mainly medical but open to all health-care staff on the island. Other users, including the public, at the discretion of the Librarian.
Lending: Reference only at present. Loan system to be introduced in the future.
Stock policy: Sold off and the remainder discarded.
Holdings: 3,000 books; 77 current journal subscriptions, 119 journal titles; 20 CD-ROMs.
Classification: NLM (Wessex adaptation).
Library management system: Heritage IV.
Computerized services: Online access to AMED; BNI; CINAHL; Embase; HMIC. Access to BNI; Cochrane Library; HMIC; MEDLINE via Ovid.
Collaborative networks: BL; BMA; JR; LIHNN; NULJ.

Norfolk & Norwich University Hospital NHS Trust: Sir Thomas Browne Library

Teaching Centre
Norfolk and Norwich University Hospital
Colney Lane
Norwich NR1 3SR
Tel: 01603 286892
Fax: 01603 287459
E-mail: bridget.cole@norfolk-norwich.thenhs.com
Librarian: Mrs Bridget Cole
Prof. staff: Mr John Losasso
Founded: 1973
Type: Multidisciplinary.
Hours open: Mon, Wed, Thurs: 9am–5.30pm; Tues: 9am–8pm; Fri: 9am–5pm.
Users: Trust employees, Norwich Community Health Trust employees, GPs, dentists, Norwich City College students and staff, USA nursing/OPT students on placement.
Lending: Members only.
Stock policy: Disposed of after offering for sale to library users.
Holdings: 10,000 books; 200 current journal subscriptions, 290 journal titles.
Classification: NLM.
Library management system: Dynix.
Computerized services: Online access via Ovid to AMED; CINAHL. Access to Cochrane Library; MEDLINE; NRR.
Special collections: Small collection of books on Norfolk doctors.
Branches: West Norwich Hospital.
Collaborative networks: ANGLES; HeLIN; NULJ.
Notes: As from October 2001 the Norfolk and Norwich Hospital Library Service and the West Norwich Hospital, Woodlands House Library will be combined. Address and phone details as above but other details may change.

Norfolk Health Authority Library

St Andrew's House

Northside
St Andrew's Business Park
Norwich NR7 0HT
Tel: 01603 307258
Fax: 01603 307258
E-mail: rosemary.stark@norfolk.nhs.uk
Librarian: Rosemary Stark
Founded: 1995
Type: Health Management; developing a multidisciplinary service.
Hours open: Mon–Fri: 9am–5pm.
Users: Health Authority staff; PCG/PCT staff. Others by prior arrangement.
Lending: To Health Authority staff in Norfolk. Borrowers must register.
Stock policy: Old stock offered to staff prior to disposal.
Holdings: 4,830 books; 47 current journal subscriptions, 87 journal titles.
Classification: NLM (Wessex adaptation).
Library management system: DB/TextWorks.
Computerized services: Online access via Ovid to AMED; CINAHL; MEDLINE. Access via NeLH to Clinical Evidence; Cochrane Library; NRR. Access to Best Evidence; BNI and HMIC.
Collaborative networks: ANGLES; BL; BMA; HeLIN.

North & East Devon Health Authority Library

Dean Clarke House
Southernhay East
Exeter
Devon EX1 1PQ
Tel: 01392 275339
E-mail: jeff.skinner@nedevon-ha.swest.nhs.uk
URL: www.ex.ac.uk/library/eml/nedhalib
Librarian: Jeff Skinner
Type: Health Management.
Hours open: Mon, Tues, Thurs: 9am–3pm; Fri: 9am–12.30pm.

Users: Health Authority staff and other health professionals in the Exeter area. Other people on request.
Lending: Normally Health Authority staff but can be flexible.
Stock policy: Usually dispose of it.
Holdings: 5,000 books; 20 current journal subscriptions, 35 journal titles.
Classification: NLM (Wessex adaptation).
Library management system: Home-made system in Sequel.
Computerized services: Access to various databases and electronic journals.
Collaborative networks: SWRLIN.

North & East Devon Partnership NHS Trust Library

Wonford House Hospital
Dryden Road
Exeter
Devon EX2 5AF
Tel: 01392 403449
Fax: 01392 403492
E-mail: mary.smith@edchs-tr.swest.nhs.uk
Librarian: Mrs Mary Smith
Type: Mental Health.
Hours open: Mon–Wed: 8.30am–4.30pm; Thurs–Fri: 8.30am–2.30pm. Registered users, 24-hour access.
Users: Employees of Trust and local PCTs. Other health professionals and university students welcome to use the library for reference only.
Lending: As above.
Stock policy: Old stock that is not kept is offered to readers with an interest in archival material. Anything too old to be of clinical value or archival use is disposed of.
Holdings: 3,000 books; 76 current journal subscriptions, 162 journal titles; 12 videos; 1 CD-ROM.
Classification: Royal College of Psychiatrists.
Library management system: Microsoft Access.

Computerized services: Online access to AMED; ASSIA; BNI; CINAHL; Embase; HMIC; MEDLINE; PsycINFO.
Collaborative networks: NAMHEL; SWRLIN.

North & Mid Hampshire Health Authority Staff Library

Education Centre
Harness House
Aldermaston Road
Basingstoke
Hampshire RG24 9NB
Tel: 01256 312231
Fax: 01256 312299 (not in library)
E-mail: natalie.grimes@gw.nm-ha.swest. nhs.uk
Librarian: Natalie Grimes
Hours open: Mon, Tues, Thurs: 1pm–5pm; Wed, Fri: 11am–4.30pm.
Collaborative networks: STLIS.

North Cumbria Acute Hospitals NHS Trust: Cumberland Infirmary Education Centre Library

Education Centre
Cumberland Infirmary
Carlisle
Cumbria CA2 7HY
Tel: 01228 814878/9
Fax: 01228 814843
E-mail: library@ncumbria-acute.nhs.uk
Librarian: Post vacant
Founded: 1986
Type: Multidisciplinary.
Hours open: Mon–Thurs: 9am–5pm; Fri: 9am–4.30pm.
Users: Health Authority staff. Restricted services available to students on placement. Paid external membership available at the discretion of the librarian.
Lending: To employees of the Health Authority. Restricted lending to students on placement and external members.

Stock policy: Books and journals discarded after varying periods.
Holdings: 12,300 books; 142 current journal subcriptions, 293 journal titles; 95 videos; 34 CD-ROMs.
Classification: NLM (Wessex adaptation).
Library management system: TINLIB.
Computerized services: Internet access to AMED; Best Evidence; CINAHL; Cochrane Library; MEDLINE; Full Text Journals @ Ovid.
Library publications: Journal holdings; library guides; online searching guides.
Special collections: Local history relating to the hospital.
Collaborative networks: HLN.

North Cumbria Acute Hospitals NHS Trust: West Cumberland Hospital Education Centre Library

Whitehaven
Cumbria CA28 8JG
Tel: 01946 693181 ext. 2537
Fax: 01946 523554
E-mail: PLIBRARY@carlh-tr.northy.nhs.uk
Librarian: Mrs Margaret A Halstead
Type: Multidisciplinary.
Hours open: Mon, Tues, Thurs: 8am–5pm; Wed: 8am–5.30pm; Fri: 8am–4.15pm.
Users: Hospital staff; health service workers within the area. Others may use the library by arrangement.
Lending: To registered borrowers. Interlibrary loans.
Stock policy: Normally dispose of, because not worth passing on.
Holdings: 6,510 books; 97 current journal subscriptions, 119 journal titles; 40 films and videos; 20 CD-ROMs.
Classification: Dewey.
Library management system: SydneyPLUS.
Computerized services: Online access to BMJ Journals; Clinical Evidence; EBMR;

Journals @ Ovid. Access to AMED; CINAHL; Cochrane Library; MEDLINE.

Library publications: Library guide; guide to online services.

Collaborative networks: HLN; NULJ; Yorkshire Health Libraries Union List.

North Cumbria Mental Health & Learning Disabilities NHS Trust Library

Geltwood House
The Carleton Clinic
Cumwhinton Drive
Carlisle
Cumbria CA1 3SX
Tel: 01228 602107
Fax: 01228 602017
E-mail: val.bye@nlhc-tr.northy.nhs.uk
Librarian: Valerie Bye
Founded: 1970s
Type: Psychiatry and Psychology.
Hours open: Mon, Thurs: 9am–4pm; Tues, Fri: 9am–12.30pm. Access at all times.
Users: Members of NHS Trust staff. Students of St Martin's College.
Lending: As above.
Stock policy: Dispose of books; offer journals to libraries in Region before disposal.
Holdings: 1,200 books; 40 current journal subscriptions, 67 journal titles; 4 CD-ROMs.
Classification: Dewey.
Computerized services: Online access to BNI. CD-ROM access to CINAHL; Cochrane Library; MEDLINE; NRR.
Collaborative networks: HLN; NULJ; PLCS.

North Derbyshire Health Library

Scarsdale
Newbold Road
Chesterfield
Derbyshire S41 7PF
Tel: 01246 231255
Fax: 01246 557704

Librarian: David Brunt
Type: Health Management.
Hours open: Mon, Wed: 9.30am–4.30pm; Fri: 9.30am–12noon.
Users: Health Authority staff. Other NHS staff in North Derbyshire.
Lending: As above.
Stock policy: Material of local interest offered to County Record Office.
Holdings: 4,500 books; 71 current journal subscriptions, 157 journal titles.
Classification: NLM.
Library management system: DB/TextWorks.
Computerized services: Internet access. Online access to Ovid.
Library publications: Library guide; monthly e-mail bulletin.
Collaborative networks: DIG.

North East Lincolnshire NHS Trust

Education Centre Library
Grimsby Hospital
Scartho Road
Grimsby
North East Lincolnshire DN33 2BA
Tel: 01472 875275
Fax: 01472 875329
Librarian: Ms Jo Thomas
Hours open: Mon–Thurs: 8.30am–8pm; Fri: 8.30am–4.30pm.
Notes: For further details see website www.telh.nhs.uk

North Essex Health Authority Library & Information Service

8 Collingwood Road
Witham
Essex CM8 2TT
Tel: 01376 302247
Fax: 01376 302357
E-mail: barbara.norrey@ne-ha.nthames. nhs.uk
Librarian: Barbara Norrey

Founded: 1995
Type: Health Policy and Public Health.
Hours open: 9.30am–4.30pm.
Users: North Essex Health Consortia staff. Outside users can be provided with information on request.
Lending: Members.
Stock policy: Pass it on to others within the Region if required.
Holdings: 3,000 books; 23 current journal subscriptions; 10 CD-ROMs; grey literature.
Classification: South Thames Regional Library West Index.
Library management system: DB/TextWorks and WebPublisher.
Computerized services: Access via Ovid to Best Evidence; CINAHL; MEDLINE; PsychLit. Access via MIRON to ASSIA; Cochrane Library; Embase; HMIC.
Library publications: Locality profiles for North Essex; mortality data for North Essex.
Collaborative networks: Eastern Region Libraries Unit; Essex Consortia Libraries Group; NTRLS.

North Essex Hospitals' Library & Information Service

Library
Colchester General Hospital
Turner Road, Colchester
Essex CO4 5JL
Tel: 01206 742146
Fax: 01206 742107
E-mail: library.service@essexrivers.nhs.uk
Librarian: Sara Stock
Prof. staff: Stephanie Picton
Type: Multidisciplinary.
Hours open: Mon–Thurs: 9am–7pm; Fri: 9am–4.40pm.
Users: Local NHS staff; students on placement, etc. Limited access to private health staff in training. Others at discretion of Librarian.
Lending: To full members.
Stock policy: Dispose of or pass to relevant departments.

Holdings: 4,460 books; 140 current journal subscriptions, 206 journal titles.
Classification: NLM.
Library management system: DB/TextWorks.
Computerized services: Access to CINAHL; Cochrane Library; HMIC; MEDLINE; NRR; PsycINFO.
Special collections: fair-sized mental health collection catering for 2 local Mental Health Trusts
Collaborative networks: NTRLS; NULJ; PLCS.

North Glamorgan NHS Trust Library

Prince Charles Hospital
Merthyr Tydfil CF47 9DT
Tel: 01685 728251
Fax: 01685 721816
E-mail: linda.foster@nglan-tr.wales.nhs.uk
Librarian: Linda Foster
Prof. staff: Sian Griffiths
Founded: 1978
Type: Multidisciplinary.
Hours open: Mon–Wed: 9am–8pm; Thurs–Fri: 9am–5pm.
Users: All registered staff of the North Glamorgan NHS Trust. GPs within the Trust area. Students of the School of Care Sciences, University of Glamorgan. Undergraduate students of the University of Wales College of Medicine.
Lending: Members only.
Holdings: 6,000 books; 194 current journal subscriptions; 207 videos; 50 CD-ROMs.
Classification: Dewey.
Library management system: LIMES.
Computerized services: Access to all databases via HOWIS including AMED; ASSIA; BNI; CancerLit; CINAHL; Cochrane Library; EBMR; Embase; HealthStar; HMIC; MEDLINE; PsycINFO; WeBNF. Access to Best Evidence; UpToDate.
Library publications: Current journals holding list; guides to searching various

databases; library guide; list of reports and grey literature; video holdings list.

Collaborative networks: AWHILES; AWHL.

North Hampshire Hospital Healthcare Library

North Hampshire Hospital
Aldermaston Road
Basingstoke
Hampshire RG21 9NA
Tel: 01256 313169
Fax: 01256 461129
E-mail: library@bas.swest.nhs.uk
URL: http://healthcarelibrary.org.uk
Librarian: Catherine Cade
Prof. staff: P. Bradley; J. Mayhew; R. Southon
Type: Multidisciplinary.
Hours open: Mon, Wed, Thurs: 8.30am–5pm; Tues: 8.30am–7pm; Fri: 8.30am–4.30pm. 24-hour access available.
Users: NHS employees in Basingstoke and the surrounding area and students on placement.
Lending: To registered users.
Stock policy: Disposal as per regional guidelines.
Holdings: 14,000 books; 150 current journal subscriptions, 200 journal titles; 150 videos.
Classification: NLM.
Library management system: Heritage.
Computerized services: Access to AMED; CINAHL; Cochrane Library; Embase; MEDLINE; PsycINFO. CD-ROM access to BNI.
Library publications: Quick Guide to Basic Literature Searching Skills; introductory guides.
Collaborative networks: HATRICS; STLIS; SWRLIN.

North Manchester Healthcare NHS Trust: Joint Education Library

Postgraduate Medical Centre
North Manchester General Hospital
Delaunays Road
Crumpsall
Manchester M8 5RN
Tel: 0161 720 2718/2722
Fax: 0161 720 2443
E-mail: Deborah.Dunton@mail.nmanhc-tr.nwest.nhs.uk
Librarian: Deborah Dunton
Founded: 1973
Type: Multidisciplinary.
Hours open: Mon–Thurs: 8.30am–8pm; Fri: 8.30am–4.30pm. July and August: Mon,Tues, Thurs: 8.30am–5pm; Wed: 8.30am–8pm; Fri: 8.30am–4.30pm.
Users: All Trust staff and Community NHS staff. Non-members may use for reference only.
Lending: To members only.
Stock policy: Sell to readers or dispose.
Holdings: 4,000 books; 100 current journal subscriptions
Classification: Dewey.
Library management system: DB/TextWorks.
Computerized services: Internet access available. CD-ROM access to BNI; CINAHL; Cochrane Library; MEDLINE.
Collaborative networks: BMA; LIHNN; NULJ.

North Middlesex Hospital NHS Trust: Ferriman Information & Library Service

North Middlesex Hospital NHS Trust
Sterling Way
Edmonton
London N18 1QX
Tel: 020 8887 2223
Fax: 020 8887 2714
E-mail: libnm1@mdx.ac.uk

Librarian: Linda Farley
Prof. staff: John Buchanan; Katrina Wilson
Founded: 1989
Type: Multidisciplinary.
Hours open: Mon, Tues, Thurs: 9am–7pm; Wed: 8am–6pm; Fri: 9am–6pm; Sat: 9am–12 noon. Vacations: Mon–Fri: 9am–6pm.
Users: Staff of North Middlesex Hospital NHS Trust; students and staff of Middlesex University; staff working within the local consortium area. Anyone else can pay to join.
Lending: To all members, and other libraries in the London NHS Region.
Stock policy: If out of date and potentially dangerous, discard. Otherwise offer for sale. Journals offered to other libraries.
Holdings: 13,500 books; 150 current journal subscriptions, 200 journal titles; 40 CD-ROMs.
Classification: NLM.
Library management system: Heritage.
Computerized services: Online access to Ovid Biomed. Access to AMED; BNI; CINAHL; Embase; MEDLINE.
Collaborative networks: NTRLS.

North Nottinghamshire Health Authority Resource Centre

Ransom Hall
Southwell Road West
Rainworth
Mansfield
Nottinghamshire NG21 0ER
Tel: 01623 414114 ext. 4584
Fax: 01623 414117
E-mail: alison.sherratt@nnotts-ha.nhs.uk
Librarian: Alison Sherratt
Hours open: Mon–Fri: 9am–5pm.
Notes: For further details see website www.telh.nhs.uk

North Nottinghamshire Resources & Information Centre

72 Portland Street
Kirkby-in-Ashfield
Nottinghamshire NG17 7AE
Tel: 01623 751984 ext. 25
Fax: 01623 752457
E-mail: jackiebetts@ach.cnhc-tr.trent.nhs.uk
Librarian: Jackie Betts (Resources and Information Manager).
Founded: 1983
Type: Multidisciplinary.
Hours open: Mon, Tues, Thurs: 9am–4.30pm; Wed: 9am–12.30pm; Fri: 9am–4pm.
Users: Anyone learning or working in North Nottinghamshire with an interest in health promotion.
Lending: Members only.
Stock policy: Disposal.
Holdings: 1,045 books; 10 current journal subscriptions; 278 films and videos; 16 CD-ROMs.
Classification: In-house.
Library management system: Headfast.
Computerized services: Internet access. Access to PatientWise.
Library publications: Newsletter.

North Staffordshire Medical Institute Library

North Staffordshire Medical Institute
Hartshill Road
Hartshill
Stoke-on-Trent
Staffordshire ST4 7NY
Tel: 01782 554198
Fax: 01782 715422
E-mail: nsmilib@dial.pipex.com
URL: www.nsmilib@dial.pipex.com
Librarian: Irene Fenton
Prof. staff: Philip Hall; Alison Hughes; David Rogers; Stephen Sharp; Susan Wright
Founded: 1965
Type: Multidisciplinary.

Hours open: Mon, Fri: 8.30am–6pm; Tues–Thurs: 8.30am–8.30pm; Sat: 9.30am–1pm.

Users: NHS staff. Other users (reference use).

Lending: To NHS staff.

Stock policy: Out-of-date stock discarded.

Holdings: 4,000 books; 300 current journal subscriptions; 20 CD-ROMs.

Classification: LC.

Library management system: Heritage.

Computerized services: Online access to AMED; Clinical Evidence; Cochrane Library; MEDLINE. Internet and CD-ROM access to CINAHL.

Library publications: Library Guide; Newsletter.

Collaborative networks: PLCS; WMRHLN.

North Tees Medical Library

Hardwick Road
Stockton-on-Tees
Co Durham TS21 2EZ
Tel: 01642 624789
E-mail: ntelib@hotmail.com
Librarian: John Blenkinsopp
Founded: 1974
Type: Multidisciplinary.
Hours open: Mon–Wed: 9am–5pm; Thurs: 9am–8pm; Fri: 9am–5pm.
Users: Staff of North Tees NHS Trust. External private members scheme (annual fee). Reference access available for all.
Lending: All registered readers.
Stock policy: Sold.
Holdings: 16,000 books; 200 current journal subscriptions, 260 journal titles; 10 films and videos; 20 CD-ROMs.
Classification: Dewey.
Library management system: Bookshelf.
Computerized services: 4 PCs with internet access. Access to AMED; Best Evidence; CINAHL; Cochrane Library; Embase: Psychiatry; MEDLINE; NRR.

Library publications: Library newsletter; series of guides.

Collaborative networks: Durham and Teeside Confederation; Northern Union List; NULJ; Yorkshire Unit List.

North Tyneside Education Centre Library

North Tyneside General Hospital
Rake Lane
North Shields
Tyne and Wear NE29 8NH
Tel: 0191 293 2761
Fax: 0191 293 2763
E-mail: educlib@hotmail.com
Librarian: Jackie McGuire
Prof. staff: Jo Grey
Founded: 1995
Type: Multidisciplinary.
Hours open: Mon–Thurs: 9am–5pm; Fri: 9am–4.30pm.
Users: Northumbria Healthcare NHS Trust staff; student nurses and student midwives. Northumberland Health Authority staff.
Lending: Northumbria Healthcare NHS Trust staff.
Stock policy: Either sold or passed on to a charity.
Holdings: 4,746 books; 179 current journal subscriptions, 229 journal titles; 275 videos; 20 CD-ROMs.
Classification: Dewey.
Library management system: SydneyPLUS.
Computerized services: Access via Ovid to AMED; CINAHL; Cochrane Library; Embase: Psychiatry; MEDLINE.
Collaborative networks: HLN.

North Warwickshire NHS Trust: Brian Oliver Centre Library

Brooklands
Coleshill Road
Marston Green
Birmingham B37 7HL

Tel: 0121 329 4923
Fax: 0121 779 4348
E-mail: margaret.wilson@nw-tr.wmids.nhs.uk
Librarian: Naomi Wills (Library Manager)
Prof. staff: Ian Keeping (Librarian)
Founded: 1998
Type: Psychiatry; Mental Health; Learning Disabilities.
Hours open: Mon–Thurs: 8.30am–4.30pm; Fri: 8.30am–4pm.
Users: Staff employed by North Warwickshire NHS Trust – doctors, nurses, care assistants, psychologists, communication therapists. Non-members can use the library for reference only.
Lending: As above.
Stock policy: Not applicable yet.
Holdings: 1,400 books; 37 current journal subscriptions; 90 journal titles; 56 videos; 5 CD-ROMs; training packs.
Classification: Own – changing to NLM (Wessex adaptation).
Computerized services: Access via Ovid to AMED; BNI; CINAHL; Embase: Psychiatry; MEDLINE; Nursing Collection.
Branches: Lea Castle Library; Manor Library, Nuneaton.

North West Health Library & Information Service

Liverpool Health Authority
24 Pall Mall
Liverpool L3 6AL
Tel: 0151 285 2010
Fax: 0151 285 2264
E-mail: library.services@liverpool-ha.nhs.uk
Librarian: Kieran Lamb
Prof. staff: Tracy Dickinson; Maureen Horrigan
Type: Health Management.
Hours open: Mon–Thurs: 9am–5pm; Fri: 9am–4.30pm.
Users: Health Authority staff in North West Region and Regional Office. Others, reference only.

Lending: As above. LIHNN and NWRLS members.
Holdings: 7,126 books; 50 current journal subscriptions, 60 journal titles; 10 videos; 32 CD-ROMs; 6,821 other materials.
Classification: BLISS.
Library management system: CAIRS.
Computerized services: Access via ADITUS portal to AMED; ASSIA for Health; BNI; CINAHL; Embase; MEDLINE; RPS e-PIC; SERFILE; SIGLE
Library publications: Library Bulletin; weekly abstracts of NHS circulars.
Special collections: Regional Grey Literature Service
Collaborative networks: LIHNN; NWRLS.

North West Region Health Care Libraries Unit

Thelwall House
Warrington Hospital
Lovely Lane
Warrington
Cheshire WA5 1QG
Tel: 01925 662587
Fax: 01925 662588
E-mail: david.stewart@warrh-tr.nwest.nhs.uk
URL: www.lihnn.org.uk
Librarian: David Stewart (Regional Director of Health Libraries)
Prof. staff: Colin Davies (Deputy Director of Health Libraries: IT); Linda Ferguson (Deputy Director of Health Libraries: CPD)
Founded: 1999
Type: Regional Co-ordinating and Development Unit.
Hours open: Mon–Fri: 9am–5pm.
Users: All library staff in the Region. NHS Trusts, Health Authorities, Postgraduate Deaneries and Workforce Development Confederations.
Lending: Staff library available to all staff in the Region.
Stock policy: Disposed of.

Holdings: 200 books; 6 current journal subscriptions.
Computerized services: LISA; Online access via ADITUS Portal to AMED; BNI; CINAHL; Embase; HMIC; MEDLINE; PsychLit.
Library publications: LIHNN Newsletter; Union List of Periodicals for NW Region.
Collaborative networks: LIHNN.

Northamptonshire Health Authority Library & Knowledge Management Services

Highfield
Cliftonville Road
Northampton NN1 5DN
Tel: 01604 615265
Fax: 01604 615270
E-mail: jane.holdsworth@northants-ha. anglox.nhs.uk
URL: 195.105.71.15/library/index.htm (NHSNet only)
Librarian: Jane Holdsworth
Prof. staff: Jane Cooper; Malcolm Robinson; Ann Skinner
Type: Multidisciplinary.
Hours open: Staffed during office hours. Access 24 hours.
Users: All NHS staff and students in Northamptonshire. Others by referral and appointment.
Lending: All members. Non-members by arrangement and fee.
Stock policy: Pass some on and dispose of some.
Holdings: 29,846 books; 548 current journal subscriptions; 235 films and videos.
Classification: NLM and Dewey.
Library management system: Unicorn.
Computerized services: Health Authority and Primary Care Intranet; Data-Star; Access to AMED; BNI; ClinPsych; Embase: Psychiatry; HMIC; MEDLINE.
Library publications: Annual Report; handouts supporting teaching programmes

on 'Finding the Evidence'; Finding Health Information on the Web.
Collaborative networks: ORLIN.

Northamptonshire Health Authority: Cripps Library

Postgraduate Centre
Northampton General Hospital NHS Trust
Northampton NN1 5BD
Tel: 01604 545258
Fax: 01604 545803
E-mail: ann.skinner@northants-ha.anglox.nhs.uk
Librarian: Ann Skinner

Northern and Yorkshire Regional Advisory Service

County Durham Health Authority
Appleton House
Lanchester Road
Durham DH1 5XZ
Tel: 0191 333 3304
Fax: 0191 333 3331
E-mail: john.hewlett@qual-perf.durham-ha. northy.nhs.uk
URL: nyrlas.nhs.uk/
Librarian: John Hewlett (Director)
Regional Librarian (ET&D): Mrs Alison Bramley, Northern and Yorkshire Regional Library Advisory Service, Department of NHS PGMDE, Willow Terrace Road, University of Leeds, Leeds, LS2 9TJ. Tel: 0113 233 1515; Fax: 0113 233 1530. E-mail: a.bramley@yorkshiredeanery.com; 106030.131@compuserve.com
Regional Librarian (IM&T): Mr David Peacock, Northumberland Health Authority, Merley Croft, Loansdean, Morpeth, Northumberland, NE61 2DL. Tel: 01670 394437. Fax: 01670 394501. E-mail: david.peacock@email.nhumberld-ha.northy. nhs.uk

Northern Devon Healthcare Trust Library

North Devon District Hospital
Raleigh Park
Barnstaple
Devon EX31 4JB
Tel: 01271 322363
Fax: 01271 322692
E-mail: library@ndevon.swest.nhs.uk
Librarian: Mrs Alison Housley
Founded: 1979
Type: Multidisciplinary.
Hours open: Mon–Fri: 8.30am–5.30pm. 24-hours access.
Users: All NHS staff working within the North Devon area for Northern Devon Healthcare Trust, North Devon Primary Care Trust and North and East Devon Partnership Trust students on placement. NHS staff from other Trusts in the Somerset, Devon and Cornwall Workforce Development Confederation area. West Country Ambulance Service Trust staff. Private membership available. Visitors, reference only.
Lending: Registered users including those with private membership.
Stock policy: Old stock either sold, sent abroad or disposed of.
Holdings: 7,000 books; 184 current journal subscriptions, 263 journal titles; 16 CD-ROMs.
Classification: NLM (Wessex adaptation).
Library management system: DB/TextWorks.
Computerized services: Online access to AMED; ASSIA for Health; BNI; CINAHL; Cochrane Library; Embase; HMIC; MEDLINE; PsycINFO. Access to BMJ Portfolio of Journals; Data-Star; Martindale.
Library publications: Accessions list; journal holdings; library guides; Schedule of Library Information Skills Courses.
Collaborative networks: NULJ; SWRLIN.

Northern Ireland Health & Social Services Library

Queen's University Medical Library
Institute of Clinical Science
Grosvenor Road
Belfast
Northern Ireland BT12 6BJ
Tel: 028 9032 2043
Fax: 028 9024 7068
E-mail: med.office@qub.ac.uk
URL: www.qub.ac.uk/lib/
Librarian: Gaynor Creighton
Prof. staff: Jean O'Connor; Mildred Saunders; Patricia Watt
Founded: 1849
Type: University Library supporting the Faculty of Medicine and Healthcare.
Hours open: Mon–Fri: 9am–10pm; Sat: 9am–12.30pm. Vacations: Mon–Fri: 9am–5.30pm; Sat: 9am–12.30pm.
Users: Staff and students of Queen's University; Members registered as employees of HPSSPS; associate (paid) members.
Lending: To registered members.
Stock policy: Some is kept for archival purposes, some withdrawn and sent abroad, and some discarded.
Holdings: 112,500 books; 800 current journal subscriptions; 100 films and videos.
Classification: LC.
Library management system: Talis.
Computerized services: Access via Ovid Biomed to BNI; CINAHL; Cochrane Library; HMIC; MEDLINE; Web of Science. CD-ROM access to Caredata; ChildData; EMIMS; HEBS; PsycINFO.
Special collections: 18th and 19th century.collections of manuscripts and books.
Branches: Altnagelvin MDEC Library; Biomedical Library, Belfast City Hospital.

Northern Ireland Regional Libraries Service

Queen's University Medical Library
Institute of Clinical Science

Grosvenor Road
Belfast
Northern Ireland BT12 6BJ
Tel: 028 9032 2043
Fax: 028 9024 7068
Librarian: Gaynor Creighton
E-mail: g.creighton@qub.ac.uk
URL: www.honni.qub.ac.uk

Northern Lincolnshire & Goole Hospitals NHS Trust Healthcare Library

Butterwick House
Scunthorpe General Hospital
Church Lane
Scunthorpe
Lincolnshire DN15 7BH
Tel: 01724 290472
Fax: 01724 290090
E-mail: healthcare.library@sgh-tr.trent.nhs.uk
URL: www.nlg.nhs.uk (hospital website)
Librarian: Vere Conolly
Founded: 1996
Type: Multidisciplinary.
Hours open: Mon–Thurs: 8.30am–5.30pm; Fri: 8.30am–5pm. 24-hour access cards available for £10 deposit.
Users: Employees of the Trust; Scunthorpe Community Trust and University of Hull students and tutors; medical students; external members (£12 p.a. fee).
Lending: All registered users have the right to borrow up to 6 items except medical students and external borrowers who are restricted to 3 items.
Stock policy: Either dispose of or, if appropriate, sell to library users.
Holdings: 10,000 books; 160 current journal subscriptions, 250 journal titles; 450 films and videos.
Classification: NLM.
Library management system: Heritage IV.
Computerized services: Online access to Biomed; BMJ Journals Online. Access to

AMED; BNI; CINAHL; Embase; MEDLINE; PsycINFO.
Collaborative networks: TRAHCLIS.

Northgate Hospital Library

Northgate and Prudhoe NHS Trust
Morpeth
Northumberland NE61 3BE
Tel: 01670 394088
Fax: 01670 394247
E-mail: Paula.Elliott@nap-tr.northy.nhs.uk
Librarian: Paula Elliott
Founded: 1996
Type: Multidisciplinary, supporting Learning and other Disabilities.
Hours open: Mon–Fri: 9am–4pm.
Users: Trust staff and students on placement at the Trust only.
Lending: As above, 4 items for 4 weeks.
Stock policy: Disposed of according to withdrawal policy.
Holdings: 3,000 books; 31 current journal subscriptions, 45 journal titles; 45 films and videos; 5 CD-ROMs; 54 training packs.
Classification: Dewey 21.
Library management system: SydneyPLUS.
Computerized services: Online access to ASSIANet. Access to AMED; CINAHL; MEDLINE; PsycINFO.
Library publications: Leaflets for borrowers.
Branches: Hunters Moor Hospital; Prudhoe Hospital.
Collaborative networks: HLN; PLCS.
Notes: The Trust will be changing its name and holdings will change as the services are reconfigured locally.

Northumberland Health Authority Library

Merley Croft
Loansdean
Morpeth
Northumberland NE61 2DL

Tel: 01670 394496
Fax: 01670 394501
E-mail: library.morpeth@nhumberld-ha.northy.nhs.uk
Librarian: Lynda Cox
Prof. staff: Vasanhi Elder
Founded: 1994
Type: Multidisciplinary.
Hours open: Mon–Fri: 9am–5pm.
Users: Primary care and community staff in Northumberland.
Lending: As above.
Stock policy: Dispose.
Holdings: 6,000 books; 100 current journal subscriptions, 150 journal titles; 20 CD-ROMs.
Classification: Own.
Computerized services: Access to AMED; CINAHL; EBMR; Embase: Psychiatry; HMIC; MEDLINE.
Library publications: Acquisitions list; nursing acquisitions list; Cutting Edge; Buzz.
Collaborative networks: BMA; HLN Union List; NULJ.

Northwick Park & St Mark's Hospitals: John Squire Medical Library

North West London Hospitals NHS Trust
Watford Road
Harrow
Middlesex HA1 3UJ
Tel: 020 8869 3322
Fax: 020 8869 3326
E-mail: jslib@clara.net
URL: www.jslib.clara.net
Librarian: Mike Kendall
Prof. staff: Jill Bruce; Jason Curtis; Lorna Finnegan; Gill Wales
Founded: 1971
Type: Multidisciplinary.
Hours open: Mon–Fri: 9am–6pm; Sat: 10am–4pm (term-time only).
Users: Those employed by Northwick Park and St Mary's NHS Trust and others who are funded to use the library. All others who have a bona fide enquiry and a need to use the resources of the library may use it on a reference only basis.
Lending: Those employed by Northwick Park and St Mary's NHS Trust and others who are funded to use the library may borrow up to 6 items at any one time.
Stock policy: Withdrawn books are offered for sale to readers, then discarded. Withdrawn journals are offered to other libraries within the London Regional Network, and then discarded.
Holdings: 14,000 books; 280 current journal subscriptions; 200 films and videos; 30 CD-ROMs.
Classification: NLM.
Library management system: DB/TextWorks.
Computerized services: Online access to Ovid Biomed and internet. Access to BNI; CINAHL; ClinPsych; Cochrane Library; MEDLINE.
Library publications: Various user guides.
Collaborative networks: London Library and Information Development Network.

Nottingham City Hospital Campus: The Children's Centre

Information and Resources Service
The Children's Centre
Hucknall Road
Nottingham NG5 1PB
Tel: 0115 962 7658
Fax: 0115 962 7915
E-mail: info_serv@childrencentre1.demon.co.uk
Librarian: Ms Lyn Nixon
Hours open: Mon–Tues: 9am–5pm; Wed–Fri: 9am–3.30pm.
Notes: For further details see website www.telh.nhs.uk

Nottingham City Hospital Postgraduate Education Centre Library

City Hospital
Hucknall Road
Nottingham NG5 1PB
Tel: 0115 969 1169 ext. 45736
E-mail: jrule@ncht.trent.nhs.uk
Librarian: John S Rule
Type: Multidisciplinary.
Hours open: Mon–Fri: 9am–5pm.
Users: Mainly NCHT staff and Nottingham University staff and students. Students of other institutions placed in Nottingham. Open to all NHS professionals.
Lending: To members only.
Stock policy: Sold off if possible. Then offered to other libraries (Ethiopia) then disposed of.
Holdings: 5,334 books; 178 current journal subscriptions, 320 journal titles; 112 videos; 3 CD-ROMs.
Classification: NLM. Modified.
Library management system: Heritage.
Computerized services: Online access to Clinical Evidence; Cochrane Library; NeLH. Internet database subscriptions to AMED; CINAHL; Embase; EBMR; MEDLINE; PreMEDLINE; PsycINFO.
Collaborative networks: Nottingham Health Information Forum.

Nottingham Health Informatics Service Library

Nottingham Health Authority
1 Standard Court
Park Row
Nottingham NG1 6GN
Tel: 0115 912 3344
Fax: 0115 912 3351
E-mail: angela.clifford@nottinghm-ha.trent.nhs.uk
Librarian: Angela Clifford (Librarian/Intelligence Co-Ordinator)
Hours open: Mon–Fri: 9am–5pm.

Notes: For further details see website www.telh.nhs.uk

Nottingham Health Informatics Service Resource Centre

Nottingham City PCT
Linden House
261 Beechdale Road
Nottingham NG8 3EY
Tel: 0115 942 8750
Fax: 0115 942 8611
E-mail: resource@nottingham-his.nhs.uk
Librarian: Des Conway
Prof. staff: Liz Doney (Primary Care Knowledge Manager); Sue Sproston (Assistant Librarian); Mandy Tidswell (Assistant Librarian)
Founded: 1991
Type: Multidisciplinary.
Hours open: Mon–Thurs: 9am–4.30pm; Fri: 9am–2pm.
Users: Open to all health and related staff working across Nottingham Health Authority. Current membership 4000. The Centre is part of the new Health Informatics Service hosted by Nottingham City PCT.
Lending: All registered clients. Student nurses restricted to 3 items.
Stock policy: Either dispose of it or leave it out for clients to take.
Holdings: 5,300 books; 100 current journal subscriptions, 105 journal titles; 2,000 films and videos; 20 CD-ROMs; 1,400 other items.
Classification: Own.
Library management system: Headfast.
Computerized services: Access via Trent Knowledge and Library Services Unit to Biomed. Access to AMED; BMJ Journals Collection; BNI; CINAHL; Embase; MEDLINE; PsychLit.
Library publications: Various newsletters and service flyers.
Special collections: drug education; health promotion; health inequalities; primary health care; nurse prescribing; sexual health and teenage pregnancies.

Collaborative networks: BL; BMA; HPRG; Nottingham Health Information Forum; NULJ; Trent Knowledge and Library Services Unit.

Nottingham Healthcare NHS Trust Medical Library

Duncan MacMillan House
Porchester Road
Mapperley
Nottingham NG3 6AA
Tel: 0115 969 1300 ext. 40760
Fax: 0115 969 1882
E-mail: library@medl.demon.co.uk
Librarian: Brian Spencer
Prof. staff: Kate Hudson
Founded: 1960
Type: Multidisciplinary; Mental Health and Learning Disabilities.
Hours open: Mon: 9am–12 noon and 12.30pm–5pm; Tues: 9am–5pm; Wed, Thurs: 9am–6pm; Fri: 9am–4.30pm.
Users: Own staff and others attending courses. External users, reference only and strictly by prior arrangement.
Lending: Own staff and students only.
Stock policy: Sometimes disposal; sometimes offered to others.
Holdings: 7,000 books; 55 current journal subscriptions, 107 journal titles; 15 videos.
Classification: Own and NLM.
Library management system: Heritage.
Computerized services: 3 Internet access points. Access to Biomed website.
Collaborative networks: HIFULOP; NULJ; eNAMHeL.

Nuffield Orthopaedic Centre NHS Trust: Girdlestone Memorial Library

Nuffield Orthopaedic Centre NHS Trust
Windmill Road
Headington
Oxford OX3 7LD
Tel: 01865 227361

Fax: 01865 227362
E-mail: gmlheh@ermine.ox.ac.uk
Librarian: Mrs Eve Hollis
Founded: 1957
Type: Multidisciplinary; Orthopaedics.
Hours open: Mon–Fri: 8am–6pm.
Users: All staff on site. Others by request.
Lending: Registered members only.
Stock policy: Pass on or discard.
Holdings: 4,000 books; 107 current journal subscriptions, 135 journal titles; 24 films and videos; 10 CD-ROMs; 8 audiotapes.
Classification: NLM.
Library management system: DB/TextWorks.
Computerized services: Online access to NHSNet and Oxford University. Access to CINAHL; Cochrane Library; Embase; MEDLINE.
Library publications: Readers Handbook; accessions list.
Special collections: History of orthopaedics.
Collaborative networks: HeLIN.

Old Hall Library

Norwich PCT HQ
Little Plumstead Hospital
Hospital Road
Norwich NR13 5EW
Tel: 01603 711407
Fax: 01603 711483
E-mail: robert.kelly@norwich-pct.nhs.uk
Librarian: Rob Kelly
Founded: 1996
Type: Multidisciplinary (mostly primary care information).
Hours open: Mon–Fri: 9am–5pm.
Users: All staff employed by the Trust. Others by arrangement.
Lending: No restrictions as yet.
Stock policy: Dispose of.
Holdings: 200 books; 20 current journal subscriptions, 33 journal titles; 49 films and videos; 5 CD-ROMs; 8,000 reports, etc.
Classification: NLM.

Library management system: Microsoft Access.

Computerized services: Online access to PubMed and general websites. Access to AMED; CINAHL; Cochrane Library.

Library publications: Current Awareness List.

Collaborative networks: HeLIN.

Oldchurch Hospital Multidisciplinary Library Information Services

Academic Centre
Oldchurch Hospital
Waterloo Road
Romford
Essex RM7 0BE
Tel: 01708 708397
Fax: 01708 708397
E-mail: karenj@romlib.demon.co.uk
Librarian: Karen Johnston
Type: Multidisciplinary Health Care.
Hours open: 9am–5pm. 24-hour coded access to registered users.
Users: Employees of Barking, Havering and Redbridge NHS Trust. Reference only to other local healthcare workers.
Lending: To all registered users/permanent employees. Limited for locum doctors – reference-only service.
Stock policy: Offered to other libraries. Sold for minimum fee 50p.
Holdings: 2,192 books; 73 current journal subscriptions, 82 journal titles; 107 films and videos; 22 CD-ROMs.
Classification: NLM.
Library management system: DB/TextWorks.
Computerized services: Ovid access to AMED; CINAHL; MEDLINE; PsycINFO. Access to BNI; Cochrane Library; MCQ databases.
Branches: Harold Wood Hospital Multidisciplinary Library.
Collaborative networks: LIBNEL.

Open University Library

Walton Hall
Milton Keynes
Buckinghamshire MK7 6AA
Tel: 01908 653530
Fax: 01908 653571
E-mail: oulibrary@open.ac.uk
URL: www.open.ac.uk/library
Librarian: Nicky Whitsed
Prof. staff: Ann Davies (Acting Assistant Director); Liz Mallett (Manager, Interactive Open Learning Centre); Evelyn Simpson (Acting Senior Librarian, IT Development Group); Richard Stubbs (Senior Librarian, Collections and Facilities); Linda Wilks (Information Manager). Plus 34 full-time librarians.
Founded: 1969.
Type: Higher Education.
Hours open: Mon–Thurs: 8.30am–7.30pm; Fri: 9am–5pm; Sat: 10am–1pm.
Users: OU staff and students; other students; local residents; local businesses.
Lending: To OU staff and students. Others on payment of a fee.
Stock policy: Passed on via British Library BookNet or donated to BookAid International.
Holdings: 185,613 books; 2,478 current journal subscriptions, 6,673 journal titles, including electronic; 23,311 films and videos; 202 CD-ROMs; 1,820 microfilm reels; 63,794 slides; 59,022 illustrations; 200 maps.
Classification: Dewey.
Library management system: Voyager.
Computerized services: See website for full lists.
Special collections: Full archive of OU course materials.
Collaborative networks: Milton Keynes Learning City Libraries Network (MKLCLN).

Ormskirk & District General Hospital: Sanderson Library

Postgraduate Graduate Medical Education Centre

Ormskirk and District General Hospital
Wigan Road
Ormskirk
Lancashire L39 2AZ
Tel: 01695 656403
Fax: 01695 656566
E-mail: ormpgmec@hotmail.com
Librarian: Michael Mason
Type: Clinical Medical.
Hours open: Mon–Fri: 9am–5pm. 24-hour access for medical staff.
Users: Medical staff, PAMs, nurses. Employees of Trust only.
Lending: All members.
Classification: Dewey.
Library management system: Heritage.
Computerized services: Access to ADITUS.
Collaborative networks: LIHNN.

Our Lady of Lourdes Hospital: Mother Mary Martin Library

North Eastern Health Board
Drogheda
County Louth
Republic of Ireland
Tel: +353 419 843696
Fax: +353 419 843626
E-mail: jean.harrison@nehb.ie
Librarian: Jean Harrison
Prof. staff: Linda Houghton
Founded: 1993
Type: Multidisciplinary.
Hours open: Mon–Thurs: 9.30am–8pm; Fri: 9.30am–5pm.
Users: Healthcare staff of North Eastern Health Board. Some non-members on payment of an annual fee.
Lending: To all healthcare staff/members of the Library service in NEHB.
Stock policy: Dispose of them.
Holdings: 7,000 books; 150 current journal subscriptions, 200 journal titles; 50 videos; 20 CD-ROMs.
Classification: Dewey.
Library management system: Heritage.

Computerized services: Access to Biomed – MEDLINE. Access to CINAHL; Cochrane Library; DARE; PsycINFO; full-text journals.
Library publications: Library information brochure; list of databases; Guide to Searching for Information; video list.
Branches: Louth County Hospital, Dundalk; Our Lady's Hospital, Navan.
Collaborative networks: Irish Healthcare Libraries Journals Holdings; NULJ.

Our Lady's Hospital for Sick Children Library

Our Lady's Hospital for Sick Children
Crumlin
Dublin 12
Republic of Ireland
Tel: +353 01 4096596
Fax: +353 01 4096596
E-mail: OLHSC.library@ucd.ie
Librarian: Suzanne Feeney
Founded: 1985
Type: Multidisciplinary; Nursing, Medical, Allied Health.
Hours open: Mon–Wed: 9.30am–8pm; Thurs-Fri: 9.30am–5pm. Vacations: Mon–Fri: 9.30am–5pm.
Users: Medical and nursing staff, students, and other hospital staff. Open to outside medical and nursing staff, students and healthcare professionals.
Lending: To Hospital staff and students attending Hospital for training .
Stock policy: Retain approximately 10 core journals. Retention policy 5 years on for other journals. Try to pass on to other libraries and charities.
Holdings: 1,500 books; 100 current journal subscriptions; 2 CD-ROMs.
Classification: Dewey.
Library management system: DB/TextWorks.
Computerized services: Cochrane Library via internet. CD-ROM access to CINAHL; MEDLINE.

Collaborative networks: Irish Healthcare Libraries Journal Holdings List.

Oxford Dementia Centre

Headington Hill Hall
Oxford Brookes University
Oxford OX3 0BP
Tel: 01865 484826
Fax: 01865 484919
E-mail: dementia-info@brookes.ac.uk
URL: www.brookes.ac.uk/dementia
Librarian: Lin Bateson
Founded: 1998
Type: Multidisciplinary Dementia Care.
Hours open: 9.30am–5pm.
Users: Oxford Brookes University staff and students. Care professionals from other organizations.
Lending: Oxford Brookes University staff and students. Photocopy service to others.
Holdings: 1,000 books and reprints; 7 current journal subscriptions; 5 films and videos.
Classification: Own.
Computerized services: All Athens pass-worded sites. Online journals subscribed to by University. Access to Stirling DSDC data-bases.
Collaborative networks: Dementia Services Development Centres.

Parkinson's Disease Society

Ray Kennedy Library
215 Vauxhall Bridge Road
London SW1V 1EJ
Tel: 020 7932 1316
Fax: 020 7233 9908
E-mail: hbarber@parkinsons.org.uk
Librarian: Helen Barber
Founded: 1991
Type: Parkinson's Disease.
Hours open: Mon–Fri: 9am–5pm.
Users: By appointment.
Lending: Reference only.
Holdings: 200 books; 26 current journal sub-scriptions; 100 videos.

Patrick McGrath Library

Broadmoor Hospital Authority
West London Mental Health NHS Trust
Crowthorne
Berkshire RG45 7EG
Tel: 01344 754400
Fax: 01344 754296
E-mail: mail@pmcg-lib.demon.co.uk
Librarian: Mrs Alison Farrar
Prof. staff: Mrs Judy Phillips
Founded: 1978
Type: Multidisciplinary.
Hours open: Mon–Thurs: 9am–5pm; Fri: 9am–4.30pm.
Users: Staff of Broadmoor. Visitors from other organizations by arrangement.
Lending: Only to staff.
Stock policy: Passed on to other libraries.
Holdings: 4,749 books; 2,900 documents; 60 current journal subscriptions.
Classification: Dewey.
Library management system: Heritage.
Computerized services: CD-ROM access to PsycINFO.
Library publications: Additions to Stock – monthly.
Special collections: Forensic Psychiatry Topic Boxes.
Collaborative networks: HeLIN; PLCS.

Pembrokeshire & Derwen NHS Trust Library & Information Centre

St David's Hospital
Carmarthen SA31 3HB
Tel: 01267 237481
Fax: 01267 237547
E-mail: toni.bolam@pdt-tr.wales.nhs.uk
Librarian: Mrs Val Bisnath
Prof. staff: Ms T Bolam
Founded: 1983
Type: Multidisciplinary Mental Health; Learning Disabilities.
Hours open: Mon–Thurs: 9am–5pm; Fri: 9am–4.30pm.

Users: All staff employed by Trust. Others considered by negotiation.

Lending: To members of Trust staff.

Stock policy: Some disposed of; some stored in an attic.

Holdings: 4,000 books; 98 current journal subscriptions; 30 videos; 50 CD-ROMs.

Classification: Own (based on NLM).

Library management system: Own (based on MS Access).

Computerized services: Online access to Data-Star. CINAHL and MEDLINE databases, etc. via CymruWeb. Access to BNI; BookData; ClinPsych; HMIC.

Library publications: Mental Health Care: A Core Collection, Tomlinsons 1999.

Collaborative networks: AWHILES; PLCS.

Pembrokeshire & Derwen NHS Trust Library Services

Withybush General Hospital
Haverfordwest
Pembrokeshire SA61 2PZ
Tel: 01437 773730/40
Fax: 01437 773740
E-mail: andrea.thomas@pdt-tr.wales.nhs.uk
Librarian: Andrea Thomas
Founded: 1969
Type: Multidisciplinary.
Hours open: Mon–Fri: 8.30am–6pm. 24-hour access.
Users: All members of the Trust, GPs, dentists and students on placement.
Lending: As above.
Stock policy: Dispose or pass it on if required.
Holdings: 5,000 books; 88 current journal subscriptions, 220 titles; 50 videos; 20 CD-ROMs.
Classification: NLM.
Library management system: Own.
Computerized services: Access via CymruWeb to AMED; ASSIA; Best Evidence; BNI Plus; CancerLit; CINAHL; Cochrane

Library; Embase; HealthStar; HMIC; MED-LINE; PsycINFO; WeBNF.

Collaborative networks: AWHILES; AWHL; NULJ.

Pembury Hospital Education Centre Library

Pembury Hospital
Pembury
Kent TN2 4QJ
Tel: 01892 823535 ext. 3119
Fax: 01892 825304
E-mail: jh165@bton.ac.uk
Librarian: Mrs J M Hurst
Type: Trust library.
Hours open: Mon, Wed: 9am–5pm; Tues,Thurs: 9am–6pm; Fri: 9am–4pm.
Users: Trust staff; Primary Care Trust staff; University of Brighton students; Health Authority.
Lending: Registered users as above.
Stock policy: Disposed of.
Holdings: 5,114 books; 88 current journal subscriptions; 238 films and videos (reference only).
Classification: NLM.
Library management system: LIBRARIAN / DB/TextWorks.
Computerized services: Access to internet and NHSNet. Access to AMED; BNI; CINAHL; ClinPsych; MEDLINE and more evidence-based databases.
Special collections: Learning disabilities
Collaborative networks: NULJ; PLCS; STLIS.

Peterborough District Hospital: Laxton Library

Postgraduate Medical Centre
Peterborough District Hospital
Thorpe Road
Peterborough
Cambridgeshire PE3 6DA
Tel: 01733 874662
Fax: 01733 347142

E-mail: laxton.library@pbh-tr.anglox.nhs.uk
Librarian: Dorothy Husband
Founded: 1973
Type: Postgraduate Medical.
Hours open: Mon–Thurs: 9am–5pm; Fri: 9am–4.30pm. 24-hour controlled access for some registered readers.
Users: Employees of Peterborough Hospitals NHS Trust. Available for reference to other local NHS staff. Other readers by appointment.
Lending: To registered members only.
Stock policy: Disposed of at varying intervals, with advice from clinical staff.
Holdings: 3,000 books; 110 current journal subscriptions.
Classification: NLM.
Library management system: DB/TextWorks.
Computerized services: Ovid databases on internet – access to AMED; CINAHL; MEDLINE and Nursing Collections 1 & 2.
Collaborative networks: Cambridgeshire Health Librarians Group. ILLs via Anglia and Oxford Scheme.

Pig Disease Information Centre

4 New Close Farm Business Park
Bar Road
Lolworth
Cambridgeshire CB3 8DS
Tel: 01954 780695
Fax: 01954 780235
E-mail: pdic@btclick.com
URL: www.pighealth.com
Librarian: Dr Michael J Meredith
Prof. staff: Paul R Meredith
Founded: 1991
Type: Veterinary.
Hours open: 10am–6pm.
Users: Veterinary surgeons, farmers, pharmaceutical industry. Others welcome by appointment.
Lending: Reference only.
Stock policy: Passed to other libraries or animal health and welfare charities.

Holdings: 350 books; 24 current journal subscriptions, 32 journal titles; 45 films and videos; 50 CD-ROMs.
Classification: Own.
Library management system: Own
Computerized services: Internet access. CD-ROM databases of swine health and production literature and conference proceedings.
Library publications: See website.
Collaborative networks: AHIS.

Pilgrim Hospital Staff Library

Pilgrim Hospital
Sibsey Road
Boston
Lincolnshire PE21 9QS
Tel: 01205 364801 ext. 2272
E-mail: Pilgrim.Library@ulh.nhs.uk
Librarian: Ann Darling
Founded: 1976
Type: Multidisciplinary.
Hours open: Mon–Fri: 9am–5pm. Access available at all times to registered members.
Users: Staff and students of NHS; staff and students of Nottingham University School of Nursing and Academic Division of Midwifery. Others for reference only at the discretion of the Librarian.
Lending: To registered members only as above.
Stock policy: Dispose of.
Holdings: 16,125 books; 205 current journal subscriptions.
Classification: Dewey.
Computerized services: Trent Consortium Ovid Biomed Service available to NHS staff. University of Nottingham networked resources available to University staff and students. CD-ROM access to HMIC.
Collaborative networks: United Lincolnshire Hospitals NHS Trust.

Pinderfields General Hospital Health Sciences Library

Pinderfields General Hospital
Aberford Road
Wakefield
West Yorkshire WF1 4DG
Tel: 01924 213705
Fax: 01924 212508
Librarian: Dianne Llewellyn
Prof. staff: Martin Saunders
Type: Multidisciplinary.
Hours open: Mon: 10am–7pm; Tues–Fri: 9am–5pm.
Users: All Trust employees. Non-employees may use for reference purposes only if telephone first.
Lending: To Trust employees and organizations with service level agreements.
Stock policy: Sold to borrowers.
Holdings: 8,000 books; 120 current journal subscriptions.
Classification: NLM (Wessex adaptation).
Library management system: DB/TextWorks.
Computerized services: Online access to Ovid. Access to BNI.
Collaborative networks: JHLS; YLI.

Plymouth Hospital NHS Trust Staff Library

Level 07
Derriford Hospital
Derriford Road
Plymouth
Devon PL6 8DH
Tel: 01752 792265
Fax: 01752 792314
E-mail: library@phnt.swest.nhs.uk
URL: www.sdhl.nhs.uk
Librarian: Samantha Brown
Prof. staff: Rosalynd Bourne; Sarah Cohen; Terry Harrison.
Type: Multidisciplinary.
Hours open: Mon–Thurs: 8.30am–5pm; Fri: 8.30am–5pm. 24-hour access by swipe card.

Users: The entire NHS healthcare community in the Region have full reference access, can borrow books and use IT facilities. Supply ILLs only to 'Core' register user base.
Lending: Private borrowers, Trust staff and community staff. Journals, reference only.
Stock policy: Local consultant sends books to a hospital in Africa. Journals offered within the Region, then the consultant, then destroyed.
Holdings: 14,500 books; 396 current journal subscriptions, 607 journal titles; 158 multimedia; e-texts, e.g. Martindale, Oxford Book of Medicine.
Classification: NLM.
Library management system: SydneyPLUS and DB/TextWorks.
Computerized services: Access to a wide range of databases via NHSNet and via internet through managed password system. Access to full-text BMJ Serials Group Journals via links from MEDLINE and other searches. 18 PCs in staff library; local intranet and website allow users to search from anywhere in the hospital. SWICE group of journals. Range of medical databases purchased as a region accessed via HCN/Optology Interface.
Library publications: What's New – on intranet; local leaflets about searching, references and the internet.
Branches: The Glenbourne Unit; Royal Eye Infirmary Medical Library; South and West Devon Health Authority Library.
Collaborative networks: SWRLIN.

Polani Research Library

Division of Medical and Molecular Genetics
Guy's, King's and St Thomas' School of Medicine
8th Floor Guy's Tower
Guy's Campus
London SE1 9RT
Tel: 020 7955 4135
Fax: 020 7955 4644
E-mail: lesley.exton@kcl.ac.uk

Librarian: Lesley Exton
Founded: 1963
Type: Medical Genetics.
Hours open: Mon–Fri: 9am–5pm.
Users: Staff of the Division of Medical and Molecular Genetics, staff and students of King's College London, visitors.
Lending: To members of the Division of Medical and Molecular Genetics only.
Stock policy: Dispose of it.
Holdings: 3,579 books; 40 current journal subscriptions, 130 journal titles; 2 films and videos; 3 CD-ROMs.
Classification: Own.
Library management system: Not computerized.

Pontefract General Infirmary

Postgraduate Medical Centre Library
Pontefract General Infirmary
Pontefract
West Yorkshire WF8 IPL
Tel: 01977 606638
Fax: 01977 606638
Librarian: Jane Smethurst
Founded: 1970
Type: Multidisciplinary.
Hours open: Mon, Wed, Thurs: 8.30am–5pm; Tues: 8.30am–5pm; Fri: 8.30am–4.30pm.
Users: Staff of Pinderfields and Pontefract Hospitals NHS Trust.
Lending: Staff of NHS Trust.
Stock policy: Sold to users, sent for overseas aid or disposed of.
Holdings: 4,500 books; 100 current journal subscriptions.
Classification: NLM (Wessex adaptation).
Library management system: DB/TextWorks.
Computerized services: Access to Ovid databases and full-text journals.
Library publications: Guide to Ovid literature searching; Library Bulletin; Library Guide; Journals Holdings List; resource guides.

Collaborative networks: YJHLS; YRAH-CLIS.
Notes: Part of Wakefield District Health Library Group.

Poole Hospital Library

Postgraduate Centre
Poole Hospital
Longfleet Road
Poole
Dorset BH15 2JB
Tel: 01202 442101
Fax: 01202 442557
E-mail: jgill@poole-tr.swest.nhs.uk
Librarian: Mr J B Gill
Prof. staff: Miss S Merner
Founded: 1972
Type: Multidisciplinary.
Hours open: Mon–Fri: 8.30am–5pm.
Users: Local NHS staff and healthcare students. External member scheme.
Lending: To NHS staff and students.
Stock policy: Out-of-date books and journals discarded, offered for sale to readers if suitable or passed to contacts for use overseas.
Holdings: 15,000 books; 150 current journal subscriptions, 200 journal titles; 150 videos; 20 CD-ROMs.
Classification: NLM (Wessex adaptation).
Library management system: Heritage.
Computerized services: Online access to AMED; ASSIA for Health; BNI; CINAHL; Cochrane Library; Embase; HMIC; MEDLINE; NRR; PsycINFO.
Library publications: Library guides.
Branches: St Ann's Hospital Library.
Collaborative networks: Dorset Circle of Libraries; NULJ; PLCS; SWRLIN.

Preston Acute Hospital NHS Trust

Library and Information Service
Royal Preston Hospital
Sharoe Green Lane
Fulwood
Preston
Lancashire PR2 9HT
Tel: 01772 710763
Fax: 01772 788472
E-mail: mandy.beaumont@patr.nhs.uk
Librarian: Mandy Beaumont
Type: Multidisciplinary.
Hours open: Mon, Wed, Thurs, Fri: 9am–5pm; Tues: 9am–7pm.
Users: Trust staff and students on placement, GPs, community staff. Non-members by appointment.
Lending: As above. Non-members, reference only.
Stock policy: Old stock is disposed of.
Holdings: 4,500 books; 125 current journal subscriptions; 180 videos.
Classification: NLM.
Library management system: Heritage.
Computerized services: Access to NHSNet. Online access to AMED; BNI; CINAHL; Embase; HMIC; MEDLINE; PsycINFO.
Library publications: Guide to Databases; Guide to Online Journals; Library Bulletin; Library Guide.
Collaborative networks: BL; BMA; LIHNN; Royal College of Surgeons.

Prestwich Hospital Professional Library

Prestwich Hospital
Bury New Road
Manchester M25 7BL
Tel: 0161 772 3518
Fax: 0161 772 3663
E-mail: JCoulshed@library.mhss-tr.nwest.nhs.uk
Librarian: John Coulshed

Prof. staff: Caroline Collinge; Valerie Hoath (jobshare).
Founded: 1954
Type: Multidisciplinary.
Hours open: Mon–Thurs: 9am–12 noon, 1pm–5pm; Fri: 9am–12 noon, 1pm–4pm.
Users: Mental Health Services of Salford staff; students on placement or on courses in the Trust.
Lending: MHSS staff and students.
Stock policy: Discard stock not borrowed for ten years.
Holdings: 6,000 books; 55 current journal subscriptions, 84 journal titles; 50 videos.
Classification: Royal College of Psychiatrists.
Library management system: DB/TextWorks; InMagic.
Computerized services: Internet access. WebSPIRS.
Library publications: Current awareness bulletins.
Collaborative networks: NORWHSLA; PLCS.

Prince Philip Hospital Multidisciplinary Library

Dafen
Llanelli
Carmarthenshire SA14 8QF
Tel: 01554 749301
Fax: 01554 749301
E-mail: annlee@princephilip.demon.co.uk
Librarian: Ann Leeuwerke
Founded: 1977
Type: Multidisciplinary.
Hours open: Mon, Tues and Thurs: 8.30am–5.30pm; Wed: 8.30am–8pm; Fri: 8.30am–5pm. 24-hour access.
Users: Employees of Carmarthenshire NHS Trust and nursing and medical students. External readers for a fee by arrangement.
Lending: To all registered users.
Stock policy: Disposed of.
Holdings: 7,000 books; 94 current journal subscriptions; 70 videos; 12 CD-ROMs.

Classification: NLM.
Library management system: Voyager.
Computerized services: Online access to ASSIA; BNI; CINAHL; Cochrane Library; Embase; MEDLINE; PsycINFO.
Library publications: Library Guide; Journal Holdings.
Collaborative networks: AWHL; AWHILES; BL; BMA; NULJ.

Princess Alexandra Hospital Medical Library

Hamstel Road
Harlow
Essex CM20 1QX
Tel: 01279 827021
Fax: 01279 445101
E-mail: lib.desk@tpah-tr.nthames.nhs.uk
Librarian: Mrs Jane Leary
Prof. staff: Post vacant
Founded: 1965
Type: Multidisciplinary.
Hours open: Mon–Fri: 9am–5pm.
Users: All local NHS healthcare professionals. Reference facilities to others.
Lending: As above.
Stock policy: Sold off or donated to Third World countries.
Holdings: 5,960 books; 135 current journal subscriptions, 355 journal titles.
Classification: NLM.
Library management system: DB/TextWorks.
Computerized services: Online access to Data-Star. Free access to EBMR and NRR. Access to Best Evidence; BNI; CINAHL; ClinPsych; Cochrane Library; MEDLINE.
Collaborative networks: Eastern Region (East) Workforce Confederation; London Region for document supply; LfN.

Princess Alice Hospice Education Library

West End Lane
Esher
Surrey KT10 8NA
Tel: 01372 461843
Fax: 01372 467771
E-mail: library@princess-alice-hospice.org.uk
Librarian: Jan Brooman
Founded: 1991
Type: Multidisciplinary.
Hours open: Mon–Fri: 9am–5pm.
Users: Staff and registered students have full facilities. Other health professionals have reference access only.
Lending: To registered users.
Stock policy: Disposed of.
Holdings: 1,750 books; 36 current journal subscriptions, 42 journal titles; 36 videos.
Classification: Own.
Library management system: Own.
Computerized services: Access to AMED; BNI; CINAHL; Cochrane Library; MEDLINE.
Collaborative networks: STLIS.

Princess Elizabeth Hospital: Institute of Health Studies Library

Princess Elizabeth Hospital
Guernsey
Channel Islands GY4 6UU
Tel: 01481 707329
Fax: 01481 700938
E-mail: vrowland@guernseydoh.org.uk
Librarian: Valerie Rowland
Founded: 1967
Type: Multidisciplinary.
Hours open: Mon–Fri: 9am–4pm. 24-hour access cards for clients.
Users: Board of Health employees. Anyone can join as an external member (for a fee). Anyone can use the library on a reference-only basis.
Lending: To members, and other libraries.
Stock policy: Retained in stack, sold off to members or recycled.
Holdings: 7,000 books; 50 current journal subscriptions; 200 videos; 6 CD-ROMs.

Classification: NLM (Wessex adaptation).
Library management system: Talis.
Computerized services: Online access to MEDLINE. Access to BNI; CINAHL; MERCK; NRR.
Collaborative networks: NULJ; SWRLIN.

Princess Marina Library

3 Alexandra Close
Princess Marina Hospital
Northampton NN5 6UH
Tel: 01604 595266/68
Fax: 01604 595267
E-mail: malcolmrobinson@northants-ha.anglox.nhs.uk
Librarian: Malcolm Robinson
Type: Health Authority.
Hours open: Mon–Fri: 9am–5pm.
Users: All NHS staff and students in Northamptonshire. Others by referral and appointment.
Lending: All members. Non-members by arrangement and fee.
Notes: For further information see Northamptonshire Health Authority entry.

Princess of Wales Hospital Postgraduate Library

Princess of Wales Hospital
Coity Road
Bridgend
Glamorgan CF31 1RQ
Tel: 01656 752532/2114/2025
Fax: 01656 752532
E-mail: bpaullada@hotmail.com
Librarian: Mrs Barbara Lynne Paullada
Prof. staff: Mr P Rawle
Founded: 1996
Type: Multidisciplinary.
Hours open: Mon–Fri: 9am–5pm.
Users: Trust employees, primary healthcare staff, students at University of Glamorgan, medical students on placement. All others at Librarian's discretion.

Lending: All registered users and members of AWHILES.
Stock policy: Offered to certain organizations who supply used medical/nursing books to Third World countries. All else disposed of.
Holdings: 4,500 books; 150 current journal subscriptions, 160 journal titles; 200 films and videos; 20 CD-ROMs.
Classification: Dewey.
Library management system: Libertas.
Computerized services: Online access to PubMed. Access via HOWIS to AMED; ASSIA; BNI; CINAHL; Embase; ENB; HealthStar; MEDLINE; PsycINFO; RCN.
Special collections: Psychiatry.
Collaborative networks: AWHILES; BL; BMA; NULJ; PCLS.

Princess Royal Hospital Health Sciences Library

Princess Royal Hospital
Lewes Road
Haywards Heath
West Sussex RH16 4EX
Tel: 01444 474968
Fax: 01444 443228
E-mail: janet_thorpe@hotmail.com
Librarian: Mrs Janet Thorpe
Founded: 1976
Type: Multidisciplinary.
Hours open: 24-hour access by card.
Users: Healthcare staff working in Mid Sussex NHS Trust.
Lending: To members.
Stock policy: Dispose of.
Holdings: 6,500 books; 140 current journal subscriptions.
Classification: NLM.
Computerized services: Internet available. Access to BNI; CINAHL; MEDLINE; PsycINFO.
Special collections: Neurology.
Collaborative networks: STLIS.

Princess Royal Hospital NHS Trust Library

Apley Castle
Telford
Shropshire TF1 6TF
Tel: 01952 641222 ext. 4440
Fax: 01952 222187
E-mail: allan.davies@prh-tr.wmids.nhs.uk
Librarian: Allan Davies
Founded: 1989
Type: Multidisciplinary.
Hours open: Mon–Thurs: 8.30am–5pm; Fri: 8.30am–4.30pm; Sat: 8.30am–12.30pm.
Users: Staff and students of the Trust, neighbouring Trusts, local NHS primary care staff and healthcare students at Staffordshire University. Others by appointment.
Lending: Restricted to members as above.
Stock policy: Put out for sale within the library.
Holdings: 9,900 books; 114 videos; 18 CD-ROMs; 42 audiocassttes..
Classification: NLM (Wessex adaption).
Library management system: Heritage.
Computerized services: CD-ROM access to ADAM; CINAHL; MEDLINE.
Library publications: Information leaflet.
Collaborative networks: SHAIR; WMRHLN.

Public Health Laboratory Service

Central Library
61 Colindale Avenue
London NW9 5HT
Tel: 020 8200 4400 ext. 4616
Fax: 020 8200 7875
E-mail: mclennett@phls.nhs.uk
URL: www.phls.co.uk
Librarian: Miss Margaret A Clennett
Prof. staff: Miss F Griffin; Mr D J Keech
Founded: 1946
Type: Infectious Diseases; Microbiology.
Hours open: Mon–Fri: 9am–5.30pm.
Users: PHLS staff. Bona fide enquirers by prior appointment.

Lending: To PHLS staff.
Stock policy: Microbiological material retained. Other material discarded.
Holdings: 9,000 books; 220 journal titles; 10 films and videos; 10 CD-ROMs.
Classification: Barnard.
Library management system: CAIRS Total Library.
Computerized services: Online access Data-Star. Access to Cochrane Library; HMIC on Internet; CD-ROM access to Ovid MEDLINE.
Library publications: Food and Environment Bulletin (Monthly); Hospital Infection and Infection Control Bulletin (Monthly); Library Bulletin (Weekly); Library Guide; List of Current Journals.
Collaborative networks: CHILL; EAHIL.

Queen Alexandra Hospital Education Centre Library

Queen Alexandra Hospital
Portsmouth
Hampshire PO6 3LY
Tel: 023 9228 6039
Fax: 023 9228 6880
E-mail: library.qah@qmail01.porthosp.swest.uk
Librarian: Helen Bingham
Prof. staff: Pip Beck (Clinical Support Librarian); Michele Game; Sue Pearse; Jan Reeves
Hours open: Mon–Fri: 8.30am–5pm.
Notes: For further details see entry for St Mary's Hospital Education Centre Library.

Queen Elizabeth Hospital NHS Trust Healthcare Library

Education Centre
Stadium Road
Woolwich
London SE18 4QH
Tel: 020 8836 6748
Fax: 020 8836 6744
E-mail: gdhlibrary@btinternet.com

URL: www.gdhlibrary.btinternet.com
Librarian: Andy Richardson (Knowledge Services Manager)
Prof. staff: Imrana Ghumra (Deputy Librarian)
Type: Multidisciplinary.
Hours open: Mon, Wed: 9am–7pm; Tues, Thurs, Fri: 9am–5pm.
Users: Acute and Community Trust staff and anyone employed within the Health Authority. Others only at the Librarian's discretion.
Lending: As above but also to libraries within the London and South Thames Region.
Stock policy: Check with other libraries first, then try to sell; otherwise disposed of.
Holdings: 6,000 books; 120 current journal subscriptions, 250 journal titles; 200 videos.
Classification: NLM.
Library management system: LIBRARIAN.
Computerized services: CD-ROM access to Cochrane Library; MEDLINE; PsycINFO.
Library publications: Healthcare Library Bulletin.
Collaborative networks: LLIDU; NULJ; PLCS; STLIS.

Queen Elizabeth Psychiatric Hospital Library

South Birmingham Mental Health NHS Trust
Mindelsohn Way
Edgbaston
Birmingham B15 2QZ
Tel: 0121 678 2059
Fax: 0121 678 2060
E-mail: qeph.librarian@sbmht.wmids.nhs.uk
Librarian: Sheryl Amesbury

Queen Margaret Hospital Education Centre Library

Whitefield Road
Dunfermline
Fife KY12 0SU
Tel: 01383 623623

Fax: 01383 627026
E-mail: qmhlibrary@yahoo.com
Librarian: Marie Smith
Founded: 1974
Type: Multidisciplinary.
Hours open: 24-hour access.
Users: NHS Trust employees. Other health professionals by request.
Lending: NHS Trust employees.
Stock policy: Passed on.
Holdings: 700 books; 50 current journal subscriptions; 5 CD-ROMs.
Classification: Own. Abridged NLM.
Library management system: Heritage.
Computerized services: Online access to Cochrane Library. Access to Best Evidence; CINAHL; MEDLINE.
Collaborative networks: BL; BMA; SHINE.

Queen Margaret University College Library

Clerwood Terrace
Edinburgh EH12 8TS
Tel: 0131 317 3301
Fax: 0131 339 7057
E-mail: library_enquiries@qmuc.ac.uk
URL: www.qmuc.ac.uk/lb/menu.htm
Librarian: Penny Aitken
Prof. staff: 11 including the Librarian.
Type: Academic.
Hours open: Mon–Wed: 9am–9pm; Thurs: 10am–9pm; Fri: 9am–5pm; Sat–Sun:1pm–5pm
Users: University College staff and students. Access for reference to other users.
Lending: To members only. Participants in the UK Libraries Plus Scheme.
Stock policy: Disposed of.
Holdings: 109,000 books; 1,015 current print journal subscriptions, 700 electronic journals; CD-ROMs superseded.
Classification: Dewey.
Library management system: SIRSI Unicorn.

Computerized services: First Search. Internet access to BNI; CINAHL; Cochrane Library; MEDLINE; PsycINFO.
Branches: Leith Campus Library, Duke Street, Edinburgh.

Queen Mary's Hospital: Charnley Library

Frognal Centre for Medical Studies
Queen Mary's Hospital
Sidcup
Kent DA14 6LT
Tel: 020 8302 2504; 020 8302 2678 ext. 4439
Fax: 020 8308 9384
E-mail: library@frognal.nildram.co.uk
val.jennings@qms-tr.sthames.nhs.uk
Librarian: Valerie Jennings
Prof. staff: Sylvia Pateman
Hours open: 8.30am–6pm. 24-hour key access.
Holdings: 120 journal titles
Computerized services: Access to BNI; CAL; Cochrane Library; HMIC; MEDLINE; NRR.
Special collections: Plastic Surgery and Medicine in WW1. Contact Dr A N Bamji for access. Includes medical records useful to genealogists.
Collaborative networks: STLIS.

Queen Mary's University Hospital Health Service Library

South West London Community Trust
Queen Mary's University Hospital
Roehampton Lane
London SW15 5PN
Tel: 020 8355 2093
Fax: 020 8355 2856
E-mail: library@swlct.sthames.nhs.uk
Librarian: Violet Bowman
Prof. staff: Pat Norman
Hours open: Mon: 9.30am–3.30pm; Wed: 9am–5pm. Swipe card for authorized users after hours.
Special collections: Rehabilitation.

Collaborative networks: STLIS.

Queen Victoria Hospital Clinical Library

East Grinstead
West Sussex RH19 3DZ
Tel: 01342 410210 ext. 266
Fax: 01342 300521
E-mail: coral.beddard@qvh-tr.sthames.nhs.uk
Librarian: Coral Beddard
Hours open: Mon, Tues, Wed: 9am–5pm; Thurs, Fri: 9am–1pm.
Holdings: 57 journal titles.
Computerized services: Access to BNI; Cochrane Library; MEDLINE.
Special collections: Treatment of burns; plastic surgery.
Collaborative networks: STLIS.

Queen's Medical Centre: Children's Health Information Centre

Children's Outpatient Department
B Floor, Queen's Medical Centre
Nottingham NG7 2UH
Tel: 0115 924 9924 ext. 41883
E-mail: lorna.patterson@mail.qmcuh-tr.trent.nhs.uk
URL: www.chic-qmc.org.uk
Librarian: Lorna Patterson/ Geraldine Gray
Founded: 1996
Type: Children's Health Information.
Hours open: Mon–Thurs: 9.30am–3.30pm; Fri: 9.30am–12.30pm.
Users: Open to all.
Lending: Open to all.
Stock policy: Dispose of it.
Holdings: 520 books; 12 current journal subscriptions; 120 videos; 20 CD-ROMs.
Classification: Own.
Computerized services: Access to LISA; AMED; Best Evidence; BNI; CINAHL; Cochrane Library; Embase; Biomed – MEDLINE; PsycINFO.

Library publications: In-house parent information leaflets.

Special collections: Books and resources for children, young people and parents on children's medical conditions and health topics.

Collaborative networks: Nottingham HIF (Health Information Forum); Patient Information Forum; LINC Health Panel via HIF; TRAHCLIS

Queen's Medical Centre: Greenfield Medical Library

A Floor, Medical School
Queen's Medical Centre
Nottingham NG7 2UH
Tel: 0115 970 9435
Fax: 0115 970 9449
E-mail: wendy.stanton@nottingham.ac.uk
URL: www.nottingham.ac.uk/library
Librarian: Wendy Stanton
Prof. staff: Nicola Darlington; Jennifer Drury; Samantha Johnson
Founded: 1968
Type: Multidisciplinary Medicine and Nursing.
Hours open: Staffed: Mon–Fri: 9am–9.45pm; Sat: 9am–5pm; Sun: 9.30am–4.45pm.
Users: University of Nottingham staff and students; staff employed by local NHS and Primary Care Trusts. Other users on application and subject to external fee. Non-members may use the library for reference only.
Lending: To members and to libraries within the Nottingham Health Community.
Stock policy: Books discarded when superseded or after 10 years. Some discarded material offered to libraries overseas.
Holdings: 65,000 books; 780 current journal subscriptions; 100 videos; 40 CD-ROMs.
Classification: Library of Congress and NLM.
Library management system: ALEPH.
Computerized services: 61 networked PCs and 2 NHS PCs. Online access to Dialog. Access via Ovid to AMED; ASSIA;

BNI; CINAHL; Cochrane Library; EBMR; Embase; HMIC; Health CD; ISTP; MEDLINE; PsycINFO.
Library publications: Library guides; guides to searching subject specific literature; training guides.
Special collections: History of medicine
Branches: School of Nursing Library, Mansfield; School of Nursing Library, Derby.
Collaborative networks: CURL; TRAHCLIS; UMSLG.

Queen's Medical Centre: HealthFacts Health Information Service

B Floor, East Block
Queen's Medical Centre
Nottingham NG7 2UH
Tel: 0115 924 9924 ext. 42301
E-mail: louise.stainsby@mail.qmcuh-tr.trent.nhs.uk
Librarian: Miss Louise Stainsby
Hours open: Mon–Fri: 10am–2pm.
Notes: For further details see website www.telh.nhs.uk

Queen's Medical Centre: NHS Library Service

c/o Room A5133
EENT
Queen's Medical Centre
Nottingham NG7 2UH
Tel: 0115 9249924 ext. 35503
E-mail: glennys.fletcher@mail.qmcmh-tr
Librarian: Glennys Fletcher
Prof. staff: Mary Leverton
Founded: 1968
Type: Workplace service.
Hours open: 24-hour access.
Users: All NHS staff employed at QMC.
Lending: Reference only.
Stock policy: Send to Sri Lanka if less than 10 years old. Otherwise dispose of.
Holdings: 5,000 books; 44 current journal subscriptions.

Classification: NLM.

Computerized services: Access through Trent to BMJ Publishing; LISA; Ovid Biomed.

Library publications: Directorate Library catalogues; combined periodicals holdings; publicity.

Collaborative networks: Nottingham Health Information Forum.

Notes: There are approximately 20 work-place libraries located in Clinical Directorates around the Trust for all major specialities.

Radcliffe Science Library

University of Oxford
Parks Road
Oxford OX1 3QP
Tel: 01865 272800
Fax: 01865 272821
E-mail: rsl.enquiries@bodley.ox.ac.uk
URL: www.bodley.ox.ac.uk/users/gac/rsl/no95.htm
Librarian: Dr Judy Palmer
Prof. staff: Yvonne Hibbott (Life and Environmental Sciences); Gabriella Netting (Reader Services)
Founded: 1749
Type: Multidisciplinary.
Hours open: Mon–Fri: 9am–10pm; Sat: 9am–1pm. Vacations: Mon–Fri: 9am–5pm; Sat: 9am–1pm.
Users: Staff and other users.
Lending: Books and journals only on inter-library loan through BLDSC.
Holdings: 350,000 books; 10,000 journal titles.
Classification: Own.
Library management system: GEAC.
Computerized services: Extensive online access. Over 44 CD-ROM databases and Windows-based databases available.
Library publications: Radcliffe Science Library – Notes for Readers.
Special collections: Portraits; various historical MS collections relating to Dr John Radcliffe (1653–1714) and other Radcliffe librarians.

Radical Resources Centre

Radical Department and Resource Centre
Mossley Hill Hospital
Park Avenue
Liverpool L18 8BU
Tel: 0151 250 6171
Fax: 0151 280 6683
E-mail: resources.radical@exchange.nmc-tr.nwest.nhs.uk
URL: www.north-mersey/radical
Librarian: Justin Karpusheff
Prof. staff: Steve Graham; Hannah Gray; Sharon Reilly
Founded: 1999
Type: Multidisciplinary.
Hours open: 9am–5pm.
Users: Employees of North Mersey Community NHS Trust and students on placement. Until discussions take place about the new organizations, Mersey Care Trust staff and Bootle and Litherland PCG.
Lending: As above.
Stock policy: Offer to other libraries via e-mail if significant amount.
Holdings: 450 books; 66 current journals subscriptions, 76 journal titles; 6 CD-ROMs; 900 other items.
Classification: DH/DSS Data Thesaurus.
Library management system: Heritage.
Computerized services: Online access to AMED; ASSIA; BNI Plus; CINAHL; Cochrane Library; Embase; HMIC; MED-LINE; PsycINFO. Access to Best Evidence.
Library publications: Newsletter.
Collaborative networks: HCLU; LIHNN; PIF; PLCS.

Rampton Hospital Staff Library

Nottinghamshire Healthcare NHS Trust
Rampton Hospital
Retford
Nottinghamshire DN22 0PD
Tel: 01777 247229
Fax: 01777 247563
Librarian: John Clark
Prof. staff: Maureen Thomas

Founded: 1973
Type: Multidisciplinary.
Hours open: Mon–Thurs: 9am–5pm; Fri: 9am–4.30pm.
Users: Employees and students at the hospital.
Lending: To members only.
Stock policy: Stock is disposed of.
Holdings: 11,000 books; 91 current journal subscriptions; 30 videos.
Classification: Dewey modified.
Library management system: Heritage.
Computerized services: Intranet access. Access to AMED; Caredata; CINAHL; Cochrane Library; Embase; MEDLINE; PsychLit.
Library publications: Current Awareness in Forensic Mental Health.
Special collections: Forensic mental health.

Ravenswood House Staff Library

Medium Secure Unit
Southampton University Hospitals NHS Trust
Knowle Hospital
Fareham
Hampshire PO17 5NA
Tel: 01329 836115
Fax: 01329 836049
E-mail: rvswood@interalpha.co.uk
Librarian: Kate Evans
Hours open: Mon–Fri: 8.30am–1.30pm.

Reaside Clinic Library

Reaside Clinic
Birmingham Great Park
Bristol Road South
Birmingham B45 9BE
Tel: 0121 678 3019
Fax: 0121 678 3089
E-mail: julie.busk@sbmht.wmids.nhs.uk
Founded: 1990
Type: Multidisciplinary.

Hours open: Mon–Thurs: 9am–5pm; Fri: 9am–4.30pm.
Users: Doctors, nurses, therapists, psychologists, students. Staff at South Birmingham Mental Health Trust. Students on placement.
Lending: As above. No lending to non-members.
Stock policy: Pass on, dispose of as necessary.
Holdings: 20 films and videos; 15 CD-ROMs.
Classification: NLM (Wessex adaptation).
Library management system: Heritage IV.
Computerized services: Internet access available. Access to Biomed; CINAHL; ClinPsych; Embase: Psychiatry; MEDLINE; NRR.
Special collections: Forensic psychiatry.
Collaborative networks: WMRHLN.

Rotherham Healthcare Library & Information Service

Libraries Suite
Rotherham District General Hospital
Moorgate Road
Rotherham
South Yorkshire S60 2UD
Tel: 01709 304525
Fax: 01709 373948
E-mail: rothlib@sheffield.ac.uk
g.l.matthews@sheffield.ac.uk
Librarian: Graham Matthews (Principal Librarian)
Prof. staff: Colin Lynch (Librarian)
Founded: 1978
Type: Multidisciplinary.
Hours open: Mon: 10.30am–8pm; Tues, Fri: 9am–5.30pm; Weds, Thurs: 9am–8pm; Sat: 9.30am–1pm. 24-hour access for selected group.
Users: All NHS staff in Rotherham and District; student nurses, midwives and medical students attached to Rotherham. Other members of the healthcare community by arrangement.

Lending: NHS staff and students as above.
Holdings: 13,000 books; 180 current journal subscriptions; 13,000 35mm clinical slides.
Classification: NLM (modified).
Library management system: Heritage IV.
Computerized services: Online access to Ovid Biomed Suite. CD-ROM access to BNI; Caredata; CINAHL; Cochrane Library; HMIC; MEDLINE.
Special collections: Patient health information; Slide Library.
Branches: Rotherham Patient Health Information Service; Wathwood Hospital Regional Psychiatric Secure Unit.
Collaborative networks: JHLS; North Trent Health Care Libraries Network; TRAHCLIS.
Notes: Rotherham Health Care Libraries Services are operated by Rotherham Borough Council, Libraries, Museums and Arts on behalf of Rotherham health community.

Rotherham Patient Health Information Service

Libraries Suite
Rotherham General Hospital
Moorgate Road
Rotherham
South Yorkshire S60 2UD
Tel: 01709 304178/307190
Fax: 01709 373948 (specify for health information)
E-mail: health.info@rgh-tr.trent.nhs.uk
Librarian: Deborah Bratton (Patient Health Information Officer)
Founded: 2001 (new development of service previously incorporated in Patients' Library).
Type: Consumer Health Information.
Hours open: Mon–Fri: 9am–5pm.
Users: Patients, carers and the general public of Rotherham.
Lending: As above, from Hospital library or via Rotherham Public Libraries.
Holdings: 3,000 books; booklets/leaflets from statutory agencies and support groups.

Classification: Helpbox v1 (under review).
Computerized services: See Rotherham Healthcare Library and Information Service.
Special collections: Consumer health information.
Collaborative networks: TRAHCLIS.
Notes: The Service is a collaboration between Rotherham NHS community and Rotherham Libraries, Museums and Arts Department.

Rotunda Hospital Library

Rotunda Hospital
Parnell Square
Dublin 1
Republic of Ireland
Tel: +353 1 8171795
Fax: +353 1 8726523
E-mail: hdelaney@rotunda.ie
URL: www.rotunda.ie
Librarian: Helen Delaney
Prof. staff: Jean Ryan
Type: Clinical Medicine; Midwifery; Education.
Hours open: Mon, Wed, Thurs: 9am–4pm; Tues: 12.30pm–6pm; Fri: 9am–2pm.
Users: Hospital staff and students attending courses at Rotunda.
Lending: Staff and current students only.
Stock policy: Dispose of or donate to other libraries or library users.
Holdings: 3,000 books; 40 current journal subscriptions; 50 CD-ROMs.
Classification: Dewey 21.
Library management system: Heritage.
Computerized services: Online access to MEDLINE via Ovid. Access to CINAHL; Cochrane Database; RCOG Dialog; SilverPlatter MEDLINE.
Library publications: Library Services Newsletter.
Special collections: Collection of staff publications; historical collection of Rotunda-related texts.
Collaborative networks: IHSLG.

Rowett Research Institute: RETO Library

Greenburn Road
Bucksburn
Aberdeen AB21 9SB
Tel: 01224 712751 ext. 4114
Fax: 01224 715349
E-mail: library@rri.sari.ac.uk
URL: www.rri.sari.ac.uk
Librarian: Mary Mowat
Founded: 1923
Type: Nutrition; Molecular Biology; Microbiology.
Hours open: Mon–Fri: 8.30am–5.30pm.
Users: Institute staff and students. Other users may use the library by appointment. Telephone enquiries are welcome.
Lending: To Institute staff only. External borrowing through BLDSC.
Stock policy: Stock offered first to other libraries.
Holdings: 15,000 books; 130 current journal subscriptions; 600 journal titles; 25,000 pamphlets.
Classification: LC.
Library management system: SydneyPLUS.
Computerized services: Online access to BIOSIS; CAB Abstracts; Dialog; MEDLINE; Web of Science.
Special collections: Rowett Archive.
Collaborative networks: BLDSC; Grampian Information.

Royal Air Force Centre of Aviation Medicine (RAFCAM) Library

RAF Henlow
Bedfordshire SG16 6DN
Tel: 01462 851515 ext. 8045
Fax: 01462 816728
E-mail: librarian@rafcam.org.uk
Librarian: Jennifer Wilkinson
Founded: 1999
Type: Aviation Medicine; Occupational Health.

Hours open: Mon–Thurs: 8.30am–5pm; Fri: 8.30am–4.30pm.
Users: Staff of the Centre and any MoD personnel requiring information on aviation medicine and related topics. Non-MoD personnel requests should be made through Officer Commanding Centre (OCCAM).
Lending: To staff of Centre and other approved borrowers.
Stock policy: Archive some old stock; dispose of out-of-date stock; offer some to libraries within the Defence Medical Library Service.
Holdings: 6,000 items.
Classification: NLM.
Library management system: Heritage IV.
Computerized services: Online access to Data-Star; Dialog. Access to Barbour Index; Health CD; MEDLINE.
Library publications: Newsletter; Additions to Stock.
Special collections: Reports from Flying Personnel Research Committee; Institute of Aviation Medicine.
Collaborative networks: Anglia and Oxford; HeLIN.

Royal Berkshire Hospital Trust Library

Postgraduate Centre
Royal Berkshire Hospital
London Road
Reading
Berkshire RG1 5AN
Tel: 0118 987 7849
Fax: 0118 987 7032
E-mail: trustlibrary@rbbh-tr.anglox.nhs.uk
Librarian: Marie Hickman
Prof. staff: Jill Duncan; Lucy Gilham
Type: Multidisciplinary.
Hours open: Mon–Fri: 9am–5pm.
Users: All Trust staff and local GPs receive the full service. Others, reference only. Members of the public, by prior appointment only.

Lending: To all Trust staff and local GPs.

Stock policy: Old stock is sold off to interested library users.

Holdings: 3,597 books; 172 current journal subscriptions, 413 journal titles; 7 CD-ROMs.

Classification: NLM.

Library management system: Heritage.

Computerized services: Access to the internet. Online access to Data-Star. Access to AMED; CINAHL; Cochrane Library; MEDLINE.

Special collections: History of medicine collection housed in separate 19th century library on Royal Berkshire Hospital site.

Branches: Battle Hospital is also serviced by this library. Please contact as above with any query relating to the library. There is no separate entry.

Collaborative networks: HeLIN.

Royal Bolton Hospital NHS Trust Education Centre Library

Education Centre
Minerva Road
Farnworth
Bolton
Lancashire BL4 0JR

Tel: 01204 390935

Fax: 01204 390795

E-mail: jean.williams@boltonh-tr.nwest.nhs.uk

Librarian: Jean Williams

Prof. staff: Pauline Francis

Founded: 1996

Type: Multidisciplinary.

Hours open: Mon–Thurs: 9am–5pm; Fri: 9am–4.30pm.

Users: Employees of the Hospital Trust; members of the Community Trust; GPs, members of Bolton Medical Institute.

Lending: To registered members.

Stock policy: Offer for sale to users, then dispose of.

Holdings: 6,200 books; 91 current journal subscriptions, 130 journal titles; 179 films and videos; 20 CD-ROMs.

Classification: NLM.

Library management system: DB/TextWorks.

Computerized services: Search facilities available from all PCs. Access to AMED; BNI; CINAHL; Embase; HMIC; MEDLINE; PsycINFO.

Collaborative networks: LIHNN.

Notes: This library developed from an amalgamation of two libraries in 1996.

Royal Bournemouth Hospital Library

Education Centre
Royal Bournemouth Hospital
Castle Lane East
Bournemouth
Dorset BH7 7DW

Tel: 01202 704270

Fax: 01202 704269

E-mail: library@rbch-tr.swest.nhs.uk

Librarian: Mrs M Hill; Mrs B Stables (job-share)

Founded: 1990

Type: Multidisciplinary.

Hours open: Mon–Fri: 8.30am–5pm.

Users: NHS staff and students. External membership scheme.

Lending: NHS staff and students.

Stock policy: Discarded, sold if suitable or made available to other countries.

Holdings: 12,000 books; 120 current journal subscriptions, 150 journal titles; 50 videos; 10 CD-ROMs.

Classification: NLM (Wessex adaptation).

Library management system: Heritage.

Computerized services: Online access to AMED; ASSIA for Health; BNI; CINAHL; Cochrane Library; Embase; HMIC; MEDLINE; NRR; PsycINFO.

Library publications: Library guides.

Collaborative networks: NULJ; SWRLIN.

Royal College of General Practitioners

Information Services Section (ISS)
14 Princes Gate
London SW7 1PU
Tel: 020 7581 3232
Fax: 020 7484 1992
E-mail: library@rcgp.org.uk
URL: www.rcgp.org.uk
Librarian: Mr Gil Richardson (Senior Information Manager)
Prof. staff: Beverley Berry (Librarian); Ellen Caswell (Information Officer); Sven Desai (Assistant Information Officer); James Hill-Walker (Webmaster); Claire Jackson (Archivist); Val Whelan (Senior Information Officer); Richard Whittome (Assistant Librarian)
Founded: 1952
Type: General Medical Practice.
Hours open: Mon–Fri: 9am–5pm. By appointment for non-members.
Users: RCGP members. Others by appointment.
Lending: Non-lending library. Searches and ILL/photocopies charged for.
Stock policy: Dispose. Pass on if needs are known.
Holdings: 5,000 books; 180 current journal subscriptions, 220 journal titles; 20 CD-ROMs.
Classification: NLM (Wessex adaptation); indexing from RCGP Thesaurus.
Library management system: InMagic DB/TextWorks V.5.
Computerized services: RCGP Library and Archives Catalogue. Online access to Data-Star; Dawson Books; Dialog; Swets. Internet access available. CD-ROM access to Cochrane Library; HMIC; MEDLINE.
Library publications: Information sheets; summary papers; briefing papers; New Books list; Journal Holdings.
Special collections: General practice theses.
Collaborative networks: BL; NTRLS.

Royal College of Midwives

Arnold Walker-Florence Mitchell Library
15 Mansfield Street
London W1M 0BE
Tel: 020 7291 9220/9221
Fax: 020 7312 3536
E-mail: library@rcm.org.uk
URL: www.rcm.org.uk
Librarian: Bryony Addis-Jones
Prof. staff: Mary Dharmachandran; Linda Forrest
Founded: 1881
Type: Nursing and Midwifery.
Hours open: Mon–Fri: 9.15am–4.45pm.
Users: Staff, RCM members and others.
Lending: To RCM members only. Books/reports; photocopies provided.
Stock policy: Permanent retention.
Holdings: 6,500 books; 65 current journal subscriptions, 110 journal titles.
Classification: Own.
Library management system: OLIB.
Computerized services: Access to BNI; Cochrane Library.
Library publications: Journal Holdings; Library Guide; Theses/Dissertations Holdings.

Royal College of Nursing

Library and Information Services
20 Cavendish Square
London W1G 0RN
Tel: 020 7647 3610
Fax: 020 7647 3420
E-mail: rcn.library@rcn.org.uk
URL: www.rcn.org.uk
Librarian: Jackie Lord
Prof. staff: Hazel Atlass; Carol Banks; Kate Clark; Sarah Cull; Elspeth Everitt; Naazlin Lalani; Bruce Payne; Helen Thomas
Founded: 1916
Type: Nursing.
Hours open: Mon, Tues, Thurs, Fri: 8.30am–7pm; Wed: 10am–7pm; Sat: 9am–5pm.

Users: RCN members; RCN staff; RCN institute students; corporate members; public for reference only (charge £5 per day).
Lending: To library members (RCN members, RCN staff, RCN institute students, corporate members).
Stock policy: Some to RCN Archives in Edinburgh; some disposed of in line with stock management policy.
Holdings: 65,000 books; 400 current journal subscriptions; 500 videos.
Classification: Own.
Library management system: Unicorn.
Computerized services: Webcat available. Access to electronic databases. Online access to BNI; CINAHL.
Special collections: Steinberg Theses.
Notes: Produces British Nursing Index.

Royal College of Nursing Wales Library

Ty Maeth
King George V Drive East
Cardiff CF14 4XZ
Tel: 029 2075 1373
Fax: 029 2068 0750
E-mail: angela.perrett@rcn.org.uk
URL: www.rcn.org.uk
Librarian: Angela Perrett
Founded: 1998
Type: Nursing.
Hours open: Mon–Fri: 8.30am–5pm.
Users: RCN members and staff. Non-members can use the library for reference only.
Lending: As above.
Stock policy: Sometimes passed on to other libraries, depending on how old stock is.
Holdings: 1,200 books; 43 current journal subscriptions.
Classification: Own.
Library management system: Unicorn.
Computerized services: Access to BNI plus; CINAHL; Cochrane Library; MEDLINE. For NHS staff only: AMED; ASSIA;

CancerLit; Embase; HealthStar; HMIC; PsycINFO.
Library publications: Library guide; useful web pages for nurses.
Collaborative networks: AWHL.

Royal College of Obstetricians & Gynaecologists

Markland Library and Information Service
27 Sussex Place
Regent's Park
London NW1 4RG
Tel: 020 7772 6385
Fax: 020 7262 8331
E-mail: library@rcog.org.uk
URL: www.rcog.org.uk
Librarian: Alice Breton
Prof. staff: Patricia Want; 2 vacancies.
Founded: 1933
Type: Specialist Medical – Obstetrics and Gynaecology.
Hours open: Mon–Fri: 9am–6pm.
Users: Staff, Fellows and members of the College. Researchers on application.
Lending: Reference only.
Stock policy: The collection is comprehensive. Duplicates may be offered to interested libraries.
Holdings: 10,000 books; 200 current journal subscriptions; CD-ROMs – Dialog; WHO; RHL.
Library management system: CALM (soon to be ADLIB).
Computerized services: Online access to Cochrane Library; DARE; EBMR; MEDLINE.
Special collections: Historical Collection in obstetrics and gynaecology.
Collaborative networks: CHILL; Medical Royal Colleges.

Royal College of Physicians & Surgeons of Glasgow Library

232–242 St Vincent Street
Glasgow G2 5RJ
Tel: 0141 227 3204
Fax: 0141 221 1804
E-mail: james.beaton@rcpsglasg.ac.uk
URL: www.rcpsglasg.ac.uk
Librarian: James Beaton
Prof. staff: Carol Parry (Archivist: Valerie MacClure)
Founded: 1698
Type: Medical.
Hours open: Mon–Fri: 9am–5pm.
Users: Members and Fellows of the College. Bona fide researchers.
Lending: Members and Fellows only.
Stock policy: Some retained, some discarded.
Holdings: 35,000 books; 70 current journal subscriptions; archival material.
Classification: NLM.
Library management system: ALICE.
Computerized services: Internet access available.
Special collections: Papers and library of William MacKenzie; library of Sir William MacEwen; 50% of the papers of Sir Ronald Ross; other personal and professional Society archives.
Collaborative networks: SHINE.

Royal College of Physicians of Edinburgh Library

9 Queen Street
Edinburgh EH12 1JQ
Tel: 0131 225 7324
Fax: 0131 220 3939
E-mail: library@rcpe.ac.uk
URL: www.rcpe.ac.uk
Librarian: Iain Milne
Prof. staff: John Dallas; Emily Simpson
Founded: 1682
Type: Medical history.
Hours open: Mon–Fri: 9am–5pm.
Users: Open access.

Lending: To members plus interlibrary loan.
Stock policy: Retain.
Holdings: 50,000 books; 50 current journal subscriptions, 1,100 journal titles; 1,000 manuscripts.
Classification: NLM.
Library management system: Softlink ALICE.
Computerized services: Medical resources on the internet and PubMed training in a computer suite.
Special collections: Many special collections providing both subject and biographical access to the history of medicine.

Royal College of Physicians of London Library

11 St Andrew's Place
London NW1 4LE
Tel: 020 7935 1174 ext. 312
Fax: 020 7486 3729
E-mail: info@rcplondon.ac.uk
URL: www.rcplondon.ac.uk
Librarian: Caroline Moss-Gibbons
Prof. staff: Julie Beckwith; Doreen Leach; Hasina Shaikh; Cathy Thornton
Founded: 1518
Type: History of Medicine, Medical Biography, UK Health Policy.
Hours open: Mon–Fri: 9am–5pm.
Users: Fellows, members and associates of the College; College staff, and bona fide researchers by appointment.
Lending: Most post-1900 books lent to Fellows, members and associates.
Stock policy: Out-of-date reference books discarded. Most clinical journals discarded after 3 years.
Holdings: 55,000 books; 100 journal titles; 43 videos; 10 CD-ROMs; 7,000 pamphlets; 200 audio tapes; 18,000 photos; 3,200 slides; archives.
Classification: UDC.
Library management system: ADLIB.

Computerized services: Online access to Data-Star; BLAISE. Access to Cochrane Library.

Library publications: Evan Bedford – Library of Cardiology Catalogue (1977); Catalogue of Engraved Portraits (1952); Roll of the Royal College of Physicians of London 3 vols; continued as Lives of the Fellows . . . (1878–); Illustrated History of the Royal College of Physicians (2001).

Special collections: Evan Bedford Library of Cardiology; Library of the 1st Marquis of Dorchester; H. M. Barlow Collection of Medical Bookplates.

Royal College of Physicians of London: Medical Education Resource Centre

Jerwood Education Centre
11 St Andrew's Place
London NW1 4LE
Tel: 020 7935 1174
E-mail: don.liu@rcplondon.ac.uk
URL: www.rcplondon.ac.uk
Librarian: Don Liu (Medical Education Resource Manager)
Prof. staff: (Learning Resources Co-ordinator to be appointed.)
Founded: 2002 (due to open in March)
Type: Medical Education.
Hours open: Mon–Fri: 9am–5pm.
Users: Fellows, members and associate members of the College; Professionals with an interest in medical education. Non-members by appointment only.
Lending: Fellows, members and associate members of the College.
Holdings: 3,000–4,000 books; 30 current journal subscriptions; 100 films and videos; 100 CD-ROMs.
Classification: UDC.
Library management system: ADLIB.
Computerized services: Access to British Education Index; Cochrane Library; ERIC; MEDLINE.

Collaborative networks: Learning and Teaching Support Network in Medicine (LTSN).

Royal College of Psychiatrists Information Services

17 Belgrave Square
London SW1X 8PG
Tel: 020 7235 2351 ext. 138
Fax: 020 7259 6303
E-mail: lhastings@rcpsych.ac.uk
URL: www.rcpsych@ac.uk/info
Librarian: Post vacant
Founded: 1895
Type: Psychiatric.
Hours open: Mon–Fri: 9.30am–4.30pm.
Users: College members, serious researchers and postgraduate students.
Lending: Reference only.
Stock policy: Pass to Institute of Psychiatry, then British Library/members.
Holdings: 3,000 books; 1,000 antiquarian books; 12 current journal subscriptions, 35 journal titles; 2 CD-ROMs.
Classification: Own.
Library management system: Heritage IV.
Computerized services: Access to Embase: Neurosciences and Psychiatry; HMIC; MEDLINE; PsycINFO.
Special collections: Antiquarian (pre-1914) book collection specializing in psychiatry and related diseases.
Collaborative networks: CHILL.

Royal College of Surgeons in Ireland

Mercer Library
Mercer Street Lower
Dublin 2
Republic of Ireland
Tel: +353 1 4022411
Fax: +353 1 4022457
E-mail: library@rcsi.ie
URL: www.rcsi.ie

Librarian: Miss B H Doran
Prof. staff: Mr H Brazier; Ms G McCabe; Ms M O'Doherty; Ms E Phillips; Ms G Smith
Founded: 1784
Type: Multidisciplinary.
Hours open: Mon–Fri: 9am–10pm.
Users: RCSI staff, students and external members.
Lending: Books only to registered members. Books and photocopies on interlibrary loan.
Stock policy: Out of date discarded occasionally.
Holdings: 80,000 books; 650 current journal subscriptions, 800 journal titles; 250 videos; 100 CD-ROMs.
Classification: Dewey.
Library management system: ALEPH.
Computerized services: Online access to Data-Star and Dialog. Access to Best Evidence; CINAHL; Cochrane Library; Ovid Biomed.
Library publications: Library guides; Periodicals List.
Special collections: Arthur Jacob Library (3,000 volmes); Butcher-Wheeler Library (500 volumes); William Doolin Collection (300 volumes); Logan Collection (500 volumes).
Branches: Beaumont Hospital Library.
Collaborative networks: ALCID; IHLG

Royal College of Surgeons of Edinburgh Library

Nicolson Street
Edinburgh EH8 9DW
Tel: 0131 527 1630/1631/1632/1702
Fax: 0131 557 6406
E-mail: library@rcsed.ac.uk
URL: www.rcsed.ac.uk
Librarian: Ms Marianne Smith
Prof. staff: Mr Simon Johnston; Mr Steve Kerr
Founded: 1699
Type: Surgical and Medical Historical.
Hours open: Mon–Fri: 9am–5pm.

Users: College Fellows and members. Enquirers on application.
Lending: Fellows and members.
Stock policy: Retain or offer to other libraries.
Holdings: 30,000 books.
Classification: Fixedshelf.
Computerized services: Information to individual applicants.
Special collections: College minutes 1505 to present; archive papers on Simpson and others.

Royal College of Surgeons of England Library & Lumley Study Centre

35–43 Lincoln's Inn Fields
London WC2A 3PE
Tel: 020 7869 6555/6556
Fax: 020 7405 4438
E-mail: library@rcseng.ac.uk
lumley@rcseng.ac.uk
URL: www.rcseng.ac.uk
Librarian: Mrs T Knight
Prof. staff: Tom Bishop; Ms Tina Craig; Wendy Paine; Carlos Sharpin; Hilary Webb
Founded: 1812
Type: All aspects of Clinical Surgery including Surgical Specialities and Dental Surgery.
Hours open: Mon, Tues, Thurs, Fri: 9.30am–5.30pm; Wed: 10am–5.30pm.
Users: College diplomates, affiliates and staff; surgical and dental trainees registered for College exams and courses; Institutional Member libraries. Researchers, doctors, dentists and postgraduate medical students not connected to the College should contact the library – access charges may apply.
Lending: Library members as above. Non-members, reference only.
Stock policy: Permanent retention.
Holdings: 60,000 books; 400 current journal subscriptions, 3,000 journal titles; 240 videos; 85 CD-ROMs.
Classification: Barnard.
Library management system: Unicorn.

Computerized services: Online access to Data-Star Web. Access to HMIC and MED-LINE via WebSPIRS; Binley's NHS Directory; Cochrane Library; Medical Directory.

Library publications: Lives of the Fellows of the Royal College of Surgeons of England; current periodicals/videos/CAL and multimedia lists.

Special collections: Printed books, manuscripts and autograph letters including the Hunter-Baillie Collection (1,500 Items); John Hunter – His Contemporaries and Pupils (1,100 Items); Lord Lister (250 Items); Richard Owen (750 Items); Arthur Keith (300 Items).

Collaborative networks: CHILL.

Royal College of Veterinary Surgeons Library & Information Service

Belgravia House
62–64 Horseferry Road
London SW1P 2AF
Tel: 020 7222 2021
Fax: 020 7222 2004
E-mail: library@rcvs.org.uk
URL: www.rcvslibrary.org.uk
Librarian: Tom Roper (Head of Library and Information Services)
Prof. staff: Vic Carbines (Systems Librarian); Jenny Harris (Reader Services Librarian)
Founded: 1844
Type: Veterinary.
Hours open: Mon–Fri: 9.15am–5pm.
Users: RCVS members, veterinary nurses, others with a bona fide research interest in animal health.
Lending: To members.
Stock policy: Kept for historical collection where appropriate.
Holdings: 25,000 books; 300 current journal subscriptions; 50 films and videos; 50 CD-ROMs.
Classification: Barnard.

Library management system: Unicorn.
Computerized services: Online access to Dialog. Access to CAB Abstracts.
Special collections: Historical collection; Henry Gray Ornithology Collection; Sir Frederick Smith Papers.
Collaborative networks: AHIS; ASVIN; Biomedical Collaboration in London: Mapping Resources for Collaborative Collection Management; CHILL.

Royal Defence Medical College Library

Horton Block
Fort Blockhouse
Haslar Road
Gosport
Hampshire PO12 2AB
Tel: 023 92 765899/765751
Fax: 023 92 765747
E-mail: library@milmed.demon.co.uk
Librarian: Paula Younger
Founded: 1997 as RDMC.
Type: MoD – Primary Care/Nursing.
Hours open: Mon–Thurs: 8am–4.30pm; Fri: 8am–3.30pm.
Users: MoD staff, mainly nurses, doctors, ODPs, teaching staff.
Lending: To MoD entitled users only.
Stock policy: Passed on to lecturers or other MoD libraries.
Holdings: 10,000 books; 200 current journal subscriptions, 300 journal titles; 300 films and videos; 250 CD-ROMs; reports, etc.
Classification: NLM.
Library management system: Heritage
Computerized services: Online access to Ovid collection. Access to BNI; CINAHL; Cochrane Library; MEDLINE.
Special collections: Tri-service video collection.
Collaborative networks: DMLS; SWR-LIN.

Royal Free & University College Medical School: Boldero Library

48 Riding House Street
London W1W 7EY
Tel: 020 7679 9454
E-mail: p.campbell@ucl.ac.uk
Librarian: Patricia Campbell
Prof. staff: Suk Ying Chu
Type: Clinical Medicine.
Hours open: Mon–Thurs: 9.30am–9pm; Fri: 9.30am–5pm. Vacations: Mon–Thurs: 9.30am–7pm; Fri: 9.30am–5pm.
Users: Members of UCL; staff of Middlesex Hospital. Others pay per visit.
Lending: To members only.
Stock policy: Offered to medical charities.
Holdings: 8,000 books; 260 current journal subscriptions; 100 videos.
Classification: NLM.
Library management system: ALEPH.
Computerized services: Access to Cochrane Library; Embase; MEDLINE; PsycINFO.
Special collections: Collection of the Institute of Urology.

Royal Free & University College Medical School: Cruciform Library

Cruciform Building
Gower Street
London WC1E 6AU
Tel: 020 7679 6079
Fax: 020 7679 6981
E-mail: clinscilib@ucl.ac.uk
URL: www.ucl.ac.uk/library
Librarian: Kate Cheney
Prof. staff: Suk Ying Chu (peripatetic)
Founded: 1906
Type: Clinical Medicine; Medical School.
Hours open: Mon–Fri: 9am–9pm; Sat: 9.30am–12.30pm.

Users: UCL staff and students; UCL Trust staff. Visitors: 2 day passes p.a. (reference only).
Lending: To UCL staff and students; UCL Trust staff.
Stock policy: Out-of-date editions of textbooks discarded.
Holdings: 15,000 books; 200 current journal subscriptions; 90 videos; 130 CD-ROMs; 20 floppy disks.
Classification: NLM.
Library management system: ALEPH.
Computerized services: Online access to MIMAS; Web of Science. Access to Cochrane Library; Embase; HMIC; MEDLINE; PsycINFO; Science Citation Index.
Library publications: Library guide.
Collaborative networks: London North Central Workforce Development Confederation; University of London.
Notes: Formerly Clinical Sciences Library.

Royal Free & University College Medical School of University College London & Royal Free Hampstead NHS Trust

Medical Library
Royal Free Hospital
Rowland Hill Street
London NW3 2PF
Tel: 020 7794 0500 ext. 3202/3
Fax: 020 7794 3534
E-mail: library@rfc.ucl.ac.uk
Librarian: Ms Betsy Anagnostelis
Prof. staff: Miss Susan Adams; Miss Rosalind Lai; Mrs Elaine Smith
Type: Academic; Clinical Medicine.
Hours open: Mon–Fri: 9am–10pm; Sat: 9am–5pm (except August).
Users: Members of UCL and the Royal Free Hampstead NHS Trust, as well as other Trusts affiliated to UCL, may use the library as full members.
Lending: To all full library members.
Stock policy: Withdrawn and disposed of.

Holdings: 10,000 books; 260 current journal subscriptions, 400 journal titles; 40 CD-ROMs.
Classification: NLM.
Library management system: ALEPH.
Computerized services: Online access to STN. Access to CINAHL; EBMR; MEDLINE; PsycINFO via Ovid Biomed. Access to Best Evidence; Cochrane Library; Health-CD; HMIC; Web of Science.

Royal Glamorgan Hospital Library

Llantrisant
Rhondda Cynon Taff CF72 8XR
Tel: 01443 443412
Fax: 01443 443242
Librarian: Post vacant
Prof. staff: Post vacant
Founded: 1998
Type: Multidisciplinary.
Hours open: Mon–Thurs: 8.30am–6pm; Fri: 8.30am–5pm.
Users: Staff of Pontypridd and Rhondda Trust; School of Care Sciences students, University of Glamorgan; students of University of Wales College of Medicine.
Lending: As above. Reference only for others.
Stock policy: Dispose of, unless of exceptional historical interest.
Holdings: 7,500 books; 80 current journal subscriptions, 185 journal titles; 150 films and videos; 20 CD-ROMs.
Classification: Dewey.
Computerized services: Access to HOWIS.
Collaborative networks: AWHILES; AWHL.

Royal Hospital for Sick Children: Forrester Cockburn Library

Royal Hospital for Sick Children
Yorkhill NHS Trust
Glasgow G3 8SJ

Tel: 0141 201 0794
Fax: 0141 201 0836
E-mail: fanderso@udcf.gla.ac.uk
Librarian: Frances Anderson
Founded: 1996
Type: Multidisciplinary Medical.
Hours open: Mon–Wed: 9am–6pm; Thurs, Fri: 9am–5pm.
Users: All Yorkhill staff. Others at the discretion of the librarian.
Lending: Yorkhill staff only.
Stock policy: Offered to staff and Glasgow University, then disposed of.
Holdings: 1,500 books; 120 films and videos; 15 CD-ROMs.
Classification: Dewey.
Computerized services: Online access to Ovid; EBSCO. Access to London Dysmorphology; NRR; POSSUM.
Collaborative networks: Glasgow NHS Libraries; SHINE.

Royal Hospital Haslar: Sir William Burnett Library

Gosport
Hampshire PO12 2AA
Tel: 023 9276 2494
Fax: 023 9276 2053
E-mail: office@haslib.demon.co.uk
URL: www.haslib.demon.co.uk/library.htm
Librarian: Michael Rowe
Prof. staff: Johanna Westwood
Founded: 1827
Type: Multidisciplinary Secondary Care.
Hours open: Mon–Thurs: 8.30am–5pm; Fri: 8.30am–4.30pm.
Users: All Defence secondary care staff.
Lending: Registered library users.
Stock policy: Dispose of or pass on.
Holdings: 8,000 books; 305 current journal subscriptions, 320 journal titles; 50 films and videos.
Classification: NLM.
Library management system: Heritage.
Computerized services: Online access to Data-Star; Dialog; Ovid Biomedical

Collections. Access to CINAHL; Cochrane Library; MDX Health Digest; MEDLINE; SportDiscus.
Library publications: Annual Report; Business Plan; various reading lists.
Special collections: Military medicine.
Collaborative networks: STLIS; SWR-LIN.

Royal Liverpool & Broadgreen University Hospitals

Broadgreen and Liverpool NHS Trust
Site Library
Broadgreen Hospital
Thomas Drive
Liverpool L14 3LB
Tel: 0151 282 6447
Fax: 0151 282 6988
E-mail: jmckie@rlbuh-tr.nwest.nhs uk
Librarian: Julie McKie
Type: Multidisciplinary.
Hours open: Mon–Thurs: 8.30am–5pm; Fri: 8.30am–4.30pm.
Users: All Trust employees, GPs and dentists. Other Trust employees by associate membership agreement.
Lending: All staff and members. Reference services only to student nurses.
Stock policy: Dispose or donate to other libraries. Book sales and donations to foreign hospitals.
Holdings: 4,500 books; 45 current journal subscriptions; 80 videos; 9 CD-ROMs.
Classification: NLM.
Library management system: ALICE.
Computerized services: Access to CINAHL; Cochrane Library; MEDLINE; NRR.
Collaborative networks: BLDSC; BMA; LIHNN; RSC.

Royal Liverpool & Broadgreen University Hospitals NHS Trust Library

Royal Liverpool University Hospital
Education Centre
Prescot Street
Liverpool L7 8XP
Tel: 0151 706 2249
Fax: 0151 706 2249
E-mail: ahall@rlbuh-tr.nwest.nhs.uk
Librarian: Angela Hall
Prof. staff: Helen Blackburn; Sarah Lewis-Newton; Julie McKie
Founded: 1980
Type: Multidisciplinary.
Hours open: Mon–Fri: 8.30am–6pm.
Users: All staff of the Royal Liverpool University Hospital. Associate membership scheme available for non-staff.
Lending: To all staff. Reference only to medical and nursing students.
Stock policy: Usually dispose of it.
Holdings: 6,000 books; 111 current journal subscriptions, 160 journal titles; 100 videos; CD-ROMs.
Classification: NLM.
Library management system: ALICE (Softlink).
Computerized services: Online access to ADITUS and NHSNet. Access to AMED; BNI; CINAHL; Embase; HMIC; MEDLINE; PsycINFO; RPS-epic.
Library publications: Newsletter.
Branches: Broadgreen Hospital Site Library.
Collaborative networks: LIHNN.

Royal National Institute for the Blind

Research Library
224 Great Portland Street
London W1N 6AA
Tel: 020 7391 2052
Fax: 020 7388 0891
E-mail: library@rnib.org.uk
URL: www.rnib.org.uk/linbrary/research
Librarian: Julian Roland
Prof. staff: Eona Bell
Founded: 1959
Hours open: Mon–Fri: 9am–5pm.

Users: Open to anyone interested in the education and rehabilitation of blind and partially sighted people.
Lending: To members and other libraries with BLDSC forms.
Stock policy: Disposed of.
Holdings: 7,000 books; 100 journal titles; 50 films and videos.
Classification: Own.
Library management system: GEAC.
Library publications: New Literature on Visual Impairment.
Special collections: Collection of early embossed literature.

Royal National Institute for Deaf People

RNID Library
Institute of Laryngology and Otology
330-332 Gray's Inn Road
London WC1X 8EE
Tel: 020 7915 1553 (voice and text)
Fax: 020 7915 1443
E-mail: rnidlib@ucl.ac.uk
URL: www.ucl.ac.uk/Library/RNID
Librarian: Mary Plackett
Founded: 1911
Type: Multidisciplinary.
Hours open: Mon–Fri: 10am–6pm.
Users: National free-access resource, for anyone with any level of interest in any aspect of hearing, speech and language.
Lending: Direct loan to UCL library borrowers and RNID London-based staff only. Interlibrary loan to others.
Stock policy: Disposed of or passed on, depending on circumstances.
Holdings: 15,000 books; 100 current journal subscriptions, 500 journal titles; small quantity of videos and CD-ROMs; archival material.
Classification: Own.
Library management system: ALEPH.
Computerized services: All those available to UCL library users.
Library publications: Reading lists and book lists on popular topics.

Royal Orthopaedic Hospital NHS Trust: Cadbury Medical Library

Research and Teaching Centre
Royal Orthopaedic Hospital NHS Trust
Woodlands, Northfield
Birmingham B31 2AP
Tel: 0121 685 4029
Fax: 0121 685 4030
E-mail: librarian@roh.ndirect.co.uk
Librarian: Judy Dawson
Founded: 1986
Type: Medical.
Hours open: Mon–Fri: 8am–7pm.
Users: All Trust employees and those in training on the Birmingham Orthopaedic Training Programme. External users by appointment.
Lending: To Trust employees and training programme staff only.
Stock policy: Stock retained if of historical interest. If not, disposed of.
Holdings: 1,600 books; 83 current journal subscriptions, 120 journal titles. 17 CD-ROMs.
Classification: NLM.
Library management system: In-house.
Computerized services: Access to AMED; CINAHL; Cochrane Library; Embase; MEDLINE; ORTHOLINE.
Library publications: Library users' guides; book-form catalogue; journals list
Collaborative networks: WISH

Royal Pharmaceutical Society of Great Britain Information Centre

1 Lambeth High Street
London SE1 7JN
Tel: 020 7735 9141
Fax: 020 7793 0232
E-mail: infocentre@rpsgb.org.uk
URL: www.rpsgb.org.uk
Librarian: Mr Roy Allcorn (Head of Information Centre)

Prof. staff: Austin Gibbons (Senior Information Pharmacist); Roddy Morrison (Librarian); Anne Walker (Assistant Librarian); Sadia Khan, Santay Patel, Rachel Norton (Information Pharmacists)
Founded: 1841
Type: Pharmacy and pharmacology.
Hours open: Mon–Wed and Fri: 9am–5pm; Thurs: 10am–5.45pm.
Users: RPSGB members; pre-registration trainees. Others on payment of a fee.
Lending: As above.
Stock policy: Offer to other libraries, sell, dump.
Holdings: 80,000 books; 350 current journal subscriptions; 15 films and videos.
Classification: UDC.
Library management system: OLIB.
Computerized services: Online access to Dialog. Access to International Pharmaceutical Abstracts; Embase; MEDLINE; Pharmline.
Library publications: Journal holdings list; Monthly Bulletin.
Special collections: Hanbury Collection.

Royal Pharmaceutical Society of Great Britain (Scottish Department)

36 York Place
Edinburgh EH1 3HU
Tel: 0131 556 4386
Fax: 0131 558 8850
E-mail: info@rpsis.com
URL: www.rpsgb.org.uk
Librarian: Christine Thomson
Founded: 1852
Type: Pharmacy and Pharmacology. Some Botany, Chemistry and Toxicology.
Hours open: Mon–Fri: 9am–1pm and 2pm–5pm.
Users: Members and library subscribers.
Lending: As above – not reference or journals.
Stock policy: Archive.
Holdings: 3,000 books; 29 journal titles.

Classification: Own.
Computerized services: CD-ROM access to BNF and Martindale.
Special collections: Historical Collection of Rare, Illustrated Botanical Works, Pharmacopoeias and Herbals.

Royal Society of Medicine Library

1 Wimpole Street
London W1G 0AE
Tel: 020 7290 2940/1/2
Fax: 020 7290 2939
E-mail: library@rsm.ac.uk
URL: www.rsm.ac.uk
Librarian: Ian Snowley (Director of Information Services)
Prof. staff: Judy Atkinson (Librarian: Enquiry and Document Delivery Services); Sheron Burton (Head of Customer Services); Nicola Howson (Librarian: Search Services); Margaret Hoye (Librarian: Bibliographic Services); Alan Turner (Librarian: Systems).
Founded: 1805
Type: Biomedical (postgraduate).
Hours open: Mon–Fri: 9am–8.30pm; Sat: 10am–5pm.
Users: Members of the Society. Non-members on application (fee payable).
Lending: To members only.
Stock policy: All stock is retained. The library goes back to 1474.
Holdings: 500,000 books; 2,000 current journal subscriptions, 10,000 journal titles.
Classification: NLM. UDC for old stock.
Library management system: Unicorn.
Computerized services: The catalogue, interlibrary loans, serials and some journals are computerized. Online access to internet; BIOSIS; Current Contents; Embase; HIST-LINE; MEDLINE; PsycINFO; SciSearch; TOXLINE (all staff mediated). CD-ROM access to Bookfind; Cochrane Library; Journal Citation Reports; Medical Directory; MEDLINE (Ovid); NRR.

Special collections: Alex Comfort Collection; MSSVD Collection; RSM Archives; photographs and portraits of medical figures.

Royal South Hants Hospital Staff Library

Southampton University Hospitals NHS Trust
Royal South Hants Hospital
Brintons Terrace
Southampton
Hampshire SO14 0YG
Tel: 02380 825651
Fax: 02380 234020
E-mail: rsh_library@excite.com
Librarian: Bobby Noyes
Prof. staff: Jane Dines; Jane Nicholson; Sara Wateridge; Linda White; Ann Woodford
Hours open: Mon–Thurs: 9am–5.30pm; Fri: 9am–5pm.
Collaborative networks: STLIS.

Royal Surrey County Hospital Library

Royal Surrey County Hospital NHS Trust
Egerton Road
Guildford
Surrey GU2 7XX
Tel: 01483 464137
Fax: 01483 576240
E-mail: library@royalsurreylibrary.org.uk
URL: www.royalsurreylibrary.org.uk
Librarian: Jonathan Hutchins
Prof. staff: Post vacant
Type: Multidisciplinary.
Hours open: Mon: 9am–7pm; Tues–Fri: 9am–5pm.
Users: Any member of NHS staff in South West.
Lending: Loans to all members.
Stock policy: Books and reports normally kept for a maximum of 10 years. Thereafter offered via local and national health library e-groups, and disposed of if unclaimed.

Holdings: 8,000 books; 160 current journal subscriptions, 230 journal titles; 50 CD-ROMs.
Classification: NLM.
Library management system: InMagic.
Computerized services: Online access to Data-Star. Internet access to AMED; CINAHL; MEDLINE; PsycINFO. CD-ROM access to BNI; HMIC.
Library publications: Monthly current awareness electronic bulletins on 20 varied topics.
Collaborative networks: BMA; NULJ; STLIS.

Royal Sussex County Hospital Library

Rosaz House
Royal Sussex County Hospital
2–4 Bristol Gate
Brighton
East Sussex BN2 5BD
Tel: 01273 664948
Fax: 01273 664949
E-mail: jil.fairclough@brighton-healthcare.nhs.uk
Librarian: Jil Fairclough
Hours open: Mon–Fri: 10am–2pm.
Computerized services: Access to BNI; CINAHL; Cochrane Library; HMIC.
Collaborative networks: STLIS.

Royal United Hospital Postgraduate Centre Library

Royal United Hospital
Bath BA1 3NG
Tel: 01225 824897/8
Fax: 01225 316575
E-mail: LIBRARY@ruh-bath.swest.nhs.uk
Librarian: David Rumsey
Prof. staff: Susan Lirav
Founded: 1967
Type: Health; Clinical Medicine.
Hours open: Mon–Thurs: 9am–5.30pm; Fri: 9am–4.30pm.

Users: NHS staff in the locality. Others by arrangement.
Lending: NHS staff in the locality. Others at discretion by arrangement.
Stock policy: Dispose.
Holdings: 157 current journal subscriptions, 208 journal titles.
Classification: NLM.
Computerized services: Online access to SW Region portfolio of databases (SWICE) – AMED; ASSIA; Embase; HMIC; MEDLINE; PsycINFO. CD-ROM access to Cochrane Library; MEDLINE and some journals.
Library publications: Journal and electronic journal list; library guide.
Special collections: History of medicine; rheumatology.
Branches: Green Lane Hospital, Devizes; Royal National Hospital for Rheumatic Diseases, Bath; St Martin's Hospital, Bath.
Collaborative networks: SWRLIN.

Royal Veterinary College Library

Royal College Street
London NW1 0TU
Tel: 020 7468 5162
Fax: 020 7468 5162
E-mail: sjackson@rvc.ac.uk
URL: www.rvc.ac.uk/libraries
Librarian: Simon Jackson (College Librarian)
Prof. staff:; Frances Houston; Elspeth Keith; Deborah Walker (Deputy College Librarian); Kate Warner
Type: Veterinary.
Hours open: Camden – Mon–Fri: 8.30-6pm. Hawkshead House – Mon–Fri: 8.45am–8.45pm; Sat: 9am–5pm; Sun: 12 noon-8pm.
Users: RVC staff and students plus M25 Consortium. Outside users by appointment.
Lending: To RVC staff and students.
Stock policy: Some archived, some disposed of, some passed on.

Holdings: 25,000 books; 368 current journal subscriptions; 70 videos; 65 CD-ROMs.
Library management system: Unicorn.
Computerized services: Online catalogue and journals. Access to CAB Abstracts; Current Contents; Embase; ISI; Web of Science.
Special collections: Historical collections. 5,000 rare books; 2,000 artefacts; Alvo College archival material.
Branches: Royal Veterinary College Library, Hawkshead House, Hawkshead Lane, North Mimms, Hatfield, Hertfordshire, AL9 7TA.
Collaborative networks: AHIS UK; M25 Consortium.

Royal Victoria Infirmary Library

Newcastle Upon Tyne Hospitals NHS Trust
Royal Victoria Infirmary
Queen Victoria Road
Newcastle-upon-Tyne NE1 4LP
Tel: 0191 282 5208
Fax: 0870 169 0295
E-mail: library@trvi.nuth.northy.nhs.uk
Librarian: Joanne Mullen
Prof. staff: Mark Chambers; Margaret Valentine
Founded: 1999
Type: Multidisciplinary.
Hours open: Mon, Tues, Fri: 9am–5pm; Wed: 9am–7pm; Thurs: 9am–6pm.
Users: All Trust staff and any health professional working in Newcastle.
Lending: To all members.
Stock policy: Put it for sale for users. Do not dispose of much stock since new books bought when opened.
Holdings: 3,200 books; 40 current journal subscriptions, 70 journal titles.
Classification: Dewey.
Library management system: SydneyPLUS.
Computerized services: All databases networked through library internet subscriptions. Access via Ovid collection to Books @ Ovid; Journals @ Ovid; AMED; CINAHL;

Cochrane Library; EBM; Embase: Psychiatry; MEDLINE; PreMEDLINE. Access via WebSPIRS to BNI Plus; Embase; HMIC; RCN Journals database; WorldInfo Nursing.

Library publications: Library Bulletin; new books list; regular spot in Hospital Bulletin.

Branches: Joint library with Freeman Hospital Library.

Collaborative networks: HLN; NULJ.

Ruth Gibbes Library

Sir Michael Sobell House
Churchill Hospital
Old Road
Headington
Oxford OX3 7LJ
Tel: 01865 225797
Fax: 01865 741862
E-mail: library@sobell-house.demon.co.uk
Librarian: Mrs Meg Roberts
Type: Palliative Care.
Hours open: Mon–Fri: 9am–4pm. Staffed Tues, Thurs, Fri.
Users: All staff within the Hospice. Contractual agreement with Oxford Brookes University for students doing palliative care diploma/degree.
Lending: Library members only. Restricted to Hospice staff and OBU students during duration of their course.
Stock policy: Pass on to another local hospice or developing countries, particularly India. Very dated stock destroyed.
Holdings: 2,000 books; 38 current journal subscriptions.
Classification: Own.
Library management system: InMagic.
Computerized services: Online access to MEDLINE. Access to Best Evidence; Cochrane Library.
Collaborative networks: HeLIN.

St Cadoc's Hospital Medical Library

St Cadoc's Hospital

Gwent Healthcare NHS Trust
Lodge Road
Caerleon
Gwent NP18 3XQ
Tel: 01633 436758
Fax: 01633 436761
E-mail: pat.colleypriest@gwent.wales.nhs.uk
Librarian: Mrs P Colleypriest
Type: Mental Health.
Hours open: 9am–5pm.
Lending: To other medical libraries.
Stock policy: Dispose of it.
Holdings: 4,000 books; 90 current journal subscriptions, 120 journal titles; 20 films and videos; 3 CD-ROMs.
Classification: Own.
Computerized services: Online access to AMED; ASSIA; BNI; CancerLit; CINAHL; Cochrane Library; EBMR: Embase; HMIC; MEDLINE; PsycINFO.
Collaborative networks: AWHL; NEWLIS; PLCS.

St Christopher's Hospice Library

St Christopher's Hospice
51–59 Lawrie Park Road
Sydenham
London SE26 6DZ
Tel: 020 8778 9252
Fax: 020 8776 9345
E-mail: denise@stchris.ftech.co.uk
Librarian: Denise Brady
Founded: 1982
Type: Multidisciplinary; Health; Special.
Hours open: Mon–Fri: 9am–5pm.
Users: Staff and students in-house. Anyone who cannot borrow can use the library by appointment with the Librarian.
Lending: To staff and students in-house only.
Stock policy: Stock no longer required given to an overseas charity.
Holdings: 4,000 books; 40 current journal subscriptions; 50 videos; 2 CD-ROMs.
Classification: In-house.

Library management system: LIBRARIAN .

Computerized services: Internet access. In-house database of 8,000 items. Can do search if required. Access to Cochrane Library; MEDLINE.

Library publications: Bookshop catalogue.

Special collections: Collection on palliative care, bereavement issues, death and dying.

Collaborative networks: STLIS.

St Columba's Hospice Clinical Library

Challenger Lodge
Boswall Road
Edinburgh EH5 3RW
Tel: 0131 551 2517/1381
Fax: 0131 551 2517
Librarian: Margaret Gill (Tuesdays)
Founded: 1991
Type: Palliative Care, Medical and Nursing.
Hours open: Open any reasonable time, including when unstaffed.
Users: Hospice staff; students; others who have a professional interest in palliative care.
Lending: Members.
Stock policy: Dispose.
Holdings: 1,700 books; 30 current journal subscriptions; 40 films and videos.
Classification: Own.
Library publications: Lookout – bimonthly current awareness bulletin.

St Francis Hospice

Education Centre
The Hall
Havering-atte-Bower
Romford
Essex RM4 1QH
Tel: 01708 758646
Fax: 01708 758641

Librarian: Susan Ellis (Education Co-ordinator).
Prof. staff: Janet Lawrence (Librarian)
Founded: 1982
Type: Palliative Care.
Hours open: 9am–5pm.
Users: Doctors, nurses, health visitors. Barking, Havering and Brentwood Healthcare Trust staff.
Lending: All applications considered. Must join the library and provide proof of identity.
Stock policy: Disposal.
Holdings: 2,000 books; 26 current journal subscriptions; 100 films and videos.
Classification: Own.
Library management system: Own.
Computerized services: Internet access available. Online access to Internurse. Access to CINAHL; Cochrane Library.
Collaborative networks: NTRLS.

St George's Library

St George's Hospital Medical School
Hunter Wing
Cranmer Terrace
London SW17 0RE
Tel: 020 8725 5466
Fax: 020 8767 4696
E-mail: s.gove@sghms.ac.uk
URL: www.sghms.ac.uk/depts/is/library
Librarian: Susan Gove
Prof. staff: Helen Alper; Sue David; Susan Gilbert; Marina Logan-Bruce; Sam Martin; Olwen Revell; Nallini Thevakarrunnai
Founded: 1977
Type: Multidisciplinary.
Hours open: Mon–Thurs: 8am–10pm; Fri: 8am–9pm; Sat: 9am–5pm. Vacations: Mon–Fri: 8am–9pm.
Users: Staff, students and official visitors of the St George's Hospital Medical School. Staff and students of the Faculty of Health and Social Care Sciences. 3 associated Trusts.
Lending: To members only.

Stock policy: Journals offered to other libraries and abroad. Books normally disposed of.
Holdings: 46,974 books; 738 current journal subscriptions; 626 videos and CD-ROMs.
Classification: LC and NLM.
Library management system: Unicorn.
Computerized services: Access to AMED; ASSIA; BNI; CINAHL; Cochrane Library; Embase; MEDLINE; PsycINFO; Web of Science. See website for details of others.
Special collections: Archives of St George's Hospital and Medical School.
Branches: Atkinson Morley's Hospital, Wimbledon; Bolingbroke Hospital, Wandsworth; Queen Mary's Hospital, Roehampton; Trinity Hospice, Clapham Common.
Collaborative networks: STLIS.

St George's Postgraduate Library

St George's Hospital
Newcastle, North Tyneside and
   Northumberland Mental Health Trust
Morpeth
Northumberland NE61 2NU
Tel: 01670 512121
Fax: 01670 395829
E-mail: sghlibrary@hotmail.com
Librarian: Miss Lisa Jenkinson
Type: Postgraduate.
Hours open: Tues–Wed: 9.30am–4.30pm; Thurs: 9.30am–3pm.
Users: Any Trust member may use the library. Non-Trust members have reference access only.
Lending: To members only. Interlibrary loan.
Stock policy: Pass it on.
Holdings: 2,000 books; 25 current journal subscriptions.
Classification: Dewey 20.
Computerized services: Access to NeLH; Ovid.

Special collections: Management book collection.
Collaborative networks: NULJ; NYR-LAS.

St Helena Hospice: Myland Hall Education Centre Library

Myland Hall
Barncroft Close
Highwoods
Colchester
Essex CO4 4SF
Tel: 01206 851560
Fax: 01206 845969
E-mail: m.hare@sthelenahospice.org.uk
URL: www.nthames-health.tpmde.ac.uk/mhec
Librarian: Millie Hare
Founded: 1987
Type: Multidisciplinary.
Hours open: Mon–Thurs: 8.30am–5pm; Fri: 8.30am–4pm.
Users: Hospice staff and volunteers' students, local health personnel and patients. Others by arrangement.
Lending: To members as above.
Stock policy: Disposed of.
Holdings: 4,000 books; 15 current journal subscriptions, 63 journal titles; 167 videos.
Classification: Own.
Library management system: LIBRARIAN .
Computerized services: Internet access available. Also extra access for students given special passwords. Access to CINAHL; Cochrane Library; NRR.
Library publications: Children and loss booklet.
Special collections: Bereavement.
Collaborative networks: Included in Union catalogue.

St Helier Hospital: Hirson Library

Wrythe Lane
Carshalton
Surrey SM5 1AA
Tel: 020 8296 2430
Fax: 020 8641 9417
E-mail: egeorge@sthelier.sghms.ac.uk
Librarian: Edward P D George
Founded: 1992, replacing existing library
Type: Multidisciplinary.
Hours open: Mon–Fri: 8.30am–6.30pm.
Users: Staff of St Helier Trust; Merton and Sutton Community Trust; Merton, Sutton and Wandsworth Health Authority; South West London Community NHS Trust; PCGs in area; medical and nursing students on placement.
Lending: All members except students.
Stock policy: Outdated stock is discarded. Recent (10 years) journals sent to Pakistan.
Holdings: 5,000 books; 187 current journal subscriptions; 30 videos; 6 CD-ROMs.
Classification: NLM.
Computerized services: Online access to Data-Star. Access to AMED; CINAHL; Clinical Evidence; ClinPsych; Cochrane Library; EBM; MEDLINE.
Branches: Sally Howell Library, Epsom General Hospital, Dorking Road, Epsom, KT18 7EG.
Collaborative networks: BMA; NULJ; STLIS.

St Loye's School of Health Studies Library

Millbrook Lane
Topsham Road
Exeter
Devon EX2 6ES
Tel: 01392 219774
Fax: 01392 435357
E-mail: g.barber@ex.ac.uk
URL: www.ex.ac.uk/stloyes
Librarian: Graeme Barber
Prof. staff: Rosemary Warren
Type: Occupational Therapy; Paramedical.
Hours open: Mon–Thurs: 9am–5.30pm; Fri: 9am–5pm.
Users: Students and staff of the School of Health Studies. Other users only by arrangement.
Lending: Students and staff of the School. Restricted to full library members.
Stock policy: Old stock discarded.
Holdings: 13,000 books; 110 current journal subscriptions, 140 journal titles; 370 videos; 10 CD-ROMs.
Classification: NLM (Wessex adaptation).
Library management system: TRAX.
Computerized services: Access to AMED via SilverPlatter; CINAHL via Ovid; Cochrane Library.
Library publications: Academic Services Guide; Behaviour and Social Science Information Guide; Biomedical Sciences Information Guide; Occupational Therapy Information Guide; Hansard Referencing Guide.
Collaborative networks: NULJ; SWRLIN.

St Luke's Hospice Library

Fobbing Farm
Nethermayne
Basildon
Essex SS16 5NJ
Tel: 01268 524973
Fax: 01268 282483
E-mail: sue@stlukeshospice.co.uk
Founded: 1997
Type: Palliative Care.
Hours open: Mon–Fri: 10am–4pm. Some sessions are missed due to volunteers not being available.
Users: Full members: anyone working at the Hospice, mainly nursing staff. Associate members: anyone wishing to join (with some references).
Lending: Books available to all members and requests from other libraries. Very restricted loan of journals.
Stock policy: Not yet applicable.

Holdings: 300 books; 11 current journal subscriptions.
Classification: NLM.
Library publications: Current library lists.
Collaborative networks: Basildon Healthcare Library.

St Martin's Hospital Library

St Martin's Hospital
Littlebourne Road
Canterbury
Kent CT1 1TD
Tel: 01227 812360
Fax: 01227 812005
E-mail: joy.sharman@ekentc-tr.sthames.nhs.uk
Librarian: Joy Sharman
Type: Multidisciplinary.
Hours open: Mon, Wed, Fri: 9am–5pm; Tues: 9am–8pm.
Users: All staff of East Kent Community Trust; Health Authority and PCG staff. Reference only for others.
Lending: Registered users only. Other libraries in South Thames scheme. External membership available on payment of fee.
Stock policy: Mostly sold on to users or given away. Journals offered to BookAid and other libraries.
Holdings: 5,241 books; 90 current journal subscriptions.
Classification: NLM.
Library management system: LIBRARIAN and DB/TextWorks.
Computerized services: Online access to Ovid Gateway via password. 8 computers with internet access. 8 CD-ROMs networked: AMED; ASSIA for Health; BNI; CINAHL; ClinPsych; HMIC; MEDLINE; Speech and Language database.
Library publications: Library Bulletin mailed to all users.
Special collections: Special strengths are mental health, community and primary care, therapies.

Collaborative networks: Canterbury Circle of Libraries; Kent County Library; NULJ; PLCS; STLIS.

St Mary's Hospital: Oliveira Library

Education Centre
St Mary's Hospital
Newport
Isle of Wight PO30 5TG
Tel: 01983 534519
Fax: 01983 521963 (not in library)
E-mail: postgradlibrary@iow.nhs.uk
Librarian: Mr G K Amos
Founded: 2000 (in its present location as a Multidisciplinary library)
Type: Multidisciplinary.
Hours open: Mon–Thurs: 9am–5pm; Fri: 9am–4pm. 24-hour access.
Users: Isle of Wight Healthcare NHS Trust staff; Primary Care Trust staff; Health Authority staff and associated bodies. Individuals outside the NHS may join as private members.
Lending: All members may borrow stock. Certain categories of student have limited borrowing.
Stock policy: Old stock is disposed of or passed on to staff or other departments.
Holdings: 5,421 books; 70 current journal subscriptions, 156 journal titles; 150 videos; sets of slides.
Classification: NLM (Wessex adaptation).
Library management system: Heritage IV.
Computerized services: Online access to Ovid databases and electronic journals. NLM; PubMed, MIRON. Internet database subscriptions presently limited to online text versions. Other sources such as health and biomedical electronic resources available via Southampton University Network.
Collaborative networks: HATRICS; STLIS; SWRLIN.
Notes: The Oliveira Library is a multidisciplinary library formed by the amalgamation of

the former Medical and Nursing libraries. The Nursing Education contract is now in the hands of Southampton University and not Portsmouth University.

St Mary's Hospital Education Centre Library

Portsmouth Hospitals NHS Trust
Education Centre
St Mary's Hospital
Portsmouth
Hampshire PO3 6AD
Tel: 023 9228 6000 ext. 4856
Fax: 023 9286 6847
E-mail:
Helen.Bingham@smail01.porthosp.swest.
nhs.uk
Librarian: Helen Bingham (Library Services Manager)
Prof. staff: Pip Beck; Pauline Blagden; Rosie Hatherley; Barbara Pitman; Jan Reeves.
Type: Multidisciplinary.
Hours open: Mon–Fri: 8.30am–5pm.
Users: NHS staff working in Portsmouth and South East Hampshire, or elsewhere in Hampshire may join as members, as may NHS students studying or on placement locally. Anyone else may use the library for reference.
Lending: To members as above.
Stock policy: Disposal.
Holdings: 15,000 books; 280 current journal subscriptions, 400 journal titles; 300 films and videos.
Classification: NLM (Wessex adaptation).
Library management system: Heritage.
Computerized services: Selection of databases via HCN and Ovid.
Branches: Library, Education Centre, Queen Alexandra Hospital, Portsmouth.
Collaborative networks: HATRICS; PLCS: STLIS; SWRLIN.
Notes: Details refer to Queen Alexandra Hospital and St Mary's.

St Mary's Hospital Learning Disabilities Library

Admin Block
St Mary's Hospital
Greenhill Road
Armley
Leeds LS12 3QE
Tel: 0113 305 5366
Fax: 0113 305 5360
E-mail: janecarlton@cwcom.net
Librarian: Jane Carlton
Type: Learning Disabilities, encompassing various disciplines.
Hours open: 9am–12 noon; 1pm–4pm.
Users: CMH Trust staff; learning disabilities staff based in Social Services.
Lending: As above.
Stock policy: Disposal.
Holdings: 500 books; 14 current journal subscriptions, 20 journal titles.
Classification: Own.
Library management system: Integer.
Library publications: Service leaflet.
Collaborative networks: Leeds Library Development Group.

St Michael's Hospice: Freda Pearce Study Centre Library

St Michael's Hospice
Bartestree
Hereford HR1 4HA
Tel: 01432 851000
Fax: 01432 851000
Librarian: Voluntary staff only.
Founded: 1985
Type: Multidisciplinary
Hours open: Mon–Fri: 9am–5pm. Other times by appointment.
Users: Staff of the Hospice. Local health and social care professionals.
Lending: Members only, i.e. staff and students on courses.
Stock policy: Disposal. Sometimes send to Tanzania.

Holdings: 350 books; 3 current journal titles; 50 films and videos; Resource folders.
Classification: Own.

St Nicholas Hospital Mental Health Library

St Nicholas Hospital
Jubilee Road
Gosforth
Newcastle-upon-Tyne NE3 3XT
Tel: 0191 213 0151 ext. 28514
Fax: 0191 213 0286
E-mail: library@medlib.demon.co.uk
Librarian: Katy Beck (Senior Library Assistant)
Founded: 1998
Type: Mental Health (Psychiatry, Psychology).
Hours open: Mon–Fri: 10am–4.30pm. 24-hour access for medical staff.
Users: All staff at NNN Mental Health Trust and all students working at St Nicholas Hospital. All healthcare community practitioners working in Newcastle and North Tyneside. Others at the discretion of library staff.
Lending: As above.
Stock policy: Old stock discarded.
Holdings: 2,000 books; 24 current journal subscriptions, 29 journal titles; 20 films and videos; 10 CD-ROMs.
Classification: Dewey.
Library management system: Limes
Computerized services: Online access to BNI; CINAHL; Embase: Psychiatry; MEDLINE; PsycINFO.
Library publications: Library guide; journal holdings list.
Collaborative networks: HLN; PLCS.

St Thomas' Hospital Library

St Thomas' Hospital
North Wing
Lambeth Palace Road
London SE1 7EH

Tel: 020 7928 9292 ext. 2507
Fax: 020 7922 8251
Librarian: Diane Finlayson
Prof. staff: Ruth Cove
Founded: 1951
Type: Health – patients and staff.
Hours open: Mon–Fri: 8.30am–5pm.
Users: All patients and staff working for Guys and St Thomas' NHS Trust.
Lending: To all in-patients and staff of the Trust.
Stock policy: Mostly disposed; some passed to the wards.
Holdings: 16,000 books; 25 journal titles; 700 films and videos; 3 CD-ROMs; radio cassettes for patients.
Classification: Dewey.
Library management system: ALICE.
Computerized services: Access to BNB; Helpbox; MDX Health Digest.
Library publications: Quarterly new book list.
Special collections: NHS administration and management; patient health information.
Collaborative networks: London NHS Region.

St Vincent's Hospital Library

Richmond Road
Fairview
Dublin 3
Republic of Ireland
Tel: +353 01 884 2474
Fax: +353 01 837 0801
E-mail: library@svhf.ie
Librarian: Eimear Burke
Founded: 1983
Type: Psychiatric Nursing; Psychiatry; Allied Health.
Hours open: Mon–Thurs: 8.30am–4.30pm; Fri: 8.30am–12.30pm.
Users: Staff and students working in the Hospital and the Eastern Regional Health Authority Area 7 (psychiatric services). Use of library for reference only, by any other person is at the discretion of the Librarian.

Phone in advance. Access is limited due to lack of staff and space.

Lending: As above. No journal loans. Visiting students on placement and external users, reference only. Interlibrary loans for journal articles only.

Stock policy: Old stock offered to staff and students in the hospital. After three months any remaining is discarded.

Holdings: 2,650 books; 29 current journal subscriptions, 47 journal titles; 61 films and videos; 8 CD-ROMs.

Classification: Dewey 19. Own for government publications.

Library management system: DB/TextWorks; DB/SearchWorks.

Computerized services: CD-ROM access to CINAHL; Cochrane Library; MEDLINE.

Library publications: Current Awareness Bulletin; library newsletter; Library Services booklet; Searching CINAHL; Searching MEDLINE; various pamphlets on particular subject areas and holdings.

Special collections: Core collection on mental health; collection of articles, leaflets and booklets written for patients and their families is available for photocopying.

Collaborative networks: BLDSC; Irish Healthcare Libraries Interlending Co-operative.

St Vincent's University Hospital Library

Education and Research Centre
Elm Park
Dublin 4
Republic of Ireland
Tel: +353 1 209 4921
Fax: +353 1 283 8123
E-mail: library.svh@ucd.ie
Librarian: Niamh Lucey (Head of Library and Information Services)
Founded: 1980
Type: Healthcare – Medical, Nursing, Allied Health, etc.

Hours open: Mon, Fri: 9.30am–5.30pm; Tues–Thurs: 9am–9pm. Study area open 24 hours.

Users: All hospital staff and any University College Dublin students training in the Hospital – all nursing, 5th- and 6th-year medical, physiotherapy and radiography. Not open to any other readers without letter of introduction from another library.

Lending: Book stock as above. Articles photocopied through Interlibrary Loan Scheme.

Stock policy: Currently old book stock held in storage. Duplicate journal issues sent to Third World medical charities.

Holdings: 5,000 books; 200 current journal subscriptions, 240 journal titles; 200 videos; 30 CD-ROMs.

Classification: Dewey.

Library management system: Filemaker Pro.

Computerized services: 17 PCs and 1 PowerMac. Online access to BNI; CINAHL; Cochrane Library; MEDLINE; PsycINFO.

Library publications: Guide to using the library.

Special collections: General medical; surgical; nursing; diagnostic imaging.

Collaborative networks: Irish Healthcare Libraries Interlibrary Loan Co-operative; LAI – HSLG.

Salford Royal Hospitals NHS Trust Medical Library

Hope Hospital
Stott Lane
Salford
Greater Manchester M6 8HD
Tel: 0161 787 5405
Fax: 0161 787 5409
E-mail: libmail@fsl.ho.man.ac.uk
URL: www.hop.man.ac.uk
Librarian: Valerie Haigh
Prof. staff: Rhona Dalton
Type: Multidisciplinary Healthcare.
Hours open: Mon–Fri: 9.15am–8pm; Sat: 9am–1pm.

Users: Hospital and community staff within the Salford area. Other users for reference only by arrangement with the Librarian.
Lending: Members only.
Stock policy: Books discarded when out of date.
Holdings: 5,092 books; 320 current journal subscriptions, 539 journal titles; 171 videos; 29 CD-ROMs.
Classification: NLM.
Library management system: DB/TextWorks.
Computerized services: Access to AMED; BNI; CINAHL; Cochrane Library; Embase; HMIC; MEDLINE; PsycINFO.
Library publications: Library Bulletin – monthly.
Special collections: Dermatology.
Collaborative networks: LIHNN.

Salisbury Healthcare NHS Trust Staff Library

Salisbury District Hospital
Salisbury
Wiltshire SP2 8BJ
Tel: 01722 336262 ext. 4432/4433
Fax: 01722 339690
E-mail: library.office@shc-tr.swest.nhs.uk
Librarian: Mrs Jenny Lang
Prof. staff: William Alexander; Janet Guy; Liz Payne
Type: Multidisciplinary.
Hours open: Mon–Fri: 9.30am–4.50pm. 24 hour access.
Users: All staff and students of the Trust; NHS staff in the area
Lending: To registered users only.
Stock policy: Some disposed of, some sold.
Holdings: 20,157 books; 225 current journal subscriptions; 150 videos.
Classification: NLM (Wessex adaptation).
Library management system: Heritage.
Computerized services: 6 PCs with internet, 3 standalone with CD-ROM. Access to

ASSIA; BNI; CINAHL; Embase; HMIC; Martindale; MEDLINE; NRR; PsychLit.
Branches: Old Manor Hospital Library.
Collaborative networks: HATRICS; PLCS; SWRLIN; WILCO.

Salomons Library

David Salomons Estate
Broomhill Road
Southborough
Tunbridge Wells
Kent TN3 0TG
Tel: 01892 507717
Fax: 01892 507719
E-mail: salomons_library@salomons.org.uk
Librarian: Gill Joye
Prof. staff: Kathy Chaney
Collaborative networks: STLIS.

Samaritans

10 The Grove
Slough
Berkshire SL1 1QP
Tel: 01753 216530
Fax: 01753 819004
E-mail: v.evans@samaritans
URL: www.samaritans.org/
Librarian: Vanessa Eden Evans
Type: Suicide; Mental Health.
Hours open: Mon–Fri: 9am–5pm.
Holdings: 1,500 books; 14 current journal subscriptions.

Sandwell Health Authority Library

Kingston House
438 High Street
West Bromwich
West Midlands B70 9LD
Tel: 0121 500 1577 (Direct line); 0121 500 1500 (Switchboard)
Fax: 0121 500 1501
E-mail: maureen.jones@sandwell-ha.wmids.nhs.uk

Librarian: Maureen Jones
Founded: 1998 (Public Health Library 1990s).
Type: Medical, Health Promotion, Health Management and Dental.
Hours open: Mon–Thurs: 10am–4pm; Fri: 10am–3pm.
Users: Health Authority staff; Sandwell Healthcare Trust staff; GPs, nurses, PAMs; outreach staff, medical and healthcare students. Non-staff members can use certain library services.
Lending: As above plus other libraries for interlending. DOH reports and local reports have a 7-day loan period.
Stock policy: Journals offered to other libraries; other items usually disposed of.
Holdings: 5,800 books; 40 current journal subscriptions, 57 journal titles; 30 films and videos.
Classification: Own.
Library management system: In development using Microsoft Access.
Computerized services: Access via NHSNet to a collection of databases via WISH. Access to Cochrane Library; Health CD. Use various websites.
Collaborative networks: WMHLN.

Sandwell Healthcare NHS Trust Clinical Library

Sandwell Healthcare NHS Trust
Lyndon
West Bromwich
West Midlands B71 4HJ
Tel: 0121 553 1831 ext. 3645; 0121 607 3551 (Direct line)
Fax: 0121 607 3397
E-mail: sanlib@dial.co.uk
Librarian: Mrs Lynne Cooper

Scarborough Hospital Library

Woodlands Drive
Scarborough
North Yorkshire YO12 6QL

Tel: 01723 342075
Fax: 01723 501594
E-mail: raya@mail.scarney.northy.nhs.uk
Librarian: Alison Ray
Founded: 1985
Type: Multidisciplinary.
Hours open: Staffed Mon–Fri: 9am–5pm; open 7am–11pm 7 days a week. Emergency access outside these hours.
Users: Anyone can use the library after registering, but not everyone can have interlibrary loans. The public may have restricted hours or access.
Lending: Anyone can borrow stock but from time to time certain items may be restricted to users on courses rather than non-organizational members.
Stock policy: Resuscitation books destroyed. Others to individuals, wards, GPs, students, depending on content and age. Some thrown away.
Holdings: 6,000 books; 90 current journal subscriptions.
Classification: NLM.
Library management system: CUADRA STAR.
Computerized services: Access to NYRLS Regional Library Databases and University of York resources. Access to AMED; Best Evidence; BNF; CINAHL; Embase; HMIC; Martindale; MEDLINE; PreMEDLINE; PsycINFO.
Library publications: Library guide and intranet page; new books and journals lists.
Collaborative networks: NYRLS.

School of Pharmacy Library

University of London
29–39 Brunswick Square
London WC1N 1AX
Tel: 020 7753 5833
Fax: 020 7753 5947
E-mail: library@ulsop.ac.uk
Librarian: Mrs Linda Lisgarten
Prof. staff: Ms C MacLeod; Ms M Wood
Founded: 1959

Type: Pharmacology; Pharmacy; Toxicology.
Hours open: Mon–Thurs: 9am–7pm; Fri:
9am–6pm. Vacations: Mon–Fri: 9am–5pm.
Users: Staff and students of the School of
Pharmacy – full service and borrowing.
Others from the University of London have
reference-only usage. Other users at the dis-
cretion of the Librarian.
Lending: To members only. To other libraries
via interlibrary loans.
Holdings: 30,000 books; 200 current journal
titles; 50 videos; 10 CD-ROMs.
Classification: UDC.
Library management system: Libertas.
Computerized services: Online access to
BIDS; Dialog. CD-ROM access to IPA;
Martindale; MEDLINE.
Library publications: Quarterly
Newsletter; numerous booklets/guides for
internal use.
Collaborative networks: M25 Libraries
Group; University of London Libraries.

Scope Library & Information Unit

6 Market Road
London N7 9PW
Tel: 020 7619 7341
Fax: 020 7619 7360
E-mail: information@scope.org.uk
URL: www.scope.org.uk
Librarian: Jonathan Clarke (Information
Officer)
Prof. staff: Post vacant
Type: Specialist Reference Library –
Cerebral Palsy and related impairments;
Disability issues; Voluntary sector issues.
Hours open: Mon–Fri: 9am–5pm.
Users: Scope staff. Disabled people, families
and carers, students and researchers – ref-
erence only.
Lending: Staff only.
Stock policy: Offered for redistribution
among Scope departments or donated to
BookAid or Scope charity shops.

Holdings: 5,000 books; 75 current journal
subscriptions; 100 films and videos; 5,000
articles and extracts.
Classification: Own.
Library management system: TINLIB.
Computerized services: Access to DLF-
Data; DISSbase; FunderFinder; MEDLINE.
Library publications: A variety of fact-
sheets on cerebral palsy, disability issues,
therapies and other relevant topics.
Special collections: Scope/Spastics
Society archive material.
Collaborative networks: ASSIGN; VOL-
SIF.

Scottish Health Service Centre

Health Management Library
Crewe Road South
Edinburgh EH4 2LF
Tel: 0131 623 2535
Fax: 0131 315 2369
E-mail: library@shsc.csa.scot.nhs.uk
URL: www.show.scot.nhs.uk/shsc/
Librarian: Gill Hewitt (Library and
Information Services Manager)
Prof. staff: Alison Bogle (Assistant Librarian)
Founded: 1967
Type: Health Management.
Hours open: Mon–Thurs: 8.30am–5pm; Fri:
8.30am–4.30pm.
Users: NHS employees throughout Scotland.
Individual and corporate membership for
non-NHS can be obtained.
Lending: To NHS employees.
Stock policy: Pass directories to other
libraries; other stock destroyed.
Holdings: 16,000 books; 113 current journal
subscriptions, 187 titles; 160 videos; 5 CD-
ROMs.
Classification: BLISS.
Library management system: Heritage
IV.
Computerized services: Online access to
Cochrane Library; IPD; MEDLINE; NRR.
Access to ASSIA; CINAHL; HealthStar;
HMIC; IMID.

Library publications: Monthly Current Awareness Bulletin

Special collections: Scotland's most comprehensive and extensive collection of healthcare management information.

Collaborative networks: SHINE.

Scottish Motor Neurone Disease Association Library & Information Service

76 Firhill Road
Glasgow G20 7BA
Tel: 0141 945 1077
Fax: 0141 945 2578
E-mail: info@scotmnd.sol.co.uk
URL: www.scotmnd.org.uk
Librarian: Sandra Wilson
Founded: 1998
Type: Medical Charity.
Hours open: Mon–Fri: 9am–5pm. The Librarian works part-time so please phone to make an appointment.
Users: Patients with Motor Neurone Disease, families and carers in Scotland. Health and social care professionals in Scotland.
Lending: As above.
Stock policy: Offered to other libraries.
Holdings: 300 books.
Classification: Own.
Computerized services: Access to Biomedical Databases via Ovid; electronic journals via Glasgow e-library (consortium agreement).
Library publications: Service leaflet; MND Information Update; reading lists for health professionals, patients, palliative care, carers, nutrition, bereavement.
Collaborative networks: SHINE.

Sheffield Centre for Health & Related Research (SCHARR)

Information Resources
Regent Court
30 Regent Street
Sheffield S1 4DA

Tel: 0114 222 5454
Fax: 0114 272 4095
E-mail: scharr-ir@sheffield.ac.uk
URL: www.shef.ac.uk/uni/academicIR-Z/scharr/
Librarian: Andrew Booth
Prof. staff: Catherine Beverley (Information Officer); Patricia Campsell (Secretary, Information Resources); Victoria Cooper (Information Assistant); Louise Falzon (Senior Information Officer); Sonia Rizzo (Junior Information Officer); Alison Winning (Information Officer/Research Support)
Founded: 1994
Type: Health Sciences.
Hours open: Mon: 9am–6pm; Tues–Fri: 9am–5pm.
Users: Academics from University of Sheffield; NHS researchers; postgraduate students (MSCs run by Scharr).
Lending: Only to internal staff.
Stock policy: Pass it on to other libraries.
Holdings: 4,500 books; 67 current journal subscriptions; 40 CD-ROMs.
Classification: NLM.
Computerized services: Internet access for staff and students. University Network access to CINAHL; Embase; MEDLINE; PsycINFO, etc. Access to Best Evidence; Cochrane Library; HealthStar; HEED; HMIC.
Collaborative networks: NULJ.

Sheffield Children's Hospital NHS Trust: Illingworth Library

Department of Paediatrics
Floor F, Stephenson Wing
Sheffield Children's Hospital NHS Trust
Western Bank
Sheffield S10 2TH
Tel: 0114 271 7347
Fax: 0114 271 7108
E-mail: s.j.massey@sheffield.ac.uk
URL: www.shef.ac.uk/childhealth/library
Librarian: Sarah Massey
Founded: 1968
Type: Multidisciplinary.

Hours open: Mon–Thurs: 9am–7pm; Fri: 9am–5pm.
Users: Health professionals of Sheffield can use the library for reference as can the public.
Lending: Anyone with a University of Sheffield library ticket.
Stock policy: Old stock is disposed of.
Holdings: 2,521 books; 58 current journal subscriptions; 95 other items.
Classification: NLM.
Library management system: Manual.

Sheffield Health Authority Library

5 Old Fulwood Road
Sheffield S10 3TG
Tel: 0114 271 1167
Fax: 0114 271 1101
E-mail: fulwood.library@sheffield-ha.nhs.uk
Librarian: Jill Rutt
Type: Multidisciplinary.
Hours open: Mon–Fri: 10am–1pm, 2pm–4.45pm.
Users: Anyone who lives or works in Sheffield can use the library although it is particularly aimed at healthcare professionals.
Lending: Members.
Stock policy: Most is disposed of although some is passed on to users of the library, where appropriate.
Holdings: 9,870 books; 48 current journal subscriptions, 85 journal titles; 580 films and videos; 21 CD-ROMs.
Classification: Own.
Library management system: LIMES.
Computerized services: Online access to Ovid Biomed databases and journals; BMJ Publishing journals.
Library publications: Resources Update: monthly bulletin of new resources; audio-visual catalogue.
Collaborative networks: Sheffield Information Organization.

Sheffield HealthLink Health Information Resource

Sheffield HealthLink
33–35 Charles Street
Sheffield S1 2HU
Tel: 0114 276 7877
Fax: 0114 272 1038
E-mail: sheffield.healthlink@sheffield-ha.nhs.uk
Librarian: Alexandra Martin (Acting Service Manager)
Hours open: Mon–Wed: 1pm–3pm. Other times by arrangement. Telephone Mon–Fri: 9.30am–4pm.
Notes: For further details see website www.telh.nhs.uk

Shelton Hospital Medical Library

Shelton Hospital
Bicton Heath
Shrewsbury
Shropshire SY3 8DN
Tel: 01743 492066
Fax: 01743 261279
Librarian: Claire Charnley (Learning Resources Centre)
Founded: Learning Resources Centre hopes to open in 2001.
Type: Now Medical Psychiatric; will be Multidisciplinary.
Hours open: 24 hour access for Medical Psychiatric staff.
Users: Medical Library – Trust staff only. Other NHS staff by arrangement. Learning Resources Centre will be all Trust staff, other NHS staff, students on local healthcare courses and certain partnership organizations e.g. social services.
Lending: Medical Library – staff only. Learning Resource Centre – most users except students, unless employed by the Trusts.
Stock policy: Still in draft.
Holdings: 1,500 books; 30 current journal subscriptions.

Classification: NLM.
Library management system: Autolib.
Computerized services: Access to Ovid databases for some categories of staff via Regional Library Unit. Access to PsychLit.
Library publications: PC Kiosk Monthly – bi-monthly.
Collaborative networks: PLCS; WMRHLN.
Notes: Converting to Learning Resources Centre.

Sherwood Forest Hospitals NHS Trust: King's Mill Centre Medical Library

King's Mill Centre for Healthcare Services NHS Trust
Mansfield Road
Sutton-in-Ashfield
Nottinghamshire NG17 4JL
Tel: 01623 622515 ext. 4009/4010
Fax: 01623 625449
Librarian: Miss Madeline Cox
Notes: For further details see website www.telh.nhs.uk

Sherwood Forest Hospitals NHS Trust: Newark Hospital Library

Newark Hospital
Boundary Lane
Newark
Nottinghamshire NG24 4DE
Tel: 01636 681681 ext. 5683
Fax: 01636 685971
Librarian: Mrs C O'Toole
Hours open: Tues: 9am–3.30pm; Fri: 9am–12 noon.
Notes: For further details see website www.telh.nhs.uk

Sir James Paget Library

JHP Healthcare NHS Trust
Lowestoft Road
Gorleston
Great Yarmouth
Norfolk NR31 6LA
Tel: 01493 452409
Fax: 01493 452878
E-mail: chris.thompson@jpaget.nhs.uk
Librarian: Mrs C A Thompson
Founded: 1974
Type: Health.
Hours open: Mon, Wed, Thurs: 8am–5.30pm; Tues: 8am–7.30pm; Fri: 8am–5pm; Sat: 9am–1.30pm.
Users: All staff employed within Great Yarmouth and Lowestoft Healthcare; nursing students at Suffolk College.
Lending: To all registered users.
Stock policy: Old stock is disposed of.
Holdings: 6,000 books; 110 current journal subscriptions.
Classification: NLM.
Computerized services: Access to CINAHL; Cochrane Library; MEDLINE.
Collaborative networks: Oxford/Anglia HCLV.

Sligo General Hospital Research & Education Centre Library

The Mall
Sligo
Republic of Ireland
Tel: 00 353 71 74604
Fax: 00 353 71 69095
E-mail: sgh.library@nwhb.ie
URL: http://homepages.iol.ie/~nwhbedu/index.html
Librarian: Helen Clark
Founded: 1998
Type: Health.
Hours open: Mon, Tues, Wed, Fri: 8.30am–9.30pm; Thurs: 9am–9.30pm; Sat: 9am–1pm.
Users: Any staff member of the North Western Health Board; general practitioners working in the region. Others may use for reference purposes only.

Lending: To members only.

Stock policy: Dispose of it.

Holdings: 2,200 books; 120 current journal subscriptions; 50 films and videos; 29 CD-ROMs.

Classification: Dewey.

Library management system: Heritage IV.

Computerized services: Online access to AMED; CINAHL; Cochrane Library; MEDLINE. Access to Best Evidence; BNI; London Dysmorphology Database.

Library publications: User guides to CINAHL and MEDLINE.

Collaborative networks: Health Services Libraries Scheme for supply of journal articles.

Smallwood Clinical Library

Moseley Hall Hospital
Alcester Road
Birmingham B13 8JL
Tel: 0121 442 4321 ext. 3479
Fax: 0121 442 3573
E-mail: alison.pope@bscht.wmids.nhs.uk
Librarian: Alison Pope
Prof. staff: Lesley Huss
Founded: 1999
Type: Multidisciplinary.
Hours open: Mon–Fri: 9am–5pm.
Users: Doctors, nurses, PAMs, community staff, management of administration. All staff with a Trust contract are allowed library membership.
Lending: As above. Placement students may use the library for reference only.
Stock policy: Currently no policy, due to age of library.
Holdings: 1,697 books; 34 current printed journal subscriptions, 66 journal titles, 32 electronic journals; 34 videos.
Classification: NLM.
Library management system: Heritage IV.

Computerized services: Access to WISH project databases – AMED; CINAHL; Embase; MEDLINE; Nursing Collection.

Collaborative networks: WMRHLN.

Solihull Hospital Staff Library

Birmingham Heartlands and Solihull NHS Trust
Education Centre
Lode Lane
Solihull
West Midlands B91 2JL
Tel: 0121 424 5195
Fax: 0121 424 4194
E-mail: sollib@hotmail.com
Librarian: Liz Preston

Somerset Partnership Library Service

Rydon House
Cheddon Road
Taunton
Somerset TA2 7AZ
Tel: 01823 333438
Fax: 01823 257407
E-mail: annette.giles@sompar.nhs.uk
Librarian: Annette Giles
Founded: 1976
Type: Multidisciplinary; Mental Health and Social Care.
Hours open: Mon–Fri: 8.30am–5pm.
Users: Full membership to any NHS employee in Somerset or student on placement. Reference-only access to anyone with a mental health information need.
Lending: To all members as above.
Stock policy: Rotated around satellite libraries until too old to be useful, then discarded.
Holdings: 6,000 books; 72 current journal subscriptions, 100 journal titles; 10 CD-ROMs.
Classification: NLM.
Library management system: DB/TextWorks.

Computerized services: Local intranet. Online access to internet. Access to AMED; ASSIA; BNI; Caredata; CINAHL; Cochrane Library; Embase; HMIC; PsycINFO; Martindale; MEDLINE.

Branches: Service consists of a main library plus 10 satellite collections.

Collaborative networks: Somerset, Devon and Cornwall Workforce Development Confederation Library Network; SWRLIN.

South Bank University Library

103 Borough Road
London SE1 0AA
Tel: 020 7815 6607
Fax: 020 7815 6699
E-mail: library@sbu.ac.uk
URL: www.sbu.ac.uk/lisa
Librarian: John Akeroyd
Founded: 1892
Type: University.
Hours open: 8.30am–9pm (term-time).
Users: Students and staff of the University.
Lending: As above.
Holdings: 500,000 books; 2,000 current journal subscriptions; 10,000 films and videos; 400 CD-ROMs.
Classification: Dewey 20.
Library management system: epixtech.
Branches: Essex and East London.
Collaborative networks: M25 Consortium.

South Cheshire Local Multidisciplinary Evidence Centre

Postgraduate Medical Centre
Mid Cheshire Health Trust
Middlewich Road
Crewe
Cheshire CW1 4QJ
Tel: 01270 612262
E-mail: linda.harrison@dial.pipex.com
URL: www.lmec.chester.ac.uk
Librarian: Linda Harrison

Founded: 2000
Type: Virtual library.
Hours open: 24-hour access.
Users: All NHS Healthcare Trust staff – MCHT and Cheshire Community Healthcare NHS Trust; 3 PCGs.
Stock policy: Current stock only.
Holdings: (700 items at Victoria Infirmary Northwich – see under Branches).
Computerized services: Access to JET Library via web. Access via ADITUS to Cochrane Library; MEDLINE, etc.
Library publications: LMEC Report – first year.
Branches: There is a Library Room at Victoria Infirmary Northwich, Cheshire.
Collaborative networks: LIHNN; South Cheshire Libraries and Information Services.

South Derby Health Authority Health Promotion Resource Centre

Derwent Support Services
2nd Floor
Boden House
Main Centre
London Road
Derby DE1 2PH
Tel: 01332 626300 ext. 6444
Fax: 01332 294891
E-mail: giulia.draper@mail.sderby-ha.trent.nhs.uk
Librarian: Mrs Giulia Draper
Hours open: Mon, Wed: 9.30am–12.30pm. Tues: by appointment only.
Notes: For further details see website www.telh.nhs.uk

South Derbyshire Health Authority Resource Centre

Derwent Court
Stuart Street
Derby DE1 2FZ
Tel: 01332 626300 ext. 6376
Librarian: Ms Heather Gardner

Hours open: Mon–Fri: 9.30am–1pm.
Notes: For further details see website www.telh.nhs.uk

South Devon Healthcare NHS Trust Library Services

Torbay Hospital
Lawes Bridge
Torquay
Devon TQ2 7AA
Tel: 01803 654704
Fax: 01803 616395
E-mail: library@sdevonhc-tr.swest.nhs.uk
URL: www.sdhl.nhs.uk
Librarian: Ms S Martin
Type: Multidisciplinary.
Hours open: Mon–Fri: 8.30am–5pm. 24-hour access.
Users: Healthcare professionals working within the Trust and within primary care.
Lending: To all members and libraries within the South West Region.
Stock policy: Books discarded after 10 years.
Holdings: 10,000 books; 120 current journal subscriptions, 150 journal titles; 20 CD-ROMs.
Classification: NLM.
Library management system: DB/TextWorks.
Computerized services: Online access to Data-Star. Internet access to AMED; ASSIA for Health; BNI; CINAHL; Cochrane Library; Embase; HMIC; MEDLINE; PsychLit.
Library publications: A Guide to Key Documents in Health Care for Nurses, Midwives and Health Visitors. 2nd ed. Published in association with University of Plymouth.
Collaborative networks: SWRLIN.

South Durham Health Care NHS Trust Medical Library

Bishop Auckland General Hospital
Cockton Hill Road
Bishop Auckland
Co Durham DL14 6AD

Tel: 01388 454000 ext. 2373
Fax: 01388 454254
E-mail: merrywet@smhc-tr.northy.nhs.uk
Librarian: Tina Merryweather
Type: Multidisciplinary.
Hours open: Mon–Thurs: 8.30am–5pm; Fri: 8.30am–4.30pm.
Users: All employees of the Trust, students, GPs within the area, some retired members.
Lending: As above. Non-members, reference only.
Stock policy: Some to departments within the hospital; rest disposed of after 'storage time'.
Holdings: 2,500 books; 50 current journals subs.
Classification: Dewey.
Library management system: Card.
Computerized services: Search facilities via Ovid to AMED, CINAHL, MEDLINE, Cochrane Library; Embase: Psychiatry. CD-ROM access to Cochrane Library; MEDLINE.

South East Region Knowledge Services Development South East

40 Eastbourne Terrace
London W2 3QR
Tel: 020 7725 2620
E-mail: mcarmel@doh.gov.uk
Librarian: Mike Carmel (Head of Knowledge Services Development South East)
Notes: See also NHS Executive South East Region (Oxford Unit); South Thames Library and Information Service; South Thames Library and Information Service Support Unit; University of Southampton: Health Sciences Library.

South Essex Health Authority Library & Information Service

Arcadia House
The Drive
Brentwood
Essex CM13 3BE

Tel: 01277 755211
Fax: 01277 755319
E-mail: seha.library@sessex-ha.nthames.nhs.uk
Librarian: Cornelia Turpin
Prof. staff: Jennifer Gray
Founded: 1996
Type: Health Management.
Hours open: Mon–Fri: 9am–5.30pm.
Users: Health Authority, Primary Care Trusts, GPs, practice nurses.
Lending: As above.
Stock policy: Dispose of books; old journals offered to other libraries.
Holdings: 2,600 books; 80 current journal subscriptions, 200 journal titles.
Classification: Own.
Library management system: DB/TextWorks to Soutron 20/20.
Computerized services: Access to AMED; ASSIA; Best Evidence; CINAHL; Clinical Evidence; ClinPsych; Cochrane Library; HMIC; MEDLINE.
Library publications: Evidence Bulletin.
Collaborative networks: North Thames Regional Documents Database and Union List of Serials; SEeLH.

South Glasgow University Hospitals NHS Trust Central Library

1345 Govan Road
Glasgow G51 4TF
Tel: 0141 201 2163
Fax: 0141 201 2133
E-mail: library@sgh.scot.nhs.uk
Librarian: Charlotte Boulnois
Founded: 1980
Type: Multidisciplinary.
Hours open: Mon–Thurs: 9am–7pm; Fri: 9am–5pm.
Users: Full usage rights to all Trust staff. Reference only to all other health professionals.
Lending: To members of the Trust/Library. To other legitimate libraries.

Stock policy: Old stock is disposed of. If one or two editions old, sent to overseas charities.
Holdings: 6,000 books; 125 current journal subscriptions, 350 journal titles; 2 CD-ROMs; 50 e-books.
Classification: Dewey (modified).
Library management system: CALM 2000.
Computerized services: Access to AMED; CINAHL; Cochrane Library; Embase; HOM-INFORM; MEDLINE; PsycINFO; RECAL; SportDiscus.
Special collections: Institute of Neurological Sciences Historical Collection.
Branches: Sister library – James Bridie Library, Victoria Infirmary, Glasgow.
Collaborative networks: GHI; Glasgow Collaboration; NULJ; PLCS; SHINE.

South Lambeth & Maudsley NHS Trust Multidisciplinary Library

108 Landor Road
Stockwell
London SW9 9NT
Tel: 020 7411 6336
Fax: 020 7411 6301
E-mail: multidisciplinary.library@slam–tr.nhs.uk
URL: http://slamlibrary.xiy.net
Librarian: Catherine Ebenezer
Type: Multidisciplinary – Mental Health and Community Health.
Hours open: Mon–Fri: 9am–5pm.
Users: Staff of SLaM Trust, local Primary Care Trusts, Lambeth Social Services, staff and students of King's College London, health professionals enrolled on courses run by the Trust.
Lending: See above.
Stock policy: Books are discarded; duplicate journals are exchanged or given to charity.
Holdings: 6,800 books; 100 current journal subscriptions, 270 journal titles; 5 videos.

Classification: NLM 4th ed. (South Thames adaptation).

Library management system: LIBRARIAN – Eurotec Consultants Management.

Computerized services: Data-Star web. All PCs have internet access. CD-ROM access to Caredata; CINAHL; ClinPsych; Cochrane Library; HMIC; MEDLINE.

Library publications: Accessions lists.

Collaborative networks: NULJ; PLCS; STLIS.

South Staffordshire Healthcare NHS Trust Library Services

St Michael's Hospital
Trent Valley Road
Lichfield
Staffordshire WS13 6EF
Tel: 01543 414555 ext. 2131
Fax: 01543 442031
E-mail: library-stm@hotmail.com
Librarian: Mrs Rosalyn Pitt
Prof. staff: Mrs Fiona Sedgley
Founded: 1979
Type: Multidisciplinary.
Hours open: Mon–Fri: 8.30am–5pm.
Users: Trust staff. Others, reference use only.
Lending: Trust staff only. Other libraries within the West Midlands Region.
Stock policy: All first editions archived. Other stock sold to Trust staff or thrown away.
Holdings: 2,450 books; 42 current journal subscriptions; 3 CD-ROMs.
Classification: NLM (Wessex adaptation).
Library management system: Heritage.
Computerized services: Online access to AMED; CINAHL; Embase: Psychiatry; MEDLINE. Access to Cochrane Library.
Library publications: Publicity leaflet.
Collaborative networks: PLCS; WMRHLN.

South Staffordshire Healthcare NHS Trust: Stafford Site Library

Education and Training Centre
St George's Hospital
Corporation Street
Stafford ST16 3AG
Tel: 01785 221584
Fax: 01785 221367
E-mail: fiona-rees@yahoo.com
Librarian: Fiona Rees
Type: Multidisciplinary.
Hours open: Mon–Fri: 9am–5pm.
Users: Any member of the South Staffordshire Healthcare NHS Trust, and associated staff working with clients.
Lending: Any member of Trust staff – no restrictions. Non-members, reference only.
Stock policy: Old stock will be put into storage and then disposed of. It would generally be too old to pass on safely.
Holdings: 3,000 books; 40 current journal subscriptions, 56 journal titles.
Classification: Dewey.
Library management system: Heritage IV.
Computerized services: Access via regional package to AMED; CINAHL; Embase: Psychiatry; MEDLINE. Access to PsycINFO.
Collaborative networks: PLCS; WMRHLN.

South Tees Medical Library

Education Centre
James Cook University Hospital
Marton Road
Middlesbrough
North Yorkshire TS4 3BW
Tel: 01642 854820
Fax: 01642 854198
E-mail: j.bethel@tees.ac.uk
Librarian: Mrs Jill Bethel
Type: Multidisciplinary.
Hours open: Mon–Fri: 9am–8.15pm; Sat: 9am–1pm.

Users: Staff from South Tees Hospitals NHS Trust and Tees and North East Yorkshire NHS Trust; students on placements in the Trusts from Universities of Teeside, Newcastle and Durham.

Lending: Books and journals, to library members only.

Stock policy: Journals discarded after 10 years. Out-of-date books are discarded.

Holdings: 13,000 books; 220 current journal subscriptions.

Classification: Dewey.

Library management system: Heritage.

Computerized services: CD-ROM access to Best Evidence; CINAHL; Cochrane Library; MEDLINE.

Collaborative networks: HLN.

South Thames Library & Information Service

Education Centre
Royal Surrey County Hospital
Egerton Road
Guildford
Surrey GU2 7XX
Tel: 01483 464082
Fax: 01483 455888
E-mail: csawers@royalsurrey.nhs.uk
Librarian: Caroline Sawers (Acting Head of Unit).
Prof. staff: Rachel Cooke; Tina Wilson

South Thames Library & Information Service Support Unit

Woodlands House
Pembury Hospital
Pembury
Tunbridge Wells
Kent TN2 4QJ
Tel: 01892 823535 ext. 3198
Fax: 01892 823647
E-mail: moya.bennett@stlis.thenhs.com
Librarian: Moya Bennett (Library Manager)

Prof. staff: Tamise Chaplin; Claire Nevill; Andy Prue (Web Development Librarian)
Hours open: Mon–Fri: 9am–5pm.

South Tyneside Hospital Education Centre Library

South Shields District Hospital
Harton Lane
South Shields
Tyne and Wear NE34 0PL
Tel: 0191 454 8888 ext. 2572
Fax: 0191 427 0096
E-mail: Maureen.Duffy@eem.sthct.northy.nhs.uk
Librarian: Mrs M Duffy
Founded: 1972
Type: Clinical Medicine.
Hours open: Mon–Thurs: 9am–5pm; Fri: 9am–4.30pm.
Users: Trust staff.
Lending: To Trust staff.
Stock policy: Old stock offered to small departmental collections and disposed of if not required.
Holdings: 4,671 books; 120 current journal subscriptions, 149 journal titles; 199 videos; 32 CD-ROMs; 58 slide sets.
Classification: Dewey.
Library management system: SydneyPLUS.
Computerized services: Online access to MEDLINE; NeLH. Access to Best Evidence; Cochrane Library. Regional deal giving access to various databases.
Collaborative networks: HLN.

South Warwickshire Medical Education Centre Library

John Turner Building
Warwick Hospital
Lakin Road
Warwick CV34 5BW
Tel: 01926 495321 ext. 4287
Fax: 01926 400895

E-mail: veronica.mitchell@swarkhops-tr.
wmids.nhs.uk
Librarian: Veronica Mitchell
Prof. staff: Nicholas Harden
Founded: 1986
Type: Dental; Multidisciplinary.
Hours open: Always open to authorized
users.
Users: Trust staff; other NHS staff in
Warwickshire. Non-NHS users by appoint-
ment.
Lending: NHS staff in South Warwickshire.
Non-NHS users may not borrow.
Stock policy: Pass on or dispose.
Holdings: 4,000 books; 73 current journal
subscriptions, 114 journal titles; 17 videos.
Classification: NLM.
Computerized services: Online access to
Ovid Biomed.
Collaborative networks: WMRHLN.

Southampton & South West Hampshire Health Authority Library

Oakley Road
Millbrook
Southampton
Hampshire SO16 4GX
Tel: 023 8072 5440
Fax: 023 8072 5565
E-mail: derek.jenkins@sswh-ha.swest.
nhs.uk
Librarian: Dr Derek Jenkins
Founded: 1991
Type: Multidisciplinary.
Hours open: Mon–Thurs: 9am–5pm; Fri:
9am–4pm.
Users: NHS staff within the Health Authority
area only.
Lending: As above plus interlibrary lending
across South West and South East Medical
Libraries.
Stock policy: Duplicates passed on to
District libraries. Old material scrapped.

Holdings: 5,000 books and documents; 8
current journal subscriptions, 30 journal
titles; 8 CD-ROMs.
Classification: NLM (SWRLIN scheme).
Library management system: Microsoft
Access for serials and loans. PROCITE for
books.
Computerized services: Online access to
Dialog and free internet sites. Access to Best
Evidence; Cochrane Library; Community
Wise; Medical Directory; NRR; via Ovid
(regional subscription) to various databases.
Collaborative networks: HATRICS;
STLIS; SWRLIN.

Southampton General Hospital Health Care Libraries Unit

Mailpoint 16
South Academic Block
Southampton General Hospital
Southampton
Hampshire SO16 6YD
Tel: 02380 796543
Fax: 02380 785648
E-mail: hclucat@soton.ac.uk
Librarian: Diane Moffat
Prof. staff: Barbara Matcham
Hours open: Mon–Fri: 8.30am–5pm.
Collaborative networks: STLIS.

Southampton General Hospital Management Library

Southampton University Hospitals NHS Trust
Mailpoint 18
Southampton General Hospital
Tremona Road
Southampton
Hampshire SO16 6YD
Tel: 02380 796037
Fax: 02380 794153
Collaborative networks: STLIS.

Southampton University Hospitals NHS Trust Staff Library

Rufus Lodge
Tatchbury Mount
Calmore
Southampton
Hampshire SO40 2RZ
Tel: 02380 874231
Fax: 02380 874225
Librarian: Ann Woodford
Prof. staff: Alison Roache
Hours open: Mon, Tues, Fri: 9.30am–12pm.
Collaborative networks: STLIS.

Southlands Hospital Health Sciences Library

Thakeham House
Southlands Hospital
Worthing and Southlands Hospitals NHS
  Trust
Shoreham-by-Sea
West Sussex BN43 6TQ
Tel: 01273 455622 ext. 3570/3774
Fax: 01273 446066
Librarian: Sue J Merriott
Prof. staff: Margaret Calver
Hours open: Tues: 9am–2pm; Thurs: 12 noon-5pm.
Holdings: 107 journal titles.
Collaborative networks: STLIS.

Southport & Ormskirk NHS Trust: Hanley Library

Postgraduate Medical Centre
Southport and Ormskirk NHS Trust
Town Lane
Southport
Merseyside PR8 6PN
Tel: 01704 704202
Fax: 01704 704454
E-mail: enidhanley@hotmail.com
Librarian: Enid Swift (Library Manager)
Founded: 1991

Type: Multidisciplinary.
Hours open: Mon–Thurs: 8.30am–5pm; Fri: 8.30am–4.30pm.
Users: Employees of Southport and Ormskirk NHS Trust. Patients allowed to use the library for reference purposes.
Lending: To employees of the Trust.
Stock policy: Normally given to charitable organizations or sent abroad to under-developed countries.
Holdings: 4,630 books; 61 current journal subscriptions, 67 journal titles; 93 videos; 14 CD-ROMs.
Classification: NLM.
Library management system: ALICE for Windows.
Computerized services: Online access via ADITUS to AMED; BNI Plus; CINAHL; Embase; MEDLINE; PsycINFO.
Collaborative networks: LIHNN.

Staffordshire General Hospital Postgraduate Medical Centre Library

Postgraduate Medical Centre
Staffordshire General Hospital
Weston Road
Stafford ST16 3SA
Tel: 01785 230638/678
Fax: 01785 230625
E-mail: lyn.brain@msgh-tr.wmids.nhs.uk
URL: www.postgrad.free-online.co.uk
Librarian: Ms L I Brain
Type: Multidisciplinary.
Hours open: Mon–Fri: 9.30am–5.30pm.
Users: Trust employees; primary care staff; community staff. Other users by arrangement.
Lending: As above. No borrowing rights for non-members.
Stock policy: Books disposed of at intervals.
Holdings: 2,200 books; 90 current journal subscriptions, 250 journal titles; 100 films and videos; 20 CD-ROMs; 20 cassettes.
Classification: NLM.

Library management system: Heritage.
Computerized services: Access via WISH including AMED; CINAHL; Embase; MEDLINE; Nursing Collection (full text). Access to Cochrane Library. Online access to various journals.
Library publications: Library leaflet; Reader's Charter; various user guides to databases.
Collaborative networks: Barnes; BL; BMA; WMRHLN.

Staffordshire University Library & Learning Resources Service

Thompson Library
College Road
Stoke
Staffordshire ST4 2XS
Tel: 01782 294443
Fax: 01782 295799
URL: www.staffs.ac.uk/services/library-and-info/library
Librarian: Liz Hart (Director)
Prof. staff: Gary Borrows (Asst Director Subject and Research Support); Jayne Everard (Head of Resources Management); Linda Goldsmith (Asst Director Information Systems and Learning Technology); Dave Parkes (Head of Operations and User Services); Janet Weaver (Head of Planning and Admin).
Type: 2 Multidisciplinary; 1 Law; 1 Health.
Hours open: Mon–Thurs: 9am–10pm; Fri: 9am–7pm; Sat, Sun: 1pm–6pm. Vacations: Mon–Fri: 9am–5pm.
Users: Students, academic staff and members of the public.
Lending: All members and affiliated colleges.
Stock policy: Pass to British Library, affiliated colleges or GAZA.
Holdings: 324,993 books and journals; 3,286 films and videos; 146 CD-ROMs.
Classification: Dewey.
Library management system: Horizon.

Special collections: A number including a mining collection and a war widows collection.
Collaborative networks: Staffordshire University Regional Federation (SURF).
Notes: The information above covers all sites: Thompson, Stoke; Law, Stoke; Nelson, Stafford; Shrewsbury.

State Hospital Staff Library

Carstairs
Lanark ML11 8RP
Tel: 01555 840293 ext. 578
E-mail: gerrymac@tsh.org.uk
Librarian: Mrs Gerry MacLean
Type: Multidisciplinary Core Forensic Psychiatry and Forensic Psychology.
Hours open: Mon–Thurs: 9am–5pm; Fri: 9am–4pm.
Users: Any staff of the State Hospital. Access, by arrangement, to all NHSIS staff. Others by arrangement with Librarian.
Lending: To all staff – no restrictions. External by arrangement with Librarian.
Stock policy: Offer to library networks or BookNet.
Holdings: 10,000 books; 56 current journal subscriptions, 112 journal titles; 6,000 offprints.
Classification: Royal College of Psychiatrists.
Library publications: Additions to stock.
Collaborative networks: BL; BMA; NULJ; PLCS; SHINE.

Stratheden Hospital Medical Library

Cupar
Fife KY15 5RR
Tel: 01334 652611 ext. 360
Fax: 01334 656560
E-mail: dorothymcginley@fife-pct.scot.nhs.uk
Librarian: Dorothy McGinley
Type: Multidisciplinary – Psychiatry; Psychology.

Hours open: Mon–Fri: 9am–5pm (staffed). 24-hour access to key holders.
Users: Employees of Fife Primary Care NHS Trust, primarily those in the Mental Health Unit. Others, reference only.
Lending: To members only. Reference books and journals not available for loan.
Stock policy: Stock is disposed of.
Holdings: 1,030 books; 32 current journal subscriptions, 87 journal titles.
Classification: NLM.
Library management system: Heritage.
Computerized services: Internet access available. Access to Cochrane Library; MEDLINE.
Library publications: Library guide; journals holdings.
Collaborative networks: BLDSC; PLCS; SHINE.

Suffolk College Nursing Library

Education Centre
Ipswich Hospital
Heath Road
Ipswich
Suffolk IP4 5PD
Tel: 01473 702547
Fax: 01473 710757
Founded:1960s.
Type: Nursing; Midwifery; Radiography.
Hours open: Mon–Thurs: 8.30am–4.30pm; Fri: 8.30am–4pm.
Users: College staff and students; health related workers.
Lending: To college staff and students. Restricted lending rights to NHS staff (ID required). Reference only to others.
Stock policy: Withdrawn stock is disposed of, not passed on to other libraries.
Holdings: 10,500 books; 60 current journal subscriptions, 104 journal titles; 200 videos.
Classification: LC and NLM.
Library management system: Dynix.
Computerized services: Internet about to be installed – for student use only. CD-ROM

access to Academic Index; ASSIA; BNI; CINAHL; Cochrane Library; Emerald Library; MEDLINE.
Library publications: In-house user guides; new books list.
Collaborative networks: HeLIN.

Suffolk Health Authority Library

Department of Public Health
PO Box 55
Foxhall Road
Ipswich
Suffolk IP3 8NN
Tel: 01473 323447
Fax: 01473 323420
E-mail: wendy.marsh@hq.suffolk-ha.anglox.nhs.uk
Librarian: Wendy Marsh
Founded: 1997
Type: Health Management.
Hours open: Mon–Fri: 8.30am–4.30pm.
Users: Health Authority staff and staff of Primary Care Groups and Trusts. Others by appointment.
Lending: As above. No lending to non-staff.
Stock policy: Dispose of out-of-date health material.
Holdings: 4,000 books; 30 current journal subscriptions, 35 journal titles; 5 CD-ROMs.
Classification: Own.
Library management system: Access.
Computerized services: 2 PCs. Access to AMED; ASSIA for Health; CINAHL; Cochrane Library; HealthStar; HMIC; MEDLINE.
Collaborative networks: Anglia and Oxford Interlibrary Loans Scheme; Suffolk and Norfolk Non Medical Education and Training Consortium Libraries Project.

Sussex Postgraduate Medical Centre Library

Brighton General Hospital
Elm Grove
Brighton
Sussex BN2 3EW
Tel: 01273 242186/242188
Fax: 01273 690032
E-mail: judy.lehmann@brighton-healthcare.nhs.uk
sharon.springham@brighton-healthcare.nhs.uk
URL: www.brighton-healthcare.nhs.uk/library/default.htm
Librarian: Judy Lehmann
Prof. staff: Sharon Springham (Deputy Head of Library Services); Jil Fairclough (Branch Librarian); Amanda Lackey (Health Authority Librarian); Vacancy (Evidence-Based Librarian)
Founded: 1967
Type: Multidisciplinary.
Hours open: Mon and Fri: 8.30am–5pm; Tues–Thurs: 8.30am–8pm.
Users: All staff of the two Trust Hospitals; all Brighton Health Authority staff; local GPs and dentists; students and staff of the Institute of Nursing and Midwifery, Brighton University. Others by arrangement.
Lending: To all members. Books only.
Stock policy: Books discarded according to South Thames stock withdrawal policy.
Holdings: 20,413 books; 368 journal titles; 50 videos; 50 CD-ROMs; 2,000 slides.
Classification: NLM.
Library management system: LIBRARIAN .
Computerized services: Access to MIRON; Ovid EBSCO Information Services. CD-ROM access to ASSIA for Health; Best Evidence; BNI; BookFind; CINAHL; ClinPsych; Cochrane Library; HMIC; MEDLINE.
Library publications: Library guide; Editor – Inset (newsletter of South Thames Libraries); electronic bulletins of library resources; full-text journals access guide.

Special collections: Evidence-based health literature; Brighton and Sussex Medico-Chirurgical Society (about 400 books on medical history); The Lancet 1832–, BMJ 1880–.
Branches: Branch Library, Rozaz House, Royal Sussex County Hospital, Brighton; Health Authority Library, East Sussex and Brighton and Hove Health Authority, Lewes, East Sussex.
Collaborative networks: NULJ; PLCS; STLIS; SWRLIN.

Sutherland Library

County Hospital
North Road
Durham DH1 4ST
Tel: 0191 3333465
E-mail: sue.graham@sunderland.ac.uk
Librarian: Sue Graham
Founded: 1995
Type: Psychiatry.
Hours open: Tues: 2pm–6pm; Thurs: 2pm–6pm.
Users: Consultants, doctors, nursing staff, community staff, therapists.
Lending: Trust staff only.
Stock policy: Dispose of it.
Holdings: 800 books; 17 current journal subscriptions, 26 journal titles.
Classification: Dewey.
Computerized services: Access to CINAHL; Cochrane Library; Embase: Psychiatry; MEDLINE.
Library publications: Library Guide to Services.
Collaborative networks: Durham and Teeside Library Alliance; HLN.

Sutton Hospital Professional Library

Chiltern Wing
Sutton Hospital
Cotswold Road
Sutton
Surrey SM2 5NF
Tel: 020 8296 4230
E-mail: kreid@sghms.ac.uk
Librarian: Karen Reid
Type: Mental Health.
Hours open: Mon, Thurs: 3pm–5pm. 24-hour access to keyholders.
Users: Staff and students at Sutton Hospital.
Lending: As above and other South Thames scheme libraries.
Holdings: 150 books; 23 current journal subscriptions, 27 journal titles.
Classification: NLM.
Computerized services: Access through Ovid to AMED; CINAHL; Clinical Evidence; EBMR; MEDLINE.
Collaborative networks: South Thames scheme for interlibrary loans.
Notes: Sutton Hospital Library is a branch of St George's Hospital Medical School Library.

Swansea NHS Trust: Singleton Hospital Staff Library

Singleton Hospital
Sketty
Swansea SA2 8QA
Tel: 01792 205666 ext. 5281
Fax: 01792 297207
E-mail: colin.engel@swansea-tr.wales.nhs.uk
Librarian: Colin Engel
Prof. staff: Helen Wright
Founded: 1973
Type: Multidisciplinary.
Hours open: Mon–Fri: 8.30am–5pm. 24-hour access for own users.
Users: Swansea NHS Trust; Swansea Bay Primary Care; Swansea Clinical School.
Lending: To library members and NHS libraries around Wales.

Stock policy: To date has been Glasgow Scheme.
Holdings: 5,000 books; 160 current journal subscriptions; 30 videos; 30 CD-ROMs.
Classification: NLM.
Library management system: Voyager.
Computerized services: Online access to Health of Wales Information Service through CymruWeb. Access to BNI; Cochrane Library; MEDLINE.
Library publications: Library guides; literature searching guides; district journals list; Audiovisual and Multimedia Resources; Training Room for Evidence and Knowledge.
Special collections: Index Medicus 1880–1966.
Branches: Sister libraries in confederation: Cefn Coed Hospital Medical Library; Staff Library Morriston Hospital.
Collaborative networks: AWHL; AWHILES.

Swindon & Marlborough NHS Trust Library

Postgraduate Centre
Princess Margaret Hospital
Okus Road
Swindon
Wiltshire SN1 4JU
Tel: 01793 426200
Fax: 01793 426816
E-mail: pmhlib@hotmail.com
Librarian: Hazel Spurrier
Founded: 1964
Type: Multidisciplinary.
Hours open: Mon–Fri: 8.30am–5.15pm.
Users: Trust staff, NHS community workers, GPs and staff. Others at Librarian's discretion.
Lending: Members. Libraries in co-operative scheme.
Stock policy: Discard.
Holdings: 4,000 books; 180 current journal subscriptions; 50 videos.
Classification: NLM.

Computerized services: Internet access to AMED; ASSIA for Health; BNI; CINAHL; Embase; HMIC; Martindale; MEDLINE; PsycINFO.
Library publications: Guide to Library Services.
Collaborative networks: SWRLIN.

Tameside Postgraduate Medical Library

Tameside Acute NHS Trust
Fountain Street
Ashton-under-Lyne
Lancashire OL6 9RW
Tel: 0161 331 6341
Fax: 0161 331 6345
Librarian: Mrs S Harrison
Founded: 1972
Type: Medical.
Hours open: Mon–Thurs: 8.30am–5pm; Fri: 8.30am–4pm.
Users: Medical staff only.
Lending: As above.
Stock policy: Disposed of after checking with other libraries.
Holdings: 2,800 books; 55 current journal subscriptions.
Classification: Own.
Library management system: DB/TextWorks.
Collaborative networks: LIHNN.

Taunton & Somerset NHS Trust Postgraduate Library

Taunton and Somerset Hospital
Taunton
Somerset TA1 5DA
Tel: 01823 342433
Fax: 01823 342434
E-mail: mcenr-s@tst.nhs.uk
Librarian: Mrs Susan McEnroe (Trust Librarian)
Prof. staff: Mrs Carol-Ann Regan
Founded: 1970
Type: Multidisciplinary.

Hours open: 24-hour access.
Users: Employees of Taunton and Somerset NHS Trust. Other members of the healthcare sector may have private membership for £25 p.a. Medical students, reference only.
Lending: Book loans to Trust employees and private members only. No journal loans.
Stock policy: Old editions and classic textbooks are offered to departments; withdrawals offered to staff; journals offered to regional libraries.
Holdings: 2,505 books; 152 current journal subscriptions.
Classification: NLM (Wessex adaptation).
Library management system: DB/TextWorks (Soutron).
Computerized services: Regional Portfolio online. Access to AMED; ASSIA for Health; BNI; CINAHL; Embase; HMIC; Martindale; MEDLINE; PsycINFO.
Collaborative networks: Somerset, Devon and Cornwall Workforce Development Confederation; SWRLIN.

Tavistock & Portman NHS Library

120 Belsize Lane
London NW3 5BA
Tel: 020 7447 3776
Fax: 020 7447 3734
E-mail: library@tavi-port.org
URL: www.tavi-port.org
Librarian: Angela Douglas
Prof. staff: Angela Hasleton; Helen Oliver.
Type: Medical – Psychosocial/Academic.
Hours open: Mon–Thurs: 9am–9pm; Fri: 10am–6pm. Vacations: 9.30am–5.30pm.
Users: Students, clinical and academic staff within Tavistock and Portman NHS Trust. Others on payment of fee.
Lending: Staff and students as above. Other members who pay, pay a special loan fee in addition.
Stock policy: Old stock is sent to BookNet.

Holdings: 16,000 books; 340 current journal subscriptions, 830 journal titles; 389 videos; 10 online databases.
Classification: BLISS.
Library management system: Unicorn.
Computerized services: Online web-based catalogue. Access to Caredata; ChildData; Cochrane Library; EBMR; Embase: Psychiatry; ERIC; MEDLINE; PsycINFO; Web of Science.
Library publications: Library guides; Guide to Internet Resources in Psychology and Social Sciences.
Collaborative networks: NTRLS.

Tayside Health Promotion Centre Library

7 Dudhope Terrace
Dundee DD3 6HG
Tel: 01382 224417/228213
Fax: 01382 226198
URL: www.show.scot.nhs.uk/thpc/v4/index.html
www.informatics-scitech.co.uk/tayside
Librarian: Dr Elspeth Henry
Type: Health Promotion.
Hours open: Mon–Fri: 9.30am–12.30pm; 1.30pm–4.30pm.
Users: Anyone resident or working in Tayside. Public and students welcome, as well as health professionals.
Lending: As above. Children need adult signature/approval.
Stock policy: Old stock is disposed of.
Holdings: 2,100 books; 35 current journal subscriptions, 42 journal titles; 250 films and videos; 10 CD-ROMs; 500 resource packs.
Classification: Own.
Library management system: HPLib 2000.
Computerized services: Access to PatientWise. CD-ROM access to HEBS Database.

Tayside Primary Care NHS Trust Library

The Carsview Centre
4 Tom McDonald Avenue
Medipark
Dundee DD2 1NH
Tel: 01382 878735
Fax: 01382 878744
E-mail: kate.harrison@tpct.scot.nhs.uk
Librarian: Kate Harrison
Founded: 1992
Type: Multidisciplinary.
Hours open: Mon–Thurs: 9am–5pm; Fri: 9am–4pm.
Users: Staff of Tayside Primary Care NHS Trust; nursing and medical students on placement. All others by arrangement with the Librarian.
Lending: Only staff and students on placement.
Stock policy: Old stock is offered then disposed of.
Holdings: 3,655 books; 93 current journal subscriptions, 187 journal titles.
Classification: Own.
Library management system: Heritage.
Computerized services: Access via Ovid to CINAHL; ClinPsych; Embase: Psychiatry.
Branches: Stalker Library, Murray Royal Hospital, Perth.
Collaborative networks: eNAMHeL; SHINE.

Ticehurst Hospital Library

Ticehurst Hospital
Ticehurst
Wadhurst
East Sussex TN5 7HU
Tel: 01580 200391 ext. 2283
Fax: 01580 201006
Librarian: T Doust
Hours open: Mon, Wed, Thurs: 3pm–5pm.
Collaborative networks: STLIS.

Tolworth Hospital Health Sciences Library

Red Lion Road
Tolworth
Surrey KT6 7QU
Tel: 020 8390 0102 ext. 5002
Fax: 020 8390 1236 (FAO Library)
E-mail: patriciaeast24@hotmail.com
Librarian: Patricia East
Founded: 1960s
Type: Multidisciplinary – Psychiatry and Psychology.
Hours open: Mon–Thurs: 9am–4pm.
Users: NHS staff and students, voluntary organizations, patients and relatives. Others at the discretion of the Librarian.
Lending: All recognized readers. Others at Librarian's discretion.
Stock policy: If it has been superseded it's usually too old for anyone, so disposed of.
Holdings: 45 current journal subscriptions, 75 journal titles; 40 videos; 6 CD-ROMs.
Classification: NLM (South Thames version).
Computerized services: Online access via Ovid to AMED; ASSIA; BNI; CINAHL; Clinical Evidence; ClinPsych; EBMR; Embase: Psychiatry; HMIC; MEDLINE and full-text journal collection.
Library publications: Journal holdings list.
Special collections: Psychiatry; Psychology.
Collaborative networks: PLCS; STLIS.

Tralee General Hospital Library

Tralee General Hospital
Tralee
Co Kerry
Republic of Ireland
Tel: +353 0 66 7184216
Fax: +353 0 66 7120627
E-mail: tghlibrary@hotmail.com
Librarian: Grainne O Mahony
Type: Medical.
Hours open: Mon, Fri: 9am–5pm; Tues, Wed, Thurs: 9am–9pm.

Users: Hospital staff, student nurses, social workers, dentists, GPs.
Lending: As above. Membership open to staff of Southern Health Board only.
Stock policy: Retain in archives.
Holdings: 2,500 books; 120 current journal subscriptions, 150 journal titles; 5 CD-ROMs.
Classification: Dewey 21.
Collaborative networks: IHLG.

Trent Knowledge & Library Services Unit

6th Floor, Boden House
Main Centre
Derby DE1 2PH
Tel: 01332 626300 ext. 6491
Fax: 01332 386545
E-mail: peter.baker@mail.sderby-ha.trent.nhs.uk
URL: telh.nhs.uk
Librarian: Peter Baker (Head of Library and Information Services)

United Bristol Healthcare Trust Learning Resource Centre (UBHT)

UBHT Education Centre
Upper Maudlin Street
Bristol BS2 8DJ
Tel: 0117 342 0105
Fax: 0117 342 0105
E-mail: ubhtirc@excite.co.uk
URL: www.ubht.nhs.uk/library
Librarian: John Sheehan
Prof. staff: Helen March; Jason Ovens
Founded: 2001
Type: Multidisciplinary Healthcare.
Hours open: Mon–Fri: 9am–5pm.
Users: UBHT staff.
Lending: UBHT staff.
Stock policy: Pass on and dispose of.
Holdings: 4,729 books; 60 current journal subscriptions, 120 journal titles; 40 videos; 20 CD-ROMs.

Classification: NLM (Wessex adaptation).
Computerized services: Access available via SWRLIN.
Collaborative networks: SWRLIN.

University College Dublin: Veterinary Medicine Library

Veterinary College
University College Dublin
Ballsbridge
Dublin 4
Republic of Ireland
Tel: +353 1 6687988
Fax: +353 1 6689732
E-mail: vetlib@ucd.ie
URL: www.ucd.ie/~library/
Librarian: Angela Hastings
Prof. staff: Rosemary Warner
Founded: 1968
Type: Veterinary.
Hours open: Mon–Fri: 9.30am–9.30pm; Sat: 9.30am–12.30pm. Vacations: Mon–Fri: 9.30am–5.30pm.
Users: Staff and students of the University. Registered external readers. Members of the veterinary profession (consultation only).
Lending: Books lent only to registered readers or via interlibrary loans.
Stock policy: Non-veterinary items discarded at intervals. Offered to other libraries or donated to charity.
Holdings: 12,000 books; 421 current journal subscriptions, 840 journal titles; 344 videos; 30 CD-ROMs.
Classification: Dewey.
Library management system: Talis.
Computerized services: Online access to Dialog. Access to AGRIS; BIOSIS; CAB; ESTA; MEDLINE; all products on the UCD Campus Network. CD-ROM access to CANIS; Clive Products; EQUUS; FELIS; electronic journal subscriptions.
Library publications: Accessions lists; library guides; newsletter.
Collaborative networks: AHIS; ASVIN; EVLG.

Notes: This library is a branch of the main UCD Library.

University College London: Thane Medical Sciences Library

Gower Street
London WC1E 6BT
Tel: 020 7679 7795/7789
Fax: 020 7679 7727
E-mail: lisa.monk@ucl.ac.uk
URL: www.ucl.ac.uk/library
Librarian: Lisa Monk
Type: Pre-clinical.
Hours open: Mon–Fri: 9.30am–7pm; Sat: 9.30am–4.30pm; Sun: check for details.
Users: Staff and students of UCL. See web page for details.
Lending: Staff and students of UCL.
Stock policy: Superseded editions of textbooks discarded or sent to store.
Holdings: 25,000 books; 450 current journal subscriptions.
Classification: GARSIDE.
Library management system: ALEPH.
Computerized services: Online access to Web of Science; CD-ROM networked access to Embase; MEDLINE.

University of Birmingham: Barnes Library

Medical School
Birmingham B15 2TT
Tel: 0121 414 3567
Fax: 0121 414 5855
E-mail: balib@bham.ac.uk
URL: www.is.bham.ac.uk/barnes
Librarian: Jean Scott
Type: Health; Life Sciences; Medical.
Hours open: Mon–Thurs: 9am–9pm; Fri: 9am–7pm; Sat: 10am–6pm. Vacations: Mon–Fri: 9am–7pm; Sat: 10am–1pm.
Users: Members of the University of Birmingham and other registered users. Others by prior appointment, for reference

only. Access control/visitor registration system in operation.

Lending: Registered borrowers only.

Stock policy: Retained in remote store – available on request.

Holdings: 93,000 books; 800 current journal subscriptions.

Classification: LC.

Library management system: Talis.

Computerized services: Wide range of networked databases and electronic journals. Numerous CD-ROMs.

Special collections: Plague (160 early vols).

University of Bristol: Dental Library

Bristol Dental Hospital
Lower Maudlin Street
Bristol BS1 2LY
Tel: 0117 928 4419
E-mail: library@bristol.ac.uk
URL: www.bris.ac.uk/is/
Librarian: Alana Farrell
Type: Dentistry.
Hours open: Mon–Wed: 9am–6.15pm; Thurs: 9.45am–6.15pm; Fri: 9am–5.45pm.
Users: University staff and students. Local NHS, dentists and others on application.
Lending: Members only or via recognized co-operative interlibrary loan schemes.
Stock policy: Duplicate copies of older books sold or discarded.
Holdings: 6,200 books; 70 current journal subscriptions, not including electronic journals.
Classification: Own.
Library management system: ALEPH.
Computerized services: Access to MEDLINE via Ovid. Access to Best Evidence; BIOSIS; Child Abuse and Neglect; CINAHL; Cochrane Library; Electronic Medicines Compendium; Embase; Health and Lifestyles; PsycINFO; Web of Science.
Collaborative networks: AULIC; SCONUL; SWRLIN.

University of Bristol: Medical Library

School of Medical Sciences
University Walk
Bristol BS8 1TD
Tel: 0117 928 7945
Fax: 0117 929 0185
E-mail: library@bristol.ac.uk
URL: www.bris.ac.uk/is/
Librarian: Fran Hazelton (Branch Supervisor)
Prof. staff: Sue Barefoot; Barbara Costello; Michael Wall
Founded: 1893
Type: Multidisciplinary.
Hours open: Mon–Wed: 8.45am–9pm; Thurs: 9.45am–9pm; Fri: 8.45am–9pm; Sat: 8.45am–4.45pm. See website for vacation opening hours.
Users: Staff and students of the University. Local NHS, GPs and others on application.
Lending: Members only or via recognized co-operative interlibrary loan schemes.
Stock policy: Duplicate copies of older books sold or discarded.
Holdings: 123,000 books; 650 current journal subscriptions, not including electronic journals.
Classification: Cunningham.
Library management system: ALEPH.
Computerized services: Access to MEDLINE via Ovid. Access to Best Evidence; BIOSIS; Child Abuse and Neglect; CINAHL; Cochrane Library; Electronic Medicines Compendium; Embase; Health and Lifestyles; PsycINFO; Web of Science.
Special collections: Medical history including books, periodicals and pamphlets; Library of Caleb Hillier Parry; mineral waters and spas.
Collaborative networks: AULIC; SCONUL; SWRLIN.

University of Bristol: Social Medicine Library

Department of Social Medicine
Canynge Hall
Whiteladies Road
Bristol BS8 2PR
Tel: 0117 928 7366
E-mail: library@bristol.ac.uk
URL: www.bris.ac.uk/is/
Librarian: Anne Dimond (Branch Supervisor)
Type: Epidemiology; Public Health Policy; Social Medicine; Primary Health Care.
Hours open: Mon–Wed, Fri: 9am–5pm; Thurs: 9.45am–5pm.
Users: University staff and students. Local NHS, GPs and others on application.
Lending: Members only or via recognized co-operative interlibrary loan schemes.
Stock policy: Duplicate copies of older books sold or discarded.
Holdings: 6,500 books; 40 current journal subscriptions, not including electronic journals.
Classification: Cunningham.
Library management system: ALEPH.
Computerized services: Access to MEDLINE via Ovid. Access to Best Evidence; BIOSIS; Child Abuse and Neglect; CINAHL; Cochrane Library; Electronic Medicines Compendium; Embase; Health and Lifestyles; PsycINFO; Web of Science.
Collaborative networks: AULIC; SCONUL; SWRLIN.

University of Bristol: Veterinary Science Library

School of Veterinary Science
Churchill Building
Langford
Bristol BS40 5DU
Tel: 0117 928 9205
E-mail: library@bristol.ac.uk
URL: www.bris.ac.uk/is/
Librarian: Valerie Warriss (Branch Supervisor)
Founded: 1950
Type: Veterinary Science.
Hours open: Mon–Wed: 8.45am–5pm; Thurs: 9.45am–5pm; Fri: 8.45am–5pm.
Users: University staff and students. Local vets and others on application.
Lending: Members only or via recognized co-operative interlibrary loan schemes.
Stock policy: Duplicate copies of older books sold or discarded.
Holdings: 25,000 books; 120 current journal subscriptions, not including electronic journals.
Classification: LC.
Library management system: ALEPH.
Computerized services: CD-ROM access to BeastCD; VetCD. Access to MEDLINE via Ovid; BIOSIS; Embase; Web of Science.
Collaborative networks: AULIC; SCONUL; SWRLIN.

University of Cambridge Library: Medical Library

Box 111
Addenbrooke's Hospital
Hills Road
Cambridge CB2 2SP
Tel: 01223 336750
Fax: 01223 331918
E-mail: library@medschl.cam.ac.uk
URL: www.medschl.cam.ac.uk/library/library.html
Librarian: P B Morgan
Prof. staff: Mrs A Collins; Mrs F W Roberts
Founded: 1973
Type: Multidisciplinary.
Hours open: Mon–Fri: 8am–10pm; Sat: 9am–9pm; Sun: 2pm–6pm.
Users: Members of Cambridge University. Local NHS staff. Local MRC staff. Others on application to the librarian.
Lending: As above.
Stock policy: Selected items transferred to Cambridge University Library. Other items disposed of.

Holdings: 35,000 books; 1,250 current journal subscriptions; 460 videos; 10 CD-ROMs.
Classification: NLM.
Library management system: Cambridge University Library.
Computerized services: Online access to Best Evidence; BIOSIS; CancerLit; Cochrane Library; Embase; PubMed; Web of Science. Access to BNI; CASP; CINAHL; HMIC; MEDLINE; PsycINFO; RCN journals database.
Library publications: Library guide; Electronic Information Resources.
Special collections: Cambridge MD and MChir theses.
Collaborative networks: HeLIN; NHS Eastern Region.

University of Cambridge: Whipple Library

Department of History and Philosophy of Science
Free School Lane
Cambridge CB2 3RH
Tel: 01223 334547
Fax: 01223 334554
E-mail: wsml@uld.cam.ac.uk
URL: www.hps.cam.ac.uk
Librarian: Dr Jill Whitelock
Founded: 1951
Type: History and Philosophy of Science, including Medicine.
Hours open: Mon–Fri: 9.30am–5.30pm. Vacations: Mon–Fri: 9.30am–5pm.
Users: Students and staff of University of Cambridge. Anyone with a genuine research interest may use the library for reading purposes on application to the Librarian.
Lending: Students and staff of University of Cambridge, visiting scholars and students from other colleges and departments in the University may apply for borrowing rights. Borrowing rights not normally granted to other categories.
Stock policy: Old stock retained.

Holdings: 24,335 books; 87 current journal subscriptions, 220 journal titles; 11 films and videos; 7 CD-ROMs; 223 theses and dissertations; 7,000 pamphlets and offprints.
Classification: Own.
Library management system: Cambridge University Union Catalogue.
Computerized services: Online access to Early English Books Online; Historical Abstracts on the Web; History of Science and Technology; Philosopher's Index; Routledge Encyclopedia of Science; Web of Science.
Special collections: Robert Whipple's Rare Books collection; Works of Robert Boyle; Phrenology Collection; Foster Pamphlet Collection; Landmarks of Science; Wellcome Iconographic Collection.

University of Central England: Nursing Library

Westbourne Road
Edgbaston
Birmingham B15 3TN
Tel: 0121 331 6011/6012
Fax: 0121 331 7180
URL: www.uce.ac.uk/library/public
Librarian: Jane Richards (Faculty Librarian)
Prof. staff: Alan Beard (Senior Assistant Librarian); Peter Ebrey (Subject Librarian); Stephen Gough (Assistant Librarian); Susan O'Sullivan (Assistant Librarian).
Founded: 1995
Type: Nursing.
Hours open: Mon–Thurs: 8.30am–9pm; Fri: 8.30am–5pm; Sat: 10am–5pm. Vacations: ask for details.
Users: Staff and students of UCE. External borrowers by fee arrangement.
Lending: As above.
Stock policy: Sell 'acceptable' old stock. Discard the rest.
Holdings: 50,000 books; 290 current journal subscriptions, 420 journal titles; 12 CD-ROMs.
Classification: Dewey.

Library management system: Talis.

Computerized services: Full range of online access. Please refer to University Library home pages.

Library publications: Various Library and Information Service and Faculty-specific guides.

Collaborative networks: WMRHLN.

University of Central Lancashire Library & Learning Resource Services

St Peter's Square
Preston
Lancashire PR1 2HE
Tel: 01772 892100
Fax: 01772 892960
E-mail: helpdesk@uclan.ac.uk
URL: www.uclan.ac.uk/library/
libhom1.htm#Basics

Type: Main university library covering Health, Nursing and allied subjects.

Hours open: See website.

Users: All registered students and staff of the University may use any of the libraries. External membership is also available, some paid and some unpaid. See website for full details.

Lending: As above.

Stock policy: See website for collection management policy.

Holdings: 500,000 books; 3,000 current printed journal subscriptions; thousands of electronic databases and full-text resources.

Classification: Dewey.

Library management system: Talis.

Computerized services: OPAC is accessible. See website for details of electronic resources.

Library publications: See website.

Branches: Clinical site libraries at Blackburn Royal Infirmary; Burnley General Hospital; Ormskirk and District General Hospital; Royal Albert Edward Infirmary, Wigan. Joint multidisciplinary services at Victoria Hospital,

Blackpool and Chorley and South Ribble District General Hospital.

Collaborative networks: BLDSC; LIHNN; NWRLS.

Notes: For opening hours and contact names see website.

University of Central Lancashire Library: Blackburn Royal Infirmary

Education Centre
Blackburn Royal Infirmary
Bolton Road
Blackburn
Lancashire BB3 3LR
Tel: 01254 294312
Fax: 01254 294318
URL: www.uclan.ac.uk/library/libclin1.htm
Collaborative networks: NULJ.

Notes: For details of opening hours and contact names see website. For users, lending services, electronic services and publications see entry for University of Central Lancashire Library and Learning Resource Services.

University of Central Lancashire Library: Burnley General Hospital

Education Centre
Burnley General Hospital
Casterton Avenue
Burnley
Lancashire BB10 2PQ
Tel: 01282 474699
Fax: 01282 474701
URL: www.uclan.ac.uk/library/libclin1.htm
Collaborative networks: NULJ.

Notes: For details of opening hours and contact names see website. For details of users, lending services, electronic services and publications see entry for University of Central Lancashire Library and Learning Resource Services.

University of Central Lancashire Library: Ormskirk and District General Hospital

Education Centre
Ormskirk and District General Hospital
Wigan Road
Ormskirk
Lancashire L39 2AZ
Tel: 01695 656790
Fax: 01695 575359
URL: www.uclan.ac.uk/library/libclin1.htm
Collaborative networks: NULJ.
Notes: For details of opening hours and contact names see website. For details of users, lending services, electronic services and publications see entry for University of Central Lancashire Library and Learning Resource Services.

University of Central Lancashire Library: Royal Albert Edward Infirmary, Wigan

Education Centre
Bernard Surgeon Suite
The Elms
Royal Albert Edward Infirmary
Wigan Lane
Wigan
Lancashire WN1 2NN
Tel: 01942 822162
Fax: 01942 822444
URL: www.uclan.ac.uk/library/libclin1.htm
Collaborative networks: NULJ.
Notes: For details of opening hours and contact names see website. For details of users, lending services, electronic services and publications see entry for University of Central Lancashire Library and Learning Resource Services.

University of Dundee School of Nursing & Midwifery Library

Ninewells
Dundee DD1 9SY
Tel: 01382 632012
Fax: 01382 640877
URL: www.dundee.ac.uk/library
Librarian: Mr Andrew Jackson
Prof. staff: Alison Aiton (Fife Campus); Donna Duff (Fife Campus); Denise Melville (Tayside Campus); Yvonne McKenzie (Tayside Campus); Norrie Sandeman (Tayside Campus)
Founded: 1967
Type: Higher Education (Nursing and Midwifery).
Hours open: Mon–Thurs: 8.45am–10pm; Fri: 8.45 am–5pm; Sat: 12 noon-4pm.
Users: Staff and students of Dundee University; NHS employees. External membership available for an annual fee.
Lending: Members only.
Stock policy: Various methods of disposal.
Holdings: 25,000 books; 300 current journal subscriptions, 500 journal titles; 1,200 videos; 25 CD-ROMs.
Classification: Dewey 20.
Library management system: Dynix.
Computerized services: Access to ASSIA; BNI; CINAHL; Cochrane Library; HEBS.
Branches: Stracathro Hospital, School of Nursing and Midwifery Library, Brechin, Angus; Gillingham Library, Perth Royal Infirmary, Perth.
Collaborative networks: BMA; NULJ; SHINE.

University of East Anglia: School of Nursing & Midwifery Library, Hellesdon Hospital

Peddars Centre
Hellesdon Hospital
Drayton High Road
Norwich NR6 5BE
Tel: 01603 421527
URL: www.lib.uea.ac.uk
Librarian: Sylvia McGregor
Prof. staff: No professional staff based on site.

Type: Nursing and Midwifery.
Hours open: Mon: 8.45am–5pm;
Tues–Thurs: 8.45am–6.30pm; Fri:
8.45am–4.30pm.
Users: Students and staff of University of
East Anglia, predominantly those in School
of Nursing and Midwifery. Open for reference
use to non-members.
Lending: As above and affiliated institutions.
External borrowers pay a fee. Others, refer-
ence use only.
Stock policy: Some older stock is trans-
ferred to the main University Library.
Withdrawn stock is discarded.
Holdings: 12,500 books; 110 current journal
subscriptions; 20 films and videos.
Classification: LC.
Library management system: Dynix.
Computerized services: Internet sub-
scriptions to CINAHL; Cochrane Library;
MEDLINE; PsycINFO; Journals @ Ovid.
Collaborative networks: ANGLES;
HeLIN.

University of East Anglia: School of Nursing and Midwifery Library, Queen Elizabeth Hospital site

Gayton Road
King's Lynn
Norfolk PE30 4ET
Tel: 01553 613959
URL: www.lib.uea.ac.uk
Librarian: Sylvia McGregor
Prof. staff: No professional staff based at
this site.
Type: Nursing and Midwifery.
Hours open: Mon, Fri: 9am–5pm; Tues,
Thurs: 9am–6pm; Wed: 9am–8pm.
Users: Students and staff of University of
East Anglia, predominantly School of
Nursing and Midwifery. Open for reference
use to non-members.
Lending: Students and staff of the University
of East Anglia and affiliated institutions.

External borrowers pay a fee. Others may
use for reference only.
Stock policy: Some older stock transferred
to main University Library. Withdrawn stock
is discarded.
Holdings: 6,500 books; 50 current journal
subscriptions; 20 films and videos.
Classification: LC.
Library management system: Dynix.
Computerized services: Access to
CINAHL; Cochrane Library; MEDLINE;
PsycINFO.
Collaborative networks: ANGLES;
HeLIN.

University of Glasgow Library

Hillhead Street
Glasgow G12 8QE
Tel: 0141 330 6704/6705
Fax: 0141 330 4952
E-mail: library@gla.ac.uk
URL: www.gla.ac.uk/library
Librarian: Andrew Wale
Prof. staff: S Ashworth; M Young
Founded: 1451
Type: Multidisciplinary.
Hours open: Mon–Fri: 8.30am–9.30pm; Sat:
9am–7.30pm; Sun: 10.30am–9.30pm.
Users: Staff and students of the University.
Graduates and bona fide researchers may
apply for external membership.
Lending: To members only.
Stock policy: Unwanted duplicates and
some superseded editions discarded.
Classification: Own.
Library management system:
Innovative Interfaces Inc.
Computerized services: Access to many
online services. Access to BIOSIS; CINAHL;
CSA; MEDLINE; Web of Science.
Special collections: Copies of Glasgow
University theses for PhD, MD, and MSc;
important historical collections of books and
manuscripts up to end of the 18th century.
Particularly strong in anatomy and
obstetrics.

Branches: James Ireland Memorial Library (dentistry); James Herriot Library (veterinary sciences).
Collaborative networks: JANET.

University of Glasgow Veterinary School: James Herriot Library

University of Glasgow
Bearsden Road
Glasgow G61 1QH
Tel: 0141 330 5708
Fax: 0141 330 4952
E-mail: vetlib@lib.gla.ac.uk
URL: www.lib.gla.ac.uk/aboutlibrary/herriot.html
Librarian: Maureen McGovern
Founded: 1994 (Vet school library 1950)
Type: Veterinary.
Hours open: Mon–Fri: 9am–5pm.
Users: Undergraduates, postgraduates, academic staff, veterinary nurses, technicians. Visitors have no borrowing rights.
Lending: To members only. Interlibrary loans requests.
Holdings: 12,627 books; 5,112 journals; 337 videos; 168 CD-ROMs.
Classification: Own.
Computerized services: Access to CAB Abstracts; EDINA-BIOSIS; MEDLINE; Web of Science.
Library publications: Newsletter.

University of Greenwich: Avery Hill Campus Library

Mansion Site
Bexley Road
Eltham
London SE9 2PQ
Tel: 020 8331 9653
E-mail: d.sheldrick@greenwich.ac.uk
Librarian: David Sheldrick
Collaborative networks: STLIS.

University of Hull Health Library

East Riding Campus
Beverley Road
Willerby
Hull
East Yorkshire HU10 6NS
Tel: 01482 466679
Fax: 01482 466680
E-mail: m.ullfors@hull.ac.uk
URL: www.hull.ac.uk/library
Librarian: Mary Ullfors (Team Leader)
Prof. staff: Elaine Houldridge (Library Skills Tutor)
Founded: 1965
Type: Nursing and Allied Health.
Hours open: Mon–Thurs: 8.30am–8pm; Fri: 8.30am–4.30pm.
Users: Staff and students of the University; NHS staff. Anyone can read or photocopy in the library.
Lending: As above. Corporate and external members can have restricted borrowing for a fee.
Stock policy: Old stock disposed of.
Holdings: 17,000 books; 164 current journal subscriptions, 180 journal titles; 560 films and videos; 20 CD-ROMs.
Classification: Dewey.
Computerized services: Access to ASSIA; CINAHL; Cochrane Library; MEDLINE; Philosopher's Index; PsycINFO, etc.
Special collections: Nursing.
Collaborative networks: NULJ.
Notes: The Health Library is a branch of University of Hull Brynmor-Jones Library.

University of Leicester: Clinical Sciences Library

University Hospitals of Leicester NHS Trust
Robert Kilpatrick Clinical Sciences Building
Leicester Royal Infirmary
PO Box 65
Leicester LE2 7LX
Tel: 0116 252 3104

Fax: 0116 252 3107
E-mail: clinlib@le.ac.uk
URL: http://www.le.ac.uk/li/clinical/clinlib.htm
Librarian: Louise Jones
Prof. staff: Joanne Dunham; Mary Edmunds Otter; Jenny Hills; Isla Kuhn; Sue Spriggs; Gemma Stephenson
Founded: 1978
Type: Multidisciplinary.
Hours open: Mon–Fri: 9am–10pm; Sat: 9am–6pm; Sun: 2pm–9pm.
Users: Staff and students of the University of Leicester and Leicester Warwick Medical School. NHS staff in Leicestershire. Other users on application and subject to a fee.
Lending: As above. External borrower ticket is available. Books and av material only.
Stock policy: Older material sent to store or discarded.
Holdings: 18,000 books; 450 current journal sunscriptions; 160 films and videos; 90 CD-ROMs.
Classification: NLM.
Library management system: Unicorn
Computerized services: Access via Internet to AMED; CINAHL; HMIC – NHS only; Cochrane Library; EBMR; EMBASE; NISS Biomed for MEDLINE and PreMEDLINE; PsycINFO; Web of Science – University only.
Library publications: Library guides; Clinical Effectiveness Update.
Special collections: Leicester Medical Society.
Collaborative networks: BMA; EMA-LINK; TRAHCLIS; UMSLG.

University of Luton: Nursing & Midwifery Library, High Wycombe

Lovelock-Jones Education Centre
Barracks Road
High Wycombe
Buckinghamshire HP11 1QN
Tel: 01494 425137
E-mail: jason.briddon@luton.ac.uk

URL: www.luton.ac.uk
Librarian: Jason Briddon
Type: Nursing and Midwifery and allied health disciplines.
Hours open: Mon–Thurs: 9am–6pm; Fri: 9am–5pm.
Users: Staff and students of University of Luton; employees of South Buckinghamshire NHS Trust.
Lending: As above.
Holdings: 8,000 books; 80 current journal subscriptions; 100 films and videos; 10 CD-ROMs.
Classification: NLM (Wessex adaptation).
Library management system: Millennium.
Computerized services: Online access to Cochrane Library; Access to BNI; CINAHL; HealthStar; HMIC; Social Services Abstracts.
Collaborative networks: HeLIN; NULJ.

University of Luton: Nursing & Midwifery Library, Stoke Mandeville

Nuffield Centre
Stoke Mandeville Hospital
Aylesbury
Buckinghamshire HP21 8AL
Tel: 01296 315900
Fax: 01296 315903
E-mail: jason.briddon@luton.ac.uk
URL: www.luton.ac.uk
Librarian: Jason Briddon
Type: Nursing and Midwifery and allied health disciplines.
Hours open: Mon–Thurs: 9am–6pm; Fri: 9am–5pm; Sat: 9.30am–2.30pm.
Users: University of Luton staff and students. Employees of local NHS Trusts – Stoke Mandeville, Vale of Aylesbury.
Lending: As above.
Holdings: 8,500 books; 90 current journal subscriptions; 150 films and videos; 10 CD-ROMs.
Classification: NLM (Wessex adaptation).

Library management system: Millennium.
Computerized services: Online access to Cochrane Library; Access to BNI; CINAHL; HealthStar; HMIC; Social Services Abstracts.
Collaborative networks: HeLIN; NULJ.

University of Manchester: ARC Epidemiology Unit, Lawrence Library

School of Epidemiology and Health Sciences
Stopford Building
Oxford Road
Manchester M13 9PT
Tel: 0161 275 3235
Fax: 0161 275 5043
E-mail: mary.ingram@man.ac.uk
Librarian: Mary Ingram
Type: Specialist library for rheumatic diseases and epidemiology
Hours open: Mon–Fri: 8.30am–4.30pm. 24-hour access.
Users: By appointment only.
Lending: Members only.
Stock policy: Passed to other libraries.
Holdings: 70 current journal subscriptions; 250 journal titles.
Classification: Own.
Computerized services: Access to all databases provided by John Rylands University Library of Manchester, via University network.
Special collections: Rheumatology; epidemiology.
Collaborative networks: LIHNN.

University of Manchester: National Primary Care Research & Development Centre Library

5th Floor
Williamson Building
Oxford Road
Manchester M13 9PL

Tel: 0161 275 7624
Fax: 0161 275 7600
E-mail: RMcNally@fs1.cpcr.man.ac.uk
URL: www.npcrdc.man.ac.uk
Librarian: Mrs Rosalind McNally
Founded: 1995
Type: Primary Care; Health Management.
Hours open: 9am–4.30pm.
Users: Members of staff of the National Primary Care R&D Centre. Access to anyone else by appointment with the Librarian.
Lending: Members of staff only.
Stock policy: Dispose of it.
Holdings: 2,000 books; 32 current journal subscriptions, 53 journal titles.
Classification: Own.
Library management system: Penlib.
Computerized services: Internet and e-mail available. Online access to Embase; HMIC; MEDLINE.
Collaborative networks: LIHNN.

University of Newcastle: Community Child Health Library

Department of Community Child Health
13 Walker Terrace
Gateshead
Tyne and Wear NE8 1EB
Tel: 0191 477 6000
Fax: 0191 477 0370
E-mail: penny.giddings@ncl.ac.uk
Librarian: Mrs Penny Giddings
Founded:1995
Type: Departmental.
Hours open: Open access. Staffed 2pm–5pm.
Users: All members of the Department. Health visitors, researchers and anyone in injury prevention, by prior appointment.
Lending: Only members of the Department.
Stock policy: Stored in attic.
Holdings: 1,500 books and reports; 16 current journal subscriptions, 26 journal titles; 16 videos; 4 CD-ROMs.
Classification: Own.

Library management system: END-NOTE and Browne.
Computerized services: Access to BIDS; CINAHL; MEDLINE; PsychLit; Web of Science via link to Newcastle University Library.
Collaborative networks: HLN.

University of Northumbria Learning Resource Centre

Coach Lane Campus
Coach Lane
Newcastle-upon-Tyne NE7 7XA
Tel: 0191 215 6540
Fax: 0191 215 6560
E-mail: in.coachlane@unn.ac.uk
URL: http://www.unn.ac.uk
Librarian: Graham Walton
Prof. staff: Pam Bailey; Paul Evans; Sheena Hanes.
Founded: 1966
Type: Multidisciplinary.
Hours open: Mon–Thurs: 9am–9pm; Fri: 9am–7pm; Sat: 9.30am–5pm; Sun: 11am–5pm. Vacations: Mon, Wed, Thurs: 9am–8pm; Tues: 9am–9pm; Fri: 9am–5pm; Sat: 1pm–5pm.
Users: University staff and students. Members of the public have access to the printed collection.
Lending: As above.
Stock policy: Sold.
Holdings: 120,000 books; 610 printed journal subscriptions, 3,000 electronic journals.
Classification: Dewey.
Library management system: Talis.
Computerized services: Access to AIDS and Cancer Research Abstracts; AMED; ASSIA; Best Evidence; BNI; Caredata; ChildData; CINAHL; Cochrane Library; HealthStar; HMIC; MEDLINE; Nursing Collections; PsycINFO; SMART; Social Work Abstracts; TRAVAX. CD-ROM access to Community Wise; Health and Lifestyle; National Surveys Guide; OECD Health Data.

Library publications: Database guides; Self Guided Tour leaflets; Database of journal articles.
Collaborative networks: HLN.

University of Nottingham: Derby School of Nursing Library

Derbyshire Royal Infirmary
London Road
Derby DE1 2QY
Tel: 01332 347141 ext. 2561/4315
Fax: 01332 290321
Librarian: Cathryn James
Type: Nursing.
Hours open: Mon–Thurs: 8.30am–5pm; Fri: 8.30am–4.30pm.
Users: University of Nottingham staff and students.
Lending: As above only.
Stock policy: Send to countries abroad; damaged stock disposed of.
Holdings: 75 journal titles; 50 CD-ROMs.
Classification: RCN.
Library management system: ALEPH.
Computerized services: Full range of databases via University of Nottingham.
Library publications: In-house publicity.

University of Nottingham: School of Nursing Library

Dukeries Centre
King's Mill Centre
Mansfield Road
Sutton-in-Ashfield
Nottingham NG17 4JL
Tel: 01623 465634/465638
Fax: 01623 465601
E-mail: sarah.carlile@nottingham.ac.uk
URL: www.nottingham.ac.uk/library/services/librarysites/mansfield.html
Librarian: Sarah Carlile
Founded: 1972
Type:; Nursing and Midwifery.

Hours open: Mon–Thu: 8.30am–4.30pm; Fri: 8.30am–4pm.

Users: Staff and students of Nottingham University. External membership reference use only, or limited membership rights on payment of a fee.

Lending: To staff and students of the University and to external members who have paid the annual fee.

Stock policy: Stock disposed of by book sales or sending to Third World countries.

Holdings: 12,000 books; 46 current journal subscriptions, 71 journal titles.

Classification: Dewey.

Library management system: Manual.

Computerized services: Internet databases and electronic journals. Access to various networked CD-ROMs; Ovid Biomed; Web of Science and others.

Library publications: Library Skills Pack; Newsletter for teaching staff.

Collaborative networks: Nottingham University Libraries; North Nottinghamshire Health Libraries; NULJ; TRAHCLIS.

University of Oxford: Institute of Health Sciences Library

Old Road
Headington
Oxford OX3 7LF
Tel: 01865 226688
Fax: 01865 226619
E-mail: library.enquiries@ihs.ox.ac.uk
URL: www.his.ox.ac.uk/library/homepage.htm
Librarian: Nicola Bexon
Founded: 1995
Type: Health Sciences Research.
Hours open: Mon–Fri: 8am–7pm. Staffed 9am–5.15pm.
Users: University employees, NHS organizations, Health Authority staff. Use of library by outside organizations is permitted.
Lending: All members.
Stock policy: Regional stock passed to other libraries. Other stock disposed of.

Holdings: 7,000 books; 60 current journal subscriptions, 80 journal titles.

Classification: NLM.

Library management system: OLIS.

Computerized services: Online access to full-text electronic journals. Access to Best Evidence; BIDS; CINAHL; Cochrane Library; Embase; LISA; MEDLINE; PsycINFO; Sociofile; Web of Science.

Special collections: Extensive statistical collection – all ONS publications in health area.

Collaborative networks: HeLIN.

University of Paisley: Royal Alexandra Hospital Campus

Department of Nursing, Midwifery and
  Health Care Library
Corsebar Road
Paisley
Renfrewshire PA2 9PN
Tel: 0141 580 4757
Fax: 0141 887 4962
E-mail: ruth.robinson@paisley.ac.uk
URL: http://library.paisley.ac.uk/libhome.htm
Librarian: Ruth Robinson
Prof. staff: Katrina Dalziel
Type: Nursing; Medicine.
Hours open: Mon–Thurs: 8.30am–4.30pm; Fri: 8.30am–4pm.
Users: Hospital staff, placement students, University staff and students. Others can apply to use the library for a fee.
Lending: All members.
Holdings: 5,600 books; 168 current journal subscriptions, 350 journal titles; 10 CD-ROMs.
Classification: Dewey 21.
Library management system: Talis.
Computerized services: Internet access available. Access to AMED; CINAHL; Cochrane Library; Embase; MEDLINE; PsycINFO; SportDiscus via Hospital subscriptions.

Branches: Multidisciplinary libraries at University campuses at Ayr, Dumfries, Paisley.
Collaborative networks: SHINE.

University of Plymouth: Plymouth Campus Library

Drake Circus
Plymouth
Devon PL4 8AA
Tel: 01752 232307
Fax: 01752 232327
URL: www.plymouth.ac.uk
Librarian: Jane Gosling; Penny Holland
Type: University library. Plymouth Campus – Science, Technology, Human Sciences, Business.
Hours open: Mon–Fri: 8.30am–10pm; Sat: 9am–5pm; Sun: 10am–6pm. Vacations: Mon–Fri: 8.30am–5pm.
Users: University of Plymouth staff and students. Associate membership available for a fee. General public have reference rights.
Lending: As above.
Stock policy: Offered for sale in library or disposed of.
Holdings: 270,000 books; 1,862 current journal subscriptions; 6,500 films and videos.
Classification: Dewey.
Library management system: Libertas.
Computerized services: See website.
Branches: Exeter Campus Library; Exmouth Campus Library; Seale Hayne Campus Library.
Collaborative networks: UK Libraries Plus.

University of Portsmouth: Frewen Library

Cambridge Road
Portsmouth
Hampshire PO1 2ST
Tel: 023 9284 3225
Fax: 023 9284 3233
URL: www.libr.port.ac.uk
Librarian: Ian Bonar (University Librarian)
Prof. staff: 22 librarians
Founded: 1977
Type: Higher Education.
Hours open: Mon–Thurs: 9am–9.45pm; Fri: 9am–8.45pm; Sat, Sun: 10am–4pm. Vacations: Mon–Fri: 9am–4.55pm; Sat, Sun: 11am–3pm.
Users: Registered staff and students of the University. External membership available.
Lending: As above.
Stock policy: Dispose of or pass on.
Holdings: 378,663 books; 3,313 current journal subscriptions; 4,442 films and videos; 1,901 CD-ROMs.
Classification: Dewey.
Library management system: Talis.
Computerized services: Access to AgeInfo; ASSIA; BNI; Caredata; Catchword; ChildData; CINAHL; Cochrane Library; MEDLINE; PsychLit; ScienceDirect; Web of Science. See website for full details.
Library publications: Library guides; Guide for External Readers.
Special collections: European Documentation Centre; law; Parliamentary papers; rare books; statistics.
Collaborative networks: SWRLIN.

University of St Andrews Library

North Street
St Andrews
Fife KY16 9TR
Tel: 01334 462281
Fax: 01334 462282
E-mail: library@st-and.ac.uk
URL: www.library.st-and.ac.uk/
Librarian: Neil Dumbleton
Prof. staff: Christine Gascoigne (Head of Special Collections); Jean Young (Head of Reference and Information Service)
Founded: 1640
Type: Multidisciplinary academic.

Hours open: Mon–Thurs: 8.45am–10pm; Fri: 8.45am–6pm; Sat: 9am–5pm; Sun: 1pm–7pm.
Users: Mainly students and staff of the University. Anyone with a good reason.
Lending: University staff and students; sixth-formers from local schools; students from Dundee University. Others on payment of membership fee.
Stock policy: No disposal.
Holdings: 650,000 books; 2,750 current journal subscriptions, 10,000 journal titles; 450 films and videos; 85 CD-ROMs.
Classification: LC.
Library management system: INNOPAC.
Computerized services: Online access to numerous databases.
Special collections: Numerous.
Collaborative networks: SCURL; Tayside and Fife Library and Information Network.

University of Sheffield Health Sciences Library: Manvers Campus Site

Humphry Davy House
Golden Smithies Lane
Manvers
Rotherham S63 7ER
Tel: 0114 222 7390
Fax: 0114 222 7399
E-mail: hsl.mc@sheffield.ac.uk
URL: www.shef.ac.uk/~lib/hsl/dvc.html
Librarian: Lyn Parker (Site Librarian)
Prof. staff: Simon Cumper
Founded: 1998
Type: Nursing
Hours open: Mon–Thurs: 9am–6pm; Fri: 9am–5pm.
Users: Staff and students of the University of Sheffield. Reference access for the general public. External borrowing on payment of a fee. Computer network restricted to members of the University.
Lending: All registered members.

Stock policy: Single copies of old editions kept in store, otherwise discarded.
Holdings: 9,200 books; 75 journal titles; 60 films and videos; 120 CD-ROMs; 250 theses.
Classification: NLM.
Library management system: Talis.
Computerized services: Access to AMED; ASSIA; Best Evidence; BNI; Caredata; CINAHL; Cochrane Library; DARE; Embase; ENB Healthcare Database; MEDLINE; PsycINFO; Web of Science.
Collaborative networks: ALL; SINTO; TRAHCLIS.

University of Sheffield Health Sciences Library: Northern General Hospital Site

Samuel Fox House
Sheffield S5 7AU
Tel: 0114 226 6801
Fax: 0114 226 6804
E-mail: hsl.ngh@sheffield.ac.uk
URL: www.shef.ac.uk/~lib/hsl/ngh.htm
Librarian: Vicky Grant; Alison Little (job-share)
Founded: 1980
Type: Multidisciplinary.
Hours open: Mon–Thurs: 9am–8pm; Fri: 9am–5pm; Sat: 9am–1pm including Easter vacation. Christmas and Summer vacations: Mon–Thurs: 9am–7pm; Fri: 9am–5pm; Sat: 9am–1pm.
Users: University of Sheffield staff and students; NHS staff employed in Sheffield. Fee-paying external members. Reference access to general public.
Lending: All registered members.
Stock policy: Single copies of old editions kept on site, otherwise discarded.
Holdings: 16,000 books; 260 current journal subscriptions; 200 films and videos; 80 CD-ROMs; 70 theses.
Classification: NLM.
Library management system: Talis.

Computerized services: Access to AMED; ASSIA; Best Evidence; BNI; CINAHL; Cochrane Library; DARE; Embase; MEDLINE; PsycINFO; Web of Science.
Collaborative networks: ALL; SINTO; TRAHCLIS.

University of Sheffield Health Sciences Library: Royal Hallamshire Hospital Site

Glossop Road
Sheffield S10 2JF
Tel: 0114 271 2030
Fax: 0114 278 0923
E-mail: hsl.rhh@sheffield.ac.uk
URL: www.shef.ac.uk/~lib/libsites/ hslindex.html
Librarian: Fiona MacGillivray (Site Librarian)
Prof. staff: Frances Ludlow; Mary Sackett; John van Loo (Health Sciences Librarian); Amanda Watkinson; Marie Willett
Founded: 1978
Type: Multidisciplinary.
Hours open: Mon–Thurs: 9am–9.30pm; Fri: 9am–5pm; Sat: 9am–1pm including Easter vacation. Christmas and Summer vacations: Mon–Thurs: 9am–7pm; Fri: 9am–5pm; Sat: 9am–12.30pm.
Users: NHS staff in Sheffield; staff and students of the University of Sheffield. Fee-paying external members. Reference access to general public.
Lending: All registered members.
Stock policy: 1 copy of superseded editions relegated to store, others discarded.
Holdings: 26,600 books; 450 current journal subscriptions; 280 videos.
Classification: NLM.
Library management system: Talis.
Computerized services: Access to AMED; ASSIA; Best Evidence; BNI; CINAHL; Cochrane Library; DARE; Embase; MEDLINE; PsycINFO; Web of Science.
Library publications: User guides.
Collaborative networks: SINTO; TRAHCLIS.

University of Southampton: Health Sciences Library

Mailpoint 883
South Academic Block
Southampton General Hospital
Southampton
Hampshire SO16 6YD
Tel: 023 8079 6541
Fax: 023 8079 8939
E-mail: hslib@soton.ac.uk
URL: www.soton.ac.uk/~library/health
Librarian: Mrs C Fowler (Head of Health Care Services Division)
Prof. staff: Mrs J Stephenson; Mrs D Morris (Library Managers); Mrs E Robertson; Miss M McKenna; Mrs S Forsey (Subject Librarians)
Founded: 1969
Type: Multidisciplinary.
Hours open: Mon–Thurs: 8.30am–9.30pm; Fri: 8.30am–6pm; Sat: 9am–5pm; Sun: 2pm–6pm. Staffed: Mon–Fri: 8.30am–6pm; Sat: 9am–12.30pm.
Users: Staff and students of University of Southampton. Staff of Southampton University Hospitals NHS Trust and other NHS staff in South East and South West Region and affiliated organizations.
Lending: Lend stock to borrowers to comply with registration criteria. Do not lend to members of the public.
Holdings: 30,001 books; 652 current journal subscriptions; 1,102 films and videos; 34 CD-ROMs; 405 other items.
Classification: NLM.
Library management system: SIRSI Unicorn.
Computerized services: Online access to Dialog. Access to ASSIA; BIDS; CSA; EDINA; Internurse; Web of Science; WebSPIRS. Access to AMED; BNI; BIOSIS previews; CINAHL; Cochrane Library; Embase; Index to Theses; MEDLINE; PsycINFO; Science and Social Science Citation Index.
Library publications: Guides and leaflets for users including searching guides for BNI,

MEDLINE, PubMed, Embase, Cochrane Library. Health and biomedical periodicals listing for University of Southampton.
Special collections: NHS management collection; audiovisual collection.
Collaborative networks: HATRICS; STLIS; SWRLIN; SWRS-SW.

University of Surrey: George Edwards Library

Stag Hill
Guildford
Surrey GU2 5XH
Tel: 01483 300800 (Jennifer Nordon)
Fax: 01483 259500
E-mail: j.nordon@surrey.ac.uk
v.cox@surrey.ac.uk
Librarian: Jennifer Nordon
Prof. staff: Vivienne Cox; Franko Kowalczuk
Collaborative networks: STLIS.

University of the West of England Library Services: Bath Campus Library

Education Centre
Royal United Hospital
Combe Park
Bath BA1 3NG
Tel: 01225 824255
Fax: 01225 824256
E-mail: Stephen.Hunt@uwe.ac.uk
URL: www.uwe.ac.uk/library/info/bath/
Librarian: Stephen Hunt
Prof. staff: None based on site. Support from Health and Social Care Faculty Librarian based at Bristol.
Founded: 1996 (as part of University)
Type: Nursing, Midwifery, Health and Social Care.
Hours open: Mon–Thurs: 8.30am–6.30pm; Fri: 8.30am–4.30pm. Vacations: Mon–Thurs: 8.30am–5pm; Fri: 8.30am–4.30pm.
Users: Students and staff of University of West of England. Members of local Health

Trusts. Any member of the public can use us for reference only.
Lending: As above. Plus paying subscribers. Participants in UK Libraries Plus or AULIC.
Stock policy: Some passed on to main library for archives. Materials over 10 years old normally given away. Material containing obsolete, possibly unsafe practices, destroyed.
Holdings: 12,000 books; 80 printed journal subscriptions, many more electronic, 120 journal titles; 150 videos; 4 CD-ROMs.
Classification: Dewey.
Library management system: Unicorn.
Computerized services: Many CD-ROM subscriptions networked by IRIS.
Library publications: Newsletter.
Collaborative networks: SWRLIN.
Notes: This library is one of 8 libraries at the University.

University of the West of England: Hartpury Campus Frank Parkinson Learning Resources Centre

Hartpury
Gloucestershire GL19 3BE
Tel: 01452 702160
Fax: 01452 702161
URL: www.uwe.ac.uk/
Librarian: Jan Nichols
Prof. staff: Andrea Baker; Hilary Cousens; Catherine Gibb
Founded: 1999
Type: Nursing and Health; Land-based Studies including Equine and Animal Science.
Hours open: Mon–Thurs: 9am–9pm; Fri: 9am–5pm; Sat: 10am–1pm. Reference only: Fri: 5pm–9pm; Sat: 1pm–5pm; Sun: 10am–5pm. Vacations: 9am–5pm.
Users: Staff and students of UWE and Hartpury College. Anyone can use the library for reference.
Lending: Staff and students of UWE and Hartpury College. Also members of local

NHS Trusts. Members of the public can pay to join.
Stock policy: Dispose of.
Holdings: 12,000 books on health; 160 current journal subscriptions on health; 800 films and videos; 98 CD-ROMs.
Classification: Dewey.
Library management system: Unicorn.
Computerized services: Internet access to CAB Abstracts; Ovid; Science Abstracts. CD-ROM access to BNI; CINAHL; Cochrane Library; GEOBASE.
Special collections: 2 photocopy collections – Gloucestershire Naturalists Society materials and the Gloucestershire Beekeepers Association materials; small bones and models collection.
Collaborative networks: SWRLIN.
Notes: This centre is a branch of UWE Library Services.

University of Ulster at Jordanstown

Shore Road
Newtown Abbey
Antrim BT37 0QB
Tel: 028 90 366964
Fax: 028 90 366849
E-mail: nd.burns@ulst.ac.uk
URL: www.ulst.ac.uk
Librarian: Niall Burns
Prof. staff: Lewis Childs; Laura Mills; Janet Peden; Liz Young.
Founded: 1974
Type: Multidisciplinary.
Hours open: 9am–10pm. Vacations: 9am–5pm.
Users: Staff and students of the University; researchers on application. Non-members for reference purposes.
Lending: Staff and students of the University. Interlibrary loans.
Stock policy: Dispose of or offer to charities.
Holdings: 25,000 books; 160 current journal subscriptions, 250 journal titles.

Classification: Dewey.
Library management system: Talis.
Computerized services: Online access to CancerLit; CINAHL; MEDLINE via Biomed. Online access to ASSIA; Cochrane Library; First Search; Proquest Health and Medical; PsycINFO; Web of Science. Access to BNI.
Branches: University of Ulster at Coleraine; University of Ulster at Magee.

University of Wales College of Medicine: Brian Cooke Dental Library

Dental School
Heath Park
Cardiff CF14 4XY
Tel: 02920 742525
Fax: 02920 743834
E-mail: denlib@cf.ac.uk
URL: www.uwcm.ac.uk/support/ information_services/libraries/librarysites/dental.htm
Librarian: Ms J Stevens
Founded: 1965
Type: Dentistry.
Hours open: Tues, Thurs, Fri: 9am–5.30pm; Mon, Wed: 9am–6pm.
Users: Staff and students of UWCM. NHS staff in Cardiff area.
Lending: As above. Others, reference only.
Stock policy: Obsolete or little-used material discarded. Two editions of standard text kept. Discarded stock sold off to students.
Holdings: 9,000 books; 150 current journal subscriptions; 130 videos; 30 CD-ROMs.
Classification: Own.
Library management system: Voyager.
Computerized services: Online access to Dialog. Access via Biomedical Data Service to CancerLit; CINAHL; MEDLINE; PreMEDLINE. Access to AMED; ASSIA Net; Best Evidence; BNI; Caredata; ClinPsych; Cochrane Library; ERIC; HMIC; HealthStar; Index to Theses; OTDBase; SMART; Web of Science; ZETOC.

Library publications: Library guide; guide to searching MEDLINE; user education materials.

Special collections: Small historical collection (240 vols.).

Collaborative networks: AWHILES; AWHL.

University of Wales College of Medicine: Cancer Research Wales Library

Velindre Hospital
Whitchurch
Cardiff CF14 2TL
Tel: 029 2031 6291
Fax: 029 2031 6927
E-mail: Bernadette.Coles@velindre-tr.wales.nhs.uk
URL: www.uwcm.ac.uk/support/ information_services/libraries/librarysites/ velindre.htm
Librarian: Bernadette Coles
Founded: 1969
Type: Multidisciplinary.
Hours open: Mon–Fri: 8.30am–4.30pm.
Users: Staff and students of UWCM.
Lending: Members only.
Stock policy: Disposed of.
Holdings: 1,200 books; 54 current journal subscriptions; 15 films and videos.
Classification: Dewey.
Library management system: Voyager.
Computerized services: Online access to Dialog. Access via Biomedical Data Service to CancerLit; CINAHL; MEDLINE; PreMEDLINE. Access to AMED; ASSIA Net; Best Evidence; BNI; Caredata; ClinPsych; Cochrane Library; ERIC; HMIC; HealthStar; Index to Theses; OTDBase; SMART; Web of Science; ZETOC.
Library publications: In-house library guide.
Collaborative networks: AWHILES; AWHL.

University of Wales College of Medicine: Cochrane Library

Llandough Hospital
Penarth
South Glamorgan CF64 2XX
Tel: 029 20715497
Fax: 029 20716497
E-mail: cochranelib@cardiff.ac.uk
URL: uwcm.ac.uk/support /information services/libraries/librarysites/ cochrane.htm
Librarian: Rosemary Soper
Founded: 1973
Type: Multidisciplinary.
Hours open: Mon–Fri: 9am–5pm.
Users: Staff and students of University of Wales College of Medicine; Cardiff and Vale NHS Trust. Others on written request.
Lending: To all registered members. Non-members on payment of external membership fee.
Stock policy: Non-unique journals disposed of after five years. Older editions of textbooks disposed of.
Holdings: 3,000 books; 87 current journal subscriptions, 110 journal titles; 50 videos.
Classification: Dewey.
Library management system: Voyager.
Computerized services: Online access to Dialog. Access via Biomedical Data Service to CancerLit; CINAHL; MEDLINE; PreMEDLINE. Access to AMED; ASSIA Net; Best Evidence; BNI; Caredata; ClinPsych; Cochrane Library; ERIC; HMIC; HealthStar; Index to Theses; OTDBase; SMART; Web of Science; ZETOC.
Publications: In-house library guides.
Special collections: Cochrane Library Archive – memorabilia relating to Archie Cochrane.
Collaborative networks: AWHILES; AWHL.

University of Wales College of Medicine: Nursing & Healthcare Studies Library

Heath Park
Cardiff CF14 4XR
Tel: 02920 742387
Fax: 02920 756431
E-mail: healthclib@cf.ac.uk
URL: www.uwcm.ac.uk
Librarian: Meg Gorman
Prof. staff: Elizabeth Morgan
Type: Nursing and Medicine.
Hours open: Oct–July: Mon–Thurs: 8.45am–8pm; Fri: 8.45am–5pm; Sat: 9am–12.30pm. July—Sept: Mon–Fri: 8.45am–5pm.
Users: Staff and students of UWCM; staff of local NHS Trusts. Anyone can use the library for reference purposes. Computer use is limited to UWCN staff and students.
Lending: As above. Students of Cardiff University. Journals for reference use only.
Stock policy: Dispose of old stock.
Holdings: 25,846 books; 160 current journal subscriptions; 70 films and videos; 7 CD-ROMs.
Classification: Dewey.
Library management system: Voyager.
Computerized services: Online access to Dialog. Access via Biomedical Data Service to CancerLit; CINAHL; MEDLINE; PreMEDLINE. Access to AMED; ASSIA Net; Best Evidence; BNI; Caredata; ClinPsych; Cochrane Library; ERIC; HMIC; HealthStar; Index to Theses; OTDBase; SMART; Web of Science; ZETOC.
Collaborative networks: AWHILES.

University of Wales College of Medicine: School of Nursing & Midwifery Studies Library

Caerleon Education Centre
Grounds of St Cadoc's Hospital
Caerleon
Newport
Gwent NP18 3XR
Tel: 01633 430919
Fax: 01633 430717
E-mail: caerleonlib@cf.ac.uk
URL: www. uwcm.ac.uk
Librarian: Meg Gorman
Prof. staff: Angela Bowyer
Founded: 1992
Type: Nursing.
Hours open: Mon–Fri: 8.30am–5pm.
Users: Staff and students of UWCM; qualified nursing staff of Gwent Healthcare Trust. Anyone can use the library for reference purposes. Computer use is limited to staff and students of UWCM.
Lending: As above. Journals are for reference use only.
Stock policy: Dispose of old stock.
Holdings: 16,894 books; 107 current journal subscriptions; 1 CD-ROM.
Classification: Dewey.
Library management system: Voyager.
Computerized services: Online access to Dialog. Access via Biomedical Data Service to CancerLit; CINAHL; MEDLINE; PreMEDLINE. Access to AMED; ASSIA Net; Best Evidence; BNI; Caredata; ClinPsych; Cochrane Library; ERIC; HMIC; HealthStar; Index to Theses; OTDBase; SMART; Web of Science; ZETOC.
Collaborative networks: AWHL; Newport Library and Information Services.

University of Wales College of Medicine: Sir Herbert Duthie Medical Library

Heath Park
Cardiff CF14 4XN
Tel: 029 2074 2875
Fax: 029 2074 3651
E-mail: duthielib@cf.ac.uk
URL: www.uwcm.ac.uk/support/
information_services/libraries
Librarian: Eiran Kelly
Prof. staff: Digna Liepa; Rowland Somers
Founded: 1947 (Present location 1971)
Type: Multidisciplinary.

Hours open: Mon–Fri: 9am–9pm; Sat: 9am–5pm. Aug/Sept: Mon–Fri: 9am–7pm; Sat: 9am–12.30pm.

Users: Staff and students of UWCM; NHS staff. Open to others for reference purposes.

Lending: As above. Limited membership rights to other identified groups.

Stock policy: Withdrawn items offered for sale to readers or where appropriate donated to libraries overseas.

Holdings: 96,000 books; 1,343 current journal subscriptions; 600 films and videos; 50 CD-ROMs; 56 maps.

Classification: Dewey.

Library management system: Voyager.

Computerized services: Online access to Dialog. Access via Biomedical Data Service to CancerLit; CINAHL; MEDLINE; PreMEDLINE. Access to AMED; ASSIA Net; Best Evidence; BNI; Caredata; ClinPsych; Cochrane Library; ERIC; HMIC; HealthStar; Index to Theses; OTDBase; SMART; Web of Science; ZETOC.

Library publications: Database search guides; department newsletter; library guides; user education material.

Special collections: History of Medicine – pre-1935 items (2,000 vols).

Collaborative networks: AWHILES.

University of Wales College of Medicine: Whitchurch Postgraduate Centre Library

Postgraduate Medical Centre
Whitchurch Hospital
Cardiff CF14 7XB
Tel: 029 2033 6382
Fax: 029 2052 0170
E-mail: kitcher@cf.ac.uk
URL: www.uwcm.ac.uk
Librarian: Mrs Hilary Kitcher
Founded: 1972
Type: Psychiatric; Multidisciplinary.
Hours open: Mon–Fri: 9am–5pm.
Users: Staff and students of UWCM. Staff of Cardiff and Vale NHS Trust.

Lending: All registered users; non-members may use library for reference purposes only. Journals may not be borrowed but photocopies may be made.

Stock policy: Withdrawn older stock is offered for sale to library users.

Holdings: 3,000 books; 88 current journal subscriptions, 120 journal titles; 40 films and videos; 10 CD-ROMs.

Classification: Dewey.

Library management system: Voyager.

Computerized services: Access to Aidsline; AMED; Best Evidence; CancerLit; CINAHL; ClinPsych; Cochrane Library; HealthStar; MEDLINE; PreMEDLINE.

Library publications: In-house journal holdings list.

Special collections: Historical psychiatry.

Collaborative networks: AWHILES; AWHL; PLCS.

University of Wales Swansea: School of Health Science Library & Information Service

Morriston Hospital
Swansea SA6 6NL
Tel: 01792 703767
Fax: 01792 799230
E-mail: s.m.storey@swansea.ac.uk
URL: www.swan.ac.uk/lis/morriston/index.htm
Librarian: Stephen Storey
Founded: 1947
Type: Nursing.
Hours open: Mon: 8.30am–9pm; Tues, Thurs, Fri: 8.30am–5pm; Wed: 9am–5pm.
Users: Staff and students of the School of Health Science have access to loan of books, interlibrary requests, etc. Others may use the library for reference.
Lending: Staff and students of the University only. Journals, reference only.
Stock policy: Withdrawn and duplicate stock offered to others by e-mail.
Holdings: 6,000 books; 123 current journal subscriptions, 243 journal titles.
Classification: NLM (Wessex adaptation).

Library management system: Voyager.
Computerized services: Online access to PubMed. Access to BNI; CINAHL; Science Direct; SwetsNet.
Library publications: List of journals held; guides to various databases.
Collaborative networks: AWHL; NULJ.

University of Warwick: Centre for Health Services Studies

Warwick Business School
Coventry
Warwickshire CV4 7AL
Tel: 02746 523985
Fax: 02476 524963
E-mail: chssdc@wbs.warwick.ac.uk
URL: http://users.wbs.warwick.ac.uk/chess/
Librarian: Diane Clay
Founded: 1984
Type: Health.
Hours open: 24-hour access by key for staff.
Users: Health researchers within the University and allied to the Warwick West Midlands Primary Care Research Network.
Lending: As above.
Stock policy: Pass on to BookAid.
Holdings: 350 books; 17 current journal subscriptions, 26 journal titles.
Classification: Dewey.
Computerized services: Online access, for NHS projects, to Aidsline; AMED; CINAHL; Embase: Psychiatry; MEDLINE; Nursing Collection; Ovid HealthStar. Access to Cochrane Library; HMIC; Ovid MEDLINE.
Library publications: See list on website.
Collaborative networks: WMRHLN.

University of Wolverhampton: Manor Learning Centre

Manor Hospital
Education and Training Centre
Moat Road
Walsall
West Midlands WS2 9PS

Tel: 01922 721172 ext. 7181
Fax: 01922 649008
E-mail: in6572@wlv.ac.uk
URL: www.wlv.ac.uk/snm
Librarian: Tanya McLaven
Type: Nursing and Midwifery.
Hours open: Mon, Wed–Fri: 9am–5pm; Tues: 9am–8pm.
Users: Students of the University of Wolverhampton; Trust employees. Free external membership. Public reference only.
Lending: University students. Restricted loans for external members.
Stock policy: Send to be recycled through Manor Hospital.
Holdings: 16,000 books; 97 current journal subscriptions, 106 journal titles; 84 films and videos; 4 CD-ROMs.
Classification: LC.
Library management system: Talis.
Computerized services: Online access to ASSIA for Health; BNI; CancerLit; ChildData; CINAHL; MEDLINE; Mental Health Collection. CD-ROM access to HMIC; NRR.
Collaborative networks: NULJ; WMRHLN.
Notes: 4 nursing sites: Burton; Manor; New Cross Hospital; Russells Hall. University sites: Compton; Dudley; Telford; Walsall; Wolverhampton.

University of Wolverhampton: New Cross Learning Centre

Education Centre
New Cross Hospital
Wolverhampton
West Midlands WV8 1EG
Tel: 01902 644805
Fax: 01902 306072
E-mail: in5468@wlv.ac.uk
Librarian: Mrs Kirstin Ewart
Founded: 1974
Type: Nursing and Midwifery.
Hours open: Mon–Fri: 9am–5pm.

Users: Students and staff of the University; Health Authority staff. External membership by annual subscription.
Lending: Books only to members.
Stock policy: Books discarded after 10 years; journals discarded after a variable number of years.
Holdings: 31,000 books; 135 current journal subscriptions; 273 videos; 200 distance learning packages.
Classification: LC.
Library management system: Talis.
Computerized services: Access to AMED; ASSIA; Best Evidence; BNI; CancerLit; ChildData; CINAHL; Cochrane Systematic Reviews; Health Management Consortium; ; MEDLINE; Nursing Collection 1&1 via WebSPIRS; InfotracWeb; Ovid Biomed; SwetsNet.
Library publications: Various tip sheets for searching databases; IT problems, etc.
Collaborative networks: NULJ; WMRHLN.

University of Wolverhampton: Russell's Hall Learning Centre

Esk House
Russell's Hall Hospital
Dudley
West Midlands DY1 2HQ
Tel: 01384 456111 ext. 2594
Fax: 01384 237543
E-mail: in5547@wlv.ac.uk
URL: www.wlv.ac.uk
Librarian: Gill Williamson
Founded: 1995
Type: Nursing.
Hours open: Mon–Tues, Thurs–Fri: 9am–5pm; Wed: 9am–8pm.
Users: Nursing students (pre- and post-registration) and other University students; University staff; Trust staff. Members of the public for a fee.
Lending: Registered members.
Stock policy: Disposal.

Holdings: 10,000 books; 85 current journal subscriptions, 104 journal titles; 9 films and videos; 21 CD-ROMs.
Classification: Dewey.
Library management system: Talis.
Computerized services: Online access to ASSIA Net: BHI net; BIDS; Butterworths; EDINA; HW Wilson; IDEAL; Index to Theses; Infotrac; MIMAS; NISS; SwetsNet; WebSPIRS.
Collaborative networks: UK Plus Scheme; reciprocal borrowing with Birmingham, Aston, Warwick and UCE Libraries.

University of York: Centre for Health Economics

NHS Centre for Reviews and Dissemination
    Information Service
Heslington
York YO1 5DD
Tel: 01904 433707
Fax: 01904 433661
E-mail: nhscrd-info@york.ac.uk
URL: www.york.ac.uk/inst/crd
Librarian: Julie Glanville
Prof. staff: Steven Duffy; Su Golder; Kate Light; Lisa Mather; Kate Misso; Kath Wright
Founded: 1989
Type: Health Economics; Health Policy; Clinical Effectiveness; Technology Assessment.
Hours open: Mon–Fri: 9am–5.15pm.
Users: Research staff of CHE and NHSCRD. Other staff and postgraduate students of the University of York. Visitors by appointment only.
Lending: Research staff of CHE and NHSCRD only.
Stock policy: Disposed of, unless required by University of York Library.
Holdings: 8,800 books; 70 current journal subscriptions, 430 journal titles; 30 CD-ROMs.
Classification: University of York.
Library management system: CAIRS.
Computerized services: Online access to Data-Star; Dialog; Ovid; STN. Access to

ARC/WinSPIRS; BIDS; EDINA; Web of Science.
Special collections: Health Economics Research Centres working papers; Technology assessment reports.

University of York: JB Morrell Library

University of York
Heslington
York YO10 5DD
Tel: 01904 433865
Fax: 01904 433866
URL: www.york.ac.uk/services/library
Librarian: Elizabeth Heaps
Prof. staff: Wayne Connolly; Christine Ellwood; Elizabeth Harbord
Founded: 1965
Type: Multidisciplinary University Library.
Hours open: Mon–Fri: 9am–10pm; Sat: 9am–5.15pm; Sun: 9am–6.30pm. Vacations: Mon–Fri: 9am–5.15pm.
Users: University staff and students. Others may use for reference purposes.
Lending: Members of the University and approved external members.
Stock policy: Under development.
Holdings: 650,000 books; 3,000 current journal subscriptions.
Classification: Own.
Library management system: Dynix.
Computerized services: Access to AMED; BNI; CINAHL; Embase; HMIC; MEDLINE, etc.
Branches: Library and Information Service Harrogate District Hospital.
Collaborative networks: RIDING; UK Libraries Plus.

Veterinary Laboratories Agency Library

New Haw
Addlestone
Surrey KT15 3NB
Tel: 01932 357314
Fax: 01932 357608
E-mail: enquiries@vla.defra.gsi.gov.uk
URL: www.defra.gov.uk/vla
Librarian: Heather Hulse
Prof. staff: Melanie French; Ellen Howard; Franko Kowalczuk
Type: Veterinary.
Hours open: Mon–Fri: 8.30am–4.30pm.
Users: Staff of the Veterinary Laboratories Agency; State Veterinary Service; Veterinary Medicines Directorate.
Lending: Loans to other government departments and through the British Library. Fee-based services are available for external users.
Holdings: 10,000 books; 300 current journal subscriptions, 500 journal titles; 122 films and videos; 6 CD-ROMs; slides.
Classification: Barnard.
Library management system: CAIRS.
Computerized services: Online access to Dialog. Access to BeastCD; CAB Abstracts; Ecctis; Justis; MEDLINE; VetCD.
Library publications: List of current periodical articles.
Special collections: Staff publications.
Collaborative networks: AHIS; CUG; SASLIC.

Victoria Hospital Health Professionals' Education Centre Library

Victoria Hospital
Whinney Heys Road
Blackpool
Lancashire FY3 8NR
Tel: 01253 303818
Fax: 01253 303818
E-mail: norma.blackburn@exch.bvh-tr.nwest.nhs.uk
Librarian: Mrs Norma Blackburn
Founded: 1974
Type: Multidisciplinary.
Hours open: Mon–Thurs: 8.45am–8.30pm; Fri: 8.45am–7.30pm.

Users: Primary, community and secondary healthcare staff, plus students on placement; student nurses and staff from the University of Central Lancashire.
Lending: To registered users.
Stock policy: Disposal.
Holdings: 13,000 books; 109 current journal subscriptions; 500 films and videos.
Classification: Dewey.
Library management system: Talis.
Computerized services: Online access to AMED; CINAHL; Embase; HMIC; MEDLINE; PsychLit. Access to Cochrane Library.
Collaborative networks: BL; BMA; LIHNN; NULJ.

Victoria Hospital Postgraduate Library

Hayfield Road
Kirkcaldy
Fife KY2 5AY
Tel: 01592 643355 ext. 8790
Fax: 01592 204599
E-mail: efpgmc_library@hotmail.com
Librarian: Dorothy McGinley
Type: Multidisciplinary – with a bias to Clinical Medicine.
Hours open: Mon–Fri: 9am–4pm. Key available out of hours.
Users: Employees of Fife Acute Hospitals NHS Trust working primarily on the Hospital site; GPs; other NHS Fife employees. Other users, reference only.
Lending: To members only.
Stock policy: Disposed of.
Holdings: 1,600 books; 84 current journal subscriptions, 190 journal titles.
Classification: NLM.
Library management system: Heritage.
Computerized services: Internet access. CD-ROM access to Cochrane Library; MEDLINE.
Library publications: Library guide; journal holdings list.
Collaborative networks: BLDSC; BMA; SHINE.

Wales Regional Libraries Service

Duthie Library
University of Wales College of Medicine
Heath Park
Cardiff CF14 4XN
Tel: 029 2074 2874
Fax: 029 2074 3574
E-mail: pritchard@cf.ac.uk
Librarian: Steve Pritchard (Director of University of Wales College of Medicine Library Services and Library Adviser to the Postgraduate Dean for Wales)

Walton Library

Medical School
University of Newcastle
Framlington Place
Newcastle-upon-Tyne NE2 4HH
Tel: 0191 222 7550
Fax: 0191 222 8102
E-mail: lib-walton-rs@ncl.ac.uk
URL: www.ncl.ac.uk/library/medical/medindex.html
Librarian: Helen MacFarlane
Prof. staff: Lynnette Bonford; Christine Cowan; Helene Farn; Linda Simpson
Founded: 1984
Type: University Medical, Dentistry, Biomedical Sciences.
Hours open: Mon–Fri: 9am–10pm; Sat: 9am–4.30pm; Sun: 11am–5.30pm. Under review – see website for full details.
Users: University staff and students; staff of the northern part of the NHS Northern and Yorkshire Region. Others on payment of fee.
Lending: All registered members; staff and research students of local universities.
Stock policy: Dispose of it.
Holdings: 36,895 books; 900 current journal subscriptions, 1,200 electronic subscriptions; 296 videos; 35 CD-ROMs.
Classification: Dewey 21.
Library management system: GEAC Advance.

Computerized services: Access to CINAHL; EBMR; MEDLINE; 6 full-text journal collections via Biomed. Access to Cochrane Library; Embase; HEED; HMIC; PsycINFO; Web of Science.
Collaborative networks: HLN; NEYAL.

Wansbeck Hospital Education Centre Library

Wansbeck Hospital
Woodhorn Lane
Ashington
Northumberland NE63 9JJ
Tel: 01670 529665
Fax: 01670 529666
E-mail: sarah.abernethy@ncl.ac.uk
Librarian: Sarah Abernethy
Type: Multidisciplinary.
Hours open: Mon–Fri: 9am–5pm.
Users: Staff of Northumbria Healthcare NHS Trust.
Lending: To members only.
Holdings: 4,000 books; 90 current journal subscriptions.
Classification: Dewey.
Library management system: SydneyPLUS.
Computerized services: Online access to Ovid. Access to CINAHL; Cochrane Library; MEDLINE.
Collaborative networks: HLN.

Warrington Hospital Library

North Cheshire Hospitals NHS Trust
Postgraduate Centre
Warrington Hospital
Lovely Lane
Warrington
Cheshire WA5 1QG
Tel: 01925 662128
Fax: 01925 662389
E-mail: warlib@yahoo.com
Librarian: Mrs Susan Harrison
Type: Multidisciplinary.

Hours open: Mon, Wed and Fri: 8.30am–5pm; Tues and Thurs: 8.30am–6.30pm.
Users: Hospital staff, nursing and medical students based at the Trust. Other health professionals may use the library for reference only.
Lending: To staff employed by the Hospital Trust and students based at the Trust, only.
Stock policy: Discarded stock disposed of.
Holdings: 7,900 books; 80 current journal subscriptions, 112 journal titles.
Classification: Dewey.
Library management system: ALICE.
Computerized services: Access to AMED; BNI; CINAHL; Embase; HMIC; MEDLINE; PsycINFO.
Collaborative networks: LIHNN.

Waterford Regional Hospital Library & Information Service

Waterford Regional Hospital
Dunmore Road
Waterford
Republic of Ireland
Tel: +353 51 842434
Fax: +353 51 848561
E-mail: library.wrh@sehb.ie
Librarian: Emma Quinn
Founded:1992 (see note)
Type: Clinical Medicine; Nursing; Health Management; Psychiatry.
Hours open: Mon–Thurs: 9.30am–9pm; Fri: 9.30am–5pm; Sat: 10am–2pm.
Users: Employees of the South Eastern Health Board and students on placement.
Lending: As above, only.
Stock policy: Pass on to other branch libraries.
Holdings: 3,000 books; 163 current journal subscriptions, 200 journal titles; 20 videos; 30 CD-ROMs.
Classification: BLISS.
Library management system: Unicorn.

Computerized services: Access to the internet on 3 PCs. Access to BNI; CINAHL; Cochrane Library; MEDLINE; OSH Plus.
Library publications: In-house library guides; guides to databases.
Collaborative networks: IHLJHI.
Notes: The Library was set up by the School of Nursing, Waterford Regional Hospital but staffed from 1992 by South Eastern Health Board. Other branches at St Joseph's Hospital, Clonmel; St Luke's Hospital, Kilkenny; Wexford General Hospital.

Wathwood Hospital Regional Secure Unit

Wathwood Hospital
Gipsy Green Lane
Wath upon Dearne
Rotherham
South Yorkshire S63 7TQ
Tel: 01709 870827
Fax: 01709 870825
E-mail: jf@wathlib.freeserve.co.uk
Librarian: Jane Fennell
Founded: 1997
Type: Forensic Psychiatry.
Hours open: Mon: 9am–4pm; Tues, Wed, Thurs: 9am–3pm; Fri: 9am–4pm.
Users: Staff of Wathwood Hospital. Others by arrangement.
Lending: As above.
Holdings: 1,000 books; 35 current journal subscriptions.
Classification: NLM (modified).
Computerized services: Online access to Ovid Biomed Suite. CD-ROM access to ASSIA; Caredata.
Library publications: Current awareness bulletins; new accessions list.
Special collections: Forensic Psychiatry.
Collaborative networks: JHLS; PLCS; TRAHCLIS.
Notes: The library is a branch of Rotherham Health Care Library and Information Service.

Weatherall Institute of Molecular Medicine Library

John Radcliffe Hospital
Headley, Headington
Oxford OX3 9DS
Tel: 01865 222362
Fax: 01865 222737
E-mail: iris.randall@molecular-medicine.ox.ac.uk
Librarian: Iris Randall
Founded: 1989
Type: Multidisciplinary.
Hours open: Mon–Fri: 8am–4pm.
Users: All staff and collaborators; Wellcome Trust Centre for Human Genetics. Anyone with a valid reason can have access during opening hours.
Lending: Reference only. Stock only loaned in exceptional circumstances.
Stock policy: Old stock offered to other libraries. Some titles go to BookAid International.
Holdings: 200 books; 116 current journal subscriptions, 131 journal titles.
Computerized services: Online access to Biomednet; Ingenta and PubMed. Access to Biological Abstracts; Current Contents Connect; Embase; MEDLINE.
Collaborative networks: Genetics Libraries Union; HeLIN; MRC info system; RESCOLINC.

Wellcome Library for the History & Understanding of Medicine

183 Euston Road
London NW1 2BE
Tel: 020 7611 8722
Fax: 020 7611 8726
E-mail: infoserv@wellcome.ac.uk
URL: www.wellcome.ac.uk/library
Librarian: David Pearson
Prof. staff: Wendy Fish (Head of Public Services); Robert Kiley (Head of Systems Strategy); Bridget Kinally (Head of Visual Resources); Zina Sabovic (Head of

Collection Management); Julia Sheppard (Head of Special Collections)

Founded: 1949

Type: History of Medicine; Science and Society; Public Understanding of Science.

Hours open: Information Service: Mon–Fri: 9am–5pm; Sat: 9am–1pm. History of Medicine Library: Mon, Wed, Fri: 9.45am–5.15pm; Tues, Thurs: 9.45am–7.15pm; Sat: 9.45am–1pm.

Users: Academic; public; health professionals. Free to all, open to all.

Lending: Reference only.

Stock policy: Retain all material except duplicates, which are offered to other libraries.

Holdings: 600,000 books; 700 current journal subscriptions, 7,000 journal titles; 13,000 films and videos; 20 CD-ROMs.

Classification: Barnard, NLM, own.

Library management system: INNOPAC.

Computerized services: Catalogue online. Access to AMED; CINAHL; Cochrane Database of Systematic Reviews; Embase; Health Reference Centre; History of Science, Medicine and Technology Database; MEDLINE.

Library publications: Current Work in the History of Medicine; SPIN (Science Policy Information News); various published catalogues.

Special collections: Extensive special collections including: 66,000 pre-1851 publications; 100,000 prints, drawings, paintings, photographs, films, etc; extensive archives and manuscripts collections including papers of Lord Lister, Family Planning Association, Edward Jenner.

Collaborative networks: CURL; RLG (Research Libraries Group); School of Advanced Study.

West Cheshire Postgraduate Medical Centre Library

Countess of Chester Hospital NHS Trust

Liverpool Road
Chester CH2 1VL

Tel: 01244 364734

Fax: 01244 364722

E-mail: librarian@coch-tr.nwest.nhs.uk

Librarian: Samantha West

Prof. staff: Tony Vyskocil (Assistant Librarian)

Founded: 1975

Type: Clinical Medicine.

Hours open: Mon–Fri: 9am–8pm.

Users: All clinicians including trainee doctors and University of Liverpool medical students; GPs and medical personnel in public and occupational health; dental personnel. Nurses, PAMs and technicians can use the library for reference.

Lending: As above.

Stock policy: Offered to other libraries then dispose of. Tend to keep last 15 years of books and journals.

Holdings: 3,500 books; 75 current journal subscriptions, 115 journal titles; 75 films and videos; 25 CD-ROMs.

Classification: LC.

Library management system: Heritage IV.

Computerized services: Internet and Microsoft Access. Online access to AMED; BNI Plus; CINAHL; Embase; HMIC; MEDLINE; Micromedic; PsycINFO via ADITUS. Access to Cochrane Database.

Collaborative networks: Cheshire Library Strategy Group; Countess of Cheshire Health Park Librarians Collaborative Group; LIHNN.

West Hertfordshire Hospitals NHS Trust Postgraduate Medical Centre Library

Postgraduate Medical Centre
Watford General Hospital
Vicarage Road
Watford
Hertfordshire WD18 0HB

Tel: 01923 217437

Fax: 01923 217909
E-mail: janet@watlib.demon.co.uk
Librarian: Janet Reynolds
Founded: 1970
Type: Multidisciplinary.
Hours open: Mon–Fri: 9am–5pm. 24-hour access for registered users.
Users: Staff of West Hertfordshire Hospitals NHS Trust; Hertfordshire Partnership Trust; PCTs in West Hertfordshire and any associated health professionals. Others, reference only by appointment.
Lending: Members only. Lend most books and videos. Limited journal loans.
Stock policy: Books – varies. Journals, if disposed of, are offered to other libraries.
Holdings: 4,500 books; 110 current journal subscriptions; 100 videos.
Classification: NLM (Wessex adaptation).
Library management system: DB/TextWorks.
Computerized services: Access to CINAHL; ClinPsych; Cochrane Library; MEDLINE.
Collaborative networks: NTRLS; NULJ.

West Kent Education Centre Library

Farnborough Hospital
Orpington
Kent BR6 8ND
Tel: 01689 814305
Fax: 01689 814307
E-mail: sandy.tarbox@bromleyhospitals.nhs.uk
Librarian: Mrs Sandra Tarbox
Founded: 1974
Type: Multidisciplinary.
Hours open: Mon–Thurs: 9am–6pm; Fri: 9am–5pm.
Users: Employees of Bromley NHS Trust, Oxleas NHS Trust; Bromley Primary Care Trust; Bromley Health. Anyone in the health profession living locally may have certain rights.
Lending: As above. Non-employees have to pay a small fee.

Stock policy: Dispose of.
Holdings: 5,000 books; 110 current journal subscriptions, 140 journal titles; 5 CD-ROMs.
Classification: NLM.
Library management system: LIBRARIAN.
Computerized services: Access to AMED; BNI; CINAHL; ClinPsych; Cochrane Library; MEDLINE.
Branches: Bromley Education Centre; Orpington Education Centre.
Collaborative networks: BL; NULJ; PLCS; STLIS.

West Kent Health Authority

Vernon Hochuli Library
Preston Hall
Aylesford
Kent ME20 7NJ
Tel: 01622 713100
Fax: 01622 719802
E-mail: jill.rutland@wken-ha.sthames.nhs.uk
Librarian: Jill Rutland
Hours open: Mon–Wed: 9am–3pm; Thurs: 9am–12.30pm.
Collaborative networks: STLIS.

West London Mental Health NHS Trust: Coombs Library

St Bernard's Wing
West London Mental Health NHS Trust
Uxbridge Road
Southall
Middlesex UB1 3EU
Tel: 020 8354 8009
Fax: 020 8354 8009
E-mail: paulv_uk@yahoo.co.uk
Librarian: Paul Valentine
Founded: 1975
Type: Multidisciplinary.
Hours open: Mon, Tues, Fri: 9am–5pm; Wed–Thurs: 9am–7pm (except August)
Users: All Trust staff, medical and nursing students; GPs. Others by arrangement.

Lending: All Trust staff. Medical and nursing students, reference only. No loans to non-members.

Stock policy: Books disposed of after 10 years, unless a 'classic text'. Journals kept according to regional policies.

Holdings: 2,700 books; 75 current journal subscriptions.

Classification: NLM.

Library management system: DB/TextWorks.

Computerized services: Internet access to Best Evidence; BNI; CINAHL; Cochrane Library; MEDLINE; PsycINFO. CD-ROM access to Embase: Psychiatry.

Library publications: Journals list; library guide.

Collaborative networks: London Region Network; PLCS; West London NHS Workforce Development Confederation.

West Middlesex University Hospital NHS Trust Library & Information Service

Twickenham Road
Isleworth
Middlesex TW7 6AF
Tel: 0208 565 5968
Fax: 0208 565 5408
E-mail: library@wmuh-tr.nthames.nhs.uk
URL: www.wmuhnhst.demon.co.uk
Librarian: Mrs P Bowen
Prof. staff: J Riste; M Walne; L Wann
Type: Multidisciplinary.
Hours open: Mon–Fri: 9.30am–5pm.
Users: All members of staff of West Middlesex Hospital NHS Trust, Hounslow and Spelthorne Mental and Community Health Trust; medical students of Imperial College and Nursing Bucks College.
Lending: As above.
Stock policy: Pass on or dispose of.
Holdings: 7,247 books; 195 current journal subscriptions, 241 journal titles; 921 videos; 6 CD-ROMs.
Classification: NLM.

Library management system: DB/TextWorks.

Computerized services: Catalogue and Microsoft. Access to AMED; Best Evidence; BookFind; CINAHL; Cochrane Library; MEDLINE; PsycINFO.

Collaborative networks: West London NHS Workforce Development Confederation.

West Midlands Health Regional Library Unit

Public Health Building
University of Birmingham
Edgbaston
Birmingham B15 3DP
Tel: 0121 414 7856
Fax: 0121 414 7855
E-mail: p.prior@hsrc.org.uk
URL: www.wish-uk.org
Librarian: Pam Prior (Regional Librarian)
Prof. staff: April Edwards (Web Development Librarian); Sarah Greening (Patient Information Officer); Stephanie Keenan (NHS/HE Liaison Librarian); Bertha Low (Digital Library lead); Rachel Whittlestone (CPD lead)
Type: Regional Co-ordinating and Development Unit.
Hours open: Mon–Fri: 9am–5pm.
Users: All library staff in the Region including Workforce Development Confederations, deanery, NHS Trust, Health Authorities and primary care.
Lending: Staff library available to all network members.
Stock policy: Disposed of.
Holdings: 150 books; 10 current journal sub-scriptions.
Library management system: Unicorn (Sirsi)
Computerized services: Online access to AMED; CINAHL; Embase: Psychiatry; MED-LINE; NeLH; Nursing Collection 1.
Library publications: e-lib review via web-site.

Collaborative networks: LINC Health Panel; Regional Librarians Group; West Midlands Health Libraries Network.

West Pennine Health Authority Library

Information Department
C Block
Westhulme Avenue
Oldham
Lancashire OL2 1PL
Tel: 0161 622 6581/5
Fax: 0161 622 6528
E-mail: diane.keenan@wpennine-ha.nwest.nhs.uk
Librarian: Diane Keenan
Prof. staff: Julie Wickham
Type: Multidisciplinary; Health Management.
Hours open: Mon–Fri: 8.30am–4.30pm.
Users: Health Authority staff; local PCGs/PCTs; practice staff; local Trusts; public health; HE/FE lecturers. Others judged on individual reasons for use.
Lending: To all healthcare and allied staff in local health community; to any library in the co-operative regional scheme in North West and Merseyside. Do not normally lend to members of the public.
Stock policy: Pass on to other libraries.
Holdings: 10,000 printed items; 12 current journal subscriptions, 24 journal titles; 4 CD-ROMs.
Classification: Own.
Library management system: Heritage.
Computerized services: Access via ADI-TUS to AMED; BNI Plus; CINAHL; Embase; HMIC; MEDLINE; PsycINFO, etc.
Library publications: Current awareness e-mail; library leaflet; weekly library update; recent acquisitions list.
Special collections: Statistics; grey literature.
Collaborative networks: LIHNN; lis-medical; Oldham Information Group; West Pennine Health Libraries Community.

West Suffolk Hospital NHS Trust Clinical Resource Centre & Library

Hardwick Lane
Bury St Edmunds
Suffolk IP33 2QZ
Tel: 01284 713343
Fax: 01284 713113
E-mail: joan.hunter@wsufftrust.org.uk
URL: www.wsufftrust.org.uk
Librarian: Mrs Joan Hunter
Founded: 1974
Type: Multidisciplinary.
Hours open: Open 24 hours, 7 days a week.
Users: All NHS staff in West of Suffolk; St Nicholas Hospice staff. Private members by arrangement.
Lending: No restrictions.
Stock policy: Dispose of.
Holdings: 12,000 books; 250 current journal subscriptions; 100 videos; 200 CD-ROMs.
Classification: NLM.
Library management system: Brown.
Computerized services: Online access to AMED; CINAHL; ClinPsych; MEDLINE. Access to AgeInfo; HMIC.
Library publications: Current awareness.
Collaborative networks: Norfolk and Suffolk Consortium Librarians Group.

West Surrey Health Authority Health Promotion Service

The White House
Crouch Oak Lane
Addlestone
Surrey KT15 2AN
Tel: 01932 854476
Fax: 01932 828397
E-mail: library@wsurreyhps2.demon.co.uk
Prof. staff: David Gray; Tricia Thompson
Hours open: 9.30am–4.30pm. Staffed 9am–5pm.
Special collections: Resources centre – video, teaching packs, etc.
Collaborative networks: STLIS.

West Surrey Health Authority Library

West Surrey Health Authority
The Ridgewood Centre
Old Bisley Road
Frimley
Camberley
Surrey GU16 5QE
Tel: 01276 605504
Fax: 01276 605491
E-mail: lilian.linden@wsurrey-ha.sthames.nhs.uk
Librarian: Jonathan Hutchins (based at Royal Surrey County Hospital)
Prof. staff: Lilian Linden
Hours open: Mon–Wed: 9am–5pm; Thurs, Fri: am or pm.
Holdings: 20 journal titles.
Collaborative networks: STLIS.

West Sussex Health Authority Library

West Sussex Health Authority
1 The Causeway
Goring-by-Sea
Worthing
West Sussex BN12 6BT
Tel: 01903 708573
Fax: 01903 700981
E-mail: information@wsussexhealth.org.uk
Librarian: Sue Merriott (based at Worthing Hospital)
Prof. staff: Ian Puttock (Head of Information Management); Wendy Sadler
Hours open: Mon–Fri: 9am–4.30pm.
Holdings: 50 journal titles.
Collaborative networks: STLIS.

West Wales General Hospital Library

West Wales General Hospital
Carmarthen NHS Trust
Glangwili
Carmarthen
Dyfed SA31 2AF
Tel: 01267 227076
Fax: 01267 223710
E-mail: librarian@carmarthen-nhs.demon.co.uk
Librarian: Mrs V E Bisnath
Founded: 1968
Type: Multidisciplinary.
Hours open: Mon–Thurs: 9am–5pm; Fri: 9am–4.30pm.
Users: Staff of the Trust, GPs, social workers and all community-based staff. Others by arrangement.
Lending: As above.
Stock policy: Dispose of old stock.
Holdings: 5,000 books;140 current journal subscriptions; 50 CD-ROMs.
Classification: NLM.
Library management system: Own.
Computerized services: Access to AMED; ASSIA; BNI; CINAHL; Cochrane Library; Embase; HealthStar; HMIC; MEDLINE; PsycINFO via Trust intranet.
Library publications: Annual Report.
Collaborative networks: AWHILES. Twinning with St David's Hospital Library, Carmarthen; Prince Philip Hospital Library, Llanelli.

Western Health Board Library Service

Library HQ
Merlin Park Hospital
Galway
Republic of Ireland
Tel: +353 91 775327
Fax: +353 91 779655
E-mail: library@bsi.ie
Librarian: Tony Linnane
Prof. staff: Petrina Mee; Julia Reynolds
Founded: 1999
Type: Multidisciplinary Healthcare.
Hours open: Mon–Fri: 9.30am–5pm.
Users: All employees of the Western Health Board; some partner organizations' staff; students of the Institute of Health Sciences.

Lending: As above. Anyone else has reference use only.

Stock policy: Do not dispose of yet, as new library.

Holdings: 12,000 books; 200 current journal subscriptions; 20 CD-ROMs.

Classification: Dewey.

Library management system: Heritage.

Computerized services: Online access to EBSCO; Ovid Biomedical and RCN. Access to AMED; BNI; CINAHL; Cochrane Library; Health Business; HealthStar; MEDLINE.

Library publications: A section in the employee newsletter.

Branches: Western Health Board Library Mayo.

Collaborative networks: Irish Healthcare Libraries Co-operative.

Westminster Library & Archives

Marylebone Information Service

Marylebone Library

Marylebone Road

London NW1 5PS

Tel: 020 7641 1039

Fax: 020 7641 1044

E-mail: m.i.s@dial.pipex.com

Librarian: Helen Rogers

Prof. staff: Ali Holder; Michael Lightowlers; Vivienne Perkins

Founded: 1950

Type: Multidisciplinary.

Hours open: Mon, Tues, Thurs, Fri: 9.30am–8pm; Wed: 10am–8pm; Sat: 9.30am–5pm; Sun: 1.30pm–5pm.

Users: Open to any member of the public.

Lending: Reference stock only. Photocopies and prints from electronic resources available.

Stock policy: Closed runs of journals are discarded. Books are discarded at varying intervals.

Holdings: 15 current journal titles.

Classification: Dewey.

Library management system: GEAC Plus.

Computerized services: Internet access (free) and CD-ROM access to health information for patients and carers.

Special collections: Health information for the general public.

Westmorland General Hospital Education Centre Library

Westmorland General Hospital

Morecambe Bay Hospitals NHS Trust

Burton Road

Kendal

Cumbria LA9 7RG

E-mail: sam.burgess@k.bay-tr.nwest.nhs.uk

Librarian: Miss Sam Burgess

Type: Multidisciplinary.

Hours open: Mon–Fri: 9am–5pm. 24-hour access for staff.

Users: Staff and students on placement. All others, reference only or at Librarian's discretion.

Lending: Members only.

Stock policy: Generally disposed of.

Holdings: 2,800 books; 52 current journal subscriptions, 92 journal titles; 15 videos; 3 CD-ROMs.

Classification: NLM.

Library management system: Heritage.

Computerized services: Online access to AMED; BNI; CINAHL; Embase; HMIC; MEDLINE; PsycINFO. CD-ROM access to CINAHL; Cochrane LIbrary; MEDLINE.

Library publications: Current awareness bulletins.

Collaborative networks: Associated Health Libraries Group; LIHNN; Morecambe Bay Hospitals NHS Trust; NULJ.

Weston Area Health Trust Staff Library

Grange Road

Weston-super-Mare

North Somerset BS23 4TQ

Tel: 01934 647166

Fax: 01934 647166

E-mail: diane.smithson@waht.swest.nhs.uk
Librarian: Diane Smithson
Founded:1989
Type: Multidisciplinary.
Hours open: 24-hour access to Trust staff.
Users: Trust staff; GPs in the area and their staff; health students while on placement with the Trust. Annual membership fee payable for others.
Lending: To users.
Stock policy: Some stock sold to users. Other material donated to developing countries.
Holdings: 4,957 books; 55 current journal subscriptions, 76 journal titles, 24 electronic journals; 67 videos; 10 CD-ROMs.
Classification: NLM.
Library management system: Access/Visual Basic database.
Computerized services: Regional subscription to AMED; ASSIA for Health; BNI; CINAHL; Embase; HMIC; Martindale; MEDLINE; PsycINFO.
Library publications: Library Guide; Beginners Guide to Literature Searching; Beginners Guide to the Internet.
Collaborative networks: SWRLIN.

Whipps Cross University Hospital Trust

Multidisciplinary Library
Medical Education Centre
Whipps Cross Hospital
London E11 1NR
Tel: 020 8535 6973
Fax: 020 8535 6973
E-mail: library@fhcare.demon.co.uk
URL: http://www.libnel.nhs.uk
Librarian: Anne Weist
Prof. staff: Susan Kerslake; Julie Anne Watson
Type: Multidisciplinary.
Hours open: Mon–Thurs: 8.15am–7.45pm; Fri: 8.15am–6.50pm. Staffed: Mon–Fri: 9am–6pm.

Users: NHS staff in North East London Health Community. Others with Librarian's permission.
Lending: NHS staff in North East London Health Community. Medical students, overnight loan only.
Stock policy: Withdrawn stock is made available to users.
Holdings: 5,800 books; 150 current journal subscriptions; 140 videos; 70 CD-ROMs.
Classification: NLM.
Library management system: DB/TextWorks.
Computerized services: Computerized Assisted Learning Room with 17 networked computers. Internet access to AMED; CINAHL; MEDLINE; PsycINFO and 24 full-text journals. CD-ROM networked access to AMED; ASSIA; CINAHL; Cochrane Library; MEDLINE.
Collaborative networks: London Libraries Information and Development Unit.

Whiston Hospital Healthcare Library

St Helen's and Knowsley Hospitals NHS Trust
Whiston Hospital
Prescot
Merseyside L35 5DR
Tel: 0151 430 1342
Fax: 0151 430 1982
Librarian: Suzanne Ford
E-mail: whistonlib@hotmail.com
Founded: 1998
Type: Multidisciplinary.
Hours open: Mon, Thurs, Fri: 9am–5pm; Tues, Wed: 9am–6pm.
Users: Staff from the Hospital Trust; Community Trust; Health Authority and primary care. All other users, reference only.
Lending: To members only.
Stock policy: Old stock is offered to users.
Holdings: 6,000 books; 135 current journal subscriptions; 98 videos; 11 CD-ROMs.
Classification: Dewey.

Library management system: Heritage IV.
Computerized services: European Business ASAP. Access to AMED; BNI; CINAHL; Embase; HMIC; MEDLINE; PsycINFO.
Collaborative networks: LIHNN; PLCS.

Wilfred Stokes Library

Stoke Mandeville Hospital
Mandeville Road
Aylesbury
Buckinghamshire HP21 8AL
Tel: 01296 315428
Fax: 01296 315475
Librarian: Ms J Kelson
Prof. staff: Post vacant
Founded: 1972
Type: Clinical Medical.
Hours open: Mon–Fri: 8.30am–5pm.
Users: Trust staff. Others may use the library for reference only.
Lending: To members only.
Stock policy: Old stock is offered to other libraries and then disposed of if not taken.
Holdings: 3,500 books; 100 current journal subscriptions; 100 videos.
Classification: NLM.
Library management system: DB/TextWorks.
Computerized services: Access to AMED; BNI; CINAHL; Embase; HMIC; MEDLINE; PsycINFO.
Special collections: Spinal Injuries Collection.
Collaborative networks: HeLIN; NULJ.

Wilson Hospital Library

Merton, Sutton and Wandsworth Health Authority
Wilson Hospital
Cranmer Road
Mitcham
Surrey CR4 4TP
Tel: 020 8687 4547

Fax: 020 8687 4436
E-mail: mswha@usa.net
Librarian: Jonathan Hutchins (based at Royal Surrey County Hospital)
Hours open: 8.30am–5pm one day a month (variable).

Wiltshire Health Authority Library

Southgate House
Pans Lane
Devizes
Wiltshire SN10 5EQ
Tel: 01380 733876
Fax: 01380 722443
E-mail: marilyn.hayes@exchange.wilts-ha.swest.nhs.uk
URL: www.healthywiltshire.org.uk
Librarian: Marilyn Hayes
Founded: 1994
Type: Health Management.
Hours open: Mon–Fri: 9am–5pm.
Users: Staff of Health Authority; Primary Care Groups; Primary Care Trusts. Others by appointment only.
Lending: As above.
Stock policy: Disposed of or recycled.
Holdings: 2,000 books and reports; 20 current journal subscriptions, 30 journal titles; 5 CD-ROMs.
Classification: NLM.
Computerized services: Access via South West Information for Clinical Effectiveness to ASSIA; BNI; CINAHL; Embase; HMIC; PsycINFO.
Special collections: DOH Circulars 1946–.
Collaborative networks: SWRLIN; WILCO (Wiltshire Libraries in Co-operation).

Winchester & Eastleigh Healthcare NHS Trust Healthcare Library

Romsey Road
Winchester

Hampshire SO22 5DG
Tel: 01962 824680
Fax: 01962 824659
E-mail: library@weht.swest.nhs.uk
URL: www.hants.org.uk/weht
Librarian: Miss B M Goddard
Prof. staff: Mrs A Day; Mrs J Dines; Mrs A Lancey
Type: Multidisciplinary.
Hours open: Mon–Fri: 8.30am–5.30pm.
Users: Local clinical staff; professions allied to medicine; managers. Reference only for members of the public.
Lending: To registered users and interlibrary loans.
Stock policy: Withdrawn old editions.
Holdings: 12,700 books; 210 journal titles.
Classification: NLM (SWRLIN adaptation).
Library management system: Heritage IV.
Computerized services: Access to Ovid Biomed; BNI Plus; CINAHL; Cochrane Library.
Collaborative networks: HATRICS; STLIS; SWRLIN.

Wishaw General Hospital

Alistair MacKenzie Library
Wishaw
South Lanarkshire ML2 0DP
Tel: 01698 361100
E-mail: julian.hodgson@laht-scot.nhs.uk
Librarian: Julian Hodgson
Type: Multidisciplinary.
Hours open: Mon–Thurs: 9am–5pm; Fri: 9am–1.30pm. Available to staff 24 hours.
Users: Staff of Lanarkshire Acute Hospitals Trust. Others by arrangement.
Lending: No restrictions.
Stock policy: Disposed of.
Holdings: 3,500 books; 120 current journals subscriptions; 80 videos; 60 CD-ROMs.
Classification: NLM.
Library management system: Cardbox Plus.

Computerized services: Online access to BNF, Caredata, Clinical Evidence, MED-LINE. Access to CINAHL.
Library publications: 'The Law': Law Hospital 1939–89 – a memoir.
Collaborative networks: SHINE.

Wolverhampton Medical Institute, The Bell Library

New Cross Hospital
Wolverhampton
West Midlands WV10 0QP
Tel: 01902 643109
Fax: 01902 723037
Librarian: Mr S Gibbens
Prof. staff: Miss Kendra Thompson
Founded: 1931
Type: Multidisciplinary.
Hours open: Mon, Wed, Thurs: 8.30am–5pm; Tues: 8.30am–7pm; Fri: 8.30am–4.30pm.
Users: All NHS employees in Wolverhampton. Non-members can use library for reference.
Lending: Members only.
Stock policy: Dispose.
Holdings: 2,200 books; 140 current journal subscriptions; 50 films and videos; 6 CD-ROMs.
Classification: NLM (Wessex adaptation).
Library management system: Heritage.
Computerized services: Online access to AMED; CINAHL; Embase: Psychiatry; MEDLINE and Full-Text Nursing Journals via WISH. Access to Cochrane Library.
Collaborative networks: Regional Library Network (Unicorn).

Women's Health Library

52 Featherstone Street
London EC1Y 8RT
Tel: 020 7251 6333
Fax: 020 7250 4152
E-mail: womenshealth@pop3.poptel.org.uk

URL: www.womenshealthlondon.org.uk
Librarian: Ingrid Smit
Founded: 1988
Type: Medical and Consumer Information for women.
Hours open: Tues, Thurs, Fri: 9.30am–1.30pm; Mon, Wed: 9.30am–4pm.
Users: Open to all members of the public, though most users are women.
Lending: Reference only.
Stock policy: Mostly disposed of, as completely superseded by more up-to-date material.
Holdings: 1,000 books; 47 current journal subscriptions, 94 journal titles; 1,480 subject folders.
Classification: Own.
Library publications: A range of newsletters, health information leaflets and factsheets.
Special collections: A wide range of topics relating to women's gynaecological and sexual health.

Worcestershire Community & Mental Health NHS Trust Library Service: Newtown Branch

Newtown Hospital
Wulstan Unit
Newtown Road
Worcester WR5 1JG
Tel: 01905 763333 ext. 33161
Fax: 01905 769813
E-mail: Elizabeth.Whitehouse@worcsh-tr.wmids.nhs.uk
Librarian: Elizabeth Whitehouse (Assistant Librarian)
Type: Multidisciplinary.
Hours open: Mon–Fri: 9am–5pm. 24-hour access.
Users: All community staff are eligible. Non-members of Trust need to contact the Librarian and in most circumstances will be allowed access for reference purposes.

Lending: As above. Journals for reference only.
Stock policy: Old stock offered to staff and secondhand booksellers. Sometimes books may be sent to Third World countries. Failing any of the above it will be destroyed.
Holdings: 1,500 books; 25 current journal subscriptions; 140 videos; 30 audio tapes.
Classification: NLM (Wessex adaptation).
Library management system: Sirsi.
Computerized services: Online access to Athens and Ovid for CINAHL; Embase: Psychiatry; MEDLINE. Access to West Midlands Regional Health Libraries Network.
Special collections: Primarily mental health materials.
Collaborative networks: WMRLN; PLCS.

Worthing & Southlands Hospitals NHS Trust Health Sciences Library

Postgraduate Medical Centre
Park Avenue
Worthing
West Sussex BN11 2HR
Tel: 01903 285025
Fax: 01903 285129
E-mail: pgmc.library.worthing@wash-tr.sthames.nhs.uk
Librarian: Mrs S J Merriott
Prof. staff: Mrs M Calver
Type: Multidisciplinary.
Hours open: Mon–Fri: 9am–5pm.
Users: Employees of Worthing and Southlands Hospitals NHS Trust; Worthing Priority Care Trust; GPs; student nurses on placement within the hospitals; West Sussex Health Authority; Sussex Ambulance Service.
Lending: Library members only. Other libraries in Interlibrary Lending Scheme.
Stock policy: Dispose or send to Third World if appropriate.
Holdings: 14,450 books; 202 current journal subscriptions; 178 videos; 36 CD-ROMs.
Classification: NLM.

Library management system:
DB/TextWorks.

Computerized services: Online access to
Ovid and HCN.

Collaborative networks: NULJ; PLCS;
STLIS.

Wotton Lawn Library, Severn NHS Trust

Horton Road
Gloucester GL1 3WL
Tel: 01452 891518
Fax: 01452 891501
E-mail: library@severn-tr.swest.nhs.uk
Librarian: Jackie Webb
Prof. staff: Chris Howarth
Founded: 1996
Type: Mental Health.
Hours open: Mon–Thurs: 8.30am–4pm; Fri:
9.30am–2.30pm.
Users: Trust members of staff only.
Lending: As above.
Stock policy: Dispose of.
Holdings: 3,000 books; 45 current journal
subscriptions.
Classification: NLM.
Computerized services: Internet sub-
scription to NHS South West Information for
Clinical Effectiveness and BMJ electronic
journals.
Collaborative networks: PLCS; SWR-
LIN.

Wrexham Medical Institute: John Spalding Library

Croesnewydd Road
Wrexham LL13 7YP
Tel: 01978 727455
Fax: 01978 727466
E-mail: mary.mckeon@new-tr.wales.nhs.uk
Librarian: Mrs Mary McKeon
Prof. staff: Mr Richard Bailey
Founded: 1963
Type: Multidisciplinary.

Hours open: Mon–Thurs: 8.30am–5pm; Fri:
8.30am–4.30pm. Open until midnight, every
day of the week.

Users: Any member of the North East Wales
NHS Trust, GPs, medical and dental students on placement in the Wrexham area.

Lending: Only members are entitled to borrow books and videos.

Stock policy: Stock is discarded at intervals.

Holdings: 4,000 books; 225 current journal
subscriptions, 245 journal titles; 370 videos;
10 CD-ROMs.

Classification: NLM.

Library management system: Heritage.

Computerized services: Online access to
AMED; ASSIA; BHI Plus; CancerLit;
CINAHL; Cochrane Database; Embase;
HealthStar; HMIC; MEDLINE; PsycINFO.
Access to ClinPsych; NRR.

Library publications: Library guides;
Video Holding List; Journal Holdings List;
New Books List; Wrexham Journal of Health
Care.

Collaborative networks: AWHILES;
AWHL; BL; BMA; College of Occupational
Therapists; Institute of Laryngology and
Otology; Royal College of Surgeons of
England.

Wrightington, Wigan & Leigh Postgraduate Education Department Library

Thomas Linacre House
Royal Albert Edward Infirmary
Wigan
Lancashire WN1 2NN
Tel: 01942 822508
Fax: 01942 822355
E-mail: Margaret.Gerrard@wiganlhs-tr.
nwest.nhs.uk
Librarian: Mrs M B Gerrard
Founded: 1974
Type: Multidisciplinary.
Hours open: Mon–Thurs: 9am–5pm; Fri:
9am–4.30pm. 24-hour access.

Users: Doctors. Open to all other Health Service staff.
Lending: No restrictions.
Stock policy: Disposed of.
Holdings: 5,000 books; 70 current journal subscriptions; 50 films and videos.
Classification: NLM.
Library management system: DB/TextWorks.
Computerized services: Online access to ADITUS. Access to Cochrane Database.
Collaborative networks: HCLU; LIHNN.

Wythenshaw Hospital Library & Information Services

Education and Resource Centre
South Manchester University Hospitals NHS Trust
Wythenshaw Hospital
Southmoor Road
Manchester M23 9LT
E-mail: library@fs1.with.man.ac.uk
URL: www.clineng1.with.man.ac.uk/library
Librarian: Donna T Schofield
Prof. staff: Ann M Coyne
Founded: 1975
Type: Multidisciplinary.
Hours open: Mon, Tues, Thurs: 9am–8.30pm; Wed, Fri: 9am–5.30pm.
Users: Employees of South Manchester University Hospitals NHS Trust; Manchester University medical students; Mental Health Partnership; South Manchester Primary Care Trusts.
Lending: As above.
Stock policy: Send to developing countries (presently via a consultant to India).
Holdings: 5,000 books; 200 current journal subscriptions, 270 journal titles; 60 videos; 10 CD-ROMs.
Classification: NLM.
Library management system: Winchill.
Computerized services: Catalogue. Access via ADITUS to MEDLINE, etc.
Library publications: The List – current awareness of new stock and library news.

Special collections: Plastic surgery; geriatric medicine; psychiatry.
Collaborative networks: BL; BMA; LIHNN; PLCS; RCSE.
Notes: There are two hospital site libraries: Withington and Wythenshaw. The two will be moving into one new building in October 2001 at Wythenshaw.

York District Hospital Library & Information Service

3rd Floor, Admin Block
York District Hospital
Wigginton Road
York YO31 8HE
Tel: 01904 454301
Fax: 01904 454330
E-mail: hslibydh@york.ac.uk
Librarian: Karen Smith
Prof. staff: Hazel Brownhill; Debra Martin
Type: Multidisciplinary.
Hours open: Mon–Thurs: 9am–8pm; Fri: 9am–5pm; Sat: 9am–12 noon.
Users: Staff of York Health Trust; staff and students of University of York. All other users need to apply to the librarian.
Lending: As above.
Stock policy: Pass on to charities, dispose of or pass on to other libraries.
Holdings: 20,000 books; 400 current journal subscriptions; 200 films and videos.
Classification: Barnard.
Library management system: Dynix.
Computerized services: Access via JANET, Ovid and SilverPlatter to multiple databases. Access to ASSIA; Cochrane Library.
Library publications: Library user guides; database training workbooks; electronic library newsletter.
Special collections: Psychiatry.
Branches: Bootham Park Hospital.
Collaborative networks: Department of Health Studies Site Librarians, University of York; NYRLAS.

Index of towns

Index of personal names

General index

This index contains only entries for hospitals, Trusts, hospices, institutions or specific library names which are mentioned in main entries but are not the title of the entry used in the A–Z sequence.

Directory of Health Library and Information Services in the United Kingdom and the Republic of Ireland

2002–3

Eleventh edition

Compiled by

Julie Ryder BA ALA
for the Health Libraries Group
of The Library Association

LIBRARY ASSOCIATION PUBLISHING
LONDON

© The Library Association 1957, 1963, 1969, 1976, 1982, 1986, 1990, 1992, 1994, 1997, 2002

Published by
Library Association Publishing
7 Ridgmount Street
London WC1E 7AE

Library Association Publishing is wholly owned by The Library Association.

First published 1957
Second edition 1963
Third edition 1969
Fourth edition 1976
Fifth edition 1982
Sixth edition 1986
Seventh edition 1990
. Eighth edition 1992
Ninth edition 1994
Tenth edition 1997
This eleventh edition 2002

Editions 1–4 entitled *Directory of medical libraries in the British Isles*
Editions 5–10 entitled *Directory of medical and health care libraries in the United Kingdom and Republic of Ireland*

British Library Cataloguing in Publication Data

A catalogue record for this book is available from the British Library.

ISBN 1-85604-378-9

Typeset from editor's disks by Library Association Publishing in Arial and Arial Heavy.
Printed and made in Great Britain by MPG Books Ltd, Bodmin, Cornwall.

Contents

Foreword

Bill Forrester, compiler and editor of the last edition of this Directory, wrote of the 'major changes' that he had introduced to the arrangement of the Directory. Julie Ryder, the editor of this, the eleventh edition, has faced major changes too; but these are the huge changes now taking place within the National Health Service.

In all four countries of the UK, the NHS is undergoing top-to-bottom review and reorganization. In England, regional offices are disappearing along with the 99 health authorities. In their place will be four regions and 29 strategic health authorities. At the same time, acute trusts are merging, mental health trusts are re-emerging and primary care trusts are being set up. Alongside all this the NHS and social services are moving ever closer.

The enormity of these changes is still sinking in and will doubtless have a profound effect on the organization of library information services in the health sector. No doubt the next edition of this Directory will look very different again.

However, despite the continuity of change in the NHS, many libraries in the health sector are long-established and this Directory will be invaluable to information professionals for several years to come.

On behalf of the Library Association's Health Libraries Group, I would like to take this opportunity of thanking all of you who have contributed to this Directory. I would also like to thank the NHS Regional Librarians Group, whose members spent time chasing up non-replies in order to make this edition more complete than ever. Finally, I would like to thank Julie Ryder, whose arduous and painstaking work has gone into making this new edition of the Directory a vital tool for all those involved in managing the knowledge base of health.

David Stewart
Chair: LA Health Libraries Group
www.la-hq.org.uk/groups/hlg/hlg.html

Preface

Welcome to the new edition.

The Directory aims to be the most comprehensive of its kind, and the title has been changed to reflect more closely the current situation. As well as the more traditional medical and nursing services it includes health promotion services, health-related charities, veterinary libraries and, for the first time, a few 'virtual' services.

In most instances the submission of a completed questionnnaire has been the criterion for inclusion, but in some cases, when no return was received, I have been specifically asked to use regional directories or website information where this would yield appropriate data upon which to build an entry.

The headings are as given on the returns, unless the library name is very specific and likely to be known only locally, or where the return was very vague – something like 'Library' – in which case I have used my own judgement.

The directory has three indexes – a town index, an index of senior staff and a general index. In this edition, in response to numerous comments, the numbers refer to page numbers and not entry numbers. Another change is that a general index replaces the hospital listing. This should make it easier to find entries – the index picks up specific library names and names of trusts or hospitals that make up part of the entry but do not form the main heading.

If you would like to purchase address labels for mailing based on this Directory, please contact: Sales Department, Library Association Publishing, 7 Ridgmount Street, London, WC1E 7AE; Tel: 020 7255 0594; Fax: 020 7255 0591; e-mail: lapublishing@la-hq.org.uk. Please send any changes to your entry to me at Julie Ryder Associates, Holmbury, Wheeler Lane, Witley, Surrey, GU8 5QU – or to julie.ryder@lineone.net if you prefer e-mail.

It is a challenging time to produce a directory like this, when change is continual. Many services have amalgamated or metamorphosed into something quite different from those appearing in the last edition; almost every service now has e-mail and most have websites. Inevitably there have also been a great many staff changes and, of course, there has been a proliferation of databases and new options for accessing information.

I would like, in particular, to express my thanks to Gillian Edwards, Margaret Forrest, William Forrester and David Stewart, as well as to the many others who have helped me to get to grips with this project.

Julie Ryder